T0214543

Lecture Notes in Artificial Intelligence 11530

Subseries of Lecture Notes in Computer Science

Series Editors

Randy Goebel
  University of Alberta, Edmonton, Canada
Yuzuru Tanaka
  Hokkaido University, Sapporo, Japan
Wolfgang Wahlster
  DFKI and Saarland University, Saarbrücken, Germany

Founding Editor

Jörg Siekmann
  DFKI and Saarland University, Saarbrücken, Germany

More information about this series at http://www.springer.com/series/1244

Dominik Endres · Mehwish Alam ·
Diana Şotropa (Eds.)

Graph-Based Representation and Reasoning

24th International Conference
on Conceptual Structures, ICCS 2019
Marburg, Germany, July 1–4, 2019
Proceedings

 Springer

Editors
Dominik Endres (iD)
Philipps-Universität Marburg
Marburg, Germany

Diana Şotropa (iD)
Babes-Bolyai University
Cluj-Napoca, Romania

Mehwish Alam (iD)
FIZ Karlsruhe – Leibniz Institute
for Information Infrastructure
Eggenstein-Leopoldshafen, Germany

ISSN 0302-9743   ISSN 1611-3349   (electronic)
Lecture Notes in Artificial Intelligence
ISBN 978-3-030-23181-1   ISBN 978-3-030-23182-8   (eBook)
https://doi.org/10.1007/978-3-030-23182-8

LNCS Sublibrary: SL7 – Artificial Intelligence

© Springer Nature Switzerland AG 2019
This work is subject to copyright. All rights are reserved by the Publisher, whether the whole or part of the material is concerned, specifically the rights of translation, reprinting, reuse of illustrations, recitation, broadcasting, reproduction on microfilms or in any other physical way, and transmission or information storage and retrieval, electronic adaptation, computer software, or by similar or dissimilar methodology now known or hereafter developed.
The use of general descriptive names, registered names, trademarks, service marks, etc. in this publication does not imply, even in the absence of a specific statement, that such names are exempt from the relevant protective laws and regulations and therefore free for general use.
The publisher, the authors and the editors are safe to assume that the advice and information in this book are believed to be true and accurate at the date of publication. Neither the publisher nor the authors or the editors give a warranty, expressed or implied, with respect to the material contained herein or for any errors or omissions that may have been made. The publisher remains neutral with regard to jurisdictional claims in published maps and institutional affiliations.

This Springer imprint is published by the registered company Springer Nature Switzerland AG
The registered company address is: Gewerbestrasse 11, 6330 Cham, Switzerland

Preface

The 24th edition of the International Conference on Conceptual Structures (ICCS 2019) took place in Marburg, Germany, during July 1–4, 2019. The origins of the conference date back to 1993 and since then the research presented at ICCS has focused on representation of and reasoning with conceptual structures in a variety of contexts. This year's edition was entitled "Graphs in Human and Machine Cognition."

The program included two keynotes: "Visualization, Reasoning, and Rationality" by Markus Knauff (University of Giessen, Germany) and "Towards a Unified Approach to Pattern Matching for Event Streams, Time Series, and Graphs" by Bernhard Seeger (University of Marburg, Germany). There were 29 submissions. Each submission was reviewed by at least two, and on average 2.9, Program Committee members. The committee decided to accept 14 long papers and six short papers, which corresponds to an acceptance rate of 50%. The decision for inclusion in this volume was taken after the authors had the chance to submit a rebuttal to their initial reviews. For the purpose of the presentation at the conference, we divided the accepted submissions into eight regular sessions and one poster session, where the short papers and posters were presented. We believe this procedure ensured that only high-quality contributions were presented at the conference. This year, we are happy to announce that two tutorials were presented at the conference: "Inference in Statistical Relational AI," by Tanya Braun and Marcel Gehrke (University of Lübeck) and "An Invitation to Formal Concept Analysis" by Tom Hanika (University of Kassel).

In addition to the regular contributions, this volume also contains the abstracts of the two keynote talks at ICCS 2019 along with the abstracts of the two tutorials that were held by members of ICCS community.

As general chair and program chairs, we would like to thank the Program Committee members and additional reviewers for their work. Without their substantial voluntary contribution it would have been impossible to ensure a high-quality conference program. We want to express our gratitude to the local organizers, who made sure that the conference ran smoothly and was a pleasant experience for all its participants. We would also like to thank Springer, EasyChair, and our supporter "*Information* — An Open Access Journal from MDPI." Our institutions, Philipps-Universität Marburg, Germany, the FIZ Karlsruhe - Leibniz Institute for Information Infrastructure, Karlsruhe, Germany, and Babes-Bolyai University, Cluj-Napoca, Romania, also provided support for our participation, for which we are grateful. Lastly, we thank the ICCS Steering Committee for their continual support, advice, and encouragement.

July 2019

Dominik Endres
Mehwish Alam
Diana Şotropa

Organization

Program Committee

Mehwish Alam	FIZ Karlsrube - Leibniz Institute for Information Infrastructure, AIFB Institute, KIT, Germany
Simon Andrews	Sheffield Hallam University, UK
Moulin Bernard	Laval University, Canada
Tanya Braun	University of Lübeck, Germany
Peggy Cellier	IRISA/INSA Rennes, France
Olivier Corby	Inria, France
Diana Cristea	Babes-Bolyai University, Romania
Madalina Croitoru	LIRMM, University of Montpellier II, France
Licong Cui	The University of Texas Health Science Center at Houston, USA
Juliette Dibie-Barthélemy	AgroParisTech, France
Florent Domenach	Akita International University, Japan
Dominik Endres	Philipps-Universität Marburg, Germany
Jérôme Euzenat	Inria and University of Grenoble Alpes, France
Catherine Faron Zucker	Université Nice Sophia Antipolis, France
Marcel Gehrke	University of Lübeck, Germany
Ollivier Haemmerlé	IRIT, University of Toulouse le Mirail, France
John Howse	University of Brighton, UK
Dmitry Ignatov	National Research University Higher School of Economics, Russia
Mateja Jamnik	University of Cambridge, UK
Adil Kabbaj	National Institute of Statistics and Applied Economics, Morocco
Hamamache Kheddouci	University Claude Bernard, France
Leonard Kwuida	Bern University of Applied Sciences, Switzerland
Steffen Lohmann	Fraunhofer, Germany
Philippe Martin	Sciences Po and CEPR, France
Amedeo Napoli	LORIA Nancy, CNRS, Inria, University of Lorraine, France
Sergei Obiedkov	Higher School of Economics, Russia
Heather D. Pfeiffer	Akamai Physics, Inc., USA
Simon Polovina	Sheffield Hallam University, UK
Uta Priss	Ostfalia University of Applied Sciences, Germany
Christian Sacarea	Babes-Bolyai University, Romania
Eric Salvat	IMERIR, France
Iain Stalker	University of Manchester, UK

Gem Stapleton   University of Brighton, UK
Diana Şotropa   Babes-Bolyai University, Romania

Additional Reviewers

Chapman, Peter
Quafafou, Mohamed
Raggi, Daniel
Shams, Zohreh
Thiéblin, Elodie
Zheng, Fengbo
Zhu, Wei

Abstracts of the Invited Talks

Recent Trends in Pattern Matching on Temporal Streams and Time Series

Bernhard Seeger

University of Marburg, Hans-Meerwein-Str. 6, 35032 Marburg, Germany
seeger@informatik.uni-marburg.de

Keywords: Pattern matching · Event streams · Situations · Time-series · Graphs

Extended Abstract

The term pattern matching is often used with very different meanings in various areas of computer science and other scientific disciplines. In computer science, pattern matching is best known from the seminal works on string searching [1]. Pattern matching is also one of the most important operators in event stream processing systems [2], in which an event stream consists of continuously arriving events each with a timestamp and payload that obey a given schema (e.g. relational or RDF). For a given event stream, usually ordered by time, event pattern matching returns all event subsequences matching a regular expression of symbols within a given time window. More precisely, event pattern matching on event streams comprises two steps. First, the incoming events are mapped to symbols using Boolean expressions on the events' payload, before the resulting symbol stream is matched using some kind of regular expression. In contrast to traditional regular expressions, event pattern matching also provides advanced features like accessing previously matched events or variable bindings, i.e., binding values of a specific event or an expression to a variable and use this variable in subsequent symbol definitions again. This leads to an operator with high expressiveness, but also makes the definition of the symbols a non-trivial task.

In this work, we will discuss recent achievements with respect to pattern matching and identify new challenging questions that might also be of interest for researchers in the area of analysis and representation of conceptual knowledge. We first question whether event processing is indeed a suitable abstraction level for users. As already mentioned, it is anything but trivial to define symbols that are required for specifying a pattern query. Instead, we argue that users prefer to use the notion of situations [3] and that we need processing systems for interval-based situation streams [4]. A situation corresponds to a period of time and an application concept for which a set of conditions holds true, while an event refers to a timestamp and a technical concept. Consider for example a car driver and a parking area. A driver is primarily interested in the time period when a parking space is available, but not the event when a car enter/leave the parking area. Our notion of situations is also in agreement with the original intention of event processing, as it is a paradigm to react to situations of interests (and not to events). Moreover, the sequential nature of regular expression based patterns has a major deficiency for situation processing. So far, the expressible temporal relationships are limited to before/after/at the same time relationships. Conditions lasting for periods of time and their temporal relationships (e.g., A happens during B) cannot or only hardly be expressed in this traditional approach. Thus, there is the need to support the full spectrum of Allen's interval algebra [5].

The second part of this work addresses the question whether such an operator is applicable to other data structures for which pattern search is of importance. First, we show its usage on time-series where the entire stream is stored in a persistent database. Such an operator is already part of the new SQL standard where it offers almost the same semantics as its streaming counterpart. While a naïve approach for processing is to stream the entire time-series into a streaming operator, this may cause serious performance problems because time-series databases tend to be very large as they keep the entire history of changes for an object. Therefore, we present the basic ideas of an index-based algorithm to exclude contiguous subsequences without matching candidates. Pattern matching from event processing is also related to graphs in two different ways. First, there is an interest in supporting so-called group patterns [6] in event streams. Based on a similarity function, e.g. spatial distance, a dynamic graph of the objects represented in the stream is first created, and then subgraphs satisfying a user-defined condition, e.g. connected component, are computed. Second, we discuss common pattern queries in graphs [7] and their relationship to the pattern operator introduced for event processing. We identify similarities and differences between these independently developed pattern languages. It remains a challenging question to answer in future research whether a single language is suitable for both scenarios.

References

1. Aho, A.V., Corasick, M.J.: Efficient string matching: an aid to bibliographic search. Commun. ACM **18**(6), 333–340 (1975)
2. Wu, E., Diao, Y., Rizvi, S.: High-performance complex event processing over streams. In: Proceedings of the 2006 ACM SIGMOD International Conference on Management of data, pp. 407–418. ACM (2006)
3. Körber, M., Glombiewski, N., Seeger, B.: TPStream: low-latency temporal pattern matching on event streams. In: EDBT, pp. 313–324 (2018)
4. Krämer, J., Seeger, B.: Semantics and implementation of continuous sliding window queries over data streams. ACM Trans. Database Syst. (TODS) **34**(1), 4 (2009)
5. Allen, J.F.: Maintaining knowledge about temporal intervals. Commun. ACM **26**(11) (1983)
6. Zheng, Y.: Trajectory data mining: an overview. ACM Trans. Intell. Syst. Technol. (TIST) **6**(3), 29 (2015)
7. Angles, R., Arenas, M., Barceló, P., Hogan, A., Reutter, J., Vrgoč, D.: Foundations of modern query languages for graph databases. ACM Comput. Surv. (CSUR) **50**(5), 68 (2017)

Visualization, Reasoning, and Rationality

Markus Knauff

Justus Liebig University, Giessen, Germany
m.knauff@uni-giessen.de

Abstract. The epistemic role of mental visualization has always been a matter of controversy. I present my cognitive research on the role of visualization in human rationality. The starting point is that the many cognitive scientists believe that visual mental images are generally functional in cognition and thus should have positive effects on human reasoning. Visualization is considered to be a good thing by most scholars. I instead argue that this is not always true. In fact, visual images can detract people from the relevant information and thus impede their reasoning. Based on this claim, I propose a spatial theory of human reasoning that solely relies on spatial representations and processes. My core idea is to draw clearly a contrast between visual images and spatial representations in reasoning and to show that only spatial representations are critical for rational reasoning. Although the approach does not rely on visual images, it explains why we often have the feeling that we think with our "mind's eye". The theory is corroborated by cognitive experiments, functional brain imaging, and computational modeling. I close with some general thoughts on the role of visualization for human rationality.

Tutorials

Inference in Statistical Relational AI

Tanya Braun ⓘ and Marcel Gehrke ⓘ

Institute of Information Systems, Universität zu Lübeck, Lübeck
{braun,gehrke}@ifis.uni-luebeck.de

Abstract. In recent years, a need for efficient inference algorithms on compact representations of large relational databases became apparent, e.g., machine learning or decision making. This need has lead to advances in probabilistic relational modelling for artificial intelligence, also known as statistical relational AI (StarAI). This tutorial provides a detailed introduction into exact inference in StarAI.

Keywords: StarAI · Exact inference · Uncertainty

Introduction

Our real world consists of many individuals or objects connected to each other, and a whole lot of uncertainty. Probabilistic relational models (PRMs) allow for modelling individuals/objects and relations between them as well as incorporating uncertainties. Random variables are used to set individuals into relations to form PRMs. Within such a model, probabilities are used to represent uncertainty. Uncertainty may range from uncertain properties of individuals over uncertain relationships among individuals to uncertain identities or even existence.

PRMs exist in the form of Markov logic networks [8] or parameterised factor models [7] among others. They allow for compactly representing a world filled with many objects and recurring patterns. Inference in such models includes answering queries, e.g., for a probability of an event or a most probable explanation of a current state of a world. Query answering algorithms aim at answering such queries in an efficient way, leveraging relational structures as much as possible.

To leverage relational structures, individuals are treated identically as long as nothing is known about them [6]. Lifting, first introduced by Poole [7], uses exchangeability of random variables and their dependencies to speed up runtimes by avoiding repeated calculations in variable elimination (VE). Variable elimination [11] is one of the standard algorithms to perform query answering in probabilistic models. Since Poole's first paper, researchers have taken up lifting and applied it to various well-understood algorithms that work on propositional models such as knowledge compilation (KC) on the basis of weighted model counting (WMC) [2] to answer queries.

Overview

This tutorial provides an overview of PRMs, inference problems in them, and inference algorithms to solve the problems with a focus on lifted inference algorithms. It provides a deeper understanding of exact inference, i.e., methods that solve an inference problem without any approximations during calculations. In this main part of the tutorial, we present algorithms that are on the one hand rooted in VE and on the other hand rooted in KC. Next to VE and KC, we delve into the specifics of

- lifted VE (LVE) [7, 9],
- the junction tree algorithm (JT) [4],
- the lifted junction tree algorithm (LJT) incorporating LVE and JT [1],
- the interface algorithm (IA) for temporal models [5], and
- the lifted dynamic junction tree algorithm, which combines LJT and IA [3] as well as
- weighted first-order model counting and first-order KC [10].

Goal: At the end of the tutorial, each participant should have an understanding of what inference algorithms are able to accomplish and how lifting is able to alleviate inference in a world full of objects and repeated structures.

References

1. Braun, T., Möller, R.: Lifted junction tree algorithm. In: Friedrich, G., Helmert, M., Wotawa, F. (eds.) KI 2016. LNCS, vol. 9904, pp. 30–42. Springer, Cham (2016). https://doi.org/10.1007/978-3-319-46073-4_3
2. Darwiche, A., Marquis, P.: A knowledge compilation map. J. Artif. Intell. Res. **17**(1), 229–264 (2002)
3. Gehrke, M., Braun, T., Möller, R.: Lifted dynamic junction tree algorithm. In: Chapman, P., Endres, D., Pernelle, N. (eds.) ICCS 2018. LNCS, vol. 10872, pp. 55–69. Springer, Cham (2018). https://doi.org/10.1007/978-3-319-91379-7_5
4. Lauritzen, S.L., Spiegelhalter, D.J.: Local computations with probabilities on graphical structures and their application to expert systems. J. Roy. Stat. Soc. Ser. B (Methodol.) **50**, 157–224 (1988)
5. Murphy, K.P.: Dynamic Bayesian Networks: Representation, Inference and Learning. Ph.D. thesis, University of California, Berkeley (2002)
6. Niepert, M., Van den Broeck, G.: Tractability through exchangeability: a new perspective on efficient probabilistic inference. In: AAAI-14 Proceedings of the 28th AAAI Conference on Artificial Intelligence, pp. 2467–2475. AAAI Press (2014)
7. Poole, D.: First-order probabilistic inference. In: IJCAI-03 Proceedings of the 18th International Joint Conference on Artificial Intelligence, pp. 985–991. IJCAI Organization (2003)
8. Richardson, M., Domingos, P.: Markov logic networks. Mach. Learn. **62**(1–2), 107–136 (2006)
9. Taghipour, N., Fierens, D., Davis, J., Blockeel, H.: Lifted variable elimination: decoupling the operators from the constraint language. J. Artif. Intell. Res. **47**(1), 393–439 (2013)

10. Van den Broeck, G., Taghipour, N., Meert, W., Davis, J., De Raedt, L.: Lifted probabilistic inference by first-order knowledge compilation. In: IJCAI-11 Proceedings of the 22nd International Joint Conference on Artificial Intelligence, pp. 2178–2185. IJCAI Organization (2011)
11. Zhang, N.L., Poole, D.: A simple approach to bayesian network computations. In: Proceedings of the 10th Canadian Conference on Artificial Intelligence, pp. 171–178. Springer (1994)

An Invitation to Formal Concept Analysis

Tom Hanika

Knowledge and Data Engineering Group, University of Kassel, Germany
tom.hanika@cs.uni-kassel.de

Abstract. This work reflects on the tutorial "a practical introduction to formal concept analysis", held at the 24th Int. Conf. on Conceptual Structures. It compiles basic notions and points to possible extensions and applications.

Keywords: Formal concept analysis · Tutorial · Clojure · Lattices · Orders

Basic Notions

Formal concept analysis (FCA) was introduced in the 1980s by Rudolf Wille [1] as an attempt to promote the communication between researchers from lattice theory and potential users from other fields of research. For this he proposed as fundamental structure *formal contexts* that are triples (G, M, I) where G (*objects*) and M (*attributes*) are sets and the relation (*incidence*) $I \subseteq G \times M$ indicates by $(g, m) \in I$ that $g \in G$ has $m \in M$. A *Galois connection* between the power sets of G and M arises naturally from I through two operators $\cdot' : \mathcal{P}(G) \to \mathcal{P}(M), G \supseteq A \mapsto \{m \in M \mid \forall g \in A : (g, m) \in I\}$ and $\cdot' : \mathcal{P}(M) \to \mathcal{P}(G), M \supseteq B \mapsto \{g \in G \mid \forall m \in B : (g, m) \in I\}$. The elements of $\mathfrak{B}(G, M, I) := \{(X, Y) \mid X \subseteq G \wedge Y \subseteq M, X' = Y \wedge Y' = X\}$ are called *formal concepts*. Using the (natural) inclusion order on G we obtain a lattice $(\mathfrak{B}(G, M, I), \subseteq)$, cf. [2]. An example context and the derived conceptual structure is shown in Fig. 1.

Mammals	carnivore	has venom	lays eggs	can fly
Platypus	×	×	×	
Spiny Anteater	×		×	
C. Vampire Bat	×	×		×

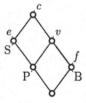

Fig. 1. Formal context (left) and line diagram of the cor. concept lattice (right).

Conceptual structures allow the analysis of complex relations in data and the discovery of dependencies within the data. For example, a valid *(attribute) implication* (dependency) in the domain shown in Fig. 1 is that an mammal that can fly and is a carnivore has a venom, denoted by $\{c, f\} \to \{v\}$. Computing all dependencies of a context and representing them using a minimal *basis* is a common task in FCA. Such a basis constitutes a closure operator on the set of attributes and allows for a compact representation of the domain knowledge as well as fast reasoning with it. All notions allow for clustering, knowledge discovery, ontology engineering, and more.

Conceptual Exploration

So far, computing concept lattices requires the availability of contexts. To comply with this requirement is often impossible in real world scenarios. Often knowledge is provided implicitly, e.g., in form of a human expert or some trained machine learning model. In these cases one can resort to an extensive set of conceptual exploration algorithms from FCA, very well collated in [3]. These algorithms are able to compute the concept lattice through queries to the domain expert in the most efficient fashion.

Tutorial Description

The objective of the tutorial is to survey basics from FCA, present contemporary notions, and promote its expansion to other Artificial Intelligence related fields. This includes classical examples and distinguished applications in knowledge discovery and social network analysis. The latter is achieved by exploiting the strong correspondence between formal contexts and bipartite graphs, which enables the transfer of FCA notions to graph theory. Furthermore, we demonstrate approaches for large data sets through employing models like probably approximately correct learning [4].

The tutorial is suitable to the general ICCS audience, i.e., no prior knowledge in FCA is needed as the tutorial is self-contained. The tutorial is addressed to theoreticians as well as practitioners from knowledge representation, ontology engineering, knowledge discovery, machine learning, and social network analysis.

Practical Computation Through Conexp-Clj

There is a plenitude of algorithms, libraries and software package at our disposal to make use of FCA. For example, github[1] counts 64 projects related to FCA. From all these conexp-clj[2], created by Daniel Borchmann, stands out for various reasons. It facilitates the use of an extensive amount of already implemented algorithms from FCA using the highly expressive functional programming language Clojure. This enables a user to express novel ideas promptly and efficiently. A short introduction into using conexp-clj as well as an outlook on features coming up is part of the tutorial.

---

[1] https://github.com.
[2] https://github.com/exot/conexp-clj.

References

1. Wille, R.: Restructuring lattice theory: an approach based on hierarchies of concepts. In: Rival, I. (ed.) Ordered Sets, NATO Advanced Study Institutes Series, vol. 83, pp. 445–470. Springer Netherlands (1982). English
2. Ganter, B., Wille, R.: Formal Concept Analysis: Mathematical Foundations, p. x+284. Springer-Verlag, Berlin (1999). https://doi.org/10.1007/978-3-642-59830-2
3. Ganter, B., Obiedkov, S.A.: Conceptual Exploration. Springer, Heidelberg (2016). https://doi.org/10.1007/978-3-662-49291-8
4. Borchmann, D., Hanika, T., Obiedkov, S.A.: On the usability of probably approximately correct implication bases. In: Bertet, K., Borchmann, D., Cellier, P., Ferré, S. (eds.) ICFCA 2017. LNCS, vol. 10308, pp. 72–88. Springer, Cham (2017). https://doi.org/10.1007/978-3-319-59271-8_5

Contents

Invited Talk

Visualization, Reasoning, and Rationality

Markus Knauff$^{(\boxtimes)}$

Justus Liebig University, Giessen, Germany
m.knauff@uni-giessen.de

Abstract. The epistemic role of mental visualization has always been a matter of controversy. I present my cognitive research on the role of visualization in human rationality. The starting point is that many cognitive scientists believe that visual mental images are generally functional in cognition and thus should have positive effects on human reasoning. Visualization is considered to be a good thing by most scholars. I instead argue that this is not always true. In fact, visual images can detract people from the relevant information and thus impede their reasoning. Based on this claim, I propose a spatial theory of human reasoning that solely relies on spatial representations and processes. My core idea is to draw clearly a contrast between visual images and spatial representations in reasoning and to show that only spatial representations are critical for rational reasoning. Although the approach does not rely on visual images, it explains why we often have the feeling that we think with our "mind's eye". The theory is corroborated by cognitive experiments, functional brain imaging, and computational modeling. I close with some general thoughts on the role of visualization for human rationality.

1 Introduction and Motivation

What is the role of *mental visualization in epistemic rationality*? Broadly speaking, research on human rationality is concerned with the acquisition, formation, and revision of beliefs, with how people reason and come to rationality justified conclusions, how they develop explanations, how they argue and deliberate, how they acquire knowledge, how they decide and judge, and about having desires, values, morality (Knauff and Spohn, in press). Typically, we distinguished between *instrumental* and *epistemic* rationality. Instrumental rationality is concerned with how people achieve goals, decide, judge, and choose between different options that have different values to the person. For instance, you decide whether you want to spend your vacation in Italy or in Greece. Maybe the food is better in Italy but the weather better in Greece. So, you weight the different options to come to a good decision. Epistemic rationality, in contrast, is concerned with good reasoning and argumentation. The question is how people draw valid conclusions from given information and how they form rational beliefs, or reject irrational beliefs. While instrumental rationality has to take values, preferences, attitudes, etc. into account, epistemic rationality, at least in principle, is concerned with good thinking, or, most broadly, with pure cognition. It is a particular

---

The text is a transcript of the invited talk at the ICCS 2019. The talk-style is partially maintained.

© Springer Nature Switzerland AG 2019
D. Endres et al. (Eds.): ICCS 2019, LNAI 11530, pp. 3–10, 2019.
https://doi.org/10.1007/978-3-030-23182-8_1

faculty of the human species. Other nonhuman animals also have to make "decisions", for instance, where to search for water. Epistemic rationality, in contrast, is the essence of our belief that humans are the only rational animals. Only humans can exchange arguments, evaluate whether their beliefs are true or false, and draw conclusions from given premises.

Logical thinking is a core requirement of epistemic rationality. This is not to deny that people sometimes also use other forms of reasoning and that the logical framework sometimes might be too narrow for explaining all facets of human epistemic rationality. It is also not to say that the human mind works like a logical theorem prover. This would be a much too narrow view on human cognition. However, the work reported here relies on the assumption that logical reasoning is at least an important part of human epistemic rationality (Knauff, in press).

Philosophers, logicians, and scholars from formal disciplines usually see the process of reasoning, and epistemic rationality in general, as inextricably linked to language. Reasoning in this view is based on language. It must not be a natural language, but any language that allows to form sentences to which we can assign truth values. There is no doubt that human cognition often relies on language-based mental representations and processes. There is a huge number of experimental findings that support this view on human reasoning (Adler and Rips 2008; Krumnack et al. 2011).

Accordingly, when you ask people how they think they sometimes say that they experience it like an inner monologue. This subjective experience is related to the language-based theories of human rationality. Yet, people also quite often report to experience their thinking as visualization, that is, they experience it as seeing at "the inner eye" or "pictures the head". This introspective experience has motivated many philosophers and psychologists to think about the role of visualization in human cognition and rationality. Hence, visualization already played a role in ancient philosophy and was since then always a matter of controversy (Mancosu 2005). Some philosophers advocated the idea of visual thinking, whereas others denied that visualization plays any role in human cognition. The former position, for instance, can be found in the semiotics of Charles Sanders Peirce, whereas philosophers such as Wittgenstein, or eminent mathematicians like Hilbert, argued against the epistemic function of visualization.

In experimental psychology, the debate about the role of visualization also has a long history, albeit it cannot be that long as in philosophy. In brief, many studies showed that visual mental imagery can help people to remember what they have experienced in the past (Kosslyn 1980). And it can help people with complex tasks or to find creative solutions for new problems (Antonietti 1991; Arnheim 1969). However, some scholars argue that people might experience the content of their thoughts as visual mental images, but this might be just an epiphenomenon, while the actual cognitive work relies on language-based representations and processes (Pylyshyn 2002, 2006) Indeed, the matter is really complex, because, on the one hand, we know that introspective experience can be fatally misguiding. An extreme position thus might be that we should not bother with visual images. Experimental psychologists usually do not trust people when they report how they think that they think. We do that with good reasons. On the other hand, it is at least irritating if psychological theories have nothing in common with the introspective experience of intelligent people. This might not be a strong argument and certainly introspection is no scientific way to evaluate theories. However, sometimes it can be the source of inspiration and the very first steps towards a theory before it is spelled out and tested with scientific methods.

In this work, I want to report the research from our group that is concerned with the role of *visual mental images in logical reasoning*. I start with two definitions: First, visual mental images are a particular kind of mental representation that is similar to representations that result for visual perception. Visual mental images can be rotated and scanned and they can be experienced as vividly as real visual perceptions. On the neural level, visual mental images should be represented and processed in visual brain areas. These areas are in the back of the brain and comprise the primary and secondary visual cortices. The most popular theory of visual mental imagery, the one developed by Kosslyn and coworkers, says that visual imagery should activate the early visual cortex, that is V1 (Kosslyn 1994; Kosslyn et al. 2001; Holmes and Kosslyn 2015; Kosslyn and Thompson 2003).

The second definition is concerned with logical reasoning. Broadly speaking, logical reasoning is concerned with performing inferences, which leads from a set of premises to a valid conclusion. If people reason logically correct, then that means that they can start from a set of true beliefs and then can be sure that derived belief is also true. The main characteristic of logic is that you can evaluate the truth of the conclusion without looking at the content of the reasoning problem. What matters is the formal structure of the argument.

2 Some Experimental Results

Many studies have shown that people often violate the principle that the content does not matter for logical validity. For instance, people have less problems to draw a logical inference, if it agrees with their prior beliefs, whereas an inference is harder if the conclusion is in contradiction to the beliefs of the person. This is the famous "belief bias" or "content effect", which has been documented in hundreds of experiments (Evans 1993; Klauer et al. 2000).

In some ways, the work reported here is concerned with a particular kind of *content effects*. In most of our experiments we varied the reasoning problems in a way that made it *easy* or *difficult* to visualize the content of the problem. For instance, I can tell you that the *Red rose is to the left of the yellow tulip, and that the yellow tulip is to the left of the orange clove*. Which relation does hold between the rose and the clove? If you think about this problem you might visualize the three flowers in a line and then mentally scan this vivid mental image to determine the relation between the two flowers. Now, I tell you that *Prof. A is smarter than Prof. B and that Prof. B is smarter than Prof. C*. Who is the smartest? This problem is much more abstract and you might not construct a visual mental image from this content.

A handful of experiments systematically varied the imageability of the content of a reasoning problem. The main hypothesis was the following: if human reasoning relies on visual mental images then reasoning should be easier if content of the problem is easy to visualize. The problem should be harder to solve if the content of the problem is difficult or almost impossible to visualize. Until recently, the evidence was equivocal.

Some researchers reported that the ease of visualization helps people to reason accurately, whereas others did not find such an affect. Visualization often was not a factor that could explain reasoning performance. An overview of this research you can find in Knauff (2009) and Knauff (2013).

In one of my early studies, I tried to understand the reasons for the inconsistency in the previous findings. Since then the topic still occupies me. In Knauff and Johnson-Laird (2002), we used four kinds of reasoning problems: *Visual problems* were problems that (other) participants in a pilot study evaluated as easy to visualize. *Visuospatial problems* were rated by the participants as easy to visualize, but they also said that they can construct a more abstract spatial representation, for instance a scale or an abstract diagram, from the content of the problem. *Purely spatial problems* were evaluated as difficult to visualize, but easy to envisage spatially. Finally, there were *abstract problems* from which the participants in the pilot study said that they do not evoke visual mental images and that they are also difficult to envisage on spatial scale, in a diagram, are similar. So, these problems are really quite abstract. Our results were astonishing: people needed the most time to reason with the visual problems. For the other problems the roughly needed the same time. It is obvious that this result does not fit with the idea that people use visual mental images to reason. In fact, the problems were harder to solve when they were easy to visualize. This result is now an established finding in the psychology of reasoning. It is called the *visual impedance effect*. Meanwhile many other groups have reported similar results (Bacon and Handley 2010; Bacon et al. 2007; Panagiotidou et al. 2018; Sato et al. 2017).

3 How Can We Explain the Visual Impedance Effect?

An answer to this question is provided by functional brain imaging experiments from our group (Knauff et al. 2003). I report these findings here just in brief. In one experiment, we used the same materials as in Knauff and Johnson-Laird (2002). When the participants had to solve these problems, they were in the scanner and had to evaluate the conclusion by pressing one of two buttons. Here is what we found: First, we found neural activity for all kinds of problems in areas of the parietal cortex. These areas are well known to be responsible for the processing of spatial information from different modalities. Our interpretation was that people solved the problems by constructing spatial mental models of the content of the reasoning problem. These problems are more abstract than visual mental images, because they just represent the spatial information relevant to the inference. The second finding, was that only the visual problems resulted in additional activity in the visual cortex. Our interpretation is that only these problems lead to visual mental images. But, from the behavioral results we know that these visual mental images can hinder reasoning.

From an evolutionary point of view, it looks surprising that humans have developed ineffective cognitive strategies that hinder them from reasoning in an optimal way. Yet, we know that evolution does not always leads to optimal features of organisms (Schurz 2011). A more psychological explanation is provided by another functional brain imaging experiment from our group (Fangmeier et al. 2006; Fangmeier and Knauff 2009). In this study, we could show that the visual cortices are only active during the understanding and integration of the premises of logical reasoning problems. Yet, when people have to actively evaluate the logical correctness of the conclusion, this activity in visual cortices disappeared. In other words, on the one hand, we found the neural correlates of visual mental imagery during the processing of the premises. On the other hand, the reasoning process itself did not rely on these visual images. We think that this is a reasonable explanation for the subjective experience of people to think at their inner eye, although the reasoning process relies on more abstract processes. As we know, people might have conscious access to the content of visual cortex, but there might have no such excess to the cognitive processes in parietal cortex. I have spelled out this theory in detail in Knauff (2013).

The *visual impedance effect* is robust and reliable across different methods and experimental paradigms. Here are a few examples: In Knauff and May (2006), we found that congenitally totally blind people are immune to the visual impedance effect, because they do not think visually (Knauff and May 2006). In another experiment, we used transcranial magnetic stimulation (TMS), which allows researchers, very roughly speaking, to produce temporal lesions in particular brain areas. In other words, we can disrupt the neural information processing in the brain areas of interest. We applied TMS to early visual cortex. And participants reasoned better in this condition than in a control condition where their ability to construct visual images in primary cortex was undisrupted (Hamburger et al. 2018). In another TMS study, we applied the TMS signal to the parietal cortex and found that this hinders people's reasoning performance. They reasoned less good when they could not construct spatial mental models in parietal cortex (Ragni et al. 2016). We also found that people who tend to think very visually show a stronger visual impedance affect than people who think more verbally (Gazzo Castañeda and Knauff 2013).

4   What Can We Learn from This Research?

Here are five take-home messages. The first message is that the *visual impedance effect* provides a new point of view to the long-lasting debates about the role of visualization in epistemic rationality. It is important to see that most of these controversies have taken place in philosophy, mathematics, and other areas. These disciplines are interested in the *normative* function of visualization. *Normative theories* are concerned with how reasoning *ought* to be, no matter whether it is performed by humans, by machines, or by any other system. These disciplines are interested in the ideal, optimal ways of reasoning. The present work, in contrast, seeks to contribute to a comprehensive *descriptive* theory of human epistemic rationality. *Descriptive theories* in psychology are concerned with *actual* human reasoning, not with idealizations. Cognitive psychologists want to understand real human reasoning that might also lead to errors. "Errors" in this context means that the inferences of real people may deviate from what we normatively would call epistemically rational. Moreover, normative theories just tell us something about the rationality of the *result* of a reasoning process. Cognitive descriptive theories are about the *processes* that lead to a certain result. The reported findings show that visualization is a part of these cognitive processes. But, these processes might be not optimal from an epistemic point of view. A more extensive discussion of this point can be found in Knauff (in press).

The second message is that it is essential to distinguish between *visual mental images* and *spatial mental models*. Visual mental images are concrete. They represent, color, shape, texture, size, etc. They also do not allow to represent indeterminacies, ambiguities, or different interpretations of the given information. You cannot imagine that the flower is red *or* yellow. If you want to do that you have to imagine two flowers. Spatial mental models are more abstract (Ragni and Knauff 2013; Knauff 2013). They represent just the information pertinent to the inference. You can imagine that one flower is to the left of another flower without accounting for the exact visual features of the flowers or the exact distance between the flowers (Knauff 1999, Knauff and May 2006; Knauff et al. 2013). The distinction between visual and spatial information processing and representation is well known from other areas of psychology, neuroscience, and linguistics (for an overview see Knauff 2013). Yet, in the psychology of reasoning, the distinction became just popular with the research that is reported here.

The third message is that introspection can be really misguiding. This by no means is new. People do not have conscious access to most of their cognitive processes.

The fourth message is that visualization in reasoning is not an epiphenomenon. The findings demonstrate that visual mental images have a causal power in reasoning. They have an effect, but this effect is not in the direction that the classical idea of visual thinking would suggest. Visualization does not help; it actually can hinder human reasoning. This is novel finding that also has consequences in many practical contexts. For instance, teachers often think that visualization helps their students to grasp complex problems. In Knauff (in press), I advise to be careful with such intuitions, which might not be supported by empirical findings (see also Mayer 2009).

The fifth message is that more work has to be done in this field. In fact, you are right when you insist that epistemic rationality and logical reasoning is a very special domain of human cognition. Hence, the reported results may just apply to this kind of problems. This is certainly true. My group is currently running experiments in many other cognitive domains to find out how general the *visual impedance effect* is. I will keep you posted!

References

Adler, J.E., Rips, L.J. (eds.): Reasoning: Studies of Human Inference and Its Foundations. Cambridge University Press, Cambridge (2008)

Antonietti, A.: Why does mental visualization facilitate problem-solving? In: Logie, R.H., Denis, M. (eds.) Mental Images in Human Cognition, pp. 211–227. Elsevier, Amsterdam (1991)

Arnheim, R.: Visual Thinking. University of California Press, Los Angeles (1969)

Bacon, A.M., Handley, S.J.: Dyslexia and reasoning: the importance of visual processes. Br. J. Psychol. **101**, 433–452 (2010)

Bacon, A.M., Handley, S.J., McDonald, E.L.: Reasoning and dyslexia: a spatial strategy may impede reasoning with visually rich information. Br. J. Psychol. **98**(1), 79–92 (2007)

Evans, J.S.B.T.: Bias and rationality. In: Manktelow, K.I., Over, D.E. (eds.) Rationality: Psychological and Philosophical Perspectives, pp. 6–30. Routledge, London (1993)

Fangmeier, T., Knauff, M., Ruff, C., Sloutsky, V.: FMRI evidence for a three-stage model of deductive reasoning. J. Cogn. Neurosci. **18**(3), 320–334 (2006)

Fangmeier, T., Knauff, M.: Neural correlates of acoustic reasoning. Brain Res. **1249**, 181–190 (2009)

Gazzo Castañeda, L.E., Knauff, M.: Individual differences, imagery and the visual impedance effect. In: Knauff, M., Pauen, M., Sebanz, N., Wachsmuth, I. (eds.) Proceedings of the 35th Annual Conference of the Cognitive Science Society, pp. 2374–2379. Cognitive Science Society, Austin (2013)

Hamburger, K., Ragni, M., Karimpur, H., Franzmeier, I., Wedell, F., Knauff, M.: TMS applied to V1 can facilitate reasoning. Exp. Brain Res. **236**, 2277–2286 (2018)

Klauer, K.C., Musch, J., Naumer, B.: On belief bias in syllogistic reasoning. Psychol. Rev. **107**, 852–884 (2000)

Knauff, M.: Visualization and rationality. In: Knauff, M., Spohn, W. (eds.) The Handbook of Rationality. MIT Press, Cambridge (in press)

Knauff, M.: Space to Reason - A Spatial Theory of Human Thought. MIT Press, Cambridge (2013)

Knauff, M.: The cognitive adequacy of Allen's interval calculus for qualitative spatial representation and reasoning. Spat. Cogn. Comput. **1**, 261–290 (1999)

Knauff, M.: A neuro-cognitive theory of deductive relational reasoning with mental models and visual images. Spat. Cogn. Comput. **9**, 109–137 (2009)

Knauff, M., Bucher, L., Krumnack, A., Nejasmic, J.: Spatial belief revision. J. Cogn. Psychol. **25**, 147–156 (2013)

Knauff, M., Johnson-Laird, P.N.: Visual imagery can impede reasoning. Mem. Cogn. **30**, 363–371 (2002)

Knauff, M., May, E.: Mental imagery, reasoning, and blindness. Q. J. Exp. Psychol. **59**(1), 161–177 (2006)

Knauff, M., Fangmeier, T., Ruff, C.C., Johnson-Laird, P.N.: Reasoning, models, and images: behavioral measures and cortical activity. J. Cogn. Neurosci. **15**, 559–573 (2003)

Knauff, M., Spohn, W.: The Handbook of Rationality. MIT Press, Cambridge (in press)

Kosslyn, S.M.: Image and Mind. Harvard University Press, Cambridge (1980)

Kosslyn, S.M.: Image and Brain. MIT Press, Cambridge (1994)

Kosslyn, S.M., Ganis, G., Thompson, W.L.: Neural foundations of imagery. Nat. Rev. Neurosci. **2**, 635–642 (2001)

Kosslyn, S.M., Thompson, W.L.: When is early visual cortex activated during visual mental imagery? Psychol. Bull. **129**(5), 723–746 (2003)

Krumnack, A., Bucher, L., Nejasmic, J., Nebel, B., Knauff, M.: A model for relational reasoning as verbal reasoning. Cogn. Syst. Res. **11**, 377–392 (2011)

Mayer, R.E.: Multimedia Learning, 2nd edn. Cambridge University Press, New York (2009)

Mancosu, P.: Visualization in logic and mathematics. In: Mancosu, P., Jørgensen, K.F., Pedersen, P.A. (eds.) Visualization, Explanation and Reasoning Styles in Mathematics, pp. 13–30. Springer, Berlin (2005). https://doi.org/10.1007/1-4020-3335-4

Holmes, E.A., Kosslyn, S.M.: Mental imagery: functional mechanisms and clinical applications. Trends Cogn. Sci. **19**(10), 590–602 (2015)

Panagiotidou, E., Serrano, F., Moreno-Rios, S.: Reasoning and reading in adults. A new reasoning task for detecting the visual impedance effect. Adv. Cogn. Psychol. **14**(4), 150–159 (2018)

Pylyshyn, Z.W.: Mental imagery: in search of a theory. Behav. Brain Sci. **25**, 157–238 (2002)

Pylyshyn, Z.W.: Seeing and Visualizing: It's Not What You Think. MIT Press, Cambridge, (2006)

Ragni, M., Franzmeier, I., Maier, S., Knauff, M.: Uncertain relational reasoning in the parietal cortex. Brain Cogn. **104**, 72–81 (2016)

Ragni, M., Knauff, M.: A theory and a computational model of spatial reasoning with preferred mental models. Psychol. Rev. **120**, 561–588 (2013)

Sato, Y., Sugimoto, Y., Ueda, K.: Real objects can impede conditional reasoning but augmented objects do not. Cogn. Sci. **42**(2), 691–707 (2017)

Schurz, G.: Evolution in Natur und Kultur. Spektrum Akademischer Verlag, Berlin (2011)

Regular Papers

Introducing Contextual Reasoning to the Semantic Web with OWL^C

Sahar Aljalbout$^{(\boxtimes)}$, Didier Buchs, and Gilles Falquet

Centre Universitaire d'informatique, University of Geneva, Geneva, Switzerland
{sahar.aljalbout,didier.buchs,gilles.falquet}@unige.ch

Abstract. Representing the context of triples and reasoning on contextualized triples is an open problem in the semantic web. In this paper, we present OWL^C: a contextual two-dimensional web ontology language. Using the first dimension, we can define contexts-dependent classes, properties, and axioms and using the second dimension, we can express knowledge about contexts which we consider formal objects, as proposed by McCarthy [17]. Moreover, we describe a contextual extension of the OWL entailment rules, and we present a new set of rules for reasoning on contexts. We demonstrate the modeling strength and reasoning capabilities of OWL^C with a practical scenario from the digital humanity domain. We chose the FDS project in virtue of its inherent contextual nature, as well as its notable complexity which allow us to highlight many issues connected with contextual knowledge representation and reasoning.

Keywords: Contexts · Contextual reasoning · OWL^C

1 Introduction

The problem of representing and reasoning on contextualized triples in RDF[1] and OWL[2] is an old and crucial problem which until today has not led to a consensus or a standard adopted by the community. We consider that triples can be enriched with two-types of contexts: (i) validity contexts which enhance the meaning of a fact such as the temporal validity. The fact itself is not sufficiently clear without validity contexts (ii) additional contexts which add to the fact without interfering with its meaning such as the provenance of the triple. A statement where both contexts are given is the following: *Saussure lived in Geneva between 1857 and 1876 as mentioned by Wikipedia*, where 1857–1876 represents the validity context (more precisely the validity time) and Wikipedia is the provenance considered as an additional context.

Contextual reasoning is more than inferring new contextual triples from existing ones, it is about understanding the situation in detail in order to generate the corresponding inferences. Currently, contextual reasoning has been

---

[1] https://www.w3.org/RDF/.
[2] https://www.w3.org/OWL/.

© Springer Nature Switzerland AG 2019
D. Endres et al. (Eds.): ICCS 2019, LNAI 11530, pp. 13–26, 2019.
https://doi.org/10.1007/978-3-030-23182-8_2

rarely explored. The effort has mainly focused on proposing approaches for encoding contexts in RDF (i.e. a language that only supports binary relations) [1,8,11,12,18] which naturally leads to no big achievements in reasoning given the limitations of RDF entailments. Considering this limited expressiveness, we take in this work a step forward and explore the benefits of having a contextual OWL. Through this paper, we answer the three following questions:

Q1. How can OWL be extended to cover the different aspects of contextual knowledge representation?
Q2. How to use contexts to enrich the entailment rules?
Q3. To what extent, our proposed approach can represent the different components of a modeling problem (i.e effectiveness)?

The first two challenges (i.e. **Q1** and **Q2**) are in fact two sides of the same coin and, consequently, they should be approached within the same, unifying framework. To achieve our goal efficiently, we propose OWL^C, a contextual two-dimensional web ontology language that is an extension of the classical OWL. We chose to answer the above questions over the real SNF[3] project of Ferdinand de Saussure [2], which is sufficiently complex and paradigmatic to contain different aspects of context-dependent knowledge.

The remainder of the paper is organized as follows: in Sect. 2, we present the Ferdinand De Saussure (FDS) use case. In Sect. 3, we discuss the requirements for contextual knowledge representation and reasoning. In Sect. 4 (resp. Sect. 5), we present a contextual extension of OWL (resp. scalable profile): OWL^C, in the style of two-dimensional logics [14]. In this extension, we allow the representation of contextual and non contextual classes, properties and axioms. The novel aspect of the representation methodology is the use of special operators for intertwining the object level (i.e. OWL^C_{core}) and the context-level (i.e. $OWL^C_{context}$). We discuss also the different types of reasoning that can be performed. Furthermore, we demonstrate the usability of OWL^C by applying it to a historical scenario in Sect. 6. Finally, in Sect. 7 we present the related works and summarize the paper in Sect. 8.

2   Motivation: FDS Use Case

An appealing application for this topic is the field of digital humanities, especially historical projects where data come from different sources and span over a wide period of time. Let us start now with the description of our use case: "the Ferdinand de Saussure project" [1,2].

Ferdinand de Saussure (1857–1913) is considered as a "formidable linguist" [2] first of all for his work in general linguistics as well as for his contributions in the rather more exclusive field of comparative grammar. However, Saussure published very little. The legacy of Saussure is fortunately not limited to

---

[3] http://www.snf.ch/fr/Pages/default.aspx.

these monographs but includes a fund of about 50,000 handwritten pages[4]. One of the major problems for Saussureans is to understand the content of these manuscripts. This is due to the following contextual problems:

- Data provenance as a context: the Saussurean manuscripts come from various sources (e.g. students notes, letters, Saussurian drafts etc.). Two different sources can state a different statement about the same idea. The provenance of a statement explains the origin of that statement. It is of major importance for Saussurians given the level of confidence that they attribute to each source.
- Time as a context: for the majority of the manuscripts, we don't know their writing date. This can be inferred by using the temporal entities and properties extracted from the transcriptions such as references, persons, events, and institutions that Saussure used to quote in his writings.

3   Requirements

In the search for a suitable formalism for representing and reasoning over contextualized knowledge, we raise the following question: *what are the minimum properties that such a formalism must have in order to best serve its purpose?* We propose and justify the following properties as a starting point for a complete answer.

Property 1: Distinction between the contextualized knowledge and the context knowledge
The union of the vocabularies used for each level must be disjoint. For example, it should be evident that the properties *time* and *provenance* belong to the contexts' knowledge. A good reason to comply with this property is to avoid user's confusion between the two levels, which naturally serve distinct purposes.

Property 2: Expressiveness of the formalism
The formalism must be able to deal with multiple contexts, the relations between them and with the possible implications that the knowledge present in any given context may have on the other contexts.

Property 3: Representation compactness
Contextual knowledge must be represented without introducing a proliferation in the number of triples (i.e. without introducing a lot of new objects or properties).

Property 4: Reasoning efficiency
The great appeal of McCarthy's theory of contexts [17] stems from the simplicity of the three postulates declaring that contexts are formal objects, that have properties and can be described in relational structures. Consequently, contextual reasoning should exploit these assumptions without increasing the computational complexity of reasoning tasks, compared to non-contextualized models.

Property 5: Preservation of reasoning cost
The contextual layer should not increase the complexity of reasoning.

---

[4] Which have been (and still) transcribed.

4   OWL 2 DL^C: A Two-Dimensional Web Ontology Language for Contexts

OWL 2 DL was designed to support the existing description logic (DL) business segment and has desirable computational properties for reasoning systems. In this section, we introduce an extension of OWL 2 DL for contexts, that we call OWL 2 DL^C. The semantics are based on the semantics of the two-dimensional description logic [14]. OWL 2 DL$^C_{core}$ is the first dimension. It is used to represent contextual object knowledge such as contextual classes, properties and axioms. OWL 2 DL$^C_{context}$ is the second dimension. It is used to represent contexts which are considered as first class citizens.

Formally speaking, an OWL 2 DL^C signature (or vocabulary) is a pair of DL signatures ($\langle N_C, N_R, N_I \rangle$, $\langle N_{KC}, N_{KR}, N_{KI} \rangle$) where:

- N_C (resp. N_{KC}) is a set of domain (resp. context) concept names,
- N_R (N_{KR}) is a set of domain (context) role names,
- N_I (N_{KI}) is a set of domain (context) individuals names.

4.1   The Contexts Language: OWL 2 DL$^C_{context}$

Contexts are considered as formal objects [17] and are of two types:

- Validity contexts: are contexts that can affect the fact itself either by enhancing its meaning, or by limiting its meaning to a given context. Fluents [20] are a typical example of validity contexts (i.e. a fluent is a temporal property whose object is subject to change over time).
- Additional contexts: supplement a fact with additional elements that do not modify its meaning. As a result, the fact is more precisely described with the additional context, but sufficiently clear without it. A typical example is the publication context which provide information about the provenance of the triple as a reference in order to support the claim.

A context type is usually characterized by a set of dimensions that describe it to a certain level of approximation. For instance, a validity context could be composed of many dimensions, such as the temporal validity, the spatial validity, etc. For example:

$$(1857, wikipedia) : LivedIn(Saussure, Geneva)$$

states that Saussure lived in Geneva during 1857 as mentioned in wikipedia. 1857 is the temporal dimension of the validity context and wikipedia is the provenance dimension considered as an additional context[5].

The axioms of the contexts language are formulas:

$$A \sqsubseteq B \mid C(a)$$

where $A \in N_{KC}$, $B \in N_{KC}$, $C \in N_{KC}$, $a \in N_{KI}$.

---

[5] In this case the individual context names N_{KI} is the cartesion product $N_{KIt} \times N_{KIp}$ of a set of temporal contexts and a set of provenance contexts.

4.2 The Core Language: OWL 2 DL$^C_{core}$

An axiom expression of the core language is either:

- a DL axiom expression on the core signature $\langle N_C, N_R, N_I \rangle$. For Example:

$$Human(Saussure)$$

- an expression of the form $K : \phi$, where K is either an individual context name (in N_{KI}) or a concept expression over the context signature $\langle N_{KC}, N_{KR}, N_{KI} \rangle$. Such an expression states that the axiom ϕ holds in the specified context or in all contexts of the specified context concept. ϕ can be:
  1. a concept axiom ($C \sqsubseteq D$, $C \equiv D$, C *disjoint* D)

$$1969 : CanVote \sqsubseteq Aged21orMore$$

  states that the axiom $CanVote \sqsubseteq Aged21orMore$ holds in the temporal context *1969*.
  2. a role axiom ($R \sqsubseteq S$, *functional*(R), *transitive*(R), ...)

$$DecentralizedCountry : hasLocalPowerIn \sqsubseteq electedLocallyIn$$

  states that in decentralized countries (contexts), a person with local power in a region had necessarily been locally elected in that region.
  3. a class or role assertion ($C(a)$, $R(a, b)$) defined on the core signature with contextual concept and role expressions

$$1857 : Professor(Saussure)$$

  which states that Saussure was a professor during 1857.

A contextual interpretation is a pair of interpretations $\mathcal{M} = (\mathcal{I}, \mathcal{J})$ where $\mathcal{I} = (\Delta, \cdot^{\mathcal{I}[.]})$ is the core interpretation, $\mathcal{J} = (\Omega, \cdot^{\mathcal{J}})$ is the context interpretation, and $\Delta \cap \Omega = \emptyset$. $\cdot^{\mathcal{I}[.]}$ is a family of interpretation functions, one for each context $k \in \Omega$. $\cdot^{\mathcal{J}}$ is the (non-contextual) interpretation function of every context in the context language. The interpretation of the class constructors of the core language is straightforward. Table 1 contains the OWL-frame like abstract syntax, the contextual description logic syntax (CDL) and the direct model theoretic semantics of OWL$^C_{core}$ basic class constructors. We only consider contextual interpretations that satisfy the *rigid designator hypothesis* [16], i.e. $i^{\mathcal{I}[k]} = i^{\mathcal{I}[k']}$ for any individual $i \in N_I$, $k \in \Omega$, and $k' \in \Omega$.

A contextual axiom $K : \phi$ is satisfied by an interpretation $\mathcal{M}$ if in every context k that belongs to the interpretation of K, the interpretation in k of the concepts, roles and individuals that appear in ϕ satisfy the axiom condition

- $\mathcal{M} \models K : C \sqsubseteq D$ iff $\forall k \in K^{\mathcal{J}} : C^{\mathcal{I}[k]} \subseteq D^{\mathcal{I}[k]}$, where $C \in N_C$ and $D \in N_C$
- $\mathcal{M} \models K : R \sqsubseteq S$ iff $\forall k \in K^{\mathcal{J}} : R^{\mathcal{I}[k]} \subseteq S^{\mathcal{I}[k]}$, where $R \in N_R$ and $S \in N_R$
- $M \models K : C(a)$ iff $\forall k \in K^{\mathcal{J}} : C(a)^{\mathcal{I}(k)}$, where $C \in N_C$ and $a \in N_I$
- $M \models K : R(a,b)$ iff $\forall k \in K^{\mathcal{J}} : R(a,b)^{\mathcal{I}(k)}$, where $R \in N_R$, $a \in N_I$ and $b \in N_I$

Table 1. OWL 2 DL$_{core}^C$ direct model theoretic semantics

Abstract syntax	CDL syntax	Semantics (interpretation in context k)
IntersectionOf(C_1 ... C_n)	$C_1 \sqcap ... \sqcap C_n$	$C_1^{\mathcal{I}[k]} \cap ... \cap C_n^{\mathcal{I}[k]}$
UnionOf(C_1 ... C_n)	$C_1 \sqcup ... \sqcup C_n$	$C_1^{\mathcal{I}[k]} \cup ... \cup C_n^{\mathcal{I}[k]}$
ComplementOf(C)	$\neg C$	$(\neg C)^{\mathcal{I}[k]} = \Delta^{\mathcal{I}[k]} \setminus C^{I[k]}$
R SomeValuesFrom(C)	$\exists(R.C)$	$x\|\exists y : (x,y) \in (R)^{\mathcal{I}[k]} and \ \ y \in (C)^{\mathcal{I}[k]}$
R AllValuesFrom(C)	$\forall(R.C)$	$x\|\forall y : (x,y) \in (R)^{\mathcal{I}[k]} \rightarrow y \in (C)^{\mathcal{I}[k]}$
OneOf(a_1 ...a_n)	$a_1 ... a_n$	$(a_1)^{\mathcal{I}[k]}, ..., (a_n)^{\mathcal{I}[k]}$

(if K is not a concept expression but a context individual name k, $K^{\mathcal{J}}$ designates the singleton $\{k^{\mathcal{J}}\}$ in the above expressions).

The interaction between the two languages is done using special operators. We introduce, in Table 2, the OWL frame-like abstract syntax and the semantics of these contexts-based concept forming operators. Examples:

- $\langle AsianCountry \rangle Professor$: the individuals that belong to the class $Professor$ in some context of type $AsianCountry$.
- $[EuropeanCountry]Professor$: the individuals that belong to the class $Professor$ in all contexts of type $EuropeanCountry$.
- $\{Switzerland\}Professor$: the individuals that belong to the class $Professor$ in $Switzerland$.

5   Reasoning with OWL^C

Inspired from OWL 2 RL[6], OWL^C is considered as a profile aimed at applications that require scalable reasoning without sacrificing too much expressive power. This is achieved by restricting the use of constructs to certain syntactic position. Using OWL^C, we can perform contextual reasoning not only on concepts or properties but also on axioms. Due to space limitations, we are only

Table 2. Semantics of the contexts-based concept forming operators.

Abstract syntax	CDL	Semantics
ConceptValuesFromSomeContext(C [K])	$\langle K \rangle C$	$x \in \Delta \mid \exists y \in K^{\mathcal{J}} : x \in C^{\mathcal{I}[y]}$
ConceptValuesFromAllContext(C [K])	$[K]C$	$x \in \Delta \mid \forall y \in K^{\mathcal{J}} \rightarrow x \in C^{\mathcal{I}[y]}$
ConceptValuesFromThisContext(C [k])	$\{k\} C$	$x \in \Delta \mid x \in C^{\mathcal{I}[k^{\mathcal{J}}]}$
PropertyValuesFromSomeContext(R [K])	$\langle K \rangle R$	$(x,z) \in \Delta \times \Delta \mid \exists y \in K^{\mathcal{J}} : (x,z) \in R^{\mathcal{I}[y]}$
PropertyValuesFromAllContext(R [K])	$[K]R$	$(x,z) \in \Delta \times \Delta \mid \forall y \in K^{\mathcal{J}} \rightarrow (x,z) \in R^{\mathcal{I}[y]}$
PropertyValuesFromThisContext(R [k])	$\{k\} R$	$(x,z) \in \Delta \times \Delta \mid (x,z) \in R^{\mathcal{I}[k^{\mathcal{J}}]}$

---

[6] https://www.w3.org/TR/owl2-profiles/#Feature_Overview_3.

able to explain two rules but in Table 3 you can find more examples. Rules are given as universally quantified first-order implications over a ternary predicate T. T represents a generalization of RDF triples thus, $T(s, p, o)$ represents a generalized RDF triple with the subject s, predicate p, and the object o. Variables in the implications are preceded with a question mark. To include the notion of

Table 3. OWL^C: Extended entailment rules for the core language

	IF	THEN
cls-com $\neg C$	T(?c$_1$, owl:complementOf, ?c$_2$) Q(?x, rdf:type, ?c$_1$, ?k) Q(?x, rdf:type, ?c$_2$, ?k)	false
cls-int1 $C \sqcap D$	T(?c, owl:intersectionOf, ?x) LIST[?x, ?c1, ..., ?cn] Q(?y, rdf:type, ?c1, ?k) Q(?y, rdf:type, ?c2, ?k) ... Q(?y, rdf:type, ?cn, ?k)	Q(?y, rdf:type, ?c, ?k)
cls-int2 $C \sqcap D$	T(?c, owl:intersectionOf, ?x) LIST[?x, ?c$_1$, ..., ?c$_n$] Q(?y, rdf:type, ?c, ?k)	Q(?y, rdf:type, ?c$_1$, ?k) Q(?y, rdf:type, ?c$_2$, ?k) ... Q(?y, rdf:type, ?c$_n$, ?k)
cls-uni $C \sqcup D$	T(?c, owl:unionOf, ?x) LIST[?x, ?c$_1$, ..., ?c$_n$] Q(?y, rdf:type, ?c$_i$, ?k)	Q(?y, rdf:type, ?c, ?k)
cls-svf1-1 $\exists R.C$	T(?x, owl:someValuesFrom, ?y) T(?x, owl:onProperty, ?p) Q(?u, ?p, ?v, ?k) Q(?v, rdf:type, ?y, ?k)	Q(?u, rdf:type, ?x, ?k)
cls-svf1-2 $\exists R.C$	T(?x, owl:someValuesFrom, ?y) T(?x, owl:onProperty, ?p) T(?u, ?p, ?v) Q(?v, rdf:type, ?y, ?k)	Q(?u, rdf:type, ?x, ?k)
cls-svf1-3 $\exists R.C$	T(?x, owl:someValuesFrom, ?y) T(?x, owl:onProperty, ?p) Q(?u, ?p, ?v, ?k) T(?v, rdf:type, ?y)	Q(?u, rdf:type, ?x, ?k)
cls-avf-1 $\forall R.C$	T(?x, owl:allValuesFrom, ?y) T(?x, owl:onProperty, ?p) Q(?u, rdf:type, ?x, ?k) Q(?u, ?p, ?v, ?k)	Q(?v, rdf:type, ?y, ?k)
cls-avf-2 $\forall R.C$	T(?x, owl:allValuesFrom, ?y) T(?x, owl:onProperty, ?p) Q(?u, rdf:type, ?x, ?k) T(?u, ?p, ?v)	Q(?v, rdf:type, ?y, ?k)
cls-avf-3 $\forall R.C$	T(?x, owl:allValuesFrom, ?y) T(?x, owl:onProperty, ?p) Q(?u, rdf:type, ?x, ?k) Q(?u, ?p, ?v, ?k)	T(?v, rdf:type, ?y)

contexts, we introduce a quaternary predicate $Q(s, p, o, k)$ where s is the subject, p is the predicate, o is the object and k is the context for which the predicate holds. If the ontology has multiple context dimensions (e.g. time and provenance) k must be understood as $k_1, \ldots, k_m$ and hence Q as a $m + 3$-ary predicate.

We can distinguish two types of object reasoning: explicit and implicit.

Implicit Contextual Reasoning. When the TBox axioms is declared as in normal OWL but the ABox is contextual.

$Professor \sqsubseteq hasColleague \textbf{ only } Professor$
$1904 : Professor(Ferdinand)$
$1904 : hasColleague(Ferdinand, Robert)$
$1880 : hasColleague(Ferdinand, Clara)$
entails $1904 : Professor(Robert)$ but not $1880 : Professor(Clara)$.

Explicit Contextual Reasoning. When the TBox axioms explicitly refer to contexts. From

$FranceBefore1944 : CanVote \sqsubseteq Man$
$FranceBefore1944 : CanVote(Alejandro)$
$FranceIn1989 : CanVote(Andros)$
we can infer $FranceBefore1944 : Man(Alejandro)$ but not $FranceIn1989 : Man(Andros)$.

Interaction between $\mathbf{OWL}_{core}^C$ and $\mathbf{OWL}_{context}^C$. The rules presented in this section let us do the interaction between the two languages. Syntactic restrictions are applied to the new constructors: an existential contextual restriction ($\langle C \rangle D$) may only appear in the left-hand side of a subclass axiom, whereas a universal contextual restriction ($[C]D$) may only appear in the right-hand side. Due to space limitations, we show some of these rules in Table 4, check [3] for more information.

Table 4. OWL^C: entailment rules for the context-based concept forming operators

	IF	THEN
cxt-svf $(\langle K \rangle D)$	$T(?e, \quad owl^c : onClass, \quad ?d)$ $T(?e, \quad owl^c : inSomeContextOf, \quad ?k)$ $Q(?x, \quad rdf:type, \quad ?d, \quad ?y)$ $T(?y, \quad rdf:type, \quad ?k)$	$T(?x, \quad rdf:type, \quad ?e)$
cxt-avf $([K]D)$	$T(?e, \quad owl^c : onClass, \quad ?d)$ $T(?e, \quad owl^c : inAllContextOf, \quad ?k)$ $T(?x, \quad rdf:type, \quad ?e)$ $Q(?x, \quad rdf:type, \quad ?d, \quad ?y)$	$T(?y, \quad rdf:type, \quad ?k)$
cxt-ov $(\{K\} D)$	$T(?e, \quad owl^c : onClass, \quad ?d)$ $T(?e, \quad owl^c : inThisContext, \quad ?k)$ $Q(?x, \quad rdf:type, \quad ?e)$	$Q(?x, \quad rdf:type, \quad ?d, \quad ?k)$

An example of the existential rule is as follow: a former president is someone who has been president in the past

$\langle PastPresidentialTerm \rangle President \sqsubseteq FormerPresident$
$1933-1945 : President(Roosvelt)$
$PastPresidentialTerm(1933-1944)$
entails $FormerPresident(Roosvelt)$

6   Use Case Implementation and Evaluation

In this section, we want to test the usability of OWL^C. We chose to test it over the FDS project. We start by defining the contexts dimensions. Then, we explain the process we followed for knowledge acquisition. Finally, we discuss the problems we encounter while encoding the formalism in RDF and we propose a practical implementation of contextual reasoning.

6.1   Definition of Context Dimensions

First step in the implementation of a contextualized knowledge graph is to decide what are the context dimensions. We choose validity time and data provenance because they are of a major importance for Saussurians as explained in Sect. 2. In order to come up with a suitable range of dimensional values, we must consider the granularity of contexts. In our use case, the main focus is on the Saussurian network (persons he cites in his manuscripts, students etc.) and events he participated too. Therefore, the data provenance will be the transcriptions from which the data was extracted. For the time dimension, the most granular value is a'year'.

6.2   Contextual Knowledge Acquisition

The acquisition of contextual knowledge was the hardest phase of this project given the fact that: (1) the information is scattered in thousands of transcriptions (2) existing natural language processing tools (to the best of our knowledge) do not extract contextual entities or more particularly n-ary relations (e.g. Saussure lived in Geneva in 1857). In many cases, information could be split over different sentences, so the problem can be hard and require "coreference resolution". The simplest way was to use existing tools to find binary relations and then parse in the vicinity of the text to find contexts such as dates/years. In cooperation with a Saussurian linguist, we did the task semi-automatically. Using Gate[7], we extracted named entities and relations from transcriptions. Time and provenance were then added to the contextual relations. Knowledge was also enriched with Wikidata[8]. We have 1032 persons. We have also showed in [1] that the FDS project contains a lot of fluent[9] relations among them: relations between persons (colleagues, studentOf, professor, spouseOf, husbandOf, educatedAt, etc.).

---

[7] https://gate.ac.uk/projects.html.
[8] https://www.wikidata.org/wiki/Wikidata.
[9] A fluent is a relation whose object is subject to change over time (e.g Saussure lives in Geneva in 1860 but in Paris in 1882).

6.3 Representing FDS with OWL^C

In this section, we explain how to encode the formalism in RDF. We start by presenting the contextual pattern we adopted and then we prove the correspondence between the OWL^C formalization and the RDF based representation.

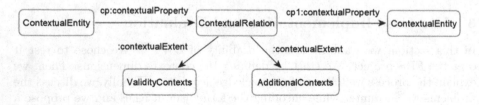

Fig. 1. Contexts in RDF.

Contexts Encoding in RDF. When it comes to encoding contexts in RDF, a lot of techniques are made available (check Sect. 7). We chose to use the n-ary pattern we presented in [1] for its compactness and intuitiveness (Fig. 1).

Mapping OWL^C to RDF. We implicitly used the standard mapping of OWL to RDF[10] for OWL_{core}^C as shown in the following example. The mapping of the context-based concept forming operators to RDF is more delicate [3]. In order to represent the contextual existential $\langle C \rangle D$ and universal operators [C]D, we designed the owl^c:contextRestriction[11] similarly to owl:Restriction. A context restriction class should have exactly two triples linking the restriction to:

1. the class (resp. property) that the restriction applies on, using the new predicate owl^c:onClass (owl:onProperty).
2. the type of the restriction: in case of a universal (resp. existential) restriction , owl^c:inAllContextOf (owl^c:inSomeContextOf) should be used.

($[EuropeanCountries]Linguists$) represents the linguists in all european countries. The mapping is as follow:

$\_ : x \quad rdf : type \quad owl^c : ContextRestriction.$
$\_ : x \quad owl^c : onClass \quad : Linguists.$
$\_ : x \quad owl^c : inAllContextOf \quad : EuropeanCountries.$

6.4 Reasoning in FDS with OWL^C

The first problem we encounter when implementing the contextual rules is that they generates a lot of objects which could not be done using SWRL[12] rules.

---

[10] https://www.w3.org/TR/owl2-mapping-to-rdf/.
[11] We actually used owlc as a prefix instead of owl^c.
[12] https://www.w3.org/Submission/SWRL/.

We choose to use SPIN[13] because it is flexible enough that you can pass parameters to them to customize their behavior. Then, they can be instantiated in any RDF or OWL ontology to add inference rules and constraint checks. Two types of rules were implemented using TopBraid Composer[14]:

OWL^C rules. Figure 2 shows the example of the *cls-int* rule encoded as a SPIN template. This template, similarly to all others, is implemented using a SPARQL INSERT request. It declares that the assertion of the same individual in two classes, holding for the same context, generates an assertion for this individual in the intersection of those classes, but also for the same holding contexts. Notice that the classes are declared as *spin:constraint*. Notice also that the query contains a filter. The existence of the filter is of a major importance, because it guarantees that an existing triple is not generated again and again, whenever the rules are running.

```
spin:body
*   INSERT {
        ?this owlc:representedBy _:b0 .
        _:b0 a owlc:ContextualRelation .
        _:b0 a ?ClassIntersection .
        _:b0 owlc:contextualExtent ?co .
    }
    WHERE {
        ?this owlc:representedBy ?cr1 .
        ?cr1 a ?FirstClass .
        ?cr1 a owlc:ContextualRelation .
        ?cr1 owlc:contextualExtent ?co .
        ?this owlc:representedBy ?cr2 .
        ?cr2 a ?SecondClass .
        ?cr2 a owlc:ContextualRelation .
        ?cr2 owlc:contextualExtent ?co .
        ?ClassIntersection owl:intersectionOf/rdf:first ?FirstClass .
        ?ClassIntersection (owl:intersectionOf/rdf:rest)/rdf:first ?SecondClass .
        FILTER NOT EXISTS {
            ?this owlc:representedBy _:0 .
            _:0 a owlc:ContextualRelation .
            _:0 a ?ClassIntersection .
            _:0 owlc:contextualExtent ?co .
        } .
    }
spin:constraint
*  Argument arg:ClassIntersection : rdfs:Class
*  Argument arg:FirstClass : rdfs:Class
*  Argument arg:SecondClass : rdfs:Class
```

Fig. 2. Template of the binary cls-int rule.

---

[13] http://spinrdf.org.
[14] https://www.topquadrant.com/tools/ide-topbraid-composer-maestro-edition/.

Domain Rules. Domain rules where added to complete the knowledge and were created with collaboration with Saussurean experts. A simple example is the following rule:
A manuscript M written by A is a letter to B and the writing time of M is [t1 ... t2] then A knows B since t1.

7   Related Works

We divide the research works into two groups: theoretical and applied.

In the theoretical group, in 2001, [10] introduced the idea of locality and compatibility where reasoning is considered mainly local and uses only part of what is potentially available. In 2003, [6] introduced the concept of distributed description logics where binary relations describe the correspondences between contexts. However, the coordination between a pair of ontologies can only happen with the use of bridge rules. In 2004, a new concept called E-connections [15] emerged: ontologies are interconnected by defining new links between individuals belonging to distinct ontologies. One major disadvantage is that it does not allow concepts to be subsumed by concepts of another ontology, which limits the expressiveness of the language. Then, in 2006, [4] attempted to extend description logics with new constructs with relative success. In 2011, a proposition was argued to use a two dimensional-description logics [14]. Results showed that this approach does not necessarily increase the computational complexity of reasoning.

In the applied group, many attempts to find a solution to the syntactic restriction of RDF binary relations emerged. Two approaches were proposed:

(a) Extending the data model and/or the semantics of RDF: the triple data structure could be extended by adding a fourth element to each triple, which is intended to express the context [8] of a set of triples [12,18].
(b) Using design patterns: It could be categorized along three axis:
   - the contextual index co is attached to the statement $R(a, b)$ and thus $R(a, b)$ holds for co such as RDF reification [5]. This method is not supported in DL reasoning.
   - the contextual index co is attached to the relation $R(a, b, co)$. An example of this representation is situation pattern [9]. In this case, we can talk about assertions as (reifying) individuals. A second example is FluentRelations [1,2].
   - the contextual index co is attached to the object terms $R(a@co, b@co)$ where co is the contextual-slice of the thing named [19,20]. This method introduces many contextualized individuals which causes objects proliferation.

Other works stand in the middle: a well defined theory implemented using semantic web languages. Among them C-OWL [7]. The idea behind is to localize the content of ontologies and to allow for explicit mappings via bridge rules. Another work [13] proposed a framework for contextual knowledge representation and reasoning (CKR) based on current RDF(S) standards. However, the expressiveness of the formalism is restricted to RDFS and there are no axioms that make it possible to explicitly use the relationships between contexts to deduce new facts or to deal with contradictions between contexts.

8 Conclusion

We identified from the state of the art approaches that the task of contextual reasoning on the semantic web is still in early stages. In our research, we intend to push this forward. Therefore, we highlighted, in Sect. 2, a minimum number of properties that a contextual reasoning formalism must have, in order to best serve its purpose. To comply with properties 1, 2, we proposed an extension of the web ontology language, that we call OWL 2 DL^C, based on a two dimensional description logic [14] with a *context-dimension* consisting of contextual entities which are possibly interlinked with semantic relations. Additionally, we proposed a profile for scalable reasoning that we called OWL^C. The formalism does not increase the complexity of reasoning making it conform with property 5. The framework has not only been presented as a theoretical framework but also it was implemented on the FDS project making it complying with properties 3 and 4. We managed to cover the requirements of Saussureans in terms of knowledge representation. What remains missing is to use the semantic relations between contexts to enrich the inference system which we plan to do in the future works.

Acknowledgement. We would like to thanks our Saussurians colleagues in particular Dr. Guiseppe Cosenza for his collaboration on FDS knowledge acquisition.

References

1. Aljalbout, S., Falquet, G.: Un modele pour la representation des connaissances temporelles dans les documents historiques. arXiv preprint arXiv:1707.08000 (2017)
2. Aljalbout, S., Falquet, G.: A semantic model for historical manuscripts. arXiv preprint arXiv:1802.00295 (2018)
3. Aljalbout, S., Falquet, G., Buchs, D.: A practical implementation of contextual reasoning on the semantic web. In: Proceedings of the 10th International Joint Conference on Knowledge Discovery, Knowledge Engineering and Knowledge Management - Volume 2: KEOD, pp. 255–262. INSTICC, SciTePress (2018)
4. Benslimane, D., Arara, A., Falquet, G., Maamar, Z., Thiran, P., Gargouri, F.: Contextual ontologies. In: Advances in Information Systems, pp. 168–176 (2006)
5. Berners-Lee, T., Hendler, J., Lassila, O., et al.: The semantic web. Sci. Ame. **284**(5), 28–37 (2001)
6. Borgida, A., Serafini, L.: Distributed description logics: assimilating information from peer sources. J. Data Semant. **1**, 153–184 (2003)
7. Bouquet, P., Giunchiglia, F., van Harmelen, F., Serafini, L., Stuckenschmidt, H.: C-OWL: contextualizing ontologies. In: Fensel, D., Sycara, K., Mylopoulos, J. (eds.) ISWC 2003. LNCS, vol. 2870, pp. 164–179. Springer, Heidelberg (2003). https://doi.org/10.1007/978-3-540-39718-2_11

8. Dividino, R., Sizov, S., Staab, S., Schueler, B.: Querying for provenance, trust, uncertainty and other meta knowledge in RDF. Web Semant. Sci. Serv. Agents World Wide Web **7**(3), 204–219 (2009)
9. Gangemi, A., Mika, P.: Understanding the semantic web through descriptions and situations. In: Meersman, R., Tari, Z., Schmidt, D.C. (eds.) OTM 2003. LNCS, vol. 2888, pp. 689–706. Springer, Heidelberg (2003). https://doi.org/10.1007/978-3-540-39964-3_44
10. Ghidini, C., Giunchiglia, F.: Local models semantics, or contextual reasoning = locality + compatibility. Artif. Intell. **127**(2), 221–259 (2001)
11. Giménez-García, J.M., Zimmermann, A., Maret, P.: NdFluents: an ontology for annotated statements with inference preservation. In: Blomqvist, E., Maynard, D., Gangemi, A., Hoekstra, R., Hitzler, P., Hartig, O. (eds.) ESWC 2017. LNCS, vol. 10249, pp. 638–654. Springer, Cham (2017). https://doi.org/10.1007/978-3-319-58068-5_39
12. Hartig, O., Thompson, B.: Foundations of an alternative approach to reification in RDF. arXiv preprint arXiv:1406.3399 (2014)
13. Joseph, M., Serafini, L.: Simple reasoning for contextualized RDF knowledge. In: WoMO, pp. 79–93 (2011)
14. Klarman, S., Gutiérrez-Basulto, V.: Two-dimensional description logics for context-based semantic interoperability. In: AAAI (2011)
15. Kutz, O., Lutz, C., Wolter, F., Zakharyaschev, M.: E-connections of abstract description systems. Artif. intell. **156**(1), 1–73 (2004)
16. LaPorte, J.: Rigid designators (2006)
17. McCarthy, J.: Generality in artificial intelligence. Commun. ACM **30**(12), 1030–1035 (1987)
18. Nguyen, V., Bodenreider, O., Sheth, A.: Don't like RDF reification?: making statements about statements using singleton property. In: Proceedings of the 23rd International Conference on World Wide Web, pp. 759–770. ACM (2014)
19. Welty, C.: Context slices: representing contexts in OWL. In: Proceedings of the 2nd International Conference on Ontology Patterns, vol. 671, pp. 59–60. CEUR-WS.org (2010)
20. Welty, C., Fikes, R., Makarios, S.: A reusable ontology for fluents in OWL. FOIS **150**, 226–236 (2006)

Graph-Based Variability Modelling: Towards a Classification of Existing Formalisms

Jessie Carbonnel[✉], David Delahaye, Marianne Huchard,
and Clémentine Nebut

LIRMM, Université de Montpellier & CNRS, Montpellier, France
{jessie.carbonnel,david.delahaye,marianne.huchard,
clementine.nebut}@lirmm.fr

Abstract. Software product line engineering is a reuse-driven paradigm for developing families of similar products from a generic product backbone with identified options. A customised product is then derived by combining the artefacts implementing the backbone with the ones implementing the chosen options. Variability analysis and representation is a central task of this paradigm: it consists in suitably defining and structuring the scope, the commonalities, and the differences between the derivable products. Several formalisms have been proposed: some are textual, such as propositional logic or constraint programming, while others are based on annotated graph representations. In this paper, we aim to survey and compare existing graph-based variability representations. Among them, conceptual structures have been used rather early and occasionally employed: this survey highlights their original position which is due to some of their properties, including canonicity and the dual view on product configurations versus their features.

Keywords: Variability · Product lines · Formal Concept Analysis

1 Introduction

Product Line Engineering (PLE) is a paradigm for developing families of similar products while lowering costs and time to market, and improving product quality and diversity of supply. PLE receives a lot of attention in many domains, like mobile phone or car manufacturing, and it encounters a growing success in the domain of software engineering where software product construction can be quite fully automated [13]. Software Product Line (SPL) Engineering is a widespread methodology, with two well identified processes. *Domain Engineering* consists in defining: (1) a model of the scope and of the variability of the product line, in particular a model of product options, (2) a generic product backbone, and (3) a set of assets (or artefacts) that implement the possible options. During *Application Engineering*, a customised product is derived by combining the artefacts of the backbone with the ones implementing the chosen options. When the

© Springer Nature Switzerland AG 2019
D. Endres et al. (Eds.): ICCS 2019, LNAI 11530, pp. 27–41, 2019.
https://doi.org/10.1007/978-3-030-23182-8_3

process is completely automated, the resulting product is an executable software, otherwise a significant part is generated.

Variability modelling is a primary task that consists in representing the common and variable aspects of products belonging to a same family. It is usually expressed in terms of *features*, where a feature is a distinguishable and visible characteristic or behaviour of a product. For instance, an e-commerce application (a product) owns a `catalog`, may implement different `payment_methods` and manage a `basket`. In this context, each product can be associated with the set of features that it possesses. A combination of features therefore represents an abstract description of the product, also called a *configuration*. A configuration set is usually presented in a tabular view depicting products against their features. Table 1 represents a set of ten configurations describing a potential family of e-commerce applications, depending on nine features, which we will use throughout the paper. A cross states that the configuration (column) possesses the feature (row). For example, $conf_1$ describes an e-commerce application proposing only a catalog depicted in a grid, and which does not implement any payment method nor basket management.

Table 1. Configuration set of a product line about e-commerce applications

Features	$conf_1$	$conf_2$	$conf_3$	$conf_4$	$conf_5$	$conf_6$	$conf_7$	$conf_8$	$conf_9$	$conf_{10}$
e_commerce	x	x	x	x	x	x	x	x	x	x
catalog	x	x	x	x	x	x	x	x	x	x
grid	x		x	x	x				x	
list		x				x	x	x		x
payment_method			x	x	x	x	x	x	x	x
credit_card			x		x	x		x	x	x
check				x	x		x	x		
basket			x	x	x	x	x	x	x	x
quick_purchase									x	x

Complying with domain and/or development constraints, all feature combinations may not be possible: for instance, two features may be incompatible. *Feature-oriented variability models* aim to document the existing features found in an SPL, as well as constraints on the way they can be combined to form a *valid configuration*, i.e., corresponding to a functional derivable product. In other words, variability models represent constraints between features to describe a configuration set delimiting the scope of an SPL. Several formalisms have been proposed for modelling and managing variability of an existing configuration set such as the one of Table 1. Some are textual, such as propositional logic or constraint programming, while others are based on annotated graph representations, which give complementary and sometimes overlapping views of variability [3,10]. Among these variability representations, conceptual structures associated to formal concept analysis [9] have been used rather early and occasionally employed, e.g., in [5,14]. A common issue faced by these graph-based models is their limited expressiveness, which may prevent them from exactly representing a given configuration set and encourage industries to use textual formalisms [12]. In this paper, we survey and compare in-use graph-based variability representations found in papers studying variability model synthesis from configuration sets [1,6–8,14,16,17]. Our objective is to identify their expressiveness limits to help practitioners choose a graphical variability representation. We highlight the particular place of conceptual structures, which are the only ones to give a canonical feature- and configuration-oriented perspective of an SPL.

The paper is organised as follows. In Sect. 2, we present the basics of the seminal in-use graph-based feature diagram representation, and we introduce feature models which are the *de facto* standard. In Sect. 3, we then establish relations between feature diagrams and propositional logic, allowing us to characterise the logical semantics of graph-based representations. In Sect. 4, we outline the different graph-based representations for variability, which are then classified, compared, and analysed in Sect. 5.

2   Feature Models and Feature Diagrams: The *de Facto* Standard for Variability Modelling

Feature Models (FMs) and Feature Diagrams (FDs) are a family of descriptive languages that aim to document variability of an SPL in terms of features and interaction between these features. For instance, they define which features require other features, or which ones are incompatible. The constraints are represented graphically by structuring the set of features in a refinement hierarchy with decorated edges to specify their dependencies, and by cross-tree constraints. The literature on PLE makes a focus on specific relations between features having in mind that FDs and FMs are used to support several tasks (e.g., defining the product line scope, and guiding its evolution and maintenance).

Figure 1 presents an FD about e-commerce applications. Feature e_commerce is the root feature. Feature catalog is mandatory, and it owns a xor-group composed of features grid and list (exactly one feature has to be present in a valid configuration). Features payment_method and basket are optional child-features of the root, and they require each other. Features credit_card and check form an or-group under payment_method (at least one of them has to be selected). Feature quick_purchase is an optional child feature of basket, and is mutually exclusive with check.

A feature combination that verifies all the constraints expressed by the FD is called a valid configuration. The set of all valid configurations is the FD *configuration semantics*. Table 1 is the configuration semantics of the FD of Fig. 1. Features that are present in all valid configurations are called *core-features* (e.g., e_commerce and catalog), and features that are present in none are called *dead-features*. Moreover, the feature hierarchy gives ontological information: for

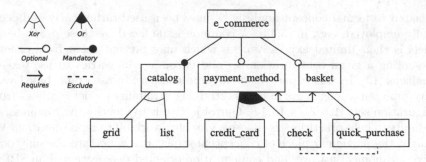

Fig. 1. Example of an FD about e-commerce applications

instance, a child feature may represent a refinement, a *part-of* or even a *use* relationship. Here, features are seen as domain concepts: this information is called the FD *ontological semantics*. A known problem in FD construction is the fact that a given configuration semantics may be represented by different ontological relationships. FDs are therefore non-canonical representations, as different FDs (i.e., presenting different ontological semantics) may be equivalent (i.e., having the same configuration semantics). Moreover, FDs are not logically complete, as some configuration sets may not be represented by this formalism (see [15]), and some authors therefore add a propositional formula to an FD.

As a consequence, She et al. [17] propose to differentiate the terms "feature diagram" and "feature model" (which is a feature diagram completed with a propositional formula), and we will use this terminology in the rest of this paper. More formally, the syntax of FDs and FMs is defined as follows:

Definition 1 (Feature Diagram [17]). *A feature diagram is defined as a tuple* $(F, E, (E_m, E_i, E_x), (G_o, G_x))$, *where* F *is a finite set of features,* $E \subseteq F \times F$ *is a set of directed child-parent edges, and* (F, E) *is a rooted tree connecting all features from* F. $E_m \subseteq E$ *is a set of mandatory edges,* $E_i \subseteq F \times F$ *is a set of cross-tree require edges such that* $E_i \cap E = \varnothing$, *and* $E_x \subseteq F \times F$ *is a set of cross-tree exclude edges such that* $E_x \cap E = \varnothing$. *The two sets* G_o *and* G_x *contain subsets of* E, *representing edges involved in or-groups and xor-groups, respectively. Two distinct subsets of* $G_o \cup G_x$ *are disjoint, and all edges in a subset have the same parent-feature.*

Definition 2 (Feature Model [17]). *A feature model is defined as a pair* (FD, φ), *where* FD *is a feature diagram, and* φ *is a propositional formula where the propositional variables are the features of the feature set* F *of* FD.

Now, consider that we have the same set of configurations as given in Table 1 without the $conf_5$ showing, among other things, that both child features of `payment_method` can be selected with a catalog displayed in a `grid`. To respect this new configuration semantics, the FD should state that selecting both `check` and `credit_card` implies to select `list`. As it is not possible to express such complex implication only by means of an FD, we must add the following formula

$\varphi' = (\text{check} \wedge \text{credit\_card}) \Rightarrow \text{list}$ to the previous FD. The FM composed of the FD of Fig. 1 and φ' therefore represents the new configuration semantics.

3   Semantics of FDs and FMs Using Propositional Logic

Mannion [11] was the first to link FDs and propositional logic. Ever since, FD ontological relationships were translated in the form of a propositional formula, where features are represented by propositional variables and relationships are defined using logical connectives. Therefore, a *logical semantics* is also associated with an FD through a propositional formula that has for models the set of valid configurations of the FD. Its use is very popular in work aiming to carry out automated analysis or reasoning over product line variability [2]. As for FDs, the logical semantics of an FM defined as $FM = (FD, \varphi)$ is $\varphi_{FD} \wedge \varphi$, where φ_{FD} is the propositional formula corresponding to the logical semantics of FD.

Table 2 presents how the ontological semantics of an FD is defined in propositional logic, giving its *logical semantics*. Two logical forms are given. The first one (column 2) is commonly used in the SPL domain and uses the following logical connectives: $\Rightarrow$ (implication), $\Leftrightarrow$ (equivalence), $\vee$ (or), and $\oplus$ (exclusive or). The second one (column 4) shows the equivalent formula in Conjunctive Normal Form (CNF), i.e., expressed as sets of clauses (a clause is a disjunction of literals, and a literal corresponds to a feature or the negation of a feature). Following the tracks of [7], and because the non-empty clauses represent implications, the logical semantics written in CNF (column 4) is appropriate to highlight the expression power of the graph-based representations.

Table 2. Logical semantics of FD constraints

Constraints	Logical semantics	Formula name	CNF form
optional	$c \Rightarrow p$	Binary	$\neg c \vee p$
mandatory	$p \Leftrightarrow c$	Implication	$\neg c \vee p, \neg p \vee c$
requires	$f_1 \Rightarrow f_2$	(BI)	$\neg f_1 \vee f_2$
exclude	$f_1 \Rightarrow \neg f_2$	Mutex (MX)	$\neg f_1 \vee \neg f_2$
or-group	$p \Leftrightarrow (c_1 \vee \ldots \vee c_n)$	OR	$\neg p \vee c_1 \vee \ldots \vee c_n$
			$\neg c_i \vee p, 1 \leq i \leq n$
xor-group	$p \Leftrightarrow (c_1 \oplus \ldots \oplus c_n)$	XOR	$\neg p \vee c_1 \vee \ldots \vee c_n$
			$\neg c_i \vee p, 1 \leq i \leq n$
			$(\neg c_i \vee \neg c_j), 1 \leq i, j \leq n, i \neq j$
core-feature	$\top \Rightarrow f_1$	CF	f_1
dead-feature	$f_1 \Rightarrow \bot$	DF	$\neg f_1$

p represents a feature in a parent position; c, c_i with $1 \leq i \leq n$, features in a child position; and f_1, f_2 any features. Columns 2 and 4 show patterns of clause sets corresponding to the FD constraints. For a clause G corresponding to the OR or XOR pattern, its associated child set is $C_G = \{c_1, \ldots, c_n\}$.

To build the formula corresponding to the logical semantics of an FD, the algorithm consists in following the FD from the root to its leaves, and applying the constructs of Table 2 to produce the clauses. The obtained formula is therefore a conjunction of expressions conforming to the patterns of clause sets of Table 2, i.e., BI, MX, OR, XOR, CF, and DF. In addition, this formula verifies two properties that follow directly from the definition of an FD: (1) presence of a root and (2) the fact that the child sets of distinct feature groups are disjoint. These properties can be formally expressed as follows:

property 1 (FD-to-CNF). Given a feature diagram FD, if φ is the logical semantics of FD then φ verifies the following properties: (a) φ is equal to a conjunction of clauses that conform to the BI, MX, OR, XOR, CF, or DF patterns; (b) φ contains at least one clause r that conforms to the CF pattern (existence of a root, which is a core-feature, i.e., present in all valid configurations); (c) for any G_i, G_j clauses of φ that conform to the OR or XOR patterns, with respective child sets C_{G_i}, C_{G_j}, $C_{G_i} \cap C_{G_j} = \emptyset$ (distinct feature group child sets are disjoint).

Conversely, any formula that can be expressed as a CNF verifying the properties (a) and (c) mentioned above in Property 1 can be represented by an FD:

property 2 (F-to-FD). A propositional logic formula φ that can be expressed as a CNF φ_{FD} can be represented by an FD if: (a) φ_{FD} is a conjunction of clauses conform to the BI, MX, OR, XOR, CF, or DF patterns, and (b) for all clauses G_i, G_j of φ_{FD} that conform to the OR or XOR patterns, with respective child sets C_{G_i}, C_{G_j}, we have $C_{G_i} \cap C_{G_j} = \emptyset$.

It should be noted that the meta-property (b) of Property 1 has been relaxed in Property 2. If no root can be identified in the formula (no clause that conforms to the CF pattern in the CNF representation of the formula) then it is always possible to complete the corresponding FD with a root feature to get a fully connected graph.

As said previously in Sect. 2, FMs have been introduced to alleviate the logical incompleteness of FDs. As a consequence, FMs are logically complete, which can be expressed by the following property:

property 3 (F-to-FM). Any propositional logic formula can be represented by an FM.

As FDs are not logically complete (i.e., they may require the addition of complementary formulas), we may wonder which kind of formulas cannot be represented as FDs, and in particular, what are the different forms of such formulas. In the following, to characterise these formulas, we will use some notations inspired by regular expressions: n represents any negative literal, p any positive literal, l^{k+} at least k times the literal l (if k is 0, l is omitted).

Any propositional formula in CNF can have three types of non-empty[1] clauses: only positive literals (p^+), only negative literals (n^+), and mixed, namely containing positive and negative literals (p^+n^+). To identify the formulas that cannot be represented by FDs, the principle is to look at the patterns of clause sets of Table 2 and identify the missing patterns. In Table 2, the BI pattern corresponds to np, the MX pattern corresponds to n^2, the OR and XOR patterns include np, np^{2+}, and n^2 (the latter for XOR), CF corresponds to p, and DF to n. We can observe that the following forms are not captured by the patterns of Table 2:

- A mixed clause with at least two negative literals (denoted by p^+n^{2+});
- A mixed clause with at least two positive literals (denoted by n^+p^{2+}), with the case of the clause np^{2+}, when it is not included in an OR or XOR pattern;
- A clause with at least two and only positive literals (denoted by p^{2+});
- A clause with at least three and only negative literals (denoted by n^{3+}); these generalised exclusion clauses will be called NAT (*Not All Together*).

These four "missing" clause patterns[2] may be needed for expressing a configuration set. The formula that completes an FD (if needed), to obtain an FM, will therefore be mainly composed of clauses that conform to these patterns.

We do not provide a proof that the set of these patterns is complete in the sense that the set of formulas that can be represented by FDs together with the set of formulas that can be represented using these patterns allows us to represent any formula. However, our approach is purely syntactical (trying to match the patterns of representable clauses and the patterns of Table 2), and the reader should be easily convinced of the completeness of this set of patterns.

4 Graph-Based Formalisms for Variability Structuring

In this section, we consider a product line variability information through a propositional formula φ defined over a set of variables $F = \{f_1, \ldots, f_k\}$. F represents the product line feature set and the models of φ the product line configuration set. In what follows, we survey graph-based variability representations used in works about FM synthesis, and we compare the variability information that they express with the one expressed by φ.

Binary Decision Graphs [1,7,17]. A Binary Decision Tree (BDT) is a canonical tree-like graph used to depict the truth table of a Boolean function of the form $\{0,1\}^k \rightarrow \{0,1\}$, which can represent a propositional formula in k variables. Each internal node represents a variable and has two outgoing edges: a

---

[1] When representing FDs, empty clauses are of little interest as any set of clauses containing an empty clause is insatisfiable, and it corresponds to an FD with no valid configuration.

[2] Let us notice that they can appear in a formula satisfying Property 2 provided that, combined with other clauses, they can disappear to the benefit of emergence of clauses of the admitted patterns BI, MX, OR, XOR, CF, or DF.

low edge and a high edge. A path from the root to a leaf corresponds to a variable assignment (i.e., a configuration): a low edge assigns the variable to 0, and a high edge assigns the variable to 1. The value of an assignment is given by the leaf (terminal node), which is equal to either 1 (valid configuration) or 0 (invalid configuration). It is an extensional representation of the configuration set. The BDT representation has redundancies, which can be avoided by node sharing, which results in a graph called **Binary Decision Diagram** (BDD) [4,7]. The term BDD usually refers to ROBDD (for Reduced Ordered Binary Decision Diagram), which is unique for a given propositional formula. A ROBDD therefore represents the set of valid configurations (models of φ), but it does not represent feature or configuration interactions. However, ROBDDs are logically complete. Figure 2 presents the ROBDD associated with the part of Table 1 restricted to features e_commerce, catalog, grid, and list.

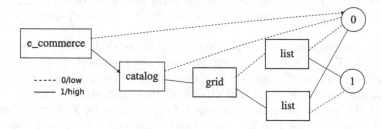

Fig. 2. ROBDD associated with the first four features of Table 1

Binary Implication Graphs [1,7,8,16,17]. A Binary Implication Graph (BIG) is a directed graph denoted by $G(V, E)$ where $V = F = \{f_1, \ldots, f_k\}$ and $E = \{(f_i, f_j) \mid \varphi \wedge (f_i \rightarrow f_j)\}$ representing binary implications (BI) between features. A feature f_i *implies* a feature f_j when each valid configuration having f_i also has f_j. BIGs are intensional representations structuring the product line feature set. This type of representation is not canonical, but its transitive closure and transitive reduction are. Figure 3 (left-hand side) presents the transitive reduction of the BIG associated with the first four features of Table 1.

Directed Hypergraphs [7]. A directed hypergraph is a directed graph generalisation where an arc can connect more than two vertices: such arcs are called hyperarcs. Vertices correspond to variables (features of F) and Boolean constants (0 and 1). A directed hypergraph can represent all types of non-empty clauses. A clause having both negative and positive literals is represented by a hyperarc $A \rightarrow B$ with $A, B \subseteq F$, A being the conjunction of the clause negative literals and B the disjunction of the clause positive literals. A clause having only negative literals is represented by a hyperarc $A \rightarrow 0$, and a clause with only positive literals is represented by a hyperarc $1 \rightarrow A$. As BIGs, their transitive reduction/closure are canonical representations, and they structure the feature set in an intensional representation. Figure 3 (right-hand side) presents the directed hypergraph transitive reduction of the first four features of Table 1.

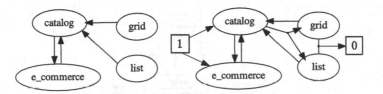

Fig. 3. Transitive reduction of the binary implication graph (left-hand side) and the directed hypergraph (right-hand side) associated with the first four features of Table 1

Mutex Graphs [16,17]. A mutex graph is an undirected graph denoted by $G(V, E)$ where $V = F = \{f_1, \ldots, f_k\}$ and $E = \{\{f_i, f_j\} \mid \varphi \wedge \neg(f_i \wedge f_j)\}$ representing mutual exclusions, also called mutex (MX) between features. Features are mutually exclusive if they cannot appear together in any valid configuration. There is a unique mutex graph associated with a propositional formula. Note that a clique in the graph represents incompatibilities inside each pair of involved features. Figure 4 (left-hand side) presents the mutex graph extracted from Table 1.

Feature Diagram Generalised Notation and Feature Graphs [7,17]. Czarnecki and Wasowski [7] propose an FD generalised notation where the feature tree may be replaced by a directed acyclic graph (encompassing require cross-tree constraints as optional relationships), feature groups may overlap, and co-occurrent features are visualised in a single node. Exclude cross-tree constraints are not represented in this formalism. This generalised notation is a canonical and intensional representation that covers the same information found in usual FDs except mutual exclusions (i.e., BI, OR and, XOR) but without the structural constraints that require expert decisions during the synthesis. An FD in generalised notation therefore represents several FDs. She et al. [17] extend this notation with mutex groups and mutual exclusions, and called this extension a feature graph. A mutex group is a set of features such that each pair is a mutex (i.e., corresponding to a clique in the mutex graph). Feature graphs depict MX in addition to FD generalised notation relationships (see the right-hand side of Fig. 4 for an example).

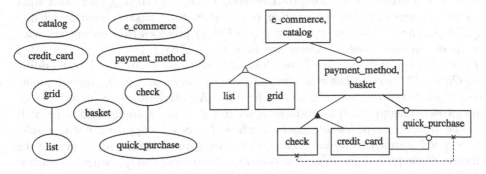

Fig. 4. Mutex graph (left-hand side) and feature graph (right-hand side) of Table 1

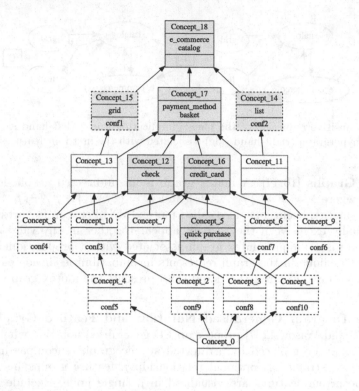

Attribute-concepts are coloured in grey and object-concepts have a dashed border.

Fig. 5. Concept lattice associated with Table 1

Conceptual Structures [9]. A set of configurations (e.g., Table 1) naturally underlies a formal context $K = (G, M, J)$ composed of configurations (G), features (M), and a binary relation (J) stating which configuration has which feature. Formal Concept Analysis (FCA) is a natural framework for variability representation: each concept $C = (E, I)$ gathers a maximal set of configurations E (extent) sharing a maximal set of features I (intent). For example, $Concept\_5$ from Fig. 5 gathers the configurations $conf9$ and $conf10$, together with their shared features $e\_commerce$, $catalog$, $payment\_method$, $basket$, $credit\_card$, and $quick\ purchase$. The concept lattice (see Fig. 5) provides the concept set with a specialisation order $\leq$, where we have $C_1 = (E_1, I_1) \leq C_2 = (E_2, I_2)$ if $E_1 \subseteq E_2$. For instance, we have $Concept\_5 \leq Concept\_16$, the latter adding to $Concept\_5$'s extent the configurations $conf3$, $conf5$, and $conf6$, and eliminating $quick\ purchase$ from the shared features. An attribute-concept $\mu(f)$ (resp. an object-concept $\gamma(c)$) introduces a feature f (resp. a configuration c), if it is the highest (resp. lowest) concept where f (resp. c) appears. For example, $Concept\_5$ is an attribute-introducer (introducing $quick\ purchase$), in grey in the figure, $Concept\_6$ is an object-introducer (introducing $conf7$), within a dashed border concept in the figure. In the representation, the features (resp. config-urations) are only written in their introducer concept and inherited top-down (resp. bottom-up). Several sub-structures are of interest for the SPL domain. The AC-poset (resp. OC-poset) is the sub-order of the concept lattice restricted to attribute-concepts (resp. object-concepts), while the AOC-poset contains both types of introducers. FCA conceptual structures are the only graph-based vari-ability representations being both intensional and extensional, and structuring both products and features. They are also canonical and logically complete.

Equivalence Class Feature Diagrams [6]. An Equivalence Class Feature Diagram (ECFD) is derived from an AC-poset. It has been introduced in [6] as an intermediate canonical structure for analysing variability. It graphically represents all the feature co-occurrences (equivalent features, like *e_commerce* and *catalog*), and all the BI (with ECFD arrows), MX, OR, and XOR that can be extracted from the concept lattice. It may also contain generalised exclu-sions (*NAT*, standing for *Not All Together*), i.e., of the form n^{3+}. The OR and XOR groups may overlap and the ECFD structure corresponds to an acyclic graph. Figure 6 (right-hand side) shows the ECFD extracted from the AC-poset of Fig. 6 (left-hand side). All the feature diagrams that have the same config-uration semantics can be embedded in the ECFD built on the formal context associated to the configuration set. It is an intensional and canonical represen-tation structuring the feature set, but it is not logically complete, as it aims to represent FD variability information.

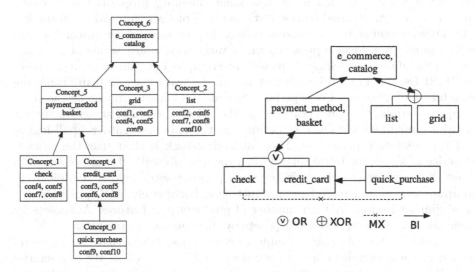

Fig. 6. AC-poset (left-hand side) and extracted ECFD (right-hand side) associated with Table 1

5 Towards a Classification of the Graph-Based Formalisms for Variability

In this section, we first compare the studied formalisms depending on the covered propositional logical expressions and the properties related to the graph-based representation. We then give examples of possible uses of this comparison.

Table 3 gathers information about the formalisms presented in the previous sections. The first two vertical parts of the table present the logical properties that are defined in Sect. 3. The first six columns state if a formalism is able to express the clause set patterns found in traditional FDs. The next four columns present the four disjunctive clause patterns that cannot be diagrammatically represented (if they are not combined with other clause patterns) in an FD. They characterise the propositional formulas that should complete the FD semantics to represent all possible configuration sets. The third vertical part of the table gives representation properties, i.e., the canonicity of the formalisms, if they structure the feature set or the product set, and if they are intensional or extensional representations. The last two columns state if the formalisms need to own a root feature, and if their feature groups are distinct (i.e., do not overlap). They correspond to the meta-properties expressed in Sect. 3. The `rooted` column is not applicable (*na*) for formalisms that do not represent binary implications, and the `distinct groups` column is not applicable for formalisms without feature groups. The formalisms that can express the ten types of clause set patterns are therefore logically complete. Aside from FMs, which are logically complete thanks to their complementary propositional formulas, three types of graph-based representations can depict all propositional formulas. ROBDDs are complete and canonical, but they do not provide feature organisation in an intensional representation of variability, which is one of the main goal of variability modelling. Directed hypergraphs have the same advantages as ROBDDs, but in addition they structure the feature set to help visualising variability information. Concept lattices and AOC-posets appear as the most complete variability representations, as they also depict and structure the set of valid configurations. These structures are the only ones gathering all logical and representation properties. Their main drawback is their size: the number of nodes in a concept lattice may grow exponentially with the size of the data input, as they organise both feature and product sets, making it difficult to compute and use to handle large product lines. Fortunately, AOC-posets have a node number limited by their number of products plus features, AC-posets by their number of features and OC-posets by their number of products.

Thanks to this table, we are able to characterise CNFs that can be represented by each formalism, as we have done for FDs in Sect. 3. We characterise a CNF by (1) a conjunction of clause set patterns of certain types and (2) some meta-properties. For a given formalism, the CNFs that can be written as a conjunction of the clause set patterns associated to this formalism (amongst the types in columns [2–11]) and that respect the corresponding meta-properties (amongst those in the last two columns) can be represented diagrammatically by this formalism. Note that our analysis reveals that the two meta-properties

Table 3. Comparison of the different graph-based variability representations depending on logical and representation properties

Formalism	np (BI)	n^2 (MX)	OR	XOR	p (CF)	n (DF)	n^{3+} (NAT)	p^+n^{2+}	n^+p^{2+}	p^{2+}	Canonical	Feature Struct.	Product Struct.	Intension	Extension	Rooted	Distinct groups
FD	x	x	x	x	x	x						x		x		x	x
FM	x	x	x	x	x	x	x	x	x	x		x		x		x	x
ROBDD	x	x	x	x	x	x	x	x	x	x	x				x		
BIG (Trans. Red)	x			x							x	x		x			na
Mutex Graph		x									x	x		x		na	na
FM Gen. Nota.	x		x	x	x	x					x	x		x			
Feature Graph	x	x	x	x	x	x					x	x		x			
Dir. Hypergraph	x	x	x	x	x	x	x	x	x	x	x	x		x			
Concept Lattice	x	x	x	x	x	x	x	x	x	x	x	x	x	x	x		
AOC-Poset	x	x	x	x	x	x	x	x	x	x	x	x	x	x	x		
AC-Poset	x	x	x	x	x	x	x	x	x	x	x	x			x		
OC-Poset	x	x	x	x	x	x	x	x	x	x	x		x	x	x		
ECFD	x	x	x	x	x	x					x	x		x			
ECFD+NAT	x	x	x	x	x	x	x				x	x		x			

are only necessary to FDs and FMs. Conversely, the comparison can be used to detect logic formulas that cannot be expressed by the existing graphical formalisms.

Our comparison may also be used to assist a designer who aims to represent the variability of a product line structured in a formalism A (for instance, which can be automatically extracted) with another formalism B (for instance, which needs an expert intervention during the synthesis). If the target formalism represents the same set or a subset of clause patterns of the ones represented by the source formalism, the transformation can be done without logical information loss. If the source formalism represents a subset of clauses of the ones represented by the target formalism, our analysis helps the designer identify the type of logical relationships that will be lost in the transformation.

6   Conclusion

Variability modelling is a central aspect in the spreading paradigm of product lines in product design and construction. Disposing of a variety of formalisms, a clear understanding of their scope and applicability, and embedding methodologies and algorithms is of major importance. In this paper, we give keys to move in these directions. The point is not to oppose the different formalisms, but to be able to use the right one at the right moment. We survey the most popular and in-use formalisms in SPL engineering research where most of the current advances are made, ranging from feature diagrams to conceptual structures. We compare and discuss them through disjunctive clauses categories that highlight their expressiveness, and through other properties such as canonicity, and whether they emphasise the relations between features, configurations, and both features and configurations. Conceptual structures play a particular role in this variety of formalisms, providing canonical representations, configuration-oriented as well as feature-oriented views, while being logically complete.

As future work, the comparison can be extended to non-Boolean formalisms including FDs with attributes or with references. FCA owns extensions, namely pattern structures and relational concept analysis, which could be used to capture new aspects of variability modelling. New graphical operators could also be imagined as a result of these studies. For identified useful transformations, we could investigate how one formalism embeds into another one, with which possible precision loss and algorithmic complexity.

References

1. Acher, M., Baudry, B., Heymans, P., Cleve, A., Hainaut, J.: Support for reverse engineering and maintaining feature models. In: Proceedings of the 7th International Workshop on Variability Modelling of Software-intensive Systems, pp. 20:1–20:8 (2013)
2. Benavides, D., Segura, S., Ruiz-Cortés, A.: Automated analysis of feature models 20 years later: a literature review. Inf. Syst. **35**(6), 615–636 (2010)
3. Bontemps, Y., Heymans, P., Schobbens, P., Trigaux, J.: Generic semantics of feature diagrams variants. In: Feature Interactions in Telecommunications and Software Systems VIII, pp. 58–77 (2005)
4. Bryant, R.E.: Graph-based algorithms for boolean function manipulation. IEEE Trans. Comput. **35**(8), 677–691 (1986)
5. Carbonnel, J., Huchard, M., Miralles, A., Nebut, C.: Feature model composition assisted by formal concept analysis. In: Proceedings of the 12th International Conference on Evaluation of Novel Approaches to Software Engineering, pp. 27–37 (2017)
6. Carbonnel, J., Huchard, M., Nebut, C.: Analyzing variability in product families through canonical feature diagrams. In: Proceedings of the 29th International Conference on Software Engineering and Knowledge Engineering, pp. 185–190 (2017)
7. Czarnecki, K., Wasowski, A.: Feature diagrams and logics: there and back again. In: Proceedings of the 11th International Software Product Line Conference, pp. 23–34 (2007)
8. Davril, J., Delfosse, E., Hariri, N., Acher, M., Cleland-Huang, J., Heymans, P.: Feature model extraction from large collections of informal product descriptions. In: Proceedings of the 9th Joint Meeting of the European Software Engineering Conference and the ACM SIGSOFT Symposium on the Foundations of Software Engineering, pp. 290–300 (2013)
9. Ganter, B., Stumme, G., Wille, R. (eds.): Formal Concept Analysis. LNCS (LNAI), vol. 3626. Springer, Heidelberg (2005). https://doi.org/10.1007/978-3-540-31881-1

10. Knüppel, A.: The role of complex constraints in feature modeling. Master's thesis, Institute of Software Engineering and Automotive Informatics, Technische Universität Carolo-Wilhelmina zu Braunschweig (2016)

11. Mannion, M.: Using first-order logic for product line model validation. In: Chastek, G.J. (ed.) SPLC 2002. LNCS, vol. 2379, pp. 176–187. Springer, Heidelberg (2002). https://doi.org/10.1007/3-540-45652-X_11

12. Mazo, R., Salinesi, C., Diaz, D., Djebbi, O., Lora-Michiels, A.: Constraints: the heart of domain and application engineering in the product lines engineering strategy. IJISMD **3**(2), 33–68 (2012)

13. Pohl, K., Böckle, G., van der Linden, F.J.: Software Product Line Engineering: Foundations, Principles, and Techniques. Springer, Heidelberg (2005). https://doi.org/10.1007/3-540-28901-1

14. Ryssel, U., Ploennigs, J., Kabitzsch, K.: Extraction of feature models from formal contexts. In: Workshop Proceedings of the 15th International Conference on Software Product Lines, vol. 2, pp. 4:1–4:8 (2011)

15. Schobbens, P., Heymans, P., Trigaux, J., Bontemps, Y.: Generic semantics of feature diagrams. Comput. Netw. **51**(2), 456–479 (2007)

16. She, S., Lotufo, R., Berger, T., Wasowski, A., Czarnecki, K.: Reverse engineering feature models. In: Proceedings of the 33rd International Conference on Software Engineering, pp. 461–470 (2011)

17. She, S., Ryssel, U., Andersen, N., Wasowski, A., Czarnecki, K.: Efficient synthesis of feature models. Inf. Softw. Technol. **56**(9), 1122–1143 (2014)

Publishing Uncertainty on the Semantic Web: Blurring the LOD Bubbles

Ahmed El Amine Djebri, Andrea G. B. Tettamanzi$^{(\boxtimes)}$, and Fabien Gandon$^{(\boxtimes)}$

Université Côte d'Azur, Inria, CNRS, I3S, Sophia Antipolis, France
djebri.emp@gmail.com, andrea.tettamanzi@univ-cotedazur.fr,
fabien.gandon@inria.fr

Abstract. The open nature of the Web exposes it to the many imperfections of our world. As a result, before we can use knowledge obtained from the Web, we need to represent that fuzzy, vague, ambiguous and uncertain information. Current standards of the Semantic Web and Linked Data do not support such a representation in a formal way and independently of any theory. We present a new vocabulary and a framework to capture and handle uncertainty in the Semantic Web. First, we define a vocabulary for uncertainty and explain how it allows the publishing of uncertainty information relying on different theories. In addition, we introduce an extension to represent and exchange calculations involved in the evaluation of uncertainty. Then we show how this model and its operational definitions support querying a data source containing different levels of uncertainty metadata. Finally, we discuss the perspectives with a view on supporting reasoning over uncertain linked data.

Keywords: Uncertainty · Linked data · Semantic web

1 Introduction

Many applications consume data from the World Wide Web either as main data to perform some analysis or as additional data to augment internal databases. However, the Web is an open world where everyone can state any information, with the possibility of altering existing assertions and publishing incorrect, ambiguous, misleading or uncertain information. In addition, users can be biased against controversial sources that might afford correct and valid information, and blindly trust some other sources. The lack of objectivity and the deficiencies of the Web are projected onto the Semantic Web [1] and the Linked Data [2], as the latter is mostly populated by harvesting existing Web resources. For instance, a huge amount of data in *Freebase* [3] was imported automatically and independently of the approval of the community. Before these external sources may be used in data mining or other data processing, their reliability must be assessed.

Uncertainty might differ from one use case to another in terms of nature and requirements. It can take the form of inconsistencies, incompleteness, ambiguity, vagueness, etc. The use of such uncertain data requires a specific representation

© Springer Nature Switzerland AG 2019
D. Endres et al. (Eds.): ICCS 2019, LNAI 11530, pp. 42–56, 2019.
https://doi.org/10.1007/978-3-030-23182-8_4

which the current standards of the Semantic Web of Linked data are not able to fulfill without extensions. Although the Semantic Web technologies have been adopted in many applications over the last two decades—recommender systems [4], news aggregators [5], and even the legal domain [6]—operating with uncertain data in such domains raises multiple questions. The main question we address in this paper is: *Can uncertainty be formalized on top of the standards of the Semantic Web to be published on the Web?*

To answer this question, we present a new vocabulary for the representation of uncertainty in the Semantic Web. The meta-Uncertainty vocabulary enables the representation of custom uncertainty approaches using standard RDF and the annotation of sentences and worlds using uncertainty values. It also allows the publishing of uncertainty calculi, enabling the reusability of uncertainty approaches. Afterward, we present an original framework enabling multi-level uncertainty mapping to sentences. The latter is mapped to a combination of their own uncertainty information and that of their context.

Section 2 describes the related work and Sect. 3 focuses on motivating scenario and the formalization of uncertainty in the Semantic Web. Section 4 addresses querying and mapping metadata about uncertainty. Section 5 is a discussion of the current state of our work before we conclude with perspectives.

2   Related Work

The study of deficiencies and uncertainty of information issued from the Web has been the object of a non-negligible part of the research work of the Semantic Web community. One of the main challenges [7] of interconnected uncertain data sources is the representation of uncertainty itself. The standardization is crucial for interoperable applications relying on the uncertain Web in which some sources have already an application-specific representation for uncertainty.

Uncertainty in the literature can be represented in many theories, each having a formal background, a set of measures and a defined calculus. Dubois et al. [8] present an overview of uncertainty representations in Artificial Intelligence and Decision Theory and discuss multiple theories, such as probability theory, the theory of evidence of Dempster-Shafer and possibility theory. Klir et al. [9] observe that dealing with uncertainty consists of four distinct levels: representation, calculus, measurement, and development of methodological aspects of the theory. Our focus in this paper is on the first two levels.

To adapt the previous uncertainty representations to fit within the Semantic Web Standards, the W3C Incubator Group URW3-XG proposed an ontology to formalize data annotation with uncertainty information [10]. The work focuses on the type and the nature of uncertainty models. However, the ontology proposed a limited set of theories for which metrics for comparison or evaluation are not offered. That does not allow evaluating uncertainty information nor comparing two uncertain statements to tell which one is more reliable. Another work presents a vocabulary for imprecise values [11]. The aim was to use the new definition to solve data fusion problems by extending RDF semantics [12] with source and interval information. This vocabulary offers to handle fuzzy or inconsistent data and is useful in time-based reasoning. Yet this vocabulary does not provide a formal definition of uncertainty.

Another part of the literature focuses on extending the current standards of the Semantic Web to fit in the existing uncertainty theories. Some authors presented probability as a *threshold* [13] or a *confidence score* [14] linked to a graph pattern. Other authors extended the OWL standard by linking a *degree of truth* with statements to enable representing Bayesian Networks [15]. More extensions propose to handle fuzzy values [16] and possibility theory [17] each using a specific set of measures depending on the theory. In general, each of these previous works focuses only on one uncertainty theory and defines a set of measurements (features) to rely on while ranking, reasoning, or aggregating uncertain data. However, limiting the representation of uncertainty to one approach per application requires implementing as many extensions as existing approaches. In that case, the problem of sharing and reusing data between the different systems persists.

To the best of our knowledge, there is no work that offers to publish uncertainty theories alongside their features and calculus. Interesting work from Dividino et al. [18] introduced the meta-knowledge mapping to statements using a non-standard representation (Quintuples) and two separated graphs (one for knowledge, another for meta-knowledge). Their framework enables the system administrator to define meta-knowledge properties and, for each property, one should define the intended semantics and the knowledge dimension inside the application in a non-standard format.

From another angle, the use of uncertain information invokes the question about context, since the reliability of information may differ from one context to another. A good reference about the importance of a context while reasoning about data validity can be found in [19]. We are interested in the case where data stated in a context can inherit its metadata.

Currently, the closest standard representation of contexts in Semantic Web is Named Graphs [20]. Data can be encapsulated inside a named graph, referenced by a URI, which can be annotated by metadata. Such representation also enables expressing and reasoning with different viewpoints without creating conflicts or inconsistencies. However, named graphs have no defined semantics in RDF other than being named containers inside the default graph. Hence, annotating a named graph does not reflect on the contained data as there is no semantic mapping between the data and their named graph. As mentioned in [21], named graphs in RDF datasets are irrelevant to determining the truth of a dataset as the latter depends on the RDF interpretation of the default graph. The document also indicates the necessity to extend RDFS [22] to support ternary relations. A simple alternative to named graphs is reification, allowing meta-statements about statements. Nevertheless, the reified statement does not necessarily assert the original one and the same problem about the propagation of the metadata from the associated context is present. A proposal in [23] approves the use of named graphs as contexts and argues that the former are already defined by a URI. In addition, the proposal extends the semantics of RDF to use inheritance in context building. Hence, the sub-contexts are more specific than the super-contexts. Nevertheless, in order for this to work at a triple level, each and every triple should have its own context with personalized metadata. Moreover, this work considers only overriding general metadata with more specific ones, hence the logic of uncertainty theory is not applied since a triple may have different aggregation and conflict resolution techniques for each uncertainty features.

3   Formalizing and Publishing Uncertainty on the Semantic Web

The first step in publishing uncertainty is to support its representation in a way that can be queried and processed. The formalism and the calculation allowed by this representation must provide results together with uncertainty meta-data that are helpful to the user in making decisions. In particular, the model we target must account for the use of different theories to represent uncertainty – for instance across different sources – and the calculus required within and between them – for instance when joining or aggregating data.

In this section we define the $mUnc$[1] vocabulary, formalized in OWL. Then we introduce an extension based on the *LDScript* function definition language [24] to define the calculus attached to a given uncertainty theory. Finally, we provide the first validation of the expressivity of our model w.r.t. the state of the art by showing how it can capture very different types of uncertainty theories.

3.1   *mUnc*: A Vocabulary for Uncertainty Theories

mUnc (for *meta-Unc*ertainty) is an OWL ontology for representing uncertainty metadata. It enables publishing uncertainty information based on uncertainty theories. Figure 1 gives an overview of the core concepts and properties of *mUnc*including: sentences, contexts (worlds) and uncertainty metadata (theories, features, calculi).

We have taken the definition of *sentence* and *world* proposed by the URW3-XG. A *sentence* is an expression evaluating a truth value, while the *world* represents the context in which a *sentence* is stated. Both sentences and worlds, can be annotated with *meta* information. For instance, the sentence ex:S1 representing the triple ⟨ex:StefanoTacconi, dbo:height, 188⟩ referring to the height of the football player is stated in the context of the French language chapter of DBpedia [25], assuming that the latter is consistent [26]. Uncertainty information is considered a specialization of the general concept of metadata. This simplifies the future extensions for other types of metadata such as provenance or trust. For the same reason, we do not include the concept of *Agent*, as it can be included using other vocabularies like W3C *PROV*[2] Ontology.

An uncertainty theory (*Uncertainty Approach*) is linked to a set of *features* and *operators*. The *features* are the metrics on which uncertainty theory is based

---

[1] http://ns.inria.fr/munc/.

[2] http://www.w3.org/TR/prov-o/.

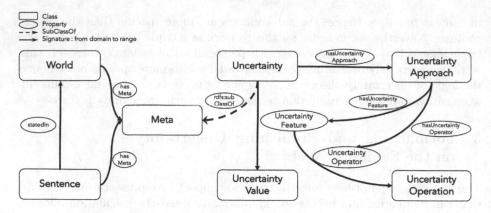

Fig. 1. Overview of the *mUnc* ontology and its core concepts

to indicate the degree of truth, credibility, or likelihood of a sentence. Each *feature* links a *value* to the *uncertainty* information. The *operators* represent the logic to apply to the previous *values*, while the *operations* are the implemented calculus for such logic. Other concepts in URW3-XG like the type or the derivation of uncertainty can be represented as features of an uncertainty approach.

To illustrate the previous definitions, we can annotate the previous sentence using probability theory. The latter can be represented using only one feature: the probability value. We choose three logical operators to include with the definition: and, or, not. Listing 1.1 shows how to assert that a sentence ex:S1 is true with a probability of 0.7.

```
ex:Probability a munc:UncertaintyApproach;
    munc:hasUncertaintyFeature ex:probabilityValue;
    munc:hasUncertaintyOperator ex:and, ex:or, ex:not.

ex:probabilityValue a munc:uncertaintyFeature;
    rdfs:range xsd:decimal.

ex:S1 munc:hasMeta [a munc:Uncertainty;
    munc:hasUncertaintyApproach ex:Probability;
    ex:probabilityValue 0.7].
```

Listing 1.1. Representing the probabilistic approach using *mUnc*

3.2   Attaching Uncertainty Calculi to Theories

Semantic Web ontology languages focus on classification ontological knowledge and do not support the provision of procedural attachments or functions inside ontologies. Our model allows linking the features of uncertainty approaches to their proper calculi (arithmetic, logical, comparison, etc). To represent the calculi, we rely on the *LDScript* function definition language [24]. This language is an ideal candidate as it is based on the SPARQL filter language and allows defining and using extension functions directly inside the Semantic Web framework. Using *LDScript*, we can define functions having a URI as a name and one or several arguments that are variables in SPARQL syntax. This enables defining uncertainty operations and link them to features using operators. To continue with the previous example, considering the fact that the sentence ex:S1 is true with a probability of 0.7, and is stated in a context ex:C1 in which all facts are considered true with a probability of 0.9, the conjunction of the two probabilities, assumed to be independent, is calculated using the formula

$$P(A \wedge B) = P(A) \times P(B). \tag{1}$$

The conjunction of the two previous values can be presented to the user using the function ex:MultiplyIndependentProbability defined using *LDScript* as shown in Listing 1.2.

```
function ex:MultiplyIndependentProbability(?pA, ?pB){
    ?pA * ?pB
}
```

Listing 1.2. Conjunction of independent probabilities using *LDScript*

Therefore, binding the function ex:MultiplyIndependentProbability (0.7, 0.9) during a SPARQL query execution will return 0.63. The former definition of the probabilistic approach using *mUnc* can be enriched by linking the URI of the function to the declared feature:

ex:ProbabilityValue ex:and ex:MultiplyIndependentProbability.

3.3   Validating the Expressivity on State of the Art Theories

As a validation of our approach, we show in this section how it supports the use of different theories to express uncertainty. A first example with the probability theory was presented in the previous section.

The enumeration of the features linked to an uncertainty theory and the comprehension of their calculus (operations) enable *mUnc* to represent existing uncertainty theories that are defined in the literature [8,9,27].

We can annotate the previous example using a possibilistic approach, with *validity* and *completeness* as features, as proposed in the work by da Costa Pereira et al. [28]. In Listing 1.3 we specify also the types for values linked to the proposed features:

```
ex:Possibility a munc:UncertaintyApproach;
    munc:hasUncertaintyFeatures ex:validity, ex:completeness;
    munc:hasUncertaintyOperators ex:and, ex:or, ex:not.
ex:validity, ex:completeness a munc:uncertaintyFeature;
    rdfs:range xsd:decimal.
```

Listing 1.3. Possibility theory using *mUnc*

The operations for such features will be different as the conjunction of two *validity* values is their maximum. The latter can be evaluated by the function ex:Max defined in the Listing 1.4. This function can be defined once and linked to any uncertainty approach.

```
function ex:Max(?v1, ?v2){
    if(?v1 >= ?v2) { ?v1 }
    else { ?v2 }
}
```

Listing 1.4. Conjunction of *validity* measures using *LDScript*

In this example we consider a sentence ex:S2 with no uncertainty information, and another sentence ex:S3 imported from another context ex:C2 having uncertainty information. The latter can be annotated with metadata about the provenance, which can be provided using *PROV* vocabulary. This enables the traceability of uncertainty information.

```
ex:S2, ex:S3 munc:statedIn ex:C1.

ex:S2 munc:hasMeta [a munc:Uncertainty;
    munc:hasUncertaintyApproach ex:Possibility;
    ex:validity 1;
    ex:completeness 0.3
    prov:wasDerivedFrom ex:ExternalSource].

ex:C1 munc:hasMeta [a munc:Uncertainty;
    munc:hasUncertaintyApproach ex:Possibility;
    ex:validity 0.8;
    ex:completeness 0.6].
```

Listing 1.5. Context annotation

Besides the existing uncertainty theories, *mUnc* can be used to define custom approaches to handle measures (datatypes) that cannot fit in the RDF standard. For example, we can define a custom approach to deal with fuzzy values using lower and upper bounds as uncertainty features, and the several functions about fuzzy values as uncertainty operations.

In the next section, we will discuss how to link between uncertainty information and sentences during the query processing.

4   Querying for Uncertain Linked Data

The presentation of uncertain linked data to the end user requires more information to be provided during the query processing, enabling him or her to rank and choose among the given answers. Since each sentence and context has its own uncertainty information, if a sentence is stated in a context, uncertainty information from both should be combined to form a result. For instance, if a sentence S in a context A has no uncertainty information, it inherits uncertainty information from A (noted as $\mathcal{U}_A$). Otherwise, S will be annotated with a combination of both $\mathcal{U}_{S_A}$ and $\mathcal{U}_A$.

4.1 Semantics of RDF with mUnc

Our work focusses on querying n uncertain data sources $s_1, s_2, ..., s_n$, each possibly containing several named graphs $G_{ij}, i \in \{1, \ldots, n\}$ representing each a set of coherent information. This means that each named graph contains a set of triples that do not lead to a contradictory reasoning. For example, if a named graph contains a triple (dbo:height, rdf:type, owl:FunctionalProperty), it cannot have both triples (ex:Person1, dbo:height, 188) and (ex:Person1, dbo:height, 195). We still can declare both triples in different named graphs. We recall here the definition of RDF Dataset and perform the link with the set of contexts.

Definition 1 *(RDF dataset). An RDF dataset of a source s_i is a collection of RDF graphs, containing one default graph G_i and a set of named graphs, each consisting of a pair (u_j, G_{ij}) where u_j is the IRI of the graph G_{ij}. The set of named graphs can be the empty set.*

As cited in [21], named graphs are suitable for context representation as they allow encapsulating a set of triples in a graph and annotate the latter with metadata. Also, each named graph can represent a vision or an opinion over the reality represented in the source. A sentence can be cited in multiple named graphs but with different uncertainty information. For example, two websites can state that tomorrow it will rain. The two websites may not be sure about that information at different levels, so they annotate the fact with different uncertainty information. Each of the previous websites can be encapsulated in a named graph representing a *context*.

Definition 2 *(Context). A context $C_{ij}, j \geq 0$ is a named graph $(u_i, G_{ij}), j \geq 0$ in the RDF Dataset of a source s_i.*

Each context can be annotated with a set of uncertainty information triples defined as follows.

Definition 3 *(Context Uncertainty). A context uncertainty $\mathcal{U}_{C_{ij}}$ is a set of pairs $(UncertaintyFeature, UncertaintyValue)$ representing the uncertainty information about the context $C_{ij}, j \geq 0$ in a datasource s_i.*

Triples in the default graph of the source s_i may present a context on their own, and they are moved to a named graph G_{i0} representing a separate context C_{i0}. The set of pairs $(\mathcal{U}_{C_{ij}}, C_{ij})$ represents the *contextual dataset* (noted as $CDS(s_i)$) of datasource s_i.

Definition 4 *(Contextual Dataset). Given a datasource s_i and a set of Contexts $C_{ij}, j \geq 0$, each annotated with a set of metadata triples $\mathcal{U}_{C_{ij}}$, a contextual* dataset $CDS(s_i)$ of a datasource s_i is a set where C_i is the default context encapsulating metadata about other contexts, C_{i0} is the context encapsulating triples which was stored in the default graph G_i of datasource s_i.

$$CDS(s_i) = \{(\mathcal{U}_{C_{ij}}, C_{ij}) \mid j \geq 0\} \tag{2}$$

Figure 2 illustrates the definition of contextual datasets.

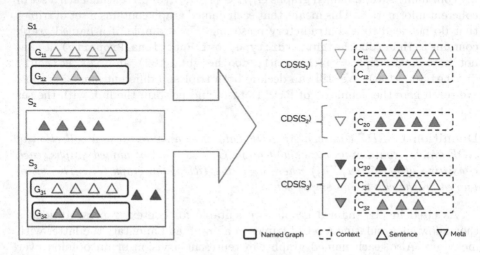

Fig. 2. Example of context encapsulation

Similar to context uncertainty, a sentence can have its own uncertainty information defined as follow.

Definition 5 *(Sentence Uncertainty). A sentence uncertainty $\mathcal{U}_{S_{C_{ij}}}$ is a set of pairs $(UncertaintyFeature, UncertaintyValue)$ representing the uncertainty information about the sentence S in a context C_{ij}.*

mUnc does not provide any extension of RDF Semantics. Instead, we rely on the SPARQL query language to provide a mapping between sentences and the uncertainty information presented to the user. Moreover, we consider *mUnc* as an approach to provide definitions of known and custom uncertainty theories, for which we do not provide any specific semantics. The possibility of defining a calculus alongside with the ontology is an alternative to generalize and to make reuse of the shared rules between uncertainty theories such as maximizing or minimizing a feature.

This process does not require a specific RDF representation (triple, quad, etc.) on data sources. It grants the possibility to unify data represented with different syntaxes (triples, quads, etc) and from several sources. For this, we extend the *Corese* semantic web engine [29] to enable loading and creating contexts in a transparent way. The process is executed while loading RDF data into *Corese*.

4.2 Query Resolution

In a semantic Web supporting the representation of uncertainty metadata, query results should include information about their uncertainty. The latter should be dependent on both sentences and their context.

Mapping each sentence S with its uncertainty information requires defining a *metadata-mapping mode* (see Table 1) to link between the metadata annotating the sentence and the one annotating the context in which the sentence is stated.

Definition 6 *(Meta-Mapping Mode). Given two sets $A = \{(x,y) \mid x \in F_1\}, B = \{(w,z) \mid w \in F_2\}$. A meta-mapping mode is the process linking A and B to a new set C where $C = \{(f,v) \mid (f,v_1) \in A, (f,v_2) \in B, v = v_1 \oplus v_2\}$.*

The meta-mapping modes are basically about choosing a set of uncertainty features, and what uncertainty value to associate to each feature based on their associated values in each of the initial sets. In the first two modes, only uncertainty information $\mathcal{U}_{C_{ij}}$ linked to the context C_{ij} is considered with a specification of the reading (distributive or collective) [18]. The third mode considers uncertainty information from the lowest level of granularity only, while the fourth mode enables inheriting context metadata but overrides the values for existing features in uncertainty information linked to the sentence.

Table 1. Metadata-mapping modes

Considered level of granularity	Mode	Explanation
Context	Inheritance	$\hat{\mathcal{U}}_{S_{C_{ij}}} = \mathcal{U}_{C_{ij}}$
Context	Distributive reading	$\mathcal{U}_{C_{ij}} = Comb(\{V_1, V_2, \ldots, V_{|C_{ij}|}\}), (F, V) \in \hat{\mathcal{U}}_{S_{C_{ij}}}$
Lowest granularity only	Override-All	$\hat{\mathcal{U}}_{S_{C_{ij}}} = \begin{cases} \mathcal{U}_{S_{C_{ij}}} & \text{if } \mathcal{U}_{S_{C_{ij}}} \neq \varnothing \\ \mathcal{U}_{C_{ij}} & \text{else} \end{cases}$
Lowest granularity first	Override if Exists	$\hat{\mathcal{U}}_{S_{C_{ij}}} = \mathcal{U}_{S_{C_{ij}}} \cup \{(F,V) \mid (F,V) \in \mathcal{U}_{C_{ij}}, F \notin \mathcal{U}_{S_{C_{ij}}}\}$
All	Combine	$\hat{\mathcal{U}}_{S_{C_{ij}}} = \{(F,V) \mid (F,V) \in \mathcal{U}_{C_{ij}}, \nexists V' (F,V') \in \mathcal{U}_{S_{C_{ij}}}\}$ $\cup \{(F,V) \mid (F,V) \in \mathcal{U}_{S_{C_{ij}}}, \nexists V'' (F,V'') \in \mathcal{U}_{C_{ij}}\}$ $\cup \{(F,V) \mid \exists V_{C_{ij}}, V_{S_{C_{ij}}} (F, V_{C_{ij}}) \in \mathcal{U}_{C_{ij}}, (F, V_{S_{C_{ij}}}) \in \mathcal{U}_{S_{C_{ij}}}, V = eval(Calculus(F), V_{C_{ij}}, V_{S_{C_{ij}}})\}$

The set of uncertainty information linked to a sentence S regarding its context is denoted as *Universal Uncertain Information Set* or $\hat{\mathcal{U}}_{S_{C_{ij}}}$ and defined as follows.

Definition 7 *(Universal Uncertain Information Set). A universal uncertain information set $\hat{\mathcal{U}}_{S_{C_{ij}}}$ of a sentence S in a context C_{ij} of the datasource s_i is a set of (UncertaintyFeature, UncertaintyValue) pairs issued by combining the sets $\mathcal{U}_{C_{ij}}, \mathcal{U}_{S_{C_{ij}}}$ using a meta-mapping mode.*

The mapping between a sentence S and its universal uncertainty information set $\hat{\mathcal{U}}_{S_{C_{ij}}}$ is a two steps process:

- Mapping both sentences and contexts to their uncertainty information. We denote $\mathcal{U}_{S_{C_{ij}}}$ the uncertainty information about the sentence S cited in the context C_{ij} and $\mathcal{U}_{C_{ij}}$ the uncertainty information about the context C_{ij}.
- $\mathcal{U}_{S_{C_{ij}}}$ is combined with $\mathcal{U}_{C_{ij}}$ using uncertainty operations linked to each feature, in order to evaluate its corresponding value in $\hat{\mathcal{U}}_{S_{C_{ij}}}$. In this step we apply the *metaList* algorithm (see Algorithm 1) translated form the formula in the fifth meta mapping-mode (see Table 1): $\hat{\mathcal{U}}_{S_{C_{ij}}} = metaList(\mathcal{U}_{S_{C_{ij}}}, \mathcal{U}_{C_{ij}})$.

Algorithm 1. *metaList*: Universal Uncertainty Information Set of a sentence S in a context C_{ij} of a datasource s_i

---

1: **procedure** METALIST$(\mathcal{U}_{S_{C_{ij}}}, \mathcal{U}_{C_{ij}})$
2:     $uncFeatures(x)$: list of all uncertainty features contained in the set x
3:     $uncValue(f, x)$: the value linked to the feature f in the set x
4:     $Operation(f)$: the uncertainty operation linked to the feature f
5:     $eval(o, v1, v2)$: execute the operation o passing the parameters $v1, v2$
6:     $\hat{\mathcal{U}}_{S_{C_{ij}}} \leftarrow \varnothing$
7:     **if** $\mathcal{U}_{S_{C_{ij}}} \neq \varnothing$ **then**
8:         **for all** $f \in uncFeatures(\mathcal{U}_{S_{C_{ij}}}) \cap uncFeatures(\mathcal{U}_{C_{ij}})$ **do**
9:             $v \leftarrow eval(Operation(f), uncValue(f, \mathcal{U}_{S_{C_{ij}}}), uncValue(f, \mathcal{U}_{C_{ij}}))$
10:             $\hat{\mathcal{U}}_{S_{C_{ij}}} \leftarrow \hat{\mathcal{U}}_{S_{C_{ij}}} \cup \{(f, v)\}$
11:         **end for**
12:         **for all** $f \in uncFeatures(\mathcal{U}_{C_{ij}}) \backslash (uncFeatures(\mathcal{U}_{S_{C_{ij}}}) \cap uncFeatures(\mathcal{U}_{C_{ij}}))$ **do**
13:             $v \leftarrow uncValue(f, \mathcal{U}_{C_{ij}})$
14:             $\hat{\mathcal{U}}_{S_{C_{ij}}} \leftarrow \hat{\mathcal{U}}_{S_{C_{ij}}} \cup \{(f, v)\}$
15:         **end for**
16:     **else**
17:         $\hat{\mathcal{U}}_{S_{C_{ij}}} \leftarrow \mathcal{U}_{C_{ij}}$
18:     **end if**
19:     **return** $\hat{\mathcal{U}}_{S_{C_{ij}}}$ ▷ the set of universal uncertainty information of the sentence S
20: **end procedure**

In our case, *Uncertainty Operations* are stored as Linked Functions. This feature in *Corese* [29] enables storing *LDScript* [24] functions in external SPARQL query files on the web to be called at the moment of query execution. The former feature permits publishing and executing the calculi of uncertainty approaches. Additionally, this approach may be extended to allow the capitalization of existing software libraries from other programming languages like C++ or Java.

5   Discussion

Compared to the previously published approaches, our work proposes an ontology to represent and formalize uncertainty, which covers also calculus. We rely on RDF standards to present existing uncertainty approaches in a machine-readable and reusable format. Our vocabulary also enables users to define their own uncertainty approaches and publish their definitions alongside with their uncertain data, allowing the reusability of the information in other Semantic Web applications.

The current representation of contexts using named graphs is limited because it requires the materialization of the graphs. Also, some sentences might be redundant in different contexts. A possible alternative would be the enrichment of RDF semantics to use `munc:statedIn` as an equivalent to storing sentences in named graphs. This gives more flexibility to the process and allows defining new methods and terms allowing context-overlapping and context-selective querying.

mUnc also enables representing uncertainty about uncertainty information, by considering the latter as sentences with uncertainty. Yet the combination of uncertainty information said about uncertainty sentences with the information provided by the sentences themselves is challenging. For the same reasons, the framework does not allow the combination of uncertainty information from multiple data sources using different uncertainty approaches. Sentences should be annotated using the same uncertainty approaches for the calculus to be executed, otherwise, this presents no problem with other metadata since they will be appended to the presented information using the *metaList* algorithm. Providing a solution for the latter problem, we can add a third step to the previous two-step process in Subsect. 4.1 corresponding to the combination of uncertainty information of identical sentences issued from different contexts with different uncertainty information. In any case, the *metaList* algorithm can be adapted to different types of metadata (ex: provenance).

A security problem about altering information can reach uncertainty calculi: altering uncertainty operations may alter the ranking of uncertain linked data and the newly generated data from it.

To the best of our knowledge, there is no previous work that offered a framework to handle uncertainty using a generic standard vocabulary to represent custom uncertainty approaches. Using our approach, uncertainty is represented using the Semantic Web standards to be publishable and reusable. In addition, the use of contexts and calculi allows more selectivity towards the metadata presented to the user and allows inferring new uncertainty information.

mUnc can extend the work by Cabrio et al. [30] by enriching the proposed fuzzy labeling algorithms with definitions of uncertainty theories suitable to the data. The Linked Data sources can adopt this approach to enrich federated queries with uncertainty information and, progressively, build a consensus-based Linked Data source. A set of other applications such as fake news detection (definition of a theory and logic for fake news), argumentation-based systems and even community-based datasources such as DBpedia can use *mUnc* to enrich their future content with uncertainty information.

6   Conclusion

In this paper, we discussed the representation and publication of uncertainty on the Semantic Web. We presented a vocabulary allowing the representation of uncertainty theories and the annotation of sentences using the Semantic Web standards. We explained the publishing of a reusable uncertainty calculi using *LDScript* and *Corese*.

Uncertainty representation is the first step of a long process, including the preliminary calculus of uncertainty values, the propagation of uncertainty among interconnecting sources. We plan to add the possibility of merging uncertain data annotated using different uncertainty approaches. We would like to implement context overlapping relying on a set of properties such as weights and thresholds, allowing the selectivity between context metadata and the optimization of the storage. Finally, this work makes a step towards inconsistency-tolerant and context-aware uncertain Web of data.

References

1. Berners-Lee, T., Hendler, J., Lassila, O.: The semantic web. Sci. Am. **284**(5), 34–43 (2001)
2. Bizer, C., Heath, T., Berners-Lee, T.: Linked data: the story so far. In: Semantic Services, Interoperability and Web Applications: Emerging Concepts, pp. 205–227. IGI Global (2011)
3. Bollacker, K., Evans, C., Paritosh, P., Sturge, T., Taylor, J.: Freebase: a collaboratively created graph database for structuring human knowledge. In: Proceedings of the 2008 ACM SIGMOD International Conference on Management of Data, pp. 1247–1250. ACM (2008)
4. Adomavicius, G., Tuzhilin, A.: Toward the next generation of recommender systems: a survey of the state-of-the-art and possible extensions. IEEE Trans. Knowl. Data Eng. **6**, 734–749 (2005)
5. Mohirta, M., Cernian, A., Carstoiu, D., Vladu, A.M., Olteanu, A., Sgarciu, V.: A semantic Web based scientific news aggregator. In: 2011 6th IEEE International Symposium on Applied Computational Intelligence and Informatics (SACI), pp. 285–289. IEEE (2011)
6. Gandon, F., Governatori, G., Villata, S.: Normative requirements as linked data. In: The 30th International Conference on Legal Knowledge and Information Systems (JURIX 2017) (2017)
7. Benslimane, D., Sheng, Q.Z., Barhamgi, M., Prade, H.: The uncertain web: concepts, challenges, and current solutions. ACM Trans. Internet Technol. (TOIT) **16**(1), 1 (2016)
8. Dubois, D., Prade, H.: Formal representations of uncertainty. In: Decision-making Process, chap. 3, pp. 85–156. Wiley (2010). https://doi.org/10.1002/9780470611876.ch3
9. Klir, G.J., Smith, R.M.: On measuring uncertainty and uncertainty-based information: recent developments. Ann. Math. Artif. Intell. **32**(1–4), 5–33 (2001)
10. Laskey, K.J., Laskey, K.B.: Uncertainty reasoning for the world wide web: report on the URW3-XG incubator group. In: URSW. Citeseer (2008)

11. Reynolds, D.: Uncertainty reasoning for linked data. In: Proceedings of the Fifth International Conference on Uncertainty Reasoning for the Semantic Web, vol. 527, pp. 85–88. CEUR-WS.org (2009)
12. Hayes, P.: RDF semantics, W3C recommendation (2004). http://www.w3.org/TR/rdf-mt/
13. McGlothlin, J.P., Khan, L.R.: Materializing and persisting inferred and uncertain knowledge in RDF datasets. In: AAAI, vol. 10, pp. 11–15 (2010)
14. d'Amato, C., Bryl, V., Serafini, L.: Semantic knowledge discovery and data-driven logical reasoning from heterogeneous data sources. In: Bobillo, F., et al. (eds.) URSW 2012, URSW 2011, URSW 2013. LNCS, vol. 8816, pp. 136–183. Springer, Cham (2014). https://doi.org/10.1007/978-3-319-13413-0_9
15. Ding, Z., Peng, Y., Pan, R.: BayesOWL: uncertainty modeling in semantic web ontologies. In: Ma, Z. (ed.) Soft Computing in Ontologies and Semantic Web, pp. 3–29. Springer, Heidelberg (2006)
16. Stoilos, G., Stamou, G.B., Tzouvaras, V., Pan, J.Z., Horrocks, I.: Fuzzy OWL: uncertainty and the semantic web. In: OWLED (2005)
17. Safia, B.B., Aicha, M.: Poss-OWL 2: possibilistic extension of OWL 2 for an uncertain geographic ontology. Procedia Comput. Sci. **35**, 407–416 (2014)
18. Dividino, R., Sizov, S., Staab, S., Schueler, B.: Querying for provenance, trust, uncertainty and other meta knowledge in RDF. Web Seman. Sci. Serv. Agents World Wide Web **7**(3), 204–219 (2009)
19. Bouquet, P., Serafini, L., Stoermer, H.: Introducing context into RDF knowledge bases. SWAP. **5**, 14–16 (2005)
20. Carroll, J.J., Bizer, C., Hayes, P., Stickler, P.: Named graphs, provenance and trust. In: Proceedings of the 14th International Conference on World Wide Web, pp. 613–622. ACM (2005)
21. Consortium, W.W.W., et al.: RDF 1.1 concepts and abstract syntax (2014)
22. Brickley, D., Guha, R.V., McBride, B.: RDF Schema 1.1. W3C recommendation 25, 2004–2014 (2014)
23. Corby, O., Faron-Zucker, C.: RDF/SPARQL design pattern for contextual metadata. In: Proceedings of the IEEE/WIC/ACM International Conference on Web Intelligence. WI 2007, pp. 470–473. IEEE Computer Society, Washington, DC (2007)
24. Corby, O., Faron-Zucker, C., Gandon, F.: LDScript: a linked data script language. In: dAmato, C., et al. (eds.) ISWC 2017. LNCS, vol. 10587, pp. 208–224. Springer, Cham (2017). https://doi.org/10.1007/978-3-319-68288-4_13
25. Bizer, C., Lehmann, J., Kobilarov, G., Auer, S., Becker, C., Cyganiak, R., Hellmann, S.: DBpedia-a crystallization point for the web of data. Web Seman. Sci. Serv. Agents World Wide Web **7**(3), 154–165 (2009)
26. Cabrio, E., Villata, S., Gandon, F.: Classifying inconsistencies in DBpedia language specific chapters. In: LREC, pp. 1443–1450 (2014)
27. Klir, G., Yuan, B.: Fuzzy Sets and Fuzzy Logic, vol. 4. Prentice Hall, Upper Saddle River (1995)
28. da Costa Pereira, C., Dubois, D., Prade, H., Tettamanzi, A.G.B.: Handling topical metadata regarding the validity and completeness of multiple-source information: a possibilistic approach. In: Moral, S., Pivert, O., Sánchez, D., Marín, N. (eds.) SUM 2017. LNCS (LNAI), vol. 10564, pp. 363–376. Springer, Cham (2017). https://doi.org/10.1007/978-3-319-67582-4_26
29. Corby, O., Zucker, C.F.: Corese: a corporate semantic web engine. In: International Workshop on Real World RDF and Semantic Web Applications, International World Wide Web Conference (2002)

30. Cabrio, E., Villata, S., Palmero Aprosio, A.: A RADAR for information reconciliation in question answering systems over linked data 1. Seman. Web **8**(4), 601–617 (2017)

Formal Context Generation Using Dirichlet Distributions

Maximilian Felde[1,2(✉)] and Tom Hanika[1,2]

[1] Knowledge and Data Engineering Group, University of Kassel, Kassel, Germany
{felde,tom.hanika}@cs.uni-kassel.de
[2] Interdisciplinary Research Center for Information System Design,
University of Kassel, Kassel, Germany

Abstract. Randomly generating formal contexts is an important task in the realm of formal concept analysis, in particular when comparing the performance of algorithms. We suggest an improved way to randomly generate formal contexts based on Dirichlet distributions. For this purpose we investigate the predominant method, coin-tossing, recapitulate some of its shortcomings and examine its stochastic model. Building upon this we propose our Dirichlet model and develop an algorithm employing this idea. Through an experimental evaluation we show that our approach is a significant improvement with respect to the variety of contexts generated.

Keywords: Formal concept analysis · Dirichlet distribution · Random context

1 Introduction

Formal concept analysis (FCA) is often used as a tool to represent and extract knowledge from data sets expressed as cross-tables between a set of objects and a set of attributes, called formal contexts. Many real-world data sets can be transformed, i.e., scaled, with little effort to be subjected to methods from FCA. There has been a great effort to develop methods to efficiently compute both formal concepts and their related properties. This has led to a multitude of algorithms at our disposal.

An important problem when investigating data sets through FCA is to decide whether an observed pattern is meaningful or not. Related fields, e.g., graph theory and ecology, employ *null model analysis*, cf. [10], a method that randomizes data sets with the constraint to preserve certain properties. This method can be easily adapted to FCA. Randomly generating formal contexts is also relevant for other applications, e.g., comparing the performance of FCA algorithms, as done in [1,8]. Both tasks can be approached by randomly generating formal contexts. Hence, one has to develop (novel) procedures to randomly generate

---

Authors are given in alphabetical order. No priority in authorship is implied.

© Springer Nature Switzerland AG 2019
D. Endres et al. (Eds.): ICCS 2019, LNAI 11530, pp. 57–71, 2019.
https://doi.org/10.1007/978-3-030-23182-8_5

formal contexts. However, methods for generating adequate random contexts
are insufficiently investigated [3].

A naïve approach for a random generation process is to uniformly draw from
the set of all formal contexts for a given set of attributes M. This approach is
infeasible as the number of formal contexts with pairwise distinct objects is $2^{2^{|M|}}$.
A related problem is the random generation of Moore families as investigated
in [6]. There, the author suggested an approach to uniformly draw from the set
of closure systems for a given set of attributes. However, this approach is not
feasible as well on attribute sets of more than seven elements.

The predominant procedure to randomly generate formal contexts is a coin-
tossing process, mainly due to the ease of use and the lack of proper alternatives.
Yet, this approach is biased to generate a certain class of contexts, as investigated
in [3]. Here we step in with a novel approach. Based upon a thorough exami-
nation of the coin-tossing approach we suggest an improved stochastic model
to randomly generate formal contexts using Dirichlet distributions. For this we
analyze the influence of the distribution parameters on the resulting contexts.
Afterwards we empirically evaluate our model on randomly generated formal
contexts with six to ten attributes. We show that our approach is a significant
improvement upon the coin-tossing process in terms of the variety of contexts
generated.

As for the structure of this paper in Sect. 2 we first give a short problem
description and recall some basic notions from FCA followed by a brief overview
of related work in Sect. 3. We proceed by stochastically modeling and examining
the coin-toss and suggest the Dirichlet model in Sect. 4. In Sect. 5 we evaluate
our model empirically and discuss our findings followed by a brief outlook on
possible applications in Sect. 6. Lastly in Sect. 7 we give our conclusions and an
outlook.

2   FCA Basics and Problem Description

We begin by recalling basic notions from formal concept analysis. For a thorough
introduction we refer the reader to [7]. A *formal context* is a triple $\mathbb{K} := (G, M, I)$
of sets. The elements of G are called *objects* and the elements of M *attributes* of
the context. The set $I \subseteq G \times M$ is called *incidence relation*, meaning $(g, m) \in
I \Leftrightarrow$ the object g has the attribute m. We introduce the common operators,
namely the *object derivation* $\cdot': \mathcal{P}(G) \rightarrow \mathcal{P}(M)$ by $A \subseteq G \mapsto A' := \{m \in
M \mid \forall g \in A\colon (g, m) \in I\}$, and the *attribute derivation* $\cdot': \mathcal{P}(M) \rightarrow \mathcal{P}(G)$ by
$B \subseteq M \mapsto B' := \{g \in G \mid \forall m \in B\colon (g, m) \in I\}$. A *formal concept* of a formal
context is a pair (A, B) with $A \subseteq G$, $B \subseteq M$ such that $A' = B$ and $B' = A$. We
then call A the *extent* and B the *intent* of the concept. With $\mathfrak{B}(\mathbb{K})$ we denote the
set of all concepts of some context $\mathbb{K}$. A pseudo-intent of $\mathbb{K}$ is a subset $P \subseteq M$
where $P \neq P''$ and $Q'' \subseteq P$ holds for every pseudo-intent $Q \subsetneq P$.

In the following we may omit *formal* when referring to formal contexts and
formal concepts. Of particular interest in the following is the class of formal contexts called *contranominal scales*. These contexts are constituted by $([n], [n], \neq)$

where $[n] := \{1, \ldots, n\}$. The number of concepts for a contranominal scale with n attributes is 2^n, thus having 2^n intents and therefore zero pseudo-intents. If a context (G, M, I) fulfills the property that for every $m \in M$ there exists an object $g \in G$ such that $g' = M \setminus \{m\}$, then (G, M, I) contains a subcontext isomorphic to a contranominal scale of size $|M|$, i.e, $\exists \hat{G} \subseteq G$ such that $(\hat{G}, M, I \cap (\hat{G} \times M)) \cong ([n], [n], \neq)$ with $n = |M|$.

In this paper we deal with the problem of randomly generating a formal context given a set of attributes. Our motivation originates in Fig. 1 where we show 5000 randomly generated contexts with ten attributes. The model used to generate these contexts is a *coin-toss*, as recalled more formally in Sect. 4. This method is the predominant approach to randomly generate formal contexts. In Fig. 1 we plotted the number of intents versus the number of pseudo-intents for each generated context and a histogram counting occurrences of pseudo-intentes. We may call this particular plotting method *I-PI plot*, where every point represents a particular combination of intent number and pseudo-intent number, called *I-PI coordinate*. Note that having the same I-PI coordinate does not imply that the corresponding contexts are isomorphic. However, different I-PI coordinates imply non-isomorphic formal contexts. The reason for employing intents and pseudo-intents is that they correspond to two fundamental features of formal contexts, namely *concept lattice* and *canonical implication base*, which we will not introduce in the realm of this work.

We observe in Fig. 1 that there appears to be a relation between the number of intents and the number of pseudo-intents. This was first mentioned in a paper by Borchmann [2]. Naturally, the question emerges whether this empirically observed correlation is based on a structural connection between intents and pseudo-intents rather than chance. As it turned out in a later study this apparent correlation is most likely the result of a systematic bias in the underlying random generation process [3].

We therefore strive after a novel approach that does not exhibit this or any other bias. Consistently with the above the I-PI coordinates and their distribution are used as an indicator for how diverse created contexts are. The coin-toss approach will serve as a baseline for this. We start by analyzing the coin-toss model which leads to a formalization fitted to the requirements of FCA in Sect. 4. This enables us to discover Dirichlet distributions as a natural generalization.

3 Related Work

The problem depicted in Sect. 2 gained not much attention in the literature so far. The first observation of the correlation between the number of intents and pseudo-intents in randomly generated contexts was by Borchmann as a side note in [2]. The phenomenon was further investigated in [3] with the conclusion that it is most likely a result of the random generation process. Their findings suggest that the coin tossing approach as basis for benchmarking algorithms is not a viable option and other ways need to be explored. Related to this is a work by Ganter on random contexts in [6]. There the author looked at a method to generate closure systems in a uniform fashion, using an elegant and conceptually simple acceptance-rejection model. However, this method is infeasible for practical use. Furthermore, the authors in [9] developed a synthetic formal context generator that employs a density measure. This generator is composed of multiple algorithms for different stages of the generation process, i.e., initialization to reach minimum density, regular filling and filling close to the maximum density. However, the survey in [3] found that the generated contexts exhibited a different type of systematic bias.

4   Stochastic Modelling

In the following we analyze and formalize a stochastic model for the coin-toss approach. By this we unravel crucial points for improving the random generation process. To enhance the readability we write $Z \sim Distribution$ to denote that Z is both a random variable following a certain Distribution and a realization of said random variable.

4.1   Coin Toss - Direct Model

Given a set of attributes M we construct $I \subseteq G \times M$ utilizing a *direct coin-toss* model as follows. We let G be a set of objects with $|G| \sim \text{DiscreteUniform}[|M|, 2^{|M|}]$ and draw a probability $p \sim \text{Uniform}(0, 1)$. For every $(g, m) \in G \times M$ we flip a binary coin denoted by $\omega_{(g,m)} \sim \text{Bernoulli}(p)$, i.e., $\omega \in \Omega = \{0, 1\}$ where $P(\omega = 1) = p$ and $P(\omega = 0) = 1 - p$, and let $X_{(g,m)}(\omega) := \{(g, m)\}$ if $\omega = 1$ and $X_{(g,m)}(\omega) := \emptyset$ if $\omega = 0$. Then we obtain the incidence relation by $I := \{X_{(g,m)}(\omega_{(g,m)}) \mid (g, m) \in G \times M\}$. Hence, I contains all those (g, m) where the coin flip was a success, i.e., $\omega = 1$. If we partition the set of coin tosses though grouping, i.e., $\{\{\omega_{(g,m)} \mid m \in M\} \mid g \in G\}$, and look for some object g at the number of successful tosses, we see that they follow a $\text{Binomial}(|M|, p)$ distribution. In detail, a binomial distribution with $|M|$ trials and a success probability of p in each trial. This means that no matter how G, M and the probability p are chosen, we always end up with a context where the number of attributes per object is the realization of a $\text{Binomial}(|M|, p)$ distributed random variable for every object $g \in G$.

Example 4.1. We generated 5000 contexts with the coin-tossing approach. A plot of their I-PI coordinates and a histogram showing the distribution of pseudo-intents are shown in Fig. 1. In the histogram we omitted the high value for zero pseudo-intents. This value emerges from the large amount of generated contranominal scales by the coin-toss model. In particular, 1714 of the contexts contain a contranominal scale and have therefore zero pseudo-intents.

We observe that most of the contexts have less than 100 pseudo-intents with varying numbers of intents between 1 and 1024. The majority of contexts has an I-PI coordinate close to an imaginary curve and the rest has, in most cases, less pseudo-intents, i.e., their I-PI coordinates lie below this curve. Looking at the histogram we observe a varying number of pseudo-intents. We have a peak at zero and a high number of 126 contexts with one pseudo-intent. Additionally there is a peak of 62 contexts with 36 pseudo-intents and a peak of 55 contexts with 73 pseudo-intents. In between we have a low between 18 to 23 pseudo-intents and one around 50.

4.2 Coin Toss - Indirect Model

In order to exhibit a critical point in the direct coin-tossing model we introduce an equivalent model using an indirect approach, called *indirect coin-toss*. Furthermore, this model serves as an intermediate stage to our proposed generation scheme.

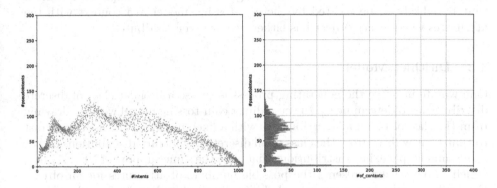

Fig. 1. Visualization of I-PI-Coordinates for Coin-Tossing, see Example 4.1

As we just established, the number of successful coin tosses, i.e., number of attributes per object, follows a binomial distribution. An indirect model that generates the same kind of formal contexts as direct coin-tossing can therefore be obtained by using a binomial distribution. In contrast to the direct model we first determine the total number of successful coin-tosses per object and pick the specific attributes afterwards. We formalize this model as follows.

Given a set of attributes M, as before, we let G be a set of objects with $|G| \sim \text{DiscreteUniform}[|M|, 2^{|M|}]$ and draw a probability $p \sim \text{Uniform}(0,1)$. For every $g \in G$ we let $\theta_g \sim \text{Binomial}(|M|, p)$ be the number of attributes associated to that object g. Hence, $\theta_g \in \{0, \ldots, |M|\}$. We let $\Theta_g := \{B \subseteq M \mid |B| = \theta_g\}$ be the set of all possible attribute combinations for g and denote by $\text{DiscreteUniform}(\Theta_g)$ the discrete uniform distribution on Θ_g. Now for every $g \in G$ we let $B_g \sim \text{DiscreteUniform}(\Theta_g)$ to obtain the set of attributes belonging to the object g and define the incidence relation by $I := \bigcup \{\{(g,m) \mid m \in B_g\} \mid g \in G\}$. This serves as a foundation for our proposed generation algorithm in Sect. 4.3. The indirect formulation reveals that the coin tossing approach is restricting the class of possible distributions for θ_g, i.e., the number of attributes

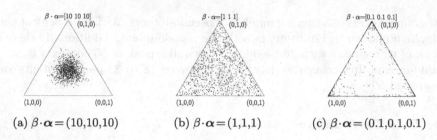

(a) $\beta\cdot\boldsymbol{\alpha}=(10,10,10)$ (b) $\beta\cdot\boldsymbol{\alpha}=(1,1,1)$ (c) $\beta\cdot\boldsymbol{\alpha}=(0.1,0.1,0.1)$

Fig. 2. Distribution of categorical probabilities of sym. Dirichlet distributions.

for the object g, to only the set of binomial ones. Thereby it introduces a systematic bias as to which contexts are being generated. An example for a context that is unlikely to be created by the coin-tossing model is a context with ten attributes where every object has either two or seven attributes.

4.3   Dirichlet Model

One way to improve the generating process is to use a broader class of discrete distributions to determine θ_g. In the indirect coin-tossing model we were drawing from the class of binomial distributions with a fixed number of trials. In contrast to that we now draw from the class of all discrete probability distributions on the same sample space, i.e., distributions that have the same support of $\{0, \ldots, |M|\}$, which in our case represents the possible numbers of attributes for an object. For finite sample spaces every probability distribution can be considered as a categorical distribution. Therefore, a common method to draw from the class of all discrete probability distributions is to employ a Dirichlet distribution. In Bayesian statistics this distribution is often utilized as prior distribution of parameters of a categorical or multinomial distribution [5].

One way to define the Dirichlet distribution is to use gamma distributions [5]. A Gamma(ρ, τ) distribution with shape parameter $\rho \geq 0$ and scale parameter $\tau > 0$ can be characterized on the real line with respect to the Lebesgue measure by a density function $f(z \mid \rho, \tau) = \frac{1}{\Gamma(\rho)\tau^\rho} \exp^{-z/\tau} z^{\rho-1} \mathbb{1}_{(0,\infty)}(z)$ if $\rho > 0$, where $\mathbb{1}_S$ denotes the indicator function on some set S and Γ denotes the gamma function. In the case of $\rho = 0$ the gamma distribution degenerates at zero. The Dirichlet$(\beta\boldsymbol{\alpha})$ distribution with parameters $\beta\boldsymbol{\alpha} = (\beta\alpha_1, \ldots, \beta\alpha_K)$, where $\beta > 0$, $\alpha_i \geq 0$ for all i and $\alpha_i > 0$ for some $i \in \{1, \ldots, K\}$ and $\sum_{i=1}^K \alpha_i = 1$, is a probability distribution on the set of K-dimensional discrete distributions. Given independent random variables $Z_1, \ldots, Z_k$ with $Z_i \sim$ Gamma$(\beta\alpha_i, 1)$ it is defined as the distribution of a random vector $(Y_1, \ldots, Y_K)$ where $Y_i = Z_i / \sum_{j=1}^k Z_j$ for $i \in \{1, \ldots, K\}$. Note that this allows for some of the variables to be degenerate

---

Algorithm 1. Dirichlet Approach

   Input : a set of attributes M
   Output: a formal context (G, M, I)

1   $N \sim \text{DiscreteUniform}[\|M\|, 2^{|M|}]$
2   $G := \{1, \ldots, N\}$
3   $\nu := (1, \ldots, 1)$ // ($|M| + 1$ **ones**)
4   $\alpha := \nu / \|\nu\|_1$
5   $\beta := |M| + 1$
6   $p \sim \text{Dirichlet}(\beta \alpha)$
7   **forall** $g \in G$ **do**
8        $\theta_g \sim \text{Categorical}(p)$
9        $\Theta_g := \{B \subseteq M \mid |B| = \theta_g\}$
10       $B_g \sim \text{DiscreteUniform}(\Theta_g)$
11       $I_g := \{(g, m) \mid m \in B_g\}$

12 $I := \bigcup_{g \in G} I_g$
13 **return** (G, M, I)

---

at zero which will be useful in the application for null models, as we will describe in Sect. 6. If $\alpha_i > 0$ for all i the random vector $(Y_1, \ldots, Y_K)$ has a density

$$f(y_1, \ldots, y_K \mid \beta \alpha_1, \ldots, \beta \alpha_K) = \frac{\Gamma(\beta)}{\prod_{i=1}^{K} \Gamma(\beta \alpha_i)} \prod_{i=1}^{K} y_i^{\beta \alpha_i - 1} \mathbb{1}_S(y_1, \ldots, y_K) \quad (1)$$

on the simplex $S = \{(y_1, \ldots, y_K) \in \mathbb{R}^K \mid y_i \geq 0, \sum_{i=1}^{K} y_i = 1\}$. Note that f in Eq. 1 is a density with respect to the $(K-1)$-dimensional Lebesgue measure and we can rewrite f as a $(K-1)$-dimensional function by letting $y_K = 1 - \sum_{i=1}^{K-1} y_i$ and using an appropriate simplex representation. Also note that the elements of $(Y_1, \ldots, Y_K)$ have the expected value $\mathbb{E}(Y_i) = \alpha_i$, the variance $\text{Var}(Y_i) = \frac{\alpha_i(1-\alpha_i)}{\beta+1}$ and the co-variance $\text{Cov}(Y_i, Y_j) = \frac{\alpha_i \alpha_j}{\beta+1}$ for $i \neq j$. Hence, the parameter α is called *base measure* or *mean* as it describes the expected value of the probability distribution and β is called *precision parameter* and describes the variance of probability distributions with regard to the base measure. A large value for β will cause the drawn distributions to be close to the base measure, a small value will cause them to be distant. A realization of a Dirichlet distributed random variable is an element of S and can therefore be seen as probability vector of a K-dimensional categorical distribution.

In Fig. 2 we illustrate the effects of varying β. We show different distributions of probabilities for three categories drawn from 3-dimensional Dirichlet distributions. The base measure α in each case is the uniform distribution, i.e., $(\frac{1}{3}, \frac{1}{3}, \frac{1}{3})$, the precision parameter $\beta \in \{30, 3, \frac{3}{10}\}$ varies. The choice of $\beta = 3$ then results in a uniform distribution on the probability simplex. For comparison we also chose $\beta = 30$ and $\beta = \frac{3}{10}$. A possible interpretation of the introduced simplex is the following. Each corner of the simplex can be thought of as one category.

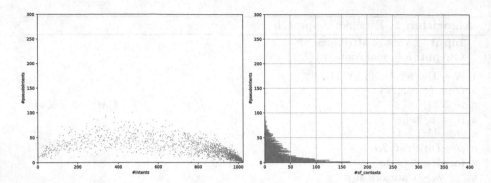

Fig. 3. Dirichlet generated contexts with $\boldsymbol{\alpha} = (\frac{1}{|M|+1}, \ldots, \frac{1}{|M|+1})$, $\beta = |M| + 1$.

The closer a point in the simplex is to a corner the more likely this category is to be drawn.

In the rest of this section we describe the model for our proposed random formal context generator. Given a set of attributes M, we let G be a set of objects with $|G| \sim \text{DiscreteUniform}[|M|, 2^{|M|}]$. We then use a probability vector $\boldsymbol{p} \sim \text{Dirichlet}(\beta\boldsymbol{\alpha})$ to determine the probabilities for an object to have 0 to $|M|$ attributes, where $\boldsymbol{\alpha} := \nu/||(\nu)||_1$ with $\nu := (1, \ldots, 1) \in \mathbb{R}^{|M|+1}$. By using $\boldsymbol{\alpha}$ as base measure and $\beta = |M|+1$, which implies $\beta\boldsymbol{\alpha} = (1, \ldots, 1)$, we draw uniformly from the set of discrete probability distributions. As a different way to determine θ_g we can therefore use $\boldsymbol{p} = (p_0, \ldots, p_{|M|})$ as probabilities of a $|M| + 1$ dimensional categorical distribution $\theta_g \sim \text{Categorical}(\boldsymbol{p})$. These categories are the numbers of attributes for an object, i.e., $P(\theta_g = c) = p_c$ for $c \in \{0, \ldots, |M|\}$. Looking back at Sect. 4.2 we replace the binomial distribution based on a uniformly distributed random variable by a categorical distribution based on a Dirichlet distributed one. Afterwards we proceed as before. We present pseudocode for the Dirichlet approach in Algorithm 1 as a further reference for the experiments in Sect. 5.

5   Experiments

In this section we present a first experimental investigation of Algorithm 1. We evaluated the results by examining the numbers of intents and pseudo-intents of generated contexts. The contexts were generated using `Python 3` and all further computations, i.e., the I-PI coordinates, were done using `conexp-clj`.[1] The generator code as well as the generated contexts can be found on GitHub.[2]

---

[1] https://github.com/exot/conexp-clj.
[2] https://github.com/maximilian-felde/formal-context-generator.

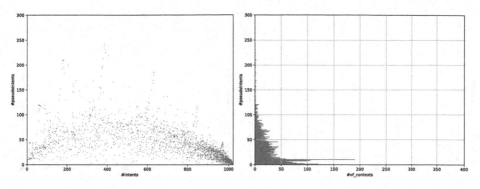

Fig. 4. Dirichlet generated contexts with $\alpha = (\frac{1}{|M|+1}, \ldots, \frac{1}{|M|+1})$, $\beta \sim \text{Uniform}(0, |M| + 1)$.

5.1 Observations

For each experiment we generated 5000 formal contexts with an attribute set M of ten attributes using Algorithm 1. We also employed slightly altered versions of this algorithm. Those alterations are concerned with the choice of β, as we will see in the following. We plotted the resulting I-PI coordinates and a histogram of the pseudo-intents for each experiment. In the histogram we omitted the value for zero pseudo-intents, i.e., the peak for contexts containing a contranominal scale of size $|M|$. A comparable experiment on ten attributes is described in Example 4.1, where a (direct) coin-toss model was utilized. The results of Example 4.1 are shown in Fig. 1. This will serve as a baseline in terms of variety and distribution of I-PI coordinates.

First we used Algorithm 1 without alterations. The results are depicted in Fig. 3. We can see that most of the generated contexts have less than 75 pseudo-intents and the number of intents varies between 1 and 1024. There is a tendency towards contexts with fewer pseudo-intents and we cannot observe any context with more than 101 pseudo-intents. The number of generated contexts containing contranominal scales of size $|M|$ was 2438. The histogram shows that the number of contexts that have a certain quantity of pseudo-intents decreases as the number of pseudo-intents increases with no significant dips or peaks. In this form the Dirichlet approach does not appear to be an improvement over the coin-tossing method. In contrary, we observe the spread of the number of pseudo-intents to be smaller than in Example 4.1.

Our next experiment was randomizing the precision parameter β between 0 and $|M|+1$, i.e., let $\beta \sim \text{Uniform}(0, |M|+1]$ in Algorithm 1, Line 5. We will refer to this alteration as variation **A**. The results are shown in Fig. 4. We can see that again many contexts have less than 100 pseudo-intents and the number of intents once again varies over the full possible range. There are 1909 contexts that contain a contranominal scale of size $|M|$. However, we notice that there is a not negligible number of contexts with over 100 and up to almost 252 pseudo-intents, which constitutes theoretical maximum [3]. Most of these gather around

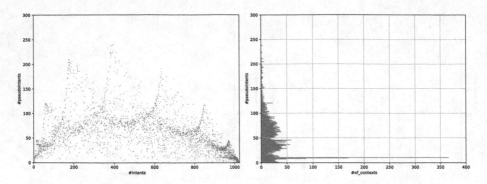

Fig. 5. Dirichlet generated contexts with $\alpha = (\frac{1}{|M|+1}, \ldots, \frac{1}{|M|+1})$, $\beta = 0.1(|M| + 1)$.

nearly vertical lines close to 75, 200, 380, 600 and 820 intents. Even though most of the contexts have an I-PI coordinate along one of those lines there are a few contexts in-between 100 and 175 pseudo-intents that do not fit this description. Looking at the histogram we can observe again that while the number of pseudo-intents increases the number of generated contexts to that pseudo-intent number decreases. This is in contrast to Example 4.1. This time, however, we can clearly see a peak at seven to ten pseudo-intents with 190 contexts having ten pseudo-intents. Apart from this we observed no other significant dips or peaks. We also tried randomizing the base measure α using Dirichlet distributions. However, this did not improve the results.

Since the last experiment revealed that small values for β resulted in a larger variety of contexts we will now investigate those in more detail. For this we introduce a constant factor c such that $\beta = c \cdot (|M| + 1)$. We find for the experiment called variation **B** the factor $c = 0.1$ suitable, as we will explain in Sect. 5.2. A plot of the results can be found in Fig. 5. We can see that most of the contexts have less than 150 pseudo-intents and the number of intents is between 1 and 1024. Furthermore, the quantity of contexts containing a contranominal scale of size $|M|$ is 1169. This number is about 700 lower than in variation **A**, roughly 500 lower compared to the coin-tossing results in Example 4.1, and over 1200 lower than in the unaltered Dirichlet approach. We can again observe the same imaginary lines as mentioned for variation **A**, with even more contrast. Finally, we observe that the space between these lines contains significantly more I-PI coordinates. Choosing even smaller values for c may result in less desirable sets of contexts. In particular, we found that lower values for c appear to increase the bias towards the imaginary lines.

The histogram (Fig. 5) of variation **B** differs distinguishably to the one in Fig. 4. The distribution of pseudo-intent numbers is more volatile and more evenly distributed. There is a first peak of 366 contexts with ten pseudo-intents, followed by a dip to eleven contexts with seventeen pseudo-intents and more relative peaks of 50 to 60 contexts each at 28, 36 and 45 pseudo-intents. After

62 pseudo-intents the number of contexts having this amount of pseudo-intents or more declines with the exception of the peak at 120 pseudo-intents.

We established that both variations of Algorithm 1 with $\beta \sim \mathrm{Uniform}(0, |M|+1)$ and $\beta = c \cdot (|M|+1)$ are improvements upon the coin-tossing approach. In order to further increase the confidence in our Dirichlet approach we have generated 100,000 contexts with the coin-tossing approach as well as with both variations for six, seven and eight attributes. We compared the distinct I-PI coordinates after certain numbers of generated contexts. The results of this experiment is shown in Fig. 6. Each subfigure shows the results for one attribute set size. We have plotted the number of generated contexts versus the number of distinct I-PI coordinates for the coin-toss (green solid line), variation **A** (orange dashed line) and variation **B** (blue dotted line). In all three plots we recognize that there is a steep increase of distinct I-PI coordinates at the beginning followed by a fast decline in new I-PI coordinates, i.e., a slow increase in the total number of distinct I-PI coordinates, for all three random generation methods. The graphs remind of sublinear growth. For all three attribute set sizes we can observe that the graphs of variation **A** and **B** lie above the graph of the coin-toss. Hence, variation **A** and **B** generated more distinct contexts compared to the coin-toss. Exemplary for $|M| = 7$ the coin-tossing approach resulted in 1963 distinct I-PI coordinates and reached them after around 99 000 generated contexts. Variation **A** generated around 19 000 contexts until it hit 1963 distinct I-PI coordinates and reached a total of around 2450 after 100,000 contexts generated. Variation **B** reached the same number of distinct I-PI values already at around 13,000 generated contexts and resulted in 2550 distinct I-PI coordinates.

5.2   Discussion

We begin the discussion by relating the parameters of the Dirichlet approach to the variety of generated contexts. Afterwards we explore the discrepancy in the quantities of contexts that contain a contranominal scale and discuss the observed imaginary lines. Lastly, we discuss the ability of the different approaches for generating pairwise distinct I-PI coordinates efficiently.

The Dirichlet approach has two parameters, one being the β parameter related to the variance of the Dirichlet distribution, the other being the α parameter which describes the expected value of the Dirichlet distribution, as explained more formally in Sect. 4.3. A large value for β results in categorical distributions that have probability vectors close to the base measure α, following from the definition. A small value for β results in categorical distributions where the probability vectors are close to the corners or edges of the simplex, see Fig. 2c. As already pointed out in Sect. 4.3, those corners of the simplex can be thought of as the categories, i.e., the possible numbers of attributes an object can have. This implies that for large β the categories are expected to be about as likely as the corresponding probabilities in the base measure. Whereas, for small β one or few particular categories are expected to be far more likely than others.

We have seen that the Dirichlet approach without alterations generated around 2450 contexts containing a contranominal scale of size $|M|$. This number

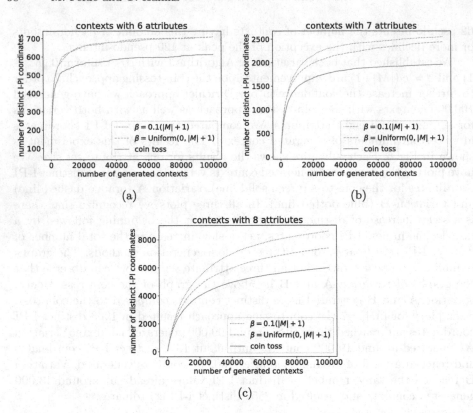

Fig. 6. Number of distinct I-PI coordinates for up to 100 000 randomly generated contexts with 6, 7 and 8 attributes (Color figure online).

was 1900 for variation **A** and 1200 for variation **B**. One reason for the huge number of contranominal scales generated by the base version of the Dirichlet approach is that most of the realizations of the Dirichlet distribution (Algorithm 1, Line 6) are inner points of the probability simplex, i.e., they lie near the centre of the simplex. These points or probability vectors result in almost balanced categorical distributions (Algorithm 1, Line 8), i.e., every category is drawn at least a few times for a fixed number of draws. This fact may explain the frequent occurrence of contranominal scales. The expected number of objects with $|M|-1$ attributes that need to be generated for a context to contain a contranominal scale is low. In more detail, we only need to hit the $|M|$ equally likely distinct objects, having $|M|-1$ attributes during the generation process. To be more precise, the mean μ_N and the standard deviation σ_N of the number of required objects with $|M|-1$ attributes can easily be computed via $\mu_N = N \sum_{k=1}^{N} \frac{1}{k}$ and $\sigma_N^2 = N \sum_{k=1}^{N} \frac{N-k}{k^2}$ with $N := \binom{|M|}{|M|-1} = |M|$, cf. [4], as this is an instance of the so-called *Coupon Collector Problem*. For example for a context with ten attributes we get $\mu_{10} \approx 29.3$ and $\sigma_{10} \approx 11.2$, hence we need to generate on average around 30 objects with nine attributes to create a contranominal scale.

Although, there is already a high probability of obtaining a contranominal scale after generating around 18 objects. This means if we generate a context with $|G| = 300$ objects and the probability for the category with nine attributes is around 10% we can expect the context to contain a contranominal scale.

If we use a lower value for β we tend to get less balanced probability vectors from the Dirichlet distribution and therefore generate less contexts that contain a contranominal scale. The pathological case is a β close to zero, which leads to contexts where all or nearly all objects have the same number of attributes. Even then we could expect at least $\frac{1}{|M|+1}$ of the contexts generated to contain a contranominal scale. In this case we basically draw from the set of categories, i.e., from the possible numbers of attributes. Those are related as corners of the simplex and the probability to land in the corner belonging to the category of $|M| - 1$ attributes is approximately $\frac{1}{|M|+1}$.

Contexts where every object has the same number of attributes are referred to as *contexts with fixed row-density* in [3]. They were used to show that the coin-tossing approach in practice does not generate a whole class of contexts. An explanation for the imaginary lines observed in Figs. 4 and 5 is that they correspond to contexts with fixed row-density, cf. [3, Fig. 5]. As pointed out in the last paragraph very low values of β the Dirichlet approach predominantly generates contexts where all objects belong to few or even only one category. This explanation is further supported by the increasing bias of the context's I-PI coordinates to form those imaginary lines for decreasing values of β. It also accounts for the peak at ten pseudo-intents in the histograms for variations **A** and **B**. This due to the fact that a fixed row-density context with density 8/10 that contains all possible objects has exactly ten pseudo-intents, cf. [3, Prop. 1]. This is again related to the *Coupon Collector Problem*. The solution to this problem yields the expected number of objects that we need in order to hit every possible combination. In particular for the case of the peak at ten pseudo-intents, $N = \binom{10}{8} = 45$, $\mu_{45} \approx 198$ and $\sigma_{45} \approx 56$, meaning if we generate a fixed row-density context with around 200 objects we can expect it to contain all possible combinations and therefore have ten pseudo-intents. This fits well with the observed 366 contexts with ten pseudo-intents in variation **B**. Consider the case that we only generate fixed row-density contexts containing all possible attribute combinations and all densities are equally likely. The expected number of contexts with eight attributes and therefore ten pseudo-intents for 5000 generated contexts then is $5000/11 \approx 455$. Naturally, variation **B** does not predominantly generate fixed row-density contexts or even fixed row-density contexts with all possible attribute combinations. Hence, the afore mentioned 366 observed contexts with ten pseudo-intents seem reasonable.

Lastly we discuss the observations from counting distinct I-PI coordinates. In Fig. 6 we can see that the Dirichlet approach results in a broader variety of contexts in comparison to the coin-tossing for any fixed number of generated contexts. All three plots show that there is an initial phase where contexts with new I-PI coordinates are frequently generated followed by a far longer part where contexts with new I-PI coordinates become increasingly rare. This is not surprising, since the number of possible I-PI coordinates is finite and the probability to re-hit increases with every distinct generated I-PI coordinate. Note that this is an effect that would also be observed when using a perfectly uniform sampling mechanism. Nonetheless what we can observe is that it takes the Dirichlet approach significantly longer, compared to the coin-tossing model, to reach a point where only few new I-PI coordinates are generated.

6   Applications

We see for our Dirichlet approach at least two major applications. For one, an improved random generation process can be used to facilitate more reliable time performance comparisons of FCA algorithms. The obtained contexts exhibit less bias and therefore a greater variety concluding in more robust runtime results.

A second application is the generation of null models for formal contexts. Null models are well employed in graph theory and are an adaption of a statistical concept. In a nutshell, the idea of null models is to generate random graphs that are in some way similar to some reference graph in order to investigate some other property in this very same reference graph. Transferring this to contexts, the idea is to randomly generate contexts that are in some way similar to some reference context. The Dirichlet approach can be employed to generate null models for a given row-sum-distribution, i.e., the distribution of the total number of attributes per object. For this null model approach one may apply Algorithm 1 with the appropriate number of objects in Line 1, the reference contexts row-sum-distribution as α in Line 4 and a large value for β, e.g., $\beta = 1000 \cdot (|M|+1)$, in Line 5.

7   Conclusions and Outlook

Analysing a stochastic model for the coin-tossing approach for randomly generating formal contexts lead in a natural way to a more sophisticated context generator. By addressing the carved out limitations of the underlying binomial model we comprehended the usefulness of Dirichlet distributions for random contexts. Based on this we developed an algorithm which can easily be implemented. This algorithm draws random contexts from a significantly larger class of contexts compared to the common coin-toss approach. We empirically evaluated this new approach for different sizes of attribute sets. The conducted experiments showed that we generated a significantly broader variety of contexts. This increased variety may enhance the reliability of random context based investigations, like algorithm performance comparisons. The novel Dirichlet approach also allows us to generate null models. This method can be employed for empirical investigations related to formal contexts, like social network analysis with FCA or ecology.

This novel approach to random formal contexts raises many questions about the relation of the data table context and Dirichlet distributions. Also, there are various unsolved problems remaining. For example, how can one minimize the amount of generated contranominal scales? Investigating base measures is a fruitful next step in order to understand their relation to real-world context generation, like null models. Furthermore, there is a lack for a characteristic description of real-world formal contexts, as done in the realm of social network analysis, for example.

References

1. Bazhanov, K., Obiedkov, S.A.: Comparing performance of algorithms for generating the Duquenne-Guigues basis. In: Napoli, A., Vychodil, V. (eds.) CLA. CEURWorkshop Proceedings, vol. 959, pp. 43–57. CEUR-WS.org (2011)
2. Borchmann, D.: Decomposing finite closure operators by attribute exploration. In: Domenach, F., Jäschke, R., Valtchev, P. (eds.) Contributions to ICFCA 2011, pp. 24–37. Univ. of Nicosia, May 2011
3. Borchmann, D., Hanika, T.: Some experimental results on randomly generating formal contexts. In: Huchard, M., Kuznetsov, S. (eds.) CLA, vol. 1624, pp. 57–69. CEUR-WS.org Proceedings (2016)
4. Dawkins, B.: Siobhan's problem: the coupon collector revisited. Am. Stat. **45**(1), 76–82 (1991)
5. Ferguson, T.S.: A Bayesian analysis of some nonparametric problems. Ann. Statist. **1**(2), 209–230 (1973)
6. Ganter, B.: Random extents and random closure systems. In: Napoli, A., Vychodil, V. (eds.) CLA. CEUR Workshop Proceedings, vol. 959, pp. 309–318. CEUR-WS.org (2011)
7. Ganter, B., Wille, R.: Formal Concept Analysis: Mathematical Foundations. Springer, Heidelberg (1999). https://doi.org/10.1007/978-3-642-59830-2
8. Kuznetsov, S.O., Obiedkov, S.A.: Comparing performance of algorithms for generating concept lattices. J. Exp. Theor. Artif. Intell. **14**(2–3), 189–216 (2002)
9. Rimsa, A., Song, M.A.J., Zárate, L.E.: SCGaz - a synthetic formal context generator with density control for test and evaluation of FCA algorithms. In: SMC, pp. 3464–3470. IEEE (2013)
10. Ulrich, W., Gotelli, N.J.: Pattern detection in null model analysis. Oikos **122**(1), 2–18 (2013)

Lifted Temporal Most Probable Explanation

Marcel Gehrke[✉][iD], Tanya Braun[iD], and Ralf Möller

Institute of Information Systems, University of Lübeck, Lübeck, Germany
{gehrke,braun,moeller}@ifis.uni-luebeck.de

Abstract. The lifted dynamic junction tree algorithm (LDJT) answers filtering and prediction queries efficiently for temporal probabilistic relational models by building and then reusing a first-order cluster representation of a knowledge base for multiple queries and time steps. Another type of query asks for a most probable explanation (MPE) for given events. Specifically, this paper contributes (i) LDJT^{mpe} to efficiently solve the temporal MPE problem for temporal probabilistic relational models and (ii) a combination of LDJT and LDJT^{mpe} to efficiently answer assignment queries for a given number of time steps.

Keywords: Relational temporal probabilistic models · Lifting · MPE · MAP

1 Introduction

Areas like healthcare, logistics, or even scientific publishing deal with probabilistic data with relational and temporal aspects and need efficient exact inference algorithms. These areas involve many objects in relation to each other with changes over time and uncertainties about object existence, attribute value assignments, or relations between objects. More specifically, publishing involves publications (the relational part) for many authors (the objects), streams of papers over time (the temporal part), and uncertainties for example due to missing or incomplete information. By performing model counting, probabilistic databases (PDBs) can answer queries for relational temporal models with uncertainties [7,8]. However, each query embeds a process behaviour, resulting in huge queries with possibly redundant information. In contrast to PDBs, we build more expressive and compact models including behaviour (offline) enabling efficient answering of more compact queries (online). For query answering, our approach performs deductive reasoning by computing marginal distributions at discrete time steps. In this paper, we study the problem of finding a MPE in temporal probabilistic relational models.

This research originated from the Big Data project being part of Joint Lab 1, funded by Cisco Systems Germany, at the centre COPICOH, University of Lübeck.

ⓒ Springer Nature Switzerland AG 2019
D. Endres et al. (Eds.): ICCS 2019, LNAI 11530, pp. 72–85, 2019.
https://doi.org/10.1007/978-3-030-23182-8_6

We [9] propose parameterised probabilistic dynamic models (PDMs) to represent probabilistic relational temporal behaviour and introduce the LDJT to exactly answer multiple filtering and prediction queries for multiple time steps efficiently. LDJT combines the advantages of the interface algorithm [15] and the lifted junction tree algorithm (LJT) [3]. Specifically, this paper contributes (i) LDJT^{mpe} to efficiently solve the temporal MPE problem for relational temporal probabilistic models and (ii) a combination of LDJT and LDJT^{mpe} to efficiently answer assignment queries, that is to say the most probable assignment for a subset of random variable (randvar).

LDJT reuses an first-order junction tree (FO jtree) structure to answer multiple queries and reuses the structure to answer queries for all time steps $t > 0$. Additionally, LDJT ensures a minimal exact inter FO jtree information propagation between time steps. In the static case, LJT^{mpe} already solves the MPE problem for relational models efficiently. We propose to combine the advances in LDJT and LJT^{mpe} to also answer temporal assignment queries efficiently.

The remainder of this paper has the following structure: We begin by recapitulating PDMs as a representation for relational temporal probabilistic models and present LDJT, an efficient reasoning algorithm for PDMs. Afterwards, we present how LJT answers queries for the MPE and LDJT^{mpe} to answer queries for the MPE in relational temporal probabilistic models. Lastly, we investigate the advantages of LDJT and LDJT^{mpe} compared to LJT and LJT^{mpe} in more depth. We conclude by looking at possible extensions.

2 Related Work

We take a look at inference for temporal propositional models, static relational models, and give an overview about research on temporal relational models.

For exact inference on temporal propositional models, a naive approach is to unroll the temporal model for a given number of time steps and use any exact inference algorithm for static, i.e., non-temporal, models. Murphy [15] proposes the interface algorithm consisting of a forward and backward pass using temporal d-separation to apply static inference algorithms to the dynamic model. For propositional temporal models, the Viterbi algorithm is one approach to calculate the MPE for events over time. Additionally, Murphy [15] presents that given a variable elimination algorithm, one can solve the Viterbi problem by calculating max-products instead of sum-products.

First-order probabilistic inference leverages the relational aspect of a static model. For models with known domain size, it exploits symmetries in a model by combining instances to reason with representatives, known as lifting [18]. Poole [18] introduces parametric factor graphs as relational models and proposes lifted variable elimination (LVE) as an exact inference algorithm on relational models. Further, de Salvo Braz [20], Milch et al. [14], and Taghipour et al. [23] extend LVE to its current form. Furthermore, there are versions of LVE to compute an MPE [2,5,21]. Lauritzen and Spiegelhalter [12] introduce the junction tree algorithm. To benefit from the ideas of the junction tree algorithm and LVE, Braun and Müller [3] present LJT, which efficiently performs exact first-order probabilistic inference on relational models given a set of queries. Additionally, Braun and Müller [5] present how to solve the MPE problem efficiently with LJT^{mpe} and how a combination of LJT and LJT^{mpe} can answer assignment queries for a subset of randvars.

To handle inference for temporal relational models most approaches are approximate. Additionally to being approximate, these approaches involve unnecessary groundings or are not designed to handle multiple queries efficiently. Ahmadi et al. [1] propose lifted belief propagation for dynamic Markov logic networks (DMLNs). Thon et al. [24] introduce CPT-L, a probabilistic model for sequences of relational state descriptions with a partially lifted inference algorithm. Geier and Biundo [11] present an online interface algorithm for DMLNs, similar to the work of Papai et al. [17]. Both approaches slice DMLNs to run well-studied MLN inference algorithms [19] on each slice. Two ways of performing online inference using particle filtering are described in [13,16]. Vlasselaer et al. [25,26] introduce an exact approach for temporal relational models, but perform inference on a ground knowledge base.

However, by using efficient inference algorithms, we calculate exact solutions for temporal relational models. Therefore, we extend LDJT, which leverages the well-studied LVE and LJT algorithms, to also answer assignment queries.

3   Parameterised Probabilistic Models

Based on [6], we present (PMs) for relational static models. Afterwards, we extend PMs to the temporal case, resulting in PDMs for relational temporal models, which, in turn, are based on [9].

3.1   Parameterised Probabilistic Models

PMs combine first-order logic with probabilistic models, representing first-order constructs using logical variables (logvars) as parameters.

Definition 1. *Let $\mathbf{L}$ be a set of logvar names, Φ a set of factor names, and $\mathbf{R}$ a set of randvar names. A parameterised randvar (PRV) 8-[$A = P(X^1, ..., X^n)$ represents a set of randvars behaving identically by combining a randvar $P \in \mathbf{R}$ with $X^1, ..., X^n \in \mathbf{L}$. If $n = 0$, the PRV is parameterless. The domain of a logvar L is denoted by $\mathcal{D}(L)$. The term range(A) provides possible values of a PRV A. Constraint $(\mathbf{X}, C_{\mathbf{X}})$ allows to restrict logvars to certain domain values and is a tuple with a sequence of logvars $\mathbf{X} = (X^1, ..., X^n)$ and a set $C_{\mathbf{X}} \subseteq \times_{i=1}^{n} \mathcal{D}(X^i)$. $\top$ denotes that no restrictions apply and may be omitted. The term $lv(Y)$ refers to the logvars in some element Y. The term $gr(Y)$ denotes the set of instances of Y with all logvars in Y grounded w.r.t. constraints.*

Let us set up a PM for publications on some topic. We model that the topic may be hot, people do research, attend conferences and publish in publications. From $\mathbf{R} = \{Hot, DoR\}$ and $\mathbf{L} = \{P, X\}$ with $\mathcal{D}(P) = \{p_1, p_2\}$ and $\mathcal{D}(X) = \{x_1, x_2, x_3\}$, we build the boolean PRVs Hot and $DoR(X)$. With $C = (X, \{x_1, x_2\})$, $gr(DoR(X)|C) = \{DoR(x_1), DoR(x_2)\}$.

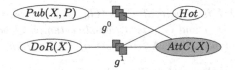

Fig. 1. Parfactor graph for G^{ex}

Definition 2. *We denote a parametric factor (parfactor) g with $\forall \mathbf{X} : \phi(\mathcal{A}) \mid C$. $\mathbf{X} \subseteq \mathbf{L}$ being a set of logvars over which the factor generalises and $\mathcal{A} = (A^1, ..., A^n)$ a sequence of PRVs. We omit $(\forall \mathbf{X} :)$ if $\mathbf{X} = lv(\mathcal{A})$. A function $\phi : \times_{i=1}^n range(A^i) \mapsto \mathbb{R}^+$ with name $\phi \in \Phi$ is defined identically for all grounded instances of $\mathcal{A}$. A list of all input-output values is the complete specification for ϕ. C is a constraint on $\mathbf{X}$. A PM $G := \{g^i\}_{i=0}^{n-1}$ is a set of parfactors and semantically represents the full joint probability distribution $P(G) = \frac{1}{Z} \prod_{f \in gr(G)} \phi(\mathcal{A}_f)$ where Z is a normalisation constant.*

Adding boolean PRVs $Pub(X, P)$ and $AttC(X)$, $G_{ex} = \{g^i\}_{i=0}^1$, $g^0 = \phi^0(Pub(X, P), AttC(X), Hot)$, $g^1 = \phi^1(DoR(X), AttC(X), Hot)$ forms a model. All parfactors have eight input-output pairs (omitted). Constraints are $\top$, i.e., the ϕ's hold for all domain values. E.g., $gr(g^1)$ contains three factors with identical ϕ. Figure 1 depicts G^{ex} as a graph with four variable nodes for the PRVs and two factor nodes for g^0 and g^1 with edges to the PRVs involved.

The semantics of a model is given by grounding and building a full joint distribution. In general, queries ask for a probability distribution of a randvar using a model's full joint distribution and fixed events as evidence.

Definition 3. *Given a PM G, a ground PRV Q and grounded PRVs with fixed range values $\mathbf{E}$, the expression $P(Q|\mathbf{E})$ denotes a query w.r.t. $P(G)$.*

3.2   Parameterised Probabilistic Dynamic Models

To define PDMs, we use PMs and the idea of how Bayesian networks give rise to dynamic Bayesian networks. We define PDMs based on the first-order Markov assumption, i.e., a time slice t only depends on the previous time slice $t - 1$. Further, the underlining process is stationary, i.e., the model behaviour does not change over time. Now, we can define PDMs.

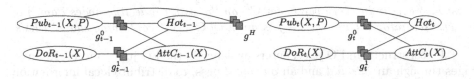

Fig. 2. $G_\rightarrow^{ex}$ the two-slice temporal parfactor graph for model G^{ex}

Definition 4. *A PDM is a pair of PMs* $(G_0, G_\rightarrow)$ *where* G_0 *is a PM representing the first time step and* $G_\rightarrow$ *is a two-slice temporal parameterised model representing* $\mathbf{A}_{t-1}$ *and* $\mathbf{A}_t$ *where* $\mathbf{A}_\pi$ *is a set of PVRs from time slice* π.

Figure 2 shows how the model G^{ex} behaves over time. $G^{ex}_\rightarrow$ consists of G^{ex} for time step $t-1$ and for time step t with inter-slice parfactor for the behaviour over time. In this example, the parfactor g^H is the inter-slice parfactors.

Definition 5. *Given a PDM G, a ground PRV* Q_t *and grounded PRVs with fixed range values* $\mathbf{E}_{0:t}$ *the expression* $P(Q_t | \mathbf{E}_{0:t})$ *denotes a query w.r.t.* $P(G)$.

The problem of answering a marginal distribution query $P(A^i_\pi | \mathbf{E}_{0:t})$ w.r.t. the model is called prediction for $\pi > t$ and filtering for $\pi = t$.

4   Lifted Dynamic Junction Tree Algorithm

To provide means to answer queries for PMs, we recapitulate LJT, mainly based on [4]. Afterwards, we present LDJT [9] consisting of FO jtree constructions for a PDM and a filtering and prediction algorithm.

4.1   Lifted Junction Tree Algorithm

LJT provides efficient means to answer queries $P(Q^i | \mathbf{E})$, with a set of query terms $\mathbf{Q}$, given a PM G and evidence $\mathbf{E}$, by performing the following steps: (i) Construct an FO jtree J for G. (ii) Enter $\mathbf{E}$ in J. (iii) Pass messages. (iv) Compute answer for each query $Q^i \in \mathbf{Q}$. We first define an FO jtree and then go through each step. To define an FO jtree, we need to define parameterised clusters (parclusters), the nodes of an FO jtree.

Definition 6. *A parcluster* $\mathbf{C}$ *is defined by* $\forall \mathbf{L} : \mathbf{A} | C$. $\mathbf{L}$ *is a set of logvars,* $\mathbf{A}$ *is a set of PRVs with* $lv(\mathbf{A}) \subseteq \mathbf{L}$, *and* C *a constraint on* $\mathbf{L}$. *We omit* $(\forall \mathbf{L} :)$ *if* $\mathbf{L} = lv(\mathbf{A})$. *A parcluster* $\mathbf{C}^i$ *can have parfactors* $\phi(\mathcal{A}^\phi) | C^\phi$ *assigned given that* *(i)* $\mathcal{A}^\phi \subseteq \mathbf{A}$, *(ii)* $lv(\mathcal{A}^\phi) \subseteq \mathbf{L}$, *and (iii)* $C^\phi \subseteq C$ *holds. We call the set of assigned parfactors a local model* G^i.
    An FO jtree for a model G is $J = (\mathbf{V}, \mathbf{E})$ *where J is a cycle-free graph, the nodes* $\mathbf{V}$ *denote a set of parcluster, and the set* $\mathbf{E}$ *edges between parclusters. An FO jtree must satisfy the following properties: (i) A parcluster* $\mathbf{C}^i$ *is a set of PRVs from G. (ii) For each parfactor* $\phi(\mathcal{A}) | C$ *in G,* $\mathcal{A}$ *must appear in some parcluster* $\mathbf{C}^i$. *(iii) If a PRV from G appears in two parclusters* $\mathbf{C}^i$ *and* $\mathbf{C}^j$, *it must also appear in every parcluster* $\mathbf{C}^k$ *on the path connecting nodes i and j in J. The separator* $\mathbf{S}^{ij}$ *of edge* $i - j$ *is given by* $\mathbf{C}^i \cap \mathbf{C}^j$ *containing shared PRVs.*

LJT constructs an FO jtree, enters evidence in the FO jtree, and passes messages through an *inbound* and an *outbound* pass, to distribute local information of the nodes through the FO jtree. To compute a message, LJT eliminates all non-separator PRVs from the parcluster's local model and received messages.

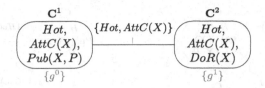

Fig. 3. FO jtree for G^{ex} (local models in grey)

After message passing, LJT answers queries. For each query, LJT finds a par-cluster containing the query term and sums out all non-query terms in its local model and received messages.

Figure 3 shows an FO jtree of G^{ex} with the local models of the parclusters and the separators as labels of edges. During the *inbound* phase of message passing, LJT sends messages from $\mathbf{C}^1$ to $\mathbf{C}^2$ and for the *outbound* phase a message from $\mathbf{C}^2$ to $\mathbf{C}^1$. If we want to know whether Hot holds, we query for $P(Hot)$ for which LJT can use either parcluster $\mathbf{C}^1$ or $\mathbf{C}^2$. Thus, LJT can sum out $AttC(X)$ and $DoR(X)$ from $\mathbf{C}^2$'s local model G^2, $\{g^1\}$, combined with the received message.

4.2   LDJT: Overview

LDJT efficiently answers queries $P(\mathbf{Q}^i_\pi|\mathbf{E}_{0:t})$, with a set of query terms $\{\mathbf{Q}_t\}^T_{t=0}$, given a PDM G and evidence $\{\mathbf{E}_t\}^T_{t=0}$, by performing the following steps:

(i) Construct offline two FO jtrees J_0 and J_t with *in-* and *out-clusters* from G.

(ii) For $t = 0$, using J_0 to enter $\mathbf{E}_0$, pass messages, answer each query term $Q^i_\pi \in \mathbf{Q}_0$, and preserve the state.

(iii) For $t > 0$, instantiate J_t for the current time step t, recover the previous state, enter $\mathbf{E}_t$ in J_t, pass messages, answer each query term $Q^i_\pi \in \mathbf{Q}_t$, and preserve the state.

Next, we show how LDJT constructs the FO jtrees J_0 and J_t with *in-* and *out-clusters*, which contain a minimal set of PRVs to m-separate the FO jtrees. M-separation means that information about these PRVs make FO jtrees independent from each other. Afterwards, we present how LDJT connects the FO jtrees for reasoning to solve the filtering and prediction problems efficiently.

4.3   LDJT: FO Jtree Construction for PDMs

LDJT constructs FO jtrees for G_0 and $G_\to$, both with an incoming and outgoing interface. To be able to construct the interfaces in the FO jtrees, LDJT uses the PDM G to identify the interface PRVs $\mathbf{I}_t$ for a time slice t, i.e., the PRVs which have successors in the next slice.

Definition 7. *The forward interface is defined as:* $\mathbf{I}_{t-1} = \{A^i_t \mid \exists\phi(\mathcal{A})|C \in G : A^i_{t-1} \in \mathcal{A} \land \exists A^j_t \in \mathcal{A}\}$.

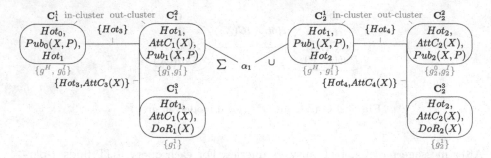

Fig. 4. Forward pass of LDJT (local models and labeling in grey)

For $G_{\rightarrow}^{ex}$, which is shown in Fig. 2, PRVs Hot_{t-1} and $Pub_{t-1}(X, P)$ have successors in the next time slice, making up $\mathbf{I}_{t-1}$. To ensure interface PRVs $\mathbf{I}$ ending up in a single parcluster, LDJT adds a parfactor g^I over the interface to the model. Thus, LDJT adds a parfactor g_0^I over $\mathbf{I}_0$ to G_0, builds an FO jtree J_0 and labels the parcluster with g_0^I from J_0 as *in-* and *out-cluster*. For $G_{\rightarrow}$, LDJT removes all non-interface PRVs from time slice $t-1$, adds parfactors g_{t-1}^I and g_t^I, and constructs J_t. Further, LDJT labels the parcluster containing g_{t-1}^I as *in-cluster* and labels the parcluster containing g_t^I as *out-cluster*.

The interface PRVs are a minimal required set to m-separate the FO jtrees. LDJT uses these PRVs as separator to connect the *out-cluster* of J_{t-1} with the *in-cluster* of J_t, allowing for reusing the structure of J_t for all $t > 0$.

4.4 LDJT: Proceeding in Time with the FO Jtree Structures

Since J_0 and J_t are static, LDJT uses LJT as a subroutine by passing on a constructed FO jtree, queries, and evidence for time step t to handle evidence entering, message passing, and query answering using the FO jtree. Further, for proceeding to the next time step, LDJT calculates an α_t message over the interface PRVs using the *out-cluster* to preserve the information about the current state. Afterwards, LDJT increases t by one, instantiates J_t, and adds α_{t-1} to the *in-cluster* of J_t. During message passing, α_{t-1} is distributed through J_t.

Figure 4 depicts how LDJT uses the interface message passing between time step one and two. First, LDJT sums out the non-interface PRV $AttC_1(X)$ from $\mathbf{C}_1^2$'s local model and the received messages and saves the result in message α_1. After increasing t by one, LDJT adds α_1 to the *in-cluster* of J_2, $\mathbf{C}_2^1$. α_1 is then distributed by message passing and accounted for when calculating α_2.

Following this procedure, LDJT can answer *filtering* and *prediction* queries. However, currently LDJT cannot answer *assignment* queries.

5 Most Probable Assignments in LJT

Let us first have a look at assignment queries and then we provide an intuition how LJT^{mpe} solves the problem based on [5].

Definition 8. *Given a PM G and evidence* **E**, *we are interested in the most probable assignment for all PRVs* **V** *in G without evidence. Thus, to solve an MPE, LJT^{mpe} computes* $\arg\max_{\mathbf{V}} P(\mathbf{V}|\mathbf{E})$.

The basic idea of calculating an MPE, compared to answering marginal distribution queries, is to use a maximisation instead of a summation to eliminate PRVs. To efficiently calculate a maximisation for relational probabilistic static models, Braun and Müller [5] propose a lifted maximisation for the current version of LVE [23] and also apply it to LJT [3].

As LJT calculates a lifted solution to the MPE problem, LJT^{mpe} uses the fact that instances behave the same for assignments. Thus, for a PRV, LJT^{mpe} only needs to store the number of instances for the range values of that PRV, which maximise the potential. Assume a MPE is that two people are doing research and one does not do research. Then, it is the same if either *alice* and *bob*, *alice* and *eve*, or *bob* and *eve* do research. Hence, LJT^{mpe} only stores a histogram encoding that two map to true and one maps to false.

To compute an MPE, LJT^{mpe} does not only need to store assignments for PRVs, but also potentials, as we want the assignment that maximises the potential. Thus, to calculate an MPE, the function ϕ in a parfactor $\phi(\mathcal{A})|C$ maps arguments to a pair of a potential and a set of histograms for already maxed out PRVs. By storing the potential and a set of histograms, LJT^{mpe} can directly read out the MPE after the last maxing out. For example after the last maxing out, a parfactor could like this: $\phi() \rightarrow (p, [6,0]_P, [3,0]_D, [3,0]_A, [1,0]_H)$.

Knowing what parfactors store computing an MPE, we now take a look at how LJT^{mpe} answers MPE queries efficiently. Algorithm 1 outlines the steps LJT^{mpe} performs. The first two steps are the same steps as for marginal queries. LJT^{mpe} first builds a corresponding FO jtree J from a PM G and enters evidence afterwards. The main difference compared to marginal queries is that LJT^{mpe} only performs an *inbound* message pass. LJT performs a complete message pass for marginal queries, to efficiently answer multiple queries. However, there only is one MPE query for a given set of evidence, for which LJT^{mpe} needs to max out all PRVs without evidence. Thus, as long as one parcluster has all the information, which a root has after an *inbound* message pass, that parcluster can answer an MPE query. The other important difference is that LJT performs a maxing out compared to a summing out to eliminate a PRV. After the *inbound* message pass, LJT^{mpe} maxes out the remaining PRVs from the root cluster of the *inbound* message passing. Lastly, LJT^{mpe} can directly read out the MPE, which lead to the highest potential.

Algorithm 1. LJT^{mpe} for PM G and Evidence **E**

---
procedure LJT$^{mpe}(G, \mathbf{E})$
    Build FO jtree J using G
    Enter **E** in J
    Perform an *inbound* message pass on J
    Answer MPE query

Figure 3 depicts an FO jtree J for our example PM G^{ex}. After the evidence entering, LJT^{mpe} performs an *inbound* message pass with, e.g., $\mathbf{C}^1$ as root. Thus, LJT^{mpe} calculates the message m^{21}: LJT^{mpe} eliminates $DoR(X)$ from $\mathbf{C}^2$ by applying lifted maxing out. For each case, where the range values of Hot and $AttC(X)$ are the same and only the range value of $DoR(X)$ differs, LJT^{mpe} keeps the higher potential of the range value and saves the assignment to max out $DoR(X)$. Hence, m^{21} contains a parfactor with 4 rows and each row contains the maximum potential and whether a true or false assignment of $DoR(X)$ leads to the potential. After LJT^{mpe} sends m^{21} to $\mathbf{C}^1$, $\mathbf{C}^1$ holds all the information necessary to answer an MPE query. In $\mathbf{C}^1$, LJT^{mpe} still has to eliminate Hot, $AttC(X)$, and $Pub(X, P)$ by applying lifted maxing out. Having eliminated all PRVs, LJT^{mpe} can return the most probable assignment given the evidence.

Another assignment query is a MAP query, where we are interested in the most probable assignment only for a subset of PRVs.

Definition 9. *Given a PM G and evidence $\mathbf{E}$, we are interested in the most probable assignment for some PRVs $\mathbf{V}$ in G without evidence. Let $\mathbf{S}$ be the remaining PRVs. To solve a MAP, LJT and LJT^{mpe} compute $\arg\max_{\mathbf{V}} \sum_{\mathbf{S}} P(\mathbf{V}|\mathbf{E})$.*

The non-commutativity of summing out and maxing out leads to a restriction of the elimination order as it forces an algorithm to sum out PRVs before maxing out query PRVs [5]. Hence, the problem of solving a MAP is in general harder [22]. To compute a lifted solution to the MAP problem, lifting imposes additional restriction on the elimination order, making the problem even harder.

However, LJT can identify harmless MAP queries. In case, a MAP queries is over all PRVs from a parcluster or from connected parclusters, LJT can use the message pass from marginal queries, in which LJT sums out PRVs. Based on the elimination order induced by separators, all other PRVs are summed out and LJT^{mpe} can calculate an MPE for the PRVs from the (connected) parcluster(s).

Assume we are interested in the assignment of Hot, $AttC(X)$, and $Pub(X, P)$. Hence, LJT needs to sum out $DoR(X)$ and LJT^{mpe} needs to max out Hot, $AttC(X)$, and $Pub(X, P)$. To answer the query, LJT^{mpe} can use $\mathbf{C}^1$. During the message pass for marginal queries, LJT calculates the message m^{21} for which it eliminates $DoR(X)$. With m^{21}, $\mathbf{C}^1$ holds all the information necessary to answer the assignment query. Thus, LJT^{mpe} can simply calculate an MPE on $\mathbf{C}^1$.

Unfortunately, LJT^{mpe} does not efficiently handle temporal aspects of PDMs. Thus, we now introduce $LDJT^{mpe}$ to efficiently answer assignment queries for relational temporal models.

6   Most Probable Assignments in LDJT

In this section, we investigate how MPE and MAP queries can be solved efficiently for temporal relational models. Further, we discuss why an efficient handling of temporal aspects is necessary.

6.1   MPE Queries

We look at temporal assignment queries and introduce how LDJT^{mpe} efficiently answers temporal assignment queries.

Definition 10. *Given a PDM G and evidence $\mathbf{E}_{0:T}$ for all time steps, we are interested in the most probable assignment for all PRVs $\mathbf{V}$ in G without evidence. Thus, to solve an temporal MPE, LDJT^{mpe} computes $\arg\max_{\mathbf{V}} P(\mathbf{V}|\mathbf{E}_{0:T})$.*

The basic idea of solving the temporal lifted MPE problem is also to use a maximisation instead of summation, which LDJT uses for marginal queries. The Viterbi algorithm is one approach to solve the temporal propositional MPE problem, which is already successfully applied to propositional temporal models by applying a max-product instead of a sum-product [15].

Algorithm 2 outlines how LDJT^{mpe} efficiently solves the temporal lifted MPE problem. The basic idea for LDJT^{mpe} is a combination from LDJT and LJT^{mpe}. The first step in Algorithm 2 is to construct FO jtree structures J_0 and J_t as described in Sect. 4.3. Using the structures, LDJT^{mpe} enters a loop where for every time step, it recovers the previous state, enters evidence for the current time steps, performs an *inbound* message pass with the *out-cluster* as root, and calculates γ_t to preserve the current time step. The main differences are that LDJT^{mpe} calculates γ_t by maxing out instead of α_t by summing out and that LDJT^{mpe} only performs an *inbound* message pass with the *out-cluster* as root. After LDJT^{mpe} propagated all the information to the last time step and thereby left the loop, it answers the MPE query.

To calculate γ_t, LDJT^{mpe} maxes out all non-interface PRVs from the *out-cluster* of J_t instead of summing them out for α_t. As LDJT^{mpe} only needs to answer one MPE query, over all time steps, it suffices to always perform an *inbound* message pass with the *out-cluster* as root. This way the *out-cluster* has all the information to calculate γ_t and for the last time step, LDJT^{mpe} uses the *out-cluster* to answer the MPE query, by maxing out the interface PRVs and reading out the most probable assignment to all PRVs without evidence.

For our example PDM G^{ex}, LDJT^{mpe} first builds FO jtree structures J_0^{ex} and J_t^{ex}, which are the same structures as for marginal queries. For time

---

Algorithm 2. LDJT^{mpe} for PDM G and Evidence $\mathbf{E}_{0:T}$

---
procedure LDJT$^{mpe}(G, \mathbf{E}_{0:T})$
    Build FO jtree J_0 and J_t using G
    $t := 0$
    while $t \neq T + 1$ **do**
        Recover previous state from γ_{t-1}
        Enter $\mathbf{E}_t$ in J_t
        Perform an *inbound* message pass on J_t with *out-cluster* as root
        Calculate γ_t
    Answer MPE query using *out-cluster* of J_T

---

step 0, LDJT^{mpe} does not have a previous state to recover. Thus, LDJT^{mpe} directly enters evidence for time step 0 in J_0^{ex}. On J_0^{ex}, LDJT^{mpe} performs an *inbound* message pass with the *out-cluster* as root and calculates γ_0 by maxing out all non-interface PRVs from the *out-cluster*. For time step 1, LDJT^{mpe} instantiates J_1^{ex} from J_t^{ex}. Figure 4 depicts the FO jtree instantiations for time step 1 and 2. LDJT^{mpe} adds γ_0 to the *in-cluster*, $\mathbf{C}_1^1$, of J_1^{ex}, enter evidence for time step 1, and performs an *inbound* message pass with $\mathbf{C}_1^2$ as root. Hence, LDJT^{mpe} calculates two messages, namely m_1^{12} and m_1^{32}. With m_1^{12} and m_1^{32}, $\mathbf{C}_1^2$ holds all the information necessary to calculate γ_1, by maxing out $AttC_1(X)$. LDJT^{mpe} proceeds in this fashion until it reaches the last time step T. In J_T^{ex} the *out-cluster* $\mathbf{C}_T^2$ holds all the information to answer the MPE query. After maxing out Hot_T, $AttC_T(X)$, and $Pub_T(X, P)$, LDJT^{mpe} can directly read out the assignments for all PRVs from each time step.

Now, we show that LDJT^{mpe} calculates the most probable assignments.

Theorem 1. *LDJT^{mpe} is sound, i.e., computes an MPE for PDM G equivalent to an MPE computed for $gr(unrolled(G))$, where unrolled returns an unrolled model for T time steps.*

Proof. LJT^{mpe} is sound. Basically, LDJT^{mpe} unrolls an FO jtree for T time steps and performs an *inbound* message pass. Thus, LDJT^{mpe} produces the same result as unrolling an FO jtree, providing it to LJT^{mpe}, and LJT^{mpe} performing an inbound message pass with one special parcluster as root. The calculations are equivalent. Hence, as LJT^{mpe} is sound, LDJT^{mpe} is also sound.

6.2   MAP Queries

Let us first define temporal MAP queries and then we introduce how a combination of LDJT, for summing out, and LDJT^{mpe}, for maxing out, can efficiently solve certain temporal MAP queries.

Definition 11. *Given a PDM G and evidence $\mathbf{E}_{0:T}$ for all time steps, we are interested in the most probable assignment for some PRVs $\mathbf{V}$ in G without evidence. Let $\mathbf{S}$ be the remaining PRVs. Thus, to solve an temporal MAP, LDJT and LDJT^{mpe} compute $\arg\max_{\mathbf{V}} \sum_{\mathbf{S}} P(\mathbf{V}|\mathbf{E}_{0:T})$.*

A combination of LDJT and LDJT^{mpe} can also answer MAP queries. Also for the combination, a MAP query over a parcluster is harmless. One feature of LDJT is that an α message separates one time slice from the next. Thus, LDJT and LDJT^{mpe} can efficiently answer MAP queries over complete time steps and reuse α messages computed while answering marginal queries. For example, we are only interested in the assignment of all PRVs from the last 20 time steps. Then, LDJT^{mpe} can instantiate J_{T-20}, add α_{T-21}, start solving an MPE, and read out at the *out-cluster* of J_T the most probable assignments for the last 20 time steps. The α_{T-21} message includes all necessary information for the summing out of all PRVs from time step 0 to $T - 21$. Therefore, in the case of MAP queries over complete time steps, the non-commutativity of summing out and maxing out does not lead to a restriction of the elimination order. Hence, using LDJT and LDJT^{mpe}, we can easily identify that MAP queries over complete time steps are harmless. Additionally, LDJT^{mpe} reuses computations from marginal queries to answer MAP queries over complete time steps.

Given both LDJT and LDJT^{mpe} are sound, soundness of the combination of both for queries over time steps follows.

6.3 Discussion

Now, we discuss how LDJT^{mpe} efficiently handels temporal aspects compared to LJT^{mpe} for MPE and MAP queries.

MPE Queries: In case we unroll a PDM into a PM and simply use LJT^{mpe}, the constructed FO jtree would not necessarily be constructed in a way to handle the temporal aspects efficiently and thus, would have an impact on the performance. However, if we unroll an FO jtree based on the structures J_0 and J_t from LDJT^{mpe}, then from a computational perspective, LJT^{mpe} and LDJT^{mpe} would perform the same calculations. Both would only perform one *inbound* message pass and by selecting the *out-cluster* of the last time step as the root also for LJT^{mpe}, then both algorithms would compute exactly the same messages.

Nonetheless, there still is a difference in the memory consumption. On the one hand, LJT^{mpe} would need to store the complete unrolled FO jtree. Thus, all messages, evidence, and local models for all time steps need to be stored in memory, which might not always be feasible for a high number of maximal time steps. On the other hand, out of the box, LDJT^{mpe} only needs to store one FO jtree, including messages, with a γ message, evidence, and local models, for the current time step. Thus, LJT^{mpe} can only perform similarly by using the FO jtree construction of LDJT^{mpe} and the memory consumption of LDJT^{mpe} is significantly lower due to the efficient handling of temporal aspects.

MAP Queries: As we have already mentioned, assignment queries over complete time steps are safe for a combination of LDJT and LDJT^{mpe}. Additionally to being safe, these queries could also be of high interest as often one is probably not interested in the assignment of all PRVs, but only in the PRVs of the last few time steps. Further, while answering marginal queries with LDJT, it can simply store the calculated α messages for assignment queries. Thus, for MAP queries over complete time steps, a combination of LDJT and LDJT^{mpe} can efficiently reuse computations and only needs to store one FO jtree at a time.

To answer MAP queries over complete time steps with a combination of LJT and LJT^{mpe}, we again could provide them with an unrolled FO jtree, analogous to the MPE queries. Here, we would again have the overhead on the memory consumption. Nonetheless, also with LJT and LJT^{mpe}, we could use the message pass of LJT, which includes a complete message pass with *inbound* and *outbound* phase, and apply LJT^{mpe} on the time slices for which we want to know the assignment. However, the combination of LJT and LJT^{mpe} does not support out of the box to dynamically add new time steps nor the separation with the α messages. Hence, a combination of LDJT and LDJT^{mpe} significantly outperforms LJT and LJT^{mpe} for MPE and MAP queries.

In general, for MPE queries the runtime results from [5] also hold for LDJT^{mpe}, if we use an unrolled FO jtree for LJT^{mpe}, as they would perform the same computations. Additionally, for MAP queries, the runtime results from [9,10] also hold for LJT^{mpe} as the assignments only induce a small overhead [5] and LJT^{mpe} efficiently handels temporal aspects of PDMs.

7   Conclusion

We present LDJT^{mpe} to efficiently solve the temporal MPE problem for temporal probabilistic relational models. The basic idea is to use lifted maxing out instead of lifted summing out, which LDJT uses, to eliminate PRVs. Additionally, we show that a combination of LDJT and LDJT^{mpe} can efficiently answer MAP queries over the last x time steps. Further, by comparing LDJT and LDJT^{mpe} against LJT and LJT^{mpe}, we show that an efficient handling of temporal aspects is necessary and that LDJT and LDJT^{mpe} significantly outperforms LJT and LJT^{mpe} for temporal models.

We currently work on extending LDJT to handle incremental changes in a PDM efficiently. Other interesting future work includes a tailored automatic learning for PDMs, parallelisation of LJT, and improved evidence entering.

References

1. Ahmadi, B., Kersting, K., Mladenov, M., Natarajan, S.: Exploiting symmetries for scaling loopy belief propagation and relational training. Mach. Learn. **92**(1), 91–132 (2013)
2. Apsel, U., Brafman, R.I.: Exploiting uniform assignments in first-order MPE. In: Proceedings of the Twenty-Eighth Conference on Uncertainty in Artificial Intelligence, pp. 74–83. AUAI Press (2014)
3. Braun, T., Möller, R.: Lifted junction tree algorithm. In: Friedrich, G., Helmert, M., Wotawa, F. (eds.) KI 2016. LNCS (LNAI), vol. 9904, pp. 30–42. Springer, Cham (2016). https://doi.org/10.1007/978-3-319-46073-4_3
4. Braun, T., Möller, R.: Preventing groundings and handling evidence in the lifted junction tree algorithm. In: Kern-Isberner, G., Fürnkranz, J., Thimm, M. (eds.) KI 2017. LNCS (LNAI), vol. 10505, pp. 85–98. Springer, Cham (2017). https://doi.org/10.1007/978-3-319-67190-1_7
5. Braun, T., Möller, R.: Lifted most probable explanation. In: Chapman, P., Endres, D., Pernelle, N. (eds.) ICCS 2018. LNCS (LNAI), vol. 10872, pp. 39–54. Springer, Cham (2018). https://doi.org/10.1007/978-3-319-91379-7_4
6. Braun, T., Möller, R.: Parameterised queries and lifted query answering. In: Proceedings of IJCAI 2018, pp. 4980–4986 (2018)
7. Dignös, A., Böhlen, M.H., Gamper, J.: Temporal alignment. In: Proceedings of the 2012 ACM SIGMOD International Conference on Management of Data, pp. 433–444. ACM (2012)

8. Dylla, M., Miliaraki, I., Theobald, M.: A temporal-probabilistic database model for information extraction. Proc. VLDB Endow. **6**(14), 1810–1821 (2013)
9. Gehrke, M., Braun, T., Möller, R.: Lifted dynamic junction tree algorithm. In: Chapman, P., Endres, D., Pernelle, N. (eds.) ICCS 2018. LNCS (LNAI), vol. 10872, pp. 55–69. Springer, Cham (2018). https://doi.org/10.1007/978-3-319-91379-7_5
10. Gehrke, M., Braun, T., Möller, R.: Preventing unnecessary groundings in the lifted dynamic junction tree algorithm. In: Mitrovic, T., Xue, B., Li, X. (eds.) AI 2018. LNCS (LNAI), vol. 11320, pp. 556–562. Springer, Cham (2018). https://doi.org/10.1007/978-3-030-03991-2_51
11. Geier, T., Biundo, S.: Approximate online inference for dynamic Markov logic networks. In: Proceedings of the 23rd IEEE International Conference on Tools with Artificial Intelligence (ICTAI), pp. 764–768. IEEE (2011)
12. Lauritzen, S.L., Spiegelhalter, D.J.: Local computations with probabilities on graphical structures and their application to expert systems. J. R. Stat. Society. Ser. B (Methodol.) **50**(2), 157–224 (1988)
13. Manfredotti, C.E.: Modeling and inference with relational dynamic Bayesian networks. Ph.D. thesis, Ph.D. dissertation, University of Milano-Bicocca (2009)
14. Milch, B., Zettlemoyer, L.S., Kersting, K., Haimes, M., Kaelbling, L.P.: lifted probabilistic inference with counting formulas. In: Proceedings of AAAI, vol. 8, pp. 1062–1068 (2008)
15. Murphy, K.P.: Dynamic Bayesian networks: representation, inference and learning. Ph.D. thesis, University of California, Berkeley (2002)
16. Nitti, D., De Laet, T., De Raedt, L.: A particle filter for hybrid relational domains. In: Proceedings of the IEEE/RSJ International Conference on Intelligent Robots and Systems (IROS), pp. 2764–2771. IEEE (2013)
17. Papai, T., Kautz, H., Stefankovic, D.: Slice normalized dynamic Markov logic networks. In: Proceedings of the Advances in Neural Information Processing Systems, pp. 1907–1915 (2012)
18. Poole, D.: First-order probabilistic inference. In: Proceedings of IJCAI, vol. 3, pp. 985–991 (2003)
19. Richardson, M., Domingos, P.: Markov logic networks. Mach. Learn. **62**(1), 107–136 (2006)
20. de Salvo Braz, R.: Lifted first-order probabilistic inference. Ph.D. thesis, Ph.D. dissertation, University of Illinois at Urbana Champaign (2007)
21. de Salvo Braz, R., Amir, E., Roth, D.: MPE and partial inversion in lifted probabilistic variable elimination. In: AAAI, vol. 6, pp. 1123–1130 (2006)
22. Sharma, V., Sheikh, N.A., Mittal, H., Gogate, V., Singla, P.: Lifted marginal MAP inference. In: UAI-18 Proceedings of the 34th Conference on Uncertainty in Artificial Intelligence, pp. 917–926. AUAI Press (2018)
23. Taghipour, N., Fierens, D., Davis, J., Blockeel, H.: Lifted variable elimination: decoupling the operators from the constraint language. J. Artif. Intell. Res. **47**(1), 393–439 (2013)
24. Thon, I., Landwehr, N., De Raedt, L.: Stochastic relational processes: efficient inference and applications. Mach. Learn. **82**(2), 239–272 (2011)
25. Vlasselaer, J., Van den Broeck, G., Kimmig, A., Meert, W., De Raedt, L.: TP-compilation for inference in probabilistic logic programs. Int. J. Approx. Reason. **78**, 15–32 (2016)
26. Vlasselaer, J., Meert, W., Van den Broeck, G., De Raedt, L.: Efficient probabilistic inference for dynamic relational models. In: Proceedings of the 13th AAAI Conference on Statistical Relational AI, AAAIWS'14-13, pp. 131–132. AAAI Press (2014)

Temporal Relations Between Imprecise Time Intervals: Representation and Reasoning

Fatma Ghorbel[1,2(✉)], Fayçal Hamdi[1], and Elisabeth Métais[1]

[1] CEDRIC Laboratory, Conservatoire National des Arts et Métiers (CNAM),
Paris, France
fatmaghorbel6@gmail.com,
{faycal.hamdi,elisabeth.metais}@cnam.fr
[2] MIRACL Laboratory, University of Sfax, Sfax, Tunisia

Abstract. Temporal data given by users are often imprecise. In this paper, we propose an approach to represent and reason about temporal relations between imprecise time intervals which are classical time intervals characterized by gradual beginnings and/or endings. It is mainly based on extending the Allen's interval algebra. It is not only suitable to express precise temporal interval relations (e.g., "Before") but also imprecise personalized ones (e.g., "Just Before"). Compared to related work, our imprecise relations are personalized, in the sense that they are not limited to a given number and their meanings are determined by a domain expert. For instance, the classic Allen's relation "Before" may be generalized in 5 imprecise relations, where "Before$_{(1)}$" means "just before" and gradually the time gap between the two intervals increases until "Before$_{(5)}$" which means "too long before". Our imprecise personalized relations are based on our extension of the Vilain and Kautz's point algebra. We showed that, unlike most related work, our temporal interval relations preserve many of the properties of the Allen's interval algebra. Furthermore, we show how they can be used for temporal reasoning by means of a transitivity table. Finally, our approach is applied to the Semantic Web. We propose a fuzzy ontology-based prototype. Inferences are done via a set of SWRL and fuzzy IF-THEN rules. We illustrate the usefulness of our approach in the context of an ontology-based memory prosthesis for Alzheimer's patients.

Keywords: Imprecise time interval · Temporal interval relation · Temporal reasoning · Allen's interval algebra · Semantic Web · Fuzzy ontology

1 Introduction

Temporal data given by users are often imprecise. For instance, in the case of information like "John was married to Maria from early 1970s to by 2016", two measures of imprecision are involved. On the one hand, "early 1970s" is imprecise in the sense that it could mean, with a decreasingly possibility, from 1970 to 1974; on the other hand, the information "by 2016" is imprecise in the sense that it could mean from 2015 to 2017. This period is represented by an imprecise time interval which is a classical time interval characterized by imprecise beginning and/or ending.

© Springer Nature Switzerland AG 2019
D. Endres et al. (Eds.): ICCS 2019, LNAI 11530, pp. 86–101, 2019.
https://doi.org/10.1007/978-3-030-23182-8_7

The Allen's interval algebra [1] is a well-known formalism to model temporal relations between time intervals. 13 relations are proposed. Their semantics are illustrated in Table 1. However, this algebra is not designed to handle situations in which time intervals are imprecise and it is not suitable to express imprecise temporal relations such as "approximately at the same time", "middle during" and "just before".

Table 1. Allen's relations between the time intervals A = $[A^-, A^+]$ (■■) and B = $[B^-, B^+]$ (▭).

Relation(A, B)	Definition	Illustration	Inverse(B, A)
Before (B)	$A^+ < B^-$		After (A)
Meets (M)	$A^+ = B^-$		Met-by (Mb)
Overlaps (O)	$(A^- < B^-) \wedge (B^- < A^+) \wedge (A^+ < B^+)$		Overlapped-by (Ob)
Starts (S)	$(A^- = B^-) \wedge (A^+ < B^+)$		Started-by (Sb)
During (D)	$(B^- < A^-) \wedge (A^+ < B^+)$		Contains (C)
Ends (E)	$(B^- < A^-) \wedge (A^+ = B^+)$		Ended-by (Eb)
Equals (Eq)	$(A^- = B^-) \wedge (A^+ = B^+)$		Equals (Eq)

Few approaches extend the Allen's interval algebra to propose temporal relations between imprecise time intervals. Only a small number of these approaches propose some imprecise temporal relations. A lot of imprecise relations are not studied by these approaches. Furthermore, most of these approaches do not preserve the properties of the original algebra and do not study the compositions of the resulting relations.

In this paper, we detail an approach to represent and reason about temporal relations between imprecise time intervals. Our approach is mainly based on extending the Allen's interval algebra. It is not only suitable to represent precise relations, but also imprecise personalized relations. Indeed, the classic Allen's relations {"Before", "After", "Overlaps", "Overlapped-by", "Starts", "Started-by", "During", "Contains", "Ends" and "Ended-by"} may be generalized in N imprecise personalized relations. Their number N and their meanings are specified by a domain expert. For instance, the classic Allen's relation After may be generalized in 3 imprecise personalized relations, where "After$_{(1)}$" means "approximately the same time"; "After$_{(2)}$" means "just after" and "After$_{(3)}$" means "long after". Our imprecise personalized relations are based on our extension of the Vilain and Kautz's point algebra [2]. Our approach preserves important properties regarding reflexivity/irreflexivity, symmetry/asymmetry and transitivity. Furthermore, we show how our temporal relations can be used for temporal reasoning by means of a transitivity table. Our approach is applied to the Semantic Web field.

The current paper is organized as follows. Related work in the field of extending the Allen's interval algebra is discussed in Sect. 2. Section 3 presents our approach to represent and reason about temporal relations between imprecise time intervals. Section 4 illustrates an application of our approach to the Semantic Web field. Section 5 draws conclusions and future research directions.

2   Related Work: Extending the Allen's Interval Algebra

A number of approaches extend the Allen's interval algebra to propose temporal relations between precise time intervals: [3, 4] and [5]. Dubois and Prade [3] discuss the approximate reasoning on dates and time intervals. They represent a precise time interval as a pair of possibility distributions that define the possible values of the endpoints of the interval. This approach allows modeling some imprecise relations such as "Long Before". Badaloni and Giacomin [5] propose a fuzzy extension of the Allen's interval algebra to handle uncertainty, called IA^{fuz}. A degree of preference ($\in [0, 1]$) is associated to each temporal interval relation, e.g., the possibility that the relation Meets holds between two time intervals is 0, 9. Imprecise temporal relations are not studied. Guesgen et al. [4] propose fuzzy temporal relations viewed as fuzzy sets of ordinary Allen's relations taking into account a neighborhood structure, a notion introduced in [6]. For instance, the temporal relation "Fuzz-Meets" covers the ordinary Allen's relation "Meets" as well as situations as "Slightly Before" and Slight "Overlap". This approach does not propose imprecise temporal relations.

Concerning imprecise time intervals, a number of approaches extend the Allen's interval algebra: [7–10] and [11]. Nagypál and Motik [9] represent these intervals as a fuzzy set. For example, "the period from the late 1920s to the early 1930s" is represented as a fuzzy set using the following semantics: (1928, 1933, 2, 2). They introduce a set of auxiliary operators on time intervals and define fuzzy counterparts of these operators. However, many of the properties of the original Allen's interval algebra are lost. For instance, the relation "Equals" is not reflexive. Thus, the compositions of the resulting relations are not studied by the authors. Imprecise temporal relations are not taken into account. Ohlbach [8] extends the Allen's interval algebra based on fuzzy sets. This approach proposes some imprecise temporal relations. However, it cannot take into account imprecise temporal relations such as "Long Before". It does not preserve many of the properties of the original Allen's interval algebra. Therefore, it is not suitable for temporal reasoning. Schockaert and Cock [9] propose a generalization of the Allen's interval algebra. This approach allows handling classical temporal relations, as well as some other imprecise relations. It preserves many of the properties of the Allen's interval algebra. The resulting relations are used for fuzzy temporal reasoning by means of a transitivity table. However, a lot of imprecise temporal relations are not studied by the authors. Sadeghi and Goertzel [10] propose an approach to handle uncertain temporal inference. The Allen's interval algebra is extended to imprecise time intervals by representing them as trapeziums with distinct beginning, middle and end. An uncertain version of the composition table is developed. Gammoudi et al. [11] generalize the Allen's relations to make them applicable to imprecise time intervals in conjunctive and disjunctive ways. The compositions of the resulting relations are not studied by the authors. Imprecise temporal interval relations are not proposed by this approach.

3 Our Approach to Represent and Reason About Temporal Relations Between Imprecise Time Intervals

Our approach consists of two phases. First, we extend the Vilain and Kautz's point algebra to propose a set of imprecise personalized time point comparators. Then, we extend the Allen's interval algebra. More precisely, we propose precise and imprecise personalized temporal relations between imprecise time intervals and we introduce a transitivity table to derive new temporal knowledge from the resulted relations. For the rest of the paper, we use the membership functions (MFs) shown in Fig. 1 [12].

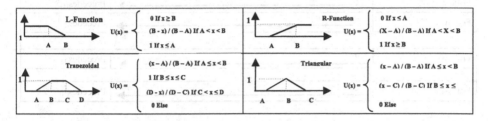

Fig. 1. L-Function, R-Function, trapezoidal and triangular membership functions [12].

3.1 Our Extension of the Vilain and Kautz's Point Algebra

Vilain and Kautz identify three precise time point comparators: "Precedes", "Same" and "Follows". However, this algebra does not introduce imprecise comparators. Based on fuzzy sets, we extend it. We generalize the two comparators Precedes and Follows to propose a set of imprecise personalized time point comparators. They are imprecise as we propose comparators such as "Just Precedes" and they are personalized as their number and meanings are set by a domain expert.

Let α and β be two parameters $\in [0, +\infty[$; let T_1 and T_2 be two time points and let N be the number of the graduality. We propose the imprecise personalized comparators {"Follows$_{(1)}^{(\alpha,\beta)}$" ... "Follows$_{(N)}^{(\alpha,\beta)}$"} to extend the precise comparator Follows. "Follows$_{(1)}^{(\alpha,\beta)}(T_1,T_2)$" means that T_1 follows T_2 w.r.t. (α, β) and $T_1 - T_2 < \alpha + \beta$. Gradually the time gap between T_1 and T_2 increases until "Follows$_{(N)}^{(\alpha,\beta)}(T_1,T_2)$" which means that T_1 follows T_2 w.r.t. (α, β) and $T_1 - T_2 > (N-1)\alpha + (N-2)\beta$. For instance, if we set N = 3, "Follows$_{(1)}^{(\alpha,\beta)}$" means "just follows"; "Follows$_{(2)}^{(\alpha,\beta)}$" means "middle follows" and "Follows$_{(3)}^{(\alpha,\beta)}$" means "long follows".

We propose the imprecise personalized comparators {"Precedes$_{(1)}^{(\alpha,\beta)}$" ... "Precedes$_{(N)}^{(\alpha,\beta)}$"} to extend the precise comparator "Precedes". "Precedes$_{(1)}^{(\alpha,\beta)}(T_1,T_2)$" means that T_1 precedes T_2 w.r.t. (α, β) and $T_1 - T_2 > -\alpha - \beta$. Gradually the time gap between T_1 and T_2 increases until "Precedes$_{(N)}^{(\alpha,\beta)}(T_1,T_2)$" which means that T_1 precedes T_2 w.r.t. (α, β) and $T_1 - T_2 < -(N-1)\alpha - (N-2)\beta$. For instance, if we set

$N = 5$, "Precedes$_{(1)}^{(\alpha,\beta)}$" means "approximately at the same time"; "Precedes$_{(2)}^{(\alpha,\beta)}$" means "just precedes"; "Precedes$_{(3)}^{(\alpha,\beta)}$" means "middle precedes"; "Precedes$_{(4)}^{(\alpha,\beta)}$" means "long precedes" and "Precedes$_{(5)}^{(\alpha,\beta)}$" means "too long precedes". Table 2 summarizes our imprecise personalized time point comparators.

Table 2. Our imprecise personalized comparators between the time points T_1 (●) and T_2 (○).

Comparator(T_1, T_2)	Illustration	Inverse(T_2, T_1)
Follows$_{(1)}^{(\alpha,\beta)}$	○ ● ————————————————————→	Precedes$_{(1)}^{(\alpha,\beta)}$
Follows$_{(2)}^{(\alpha,\beta)}$	○ ● ————————————————————→	Precedes$_{(2)}^{(\alpha,\beta)}$
	...	
Follows$_{(k)}^{(\alpha,\beta)}$	○ ● ————————————→	Precedes$_{(k)}^{(\alpha,\beta)}$
	...	
Follows$_{(N)}^{(\alpha,\beta)}$	○ ● ——→	Precedes$_{(N)}^{(\alpha,\beta)}$

{"Follows$_{(1)}^{(\alpha,\beta)}$" … "Follows$_{(N)}^{(\alpha,\beta)}$"} and {"Precedes$_{(1)}^{(\alpha,\beta)}$"… "Precedes$_{(N)}^{(\alpha,\beta)}$"} are defined as fuzzy sets. "Follows$_{(1)}^{(\alpha,\beta)}$" has the R-Function MF which has the parameters $A = \alpha$ and $B = (\alpha + \beta)$. All comparators {"Follows$_{(2)}^{(\alpha,\beta)}$"… "Follows$_{(N-1)}^{(\alpha,\beta)}$"} have the trapezoidal MF which has the parameters $A = ((k - 1) + (k - 2)\,\alpha)$, $B = ((k - 1)(\alpha + \beta))$, $C = (k\,\alpha + (k - 1)\,\beta)$ and $D = (k\,(\alpha + \beta))$. "Follows$_{(N)}^{(\alpha,\beta)}$" has the L-Function MF which has the parameters $A = ((N - 1)\,\alpha + (N - 2)\,\beta)$ and $B = ((N - 1)(\alpha + \beta))$. "Precedes$_{(1)}^{(\alpha,\beta)}$" has the R-Function MF which has the parameters $A = (-\,\alpha - \beta)$ et $B = (-\alpha)$. All comparators {"Precedes$_{(2)}^{(\alpha,\beta)}$"… "Precedes$_{(N-1)}^{(\alpha,\beta)}$"} have the trapezoidal MF which has the parameters $A = (-k\,(\alpha + \beta))$, $B = (-k\,\alpha - (k -1)\,\beta)$, $C = (-(k - 1)(\alpha + \beta))$ and $D = (-(k - 1)\,\alpha - (k - 2)\,\beta)$. "Precedes$_{(N)}^{(\alpha,\beta)}$" has the L-Function MF which has the parameters $A = (-(N -1)(\alpha + \beta))$ and $B = (-(N - 1)\,\alpha - (N - 2)\,\beta)$. Figure 2 shows the MFs associated to the proposed comparators.

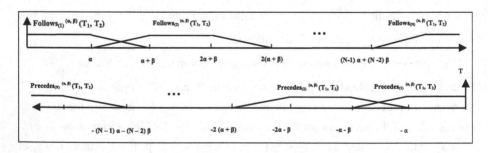

Fig. 2. Our imprecise personalized time point comparators.

We have the following formulas:

$$Follows_{(k)}^{(\alpha,\beta)}(T_1,T_2) = Precedes_{(k)}^{(\alpha,\beta)}(T_2,T_1)(k \in [1,N]) \tag{1}$$

$$Follows_{(k)}^{(\alpha,\beta)}(T_1,T_2) = 1 - Precedes_{(k)}^{(\alpha,\beta)}(T_1,T_2)(k \in [1,N]) \tag{2}$$

$$Follows(T_1,T_2) = \sum Follows_{(k)}^{(\alpha,\beta)}(T_1,T_2)(k \in [1,N]) \tag{3}$$

$$Precedes_{(k)}^{(\alpha,\beta)}(T_1,T_2) = Follows_{(k)}^{(\alpha,\beta)}(T_2,T_1)(k \in [1,N]) \tag{4}$$

$$Precedes_{(k)}^{(\alpha,\beta)}(T_1,T_2) = 1 - Follows_{(k)}^{(\alpha,\beta)}(T_2,T_1)(k \in [1,N]) \tag{5}$$

$$Precedes(T_1,T_2) = \sum Precedes_{(k)}^{(\alpha,\beta)}(T_1,T_2)(k \in [1,N]) \tag{6}$$

Example 1: Assume that $T_1 = 1974$ and $T_2 = 2017$. Using $N = 3$, $\alpha = 10$ years and $\beta = 20$ years ("$Precedes_{(1)}^{(10,20)}$" means "just precedes", "$Precedes_{(2)}^{(10,20)}$" means "middle precedes" and "$Precedes_{(3)}^{(10,20)}$" means "long precedes"), we obtain:

$Precedes_{(1)}^{(10,20)}(T_1,T_2) = 0$	$Precedes_{(2)}^{(10,20)}(T_1,T_2) = 0,85$
$Precedes_{(3)}^{(10,20)}(T_1,T_2) = 0,15$	$Precedes(T_1,T_2) = 1$

expressing that 1974 occurred "middle precedes" 2017 to a high degree and 1974 occurred "just precedes" 2017 to a low degree. On the other hand, using $N = 5$, $\alpha = 10$ years and $\beta = 5$ years ("$Precedes_{(1)}^{(10,20)}$" means "approximately at the same time", "$Precedes_{(2)}^{(10,20)}$" means "just precedes", "$Precedes_{(3)}^{(10,20)}$" means "middle precedes", "$Precedes_{(4)}^{(10,20)}$" means "long precedes" and "$Precedes_{(5)}^{(10,20)}$" means "too long precedes"), we obtain:

$Precedes_{(1)}^{(10,5)}(T_1,T_2) = 0$	$Precedes_{(2)}^{(10,5)}(T_1,T_2) = 0$
$Precedes_{(3)}^{(10,5)}(T_1,T_2) = 0,4$	$Precedes_{(4)}^{(10,5)}(T_1,T_2) = 0,6$
$Precedes_{(5)}^{(10,5)}(T_1,T_2) = 0$	$Precedes(T_1,T_2) = 1$

expressing that 1974 occurred "long precedes" 2017 to a high degree.

3.2 Our Extension of the Allen's Interval Algebra

We extend the Allen's interval algebra. First, we propose temporal relations between imprecise time intervals. Then, we introduce our transitivity table to reason about the resulting relations.

Let $I = [I^-, I^+]$ be an imprecise time interval. The imprecision is represented by a disjunction of mutually exclusive elements; one of them is the true value [11]. The imprecise beginning bound I^- could be one of the disjunctive ascending set $\{I^{-(1)} \ldots I^{-(B)}\}$ and the imprecise ending bound I^+ could be one of the disjunctive ascending set $\{I^{+(1)} \ldots I^{+(E)}\}$. Each element has its own possibility that it may be held. We represent each imprecise bound as a fuzzy set. The domain expert associates the corresponding MF. For instance, if we have the information "John was starting his PhD study in 1963 and was graduated in late 1960s", the beginning bound is precise. The ending bound is imprecise, in the sense that it could mean, with an increasingly possibility, 1966, 1967, 1968, 1969 or 1970. It is represented as a fuzzy set which has the triangular membership function (A = 1966 and B = C = 1970).

Our Temporal Relations between Imprecise Time Intervals. We propose precise and imprecise personalized temporal relations between imprecise time intervals.

Precise Temporal Interval Relations: We redefine the 13 Allen's relations to propose precise temporal relations between imprecise time intervals. We are based on the Vilain and Kautz's point algebra. For instance, the relation "Before" between the two imprecise time intervals $I = [I^-, I^+]$ and $J = [J^-, J^+]$ is redefined as:

$$\forall I^{+(i)} \in I^+, \forall J^{-(j)} \in J^- / Precedes\left(I^{+(i)}, J^{-(j)}\right) \tag{7}$$

This means that the most recent time point of I^+ ($I^{+(E)}$) ought to precede the oldest time point of J^- ($J^{-(1)}$):

$$Precedes\left(I^{+(E)}, J^{-(1)}\right) \tag{8}$$

In a similar way, we redefine the other Allen's relations, as shown in Table 3.

Table 3. Our precise temporal relations between the imprecise time intervals I and J.

Relation (I, J)	Definition	Inverse (J, I)
Before	Precedes $(I^{+(E)}, J^{-(1)})$	After
Meets	Min(Same$(I^{+(1)}, J^{-(1)}) \wedge$ Same$(I^{+(E)}, J^{-(B)})$)	Met-by
Overlaps	Min (Precedes$(I^{-(B)}, J^{-(1)}) \wedge$ Precedes$(J^{-(B)}, I^{+(1)}) \wedge$ Precedes$(I^{+(E)}, J^{+(1)})$)	Overlapped-by
Starts	Min(Same$(I^{-(1)}, J^{-(1)}) \wedge$ Same$(I^{-(B)}, J^{-(B)}) \wedge$ Precedes$(I^{+(E)}, J^{+(1)})$)	Started-by
During	Min (Precedes$(J^{-(B)}, I^{-(1)}) \wedge$ Precedes$(I^{+(E)}, J^{+(1)})$)	Contains
Ends	Min(Precedes$(J^{-(B)}, I^{-(1)}) \wedge$ Same$(I^{+(1)}, J^{+(1)}) \wedge$ Same$(I^{+(E)}, J^{+(E)})$)	Ended-by
Equals	Min(Same$(I^{-(1)}, J^{-(1)}) \wedge$ Same$(I^{-(B)}, J^{-(B)}) \wedge$ Same$(I^{+(1)}, J^{+(1)}) \wedge$ Same$(I^{+(E)}, J^{+(E)})$)	Equals

<u>Imprecise Personalized Temporal Interval Relations</u>: We also define imprecise personalized temporal relations between imprecise time intervals. The aim is to provide a way to model gradual, linguistic-like description of temporal interval relations. Compared to related work, our work is not limited to a given number of imprecise relations. It is possible to determinate the level of precision that it should be in a given context. The Allen's relations {"Before", "After", "Overlaps", "Overlapped-by", "Starts", "Started-by", "During", "Contains", "Ends" and "Ended-by"} are generalized in N imprecise relations. Their number and meanings are set by a domain expert. For instance, the classic Allen's relation "Before" may be generalized in N imprecise relations {"Before$_{(1)}^{(\alpha,\beta)}$" ... "Before$_{(N)}^{(\alpha,\beta)}$"}, where "Before$_{(1)}^{(\alpha,\beta)}$(I, J)" means I "just before" J; and gradually the time gap between the ending bound of I and the beginning bound of J increase until "Before$_{(N)}^{(\alpha,\beta)}$(I, J)". Our imprecise personalized temporal relations are based on our extension of the Vilain and Kautz's point algebra. For instance, "Before$_{(k)}^{(\alpha,\beta)}$(I, J)" is defined as:

$$\forall I^{+\,(i)} \in I^+ , \forall J^{-\,(j)} \in J^- / Precedes_{(k)}^{(\alpha,\beta)}\left(I^{+\,(i)}, J^{-(j)}\right) \qquad (9)$$

This means that the most recent time point of I^+ ($I^{+(E)}$) ought to precede the oldest time point of J^- ($J^{-(1)}$):

$$Precedes_{(k)}^{(\alpha,\beta)}\left(I^{+\,(E)}, J^{-(1)}\right) \qquad (10)$$

In a similar way, we define the other interval relations, as shown in Table 4.

Table 4. Our imprecise personalized temporal relations between the imprecise time intervals I and J.

Relation (I, J)	Definition	Inverse (J, I)
Before$_{(k)}^{(\alpha,\beta)}$	Precedes$_{(k)}^{(\alpha,\beta)}$($I^{+(E)}, J^{-(1)}$)	After$_{(k)}^{(\alpha,\beta)}$
Overlaps$_{(k)}^{(\alpha,\beta)}$	Min(Precedes$^{(\alpha,\beta)}$($I^{-(B)}, J^{-(1)}$) $\wedge$ Precedes$^{(\alpha,\beta)}$($J^{-(B)}, I^{+(1)}$) $\wedge$ Precedes$_{(k)}^{(\alpha,\beta)}$($I^{+(E)}, J^{+(1)}$))	Overlapped $-$ by$_{(k)}^{(\alpha,\beta)}$
Starts$_{(k)}^{(\alpha,\beta)}$	Min(Same($I^{-(1)}, J^{-(1)}$) $\wedge$ Same($I^{-(B)}, J^{-(B)}$) $\wedge$ Precedes$_{(k)}^{(\alpha,\beta)}$($I^{+(E)}, J^{+(1)}$))	Started $-$ by$_{(k)}^{(\alpha,\beta)}$
During$_{(k)}^{(\alpha,\beta)}$	Min(Precedes$_{(k)}^{(\alpha,\beta)}$($J^{-(B)}, I^{-(1)}$) $\wedge$ Precedes$^{(\alpha,\beta)}$($I^{+(E)}, J^{+(1)}$))	Contains$_{(k)}^{(\alpha,\beta)}$
Ends$_{(k)}^{(\alpha,\beta)}$	Min(Precedes$_{(k)}^{(\alpha,\beta)}$($J^{-(B)}, I^{-(1)}$) $\wedge$ Same($I^{+(1)}, J^{+(1)}$) $\wedge$ Same ($I^{+(E)}, J^{+(E)}$))	Ended $-$ by$_{(k)}^{(\alpha,\beta)}$

Note that the definitions of the proposed temporal relations coincide with Allen's original definitions if each α and β equals zero; N equals one and I and J are precise time intervals.

The precise temporal relations may be calculated from the imprecise personalized ones as follows:

$$\text{Before}(I, J) = \sum \text{Before}_{(k)}^{(\alpha,\beta)}(I, J)(k \in [1, N]) \tag{11}$$

$$\text{After}(I, J) = \sum \text{After}_{(k)}^{(\alpha,\beta)}(I, J)(k \in [1, N]) \tag{12}$$

$$\text{Overlaps}(I, J) = \sum \text{Overlaps}_{(k)}^{(\alpha,\beta)}(I, J)(k \in [1, N]) \tag{13}$$

$$\text{Overlapped-by}(I, J) = \sum \text{Overlapped-by}_{(k)}^{(\alpha,\beta)}(I, J)(k \in [1, N]) \tag{14}$$

$$\text{Starts}(I, J) = \sum \text{Starts}_{(k)}^{(\alpha,\beta)}(I, J)(k \in [1, N]) \tag{15}$$

$$\text{Started-by}(I, J) = \sum \text{Started-by}_{(k)}^{(\alpha,\beta)}(I, J)(k \in [1, N]) \tag{16}$$

$$\text{During}(I, J) = \sum \text{During}_{(k)}^{(\alpha,\beta)}(I, J)(k \in [1, N]) \tag{17}$$

$$\text{Contains}(I, J) = \sum \text{Contains}_{(k)}^{(\alpha,\beta)}(I, J)(k \in [1, N]) \tag{18}$$

$$\text{Ends}(I, J) = \sum \text{Ends}_{(k)}^{(\alpha,\beta)}(I, J)(k \in [1, N]) \tag{19}$$

$$\text{Ended-by}(I, J) = \sum \text{Ended-by}_{(k)}^{(\alpha,\beta)}(I, J)(k \in [1, N]) \tag{20}$$

Our temporal relations preserve many properties of the Allen's algebra. We obtain generalizations of the reflexivity/irreflexivity, symmetry/asymmetry and transitivity properties. Let $K = [K^-, K^+]$ be imprecise time interval.

Reflexivity/Irreflexivity: The temporal relations {"Before", "After", "Meets", "Met-by", "Overlaps", "Overlapped-by", "Starts", "Started-by", "During", "Contains", "Ends", "Ended-by", "Before$_{(k)}^{(\alpha,\beta)}$", "After$_{(k)}^{(\alpha,\beta)}$", "Overlaps$_{(k)}^{(\alpha,\beta)}$", "Overlapped-by$_{(k)}^{(\alpha,\beta)}$", "Starts$_{(k)}^{(\alpha,\beta)}$", "Started-by$_{(k)}^{(\alpha,\beta)}$", "During$_{(k)}^{(\alpha,\beta)}$", "Contains$_{(k)}^{(\alpha,\beta)}$", "Ends$_{(k)}^{(\alpha,\beta)}$" and "Ended-by$_{(k)}^{(\alpha,\beta)}$"} are irreflexive, i.e., let R be one of the aforementioned relations. It holds that

$$R(I, I) = 0$$
$$(e.g., Before_{(k)}^{(\alpha,\beta)}(I, I) = Precedes_{(k)}^{(\alpha,\beta)}\left(I^{+(E)}, I^{-(1)}\right) = 0 \, as \, I^{+(E)} - I^{-(1)} > 0) \tag{21}$$

Furthermore, the relation "Equals" is reflexive. It holds that

$$Equals(I, I) = 1 \tag{22}$$

Symmetry/Asymmetry: The temporal relations {"Before", "After", "Meets", "Met-by", "Overlaps", "Overlapped-by", "Starts", "Started-by", "During", "Contains", "Ends", "Ended-by", "Before$_{(k)}^{(\alpha,\beta)}$", "After$_{(k)}^{(\alpha,\beta)}$", "Overlaps$_{(k)}^{(\alpha,\beta)}$", "Overlapped-by$_{(k)}^{(\alpha,\beta)}$", "Starts$_{(k)}^{(\alpha,\beta)}$", "Started-by$_{(k)}^{(\alpha,\beta)}$", "During$_{(k)}^{(\alpha,\beta)}$", "Contains$_{(k)}^{(\alpha,\beta)}$", "Ends$_{(k)}^{(\alpha,\beta)}$" and "Ended-by$_{(k)}^{(\alpha,\beta)}$"} are asymmetric, i.e., let R be one of the aforementioned relations. It holds that

$$R(I, J) \, and \, R(J, I) = \, > I = J \tag{23}$$

Furthermore, the relation "Equals" is symmetric. It holds that

$$Equals(I, J) = Equals(J, I) \tag{24}$$

Transitivity: The temporal relations {"Before", "After", "Overlaps", "Overlapped-by", "Starts", "Started-by", "During", "Contains", "Equals", "Before$_{(k)}^{(\alpha,\beta)}$", "After$_{(k)}^{(\alpha,\beta)}$", "Overlaps$_{(k)}^{(\alpha,\beta)}$", "Overlapped-by$_{(k)}^{(\alpha,\beta)}$", "Starts$_{(k)}^{(\alpha,\beta)}$", "Started-by$_{(k)}^{(\alpha,\beta)}$", "During$_{(k)}^{(\alpha,\beta)}$" and "Contains$_{(k)}^{(\alpha,\beta)}$"} are transitive, i.e., let R be one of the aforementioned relations. It holds that

$$R(I, J) \, and \, R(J, K) = \, > R(I, K) \tag{25}$$

For instance, we can deduce from "Before$_{(k)}^{(\alpha,\beta)}(I, J)$" and "Before$_{(k)}^{(\alpha,\beta)}(J, K)$" that "Before$_{(k)}^{(\alpha,\beta)}(I, K)$" holds. Indeed by "Before$_{(k)}^{(\alpha,\beta)}(I, J)$", we have "Precedes$_{(k)}^{(\alpha,\beta)}(I^{+(E)}, J^{-(1)})$", and by "Before$_{(k)}^{(\alpha,\beta)}(J, K)$", we have "Precedes$_{(k)}^{(\alpha,\beta)}(J^{+(E)}, K^{-(1)})$". From "Precedes$_{(k)}^{(\alpha,\beta)}$ $(I^{+(E)}, J^{-(1)})$" and "Precedes$_{(k)}^{(\alpha,\beta)}(J^{+(E)}, K^{-(1)})$", we conclude "Precedes$_{(k)}^{(\alpha,\beta)}$ $(I^{+(E)}, K^{-(1)})$", or in other words, "Before$_{(k)}^{(\alpha,\beta)}(I, K)$".

Example 2: Let $I_1 = [I_1^-, I_1^+]$, $I_2 = [I_2^-, I_2^+]$ and $I_3 = [I_3^-, I_3^+]$ be imprecise time intervals; where I_1^- is represented using the L-function MF (A = 1960 and B = 1963); I_1^+ is represented using the R-function MF (A = 1971 and B = 1974); I_2^- is represented using the L-function MF (A = 1940 and B = 1943); I_2^+ is represented using the R-function MF (A = 1971 and B = 1974); I_3^- is represented using the L-function MF (A = 2017 and B = 2020) and I_3^+ is represented using the R-function MF (A = 2030 and B = 2033). Using N = 3, α = 10 years and β = 20 years, we obtain:

Ends $(I_1, I_2) = 1$	Before $(I_2, I_3) = 1$
$\text{End}_{(1)}^{(10,20)}(I_1, I_2) = 0,65$	$\text{Before}_{(1)}^{(10,20)}(I_2, I_3) = 0$
$\text{End}_{(2)}^{(10,20)}(I_1, I_2) = 0,35$	$\text{Before}_{(2)}^{(10,20)}(I_2, I_3) = 0,85$
$\text{End}_{(3)}^{(10,20)}(I_1, I_2) = 0$	$\text{Before}_{(3)}^{(10,20)}(I_2, I_3) = 0,15$

Reasoning About Temporal Relations Between Imprecise Time Intervals: Transitivity Table. The crux of the Allen's interval algebra is the transitivity table. This table lets us reason from R_1 (A, B) and R_2 (B, C) to R_3 (A, C), where $A = [A^-, A^+]$, $B = [B^-, B^+]$ and $C = [C^-, C^+]$ are precise time intervals and R_1, R_2 and R_3 are the Allen's interval relations. For instance, using the Allen's original definitions, we can deduce from "During(A, B)" and "Meet(B, C)" that "Before(A, C)" holds. Indeed by "During (A, B)", we have $(A^- > B^-)$ and $(A^+ < B^+)$, and by "Meet(B, C)", we have $B^+ = C^-$. From $(A^+ < B^+)$ and $(B^+ = C^-)$, we conclude, or in other words, "Before(A, C)". As our temporal relations preserve the properties of the Allen's original algebra, we generalize such deductions using the three imprecise time intervals $I = [I^-, I^+]$, $J = [J^-, J^+]$ and $K = [K^-, K^+]$. Based on Table 3, we can deduce from "During(I, J)" and "Meet(J, K)" that "Before(I, K)" holds. Indeed by "During(I, J)", we have "$\text{Min}(\text{Precedes}(J^{-(B)}, I^{-(1)}) \wedge \text{Precedes}(I^{+(E)}, J^{+(1)}))$", and by "Meet(J, K)", we have "$\text{Min}(\text{Same}(J^{+(1)}, K^{-(1)}) \wedge \text{Same}(J^{+(E)}, K^{-(B)}))$". From "$\text{Precedes}(I^{+(E)}, J^{+(1)})$" and "Same $(J^{+(1)}, K^{-(1)})$", we conclude, or in other words, "Before(I, K)". When considering only precise relations, our transitivity table coincides with Allen's one. We can also make such deduction when considering imprecise personalized relations. For instance, we can deduce from "Ends(I, J)" and "$\text{Before}_{(k)}^{(\alpha,\beta)}(J, K)$" which holds with a degree $D_{(k)}$ that "$\text{Before}_{(k)}^{(\alpha,\beta)}(I, K)$" holds with a degree $D_{(k)}$ $(\min(1, D_{(k)}))$ and "Before (I, K)". Table 5 shows a part of our transitivity table.

Table 5. A part of our transitivity table.

	B	$B_{(1)}$	$B_{(k)}$	$B_{(N)}$	M	O	$O_{(1)}$	$O_{(k)}$	$O_{(N)}$	E	$E_{(1)}$	$E_{(k)}$	$E_{(N)}$	D
B	B	B	B	B $B_{(N)}$	B	B	B	B	B $B_{(N)}$	B	B	B	B	B
$B_{(1)}$	B	B	B	B $B_{(N)}$	B	B	B	B	B $B_{(N)}$	B $B_{(1)}$	B $B_{(1)}$	B $B_{(1)}$	B $B_{(1)}$	B
$B_{(k)}$	B	B	B	B $B_{(N)}$	B	B	B	B	B $B_{(N)}$	B $B_{(k)}$	B $B_{(k)}$	B $B_{(k)}$	B $B_{(k)}$	B
$B_{(N)}$	B $B_{(N)}$	B $B_{(N)}$	B $B_{(N)}$	B $B_{(N)}$	B $B_{(N)}$	B $B_{(N)}$		B $B_{(N)}$	B $B_{(N)}$	B $B_{(N)}$	B $B_{(N)}$	B $B_{(N)}$	B $B_{(N)}$	B $B_{(N)}$
M	B	B	B	B $B_{(N)}$	B	B	B $B_{(1)}$	B $B_{(k)}$	B $B_{(N)}$	M	M	M	M	B
O	B	B	B	B $B_{(N)}$	B	B O M	B O M	B O M	B O M	O D S	O D S	O D S	O D S	B O M D S

Table 5. (*continued*)

	B	B$_{(1)}$	B$_{(k)}$	B$_{(N)}$	M	O	O$_{(1)}$	O$_{(k)}$	O$_{(N)}$	E	E$_{(1)}$	E$_{(k)}$	E$_{(N)}$	D
O$_{(1)}$	B	B	B	B B$_{(N)}$	B	B O M	B O M	B O M	B O M	O D S	O D S	O D S	O D S	B O M D S
O$_{(k)}$	B	B	B	B B$_{(N)}$	B	B O M	B O M	B O M	B O M	O D S	O D S	O D S	O D S	B O M D S
O$_{(N)}$	B	B	B	B B$_{(N)}$	B	B O M	B O M	B O M	B O M	O D S	O D S	O D S	O D S	B O M

Example 3: Let $I_1 = [I_1^-, I_1^+]$, $I_2 = [I_2^-, I_2^+]$ and $I_3 = [I_3^-, I_3^+]$ be the imprecise time intervals mentioned in Example 2. We use $N = 3$, $\alpha = 10$ years and $\beta = 20$ years. Based on the transitivity relation that allows inferring "Before$_{(k)}^{(\alpha,\beta)}(I_1, I_3)$" from "Ends (I_1, I_2)" and "Before$_{(k)}^{(\alpha,\beta)}(I_2, I_3)$", we automatically infer from the results shown in Example 2 the following relations:

$$\text{Before}_{(1)}^{(\alpha,\beta)}(I_1, I_3) = 0 \qquad \Big| \text{Before}_{(2)}^{(\alpha,\beta)}(I_1, I_3) = 0,85 \qquad \Big| \text{Before}_{(3)}^{(\alpha,\beta)}(I_1, I_3) = 0,15$$

Note that we have the same results if we calculate "Before$_{(1)}^{(\alpha,\beta)}(I_1, I_3)$", "Before$_{(2)}^{(\alpha,\beta)}(I_1, I_3)$" and "Before$_{(3)}^{(\alpha,\beta)}(I_1, I_3)$" based on Table 4.

4 Application to the Semantic Web

Our approach is applied to the Semantic Web. First, we implement a prototype based on a temporal fuzzy ontology. Then, we integrate it in the Captain Memo memory prosthesis [17].

4.1 Our Fuzzy Ontology-Based Prototype

We propose a JAVA-based prototype that implements our approach. It is based on a temporal fuzzy ontology and allows users to interact through user interfaces.

Our ontology is implemented using Fuzzy OWL 2 [14]. We use the ontology editor PROTÉGÉ version 4.3 and the Fuzzy OWL 2 PROTÉGÉ's plug-in version 2.21[1] to

---

[1] http://www.umbertostraccia.it/cs/software/FuzzyOWL/index.html.

edit it. Inferences are done via a set of SWRL and fuzzy IF-THEN rules. We use the Pellet [15] and FuzzyDL [16] reasoners. We associate a SWRL rule for each precise temporal relation to deduce it from the imprecise time intervals entered by the user or each transitivity relation that implies only precise temporal relations. For instance, based on Table 3, we associate two precise rules to infer "During(I, J)" and "Meets(J, K)", where $I = [I^-, I^+]$, $J = [J^-, J^+]$ and $K = [K^-, K^+]$ be imprecise time intervals. Based on our transitivity table, we can infer "Before(I, K)" as the following:

TimeInterval (?I) $\wedge$ TimeInterval (?J) $\wedge$ HasBeginningTo (?J, ?$J^{-(B)}$,) $\wedge$ HasBeginningFrom (?I, ?$I^{-(1)}$) $\wedge$ HasEndTo (?I, ?$I^{+(E)}$) $\wedge$ HasEndFrom (?J, ?$J^{+(1)}$) $\wedge$ swrlb:lessThan (?$J^{-(B)}$, ?$I^{-(1)}$) $\wedge$ swrlb:lessThan (?$I^{+(E)}$, ?$J^{+(1)}$) $\rightarrow$ During (?I, ?J)
TimeInterval (?J) $\wedge$ TimeInterval (?K) $\wedge$ HasEndFrom (?J, ?$K^{+(1)}$) $\wedge$ HasBeginningFrom (?K, ?$K^{-(1)}$) $\wedge$ HasEndTo (?J, ?$J^{+(E)}$) $\wedge$ HasBeginningTo (?K, ?$K^{-(B)}$) $\wedge$ swrlb:equal (?$J^{+(E)}$,? $K^{-(B)}$) $\wedge$ swrlb:equal (?$J^{+(1)}$, ?$K^{-(1)}$)$\rightarrow$ Meets (?J, ?K)
During (?I, ?J) $\wedge$ Meets (?J, ?K) $\rightarrow$ Before (?I, ?K)

We associate a fuzzy IF-THEN rule for each imprecise personalized temporal relation deduced from imprecise time intervals entered by the user or each transitivity relation that implies imprecise personalized temporal relations. Rules are expressed with the Mamdani structure. For instance, to infer "$Before_{(1)}^{(\alpha,\beta)}$(I, J)", we define an input fuzzy variable named "$VarPrecedes_{(1)}$" which have the same MF than that the one associated to "$Precedes_{(1)}^{(\alpha,\beta)}$". We define one output fuzzy variable "$VarBefore_{(1)}$" which has the L-function MF (A = 0 and B = 1). $VarPrecedes_{(1)}$ is instantiated with $(I^{+(E)} - J^{-(1)})$. The associated rule is the following:

(define-concrete-feature VarPrecedes$_{(1)}$ real) (define-concrete-feature VarBefore$_{(1)}$
real)
(define-fuzzy-concept Fulfilled Right-shoulder(0,$-\alpha -\beta$,$-\alpha$,0)) (define-fuzzy-concept
True Right-shoulder(0, 0, 1, 1))
(define-concept Rule0 (g-and (some VarPrecedes$_{(1)}$ Fulfilled) (some VarBefore$_{(1)}$
True)))
(instance facts (= VarPrecedes$_{(1)}$ ($I^{+(E)} - J^{-(1)}$)))

The general architecture of our prototype is composed of three main components: Ontology Population, Qualitative Temporal Data Inference and Querying. First, the users instantiate the ontology via the user interface shown in Fig. 3. After each user' new input data, the Qualitative Temporal Data Inference component is automatically executed. It is based on the proposed SWRL and fuzzy IF-THEN rules. The third component allows users to query the ontology. We use SPARQL for the crisp part of the ontology. For the fuzzy part, we use the query syntax related to the FuzzyDL reasoner. In Fig. 3, we show all saved imprecise time intervals using the following rule: (all instances? TimeInterval).

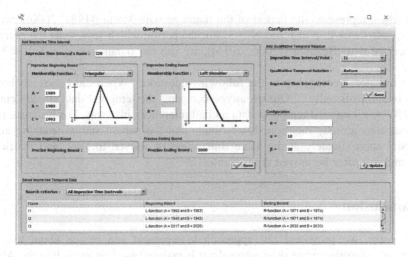

Fig. 3. Ontology population user interface.

4.2 Application to the Captain Memo Memory Prosthesis

In the context of the VIVA project[2], we are suggesting the Captain Memo memory prosthesis, to assist Alzheimer's patients in overcoming mnesic problems. This prosthesis supplies a set of services. Among these services, one is devoted to "remember thing(s) about people" i.e., it helps the Alzheimer's patient to remember their convivial surroundings and relatives. It is based on PersonLink [18] which is a multicultural and multilingual OWL 2 ontology for storing, modeling and reasoning about family relations. Interpersonal relations change over time. However, temporal data given by Alzheimer's patients are often imprecise. e.g., "I taught at the Sorbonne University from by 1980 to late 1990s" and "I traveled to India in early 1980s". We use the approach detailed in this paper to manage the temporal dimension in PersonLink.

Alzheimer's patients present own characteristics that differ from other user groups, parts of them are related to Alzheimer's disease and the other parts are related to the normal effects of aging. We note that they give dates in reference to other dates or events e.g., "My daughter was born when I was in Paris. However, my son was born when I was in Nantes", "I bought a house when I was a teacher at the Sorbonne University" and "I was two teacher contracts when I was a PhD student" and "My sister was married before moving to Paris". An interesting point in this work is to deal with a personalized slicing of the person's life in order to sort the different events. For each user, we define their slices of life. They serve as reference intervals. For each slice of life, we define its own parameters α, β and N. For instance, for the reference interval which represents the period of living in Paris ([1979, Now]), we use the parameters $\alpha = 5$, $\beta = 3$ and N = 5. However, for the period which represents the period of living in Nantes ([1971, 1979]), we use the parameters $\alpha = 2$, $\beta = 1$ and N = 3. For the

---

[2] «Vivre à Paris avec Alzheimer en 2030 grâce aux nouvelles technologies», http://viva.cnam.fr/.

period which represents the period of the marriage with Maria ([1981, 2000]), we use the parameters $\alpha = 2$, $\beta = 1$ and $N = 3$. For the period which represents the period of the marriage with Béatrice ([2006, 2016]), we use the parameters $\alpha = 2$, $\beta = 3$ and $N = 3$.

For instance, in response to the following question: "When did I start teaching at the Sorbonne University?". Our prototype compares the temporal data already entered "by 1980" to all entered temporal data and all references intervals. For instance, using the parameters already mentioned, we obtain that the patient started teaching at this university approximately at the same time when he moved to Paris and married to Maria and just after he moved from Nantes.

5 Conclusion

In this paper, we presented our approach to represent and reason about temporal relations between imprecise time intervals. It is mainly based on extending the Allen's interval algebra. We proposed precise and imprecise temporal relations. Compared to related work, our imprecise relations are personalized as their number and their meanings are set by a domain expert. They are based on our extension, with an imprecise personalized view, of the Vilain and Kautz's point algebra. Unlike existing approaches, generalizations of important properties of Allen's interval relations are valid, in particular those related to reflexivity/irreflexivity, symmetry/asymmetry and transitivity. We introduced a transitivity table to reason about the resulting temporal relations. Finally, we have applied our work to the Semantic Web field. We proposed a fuzzy ontology-based prototype. This prototype has been integrated in the Captain Memo memory prosthesis to handle imprecise time intervals in the context of the PersonLink ontology.

The Allen's interval algebra is not intended to relate an interval with a time instant or even two time instants. We plan propose temporal relations that may hold between two imprecise time points or an imprecise time interval and an imprecise time point and we will define the composition of the resulting relations.

References

1. Allen, J.F.: Maintaining knowledge about temporal intervals. Commun. ACM **26**, 832–843 (1983)
2. Vilain, M.B., Kautz, H.A.: Constraint propagation algorithms for temporal reasoning. In: Readings in Qualitative Reasoning About Physical Systems, pp. 377–382 (1986)
3. Dubois, D., Prade, H.: Processing fuzzy temporal knowledge. IEEE Trans. Syst. Man Cybern. **19**, 729–744 (1989)
4. Guesgen, H.W., Hertzberg, J., Philpott, A.: Towards implementing fuzzy Allen relations. In: ECAI-94 Workshop on Spatial and Temporal Reasoning, pp. 49–55 (1994)
5. Badaloni, S., Giacomin, M.: The algebra IA^{fuz}: a framework for qualitative fuzzy temporal reasoning. Artif. Intell. **170**(10), 872–908 (2006)
6. Freksa, C.: Temporal reasoning based on semi-intervals. Artif. Intell. **54**(1), 199–227 (1992)

7. Nagypál, Gábor, Motik, Boris: A fuzzy model for representing uncertain, subjective, and vague temporal knowledge in ontologies. In: Meersman, Robert, Tari, Zahir, Schmidt, Douglas C. (eds.) OTM 2003. LNCS, vol. 2888, pp. 906–923. Springer, Heidelberg (2003). https://doi.org/10.1007/978-3-540-39964-3_57

8. Ohlbach, H.J.: Relations between fuzzy time intervals. In: International Symposium on Temporal Representation and Reasoning, pp. 44–51 (2004)

9. Schockaert, S., Cock, M.D.: Temporal reasoning about fuzzy intervals. Artif. Intell. **172**(8), 1158–1193 (2008)

10. Sadeghi, K.M.M., Goertzel, B.: Uncertain interval algebra via fuzzy/probabilistic modeling. In: FUZZ-IEEE 2014, pp. 591–598 (2014)

11. Gammoudi, A., Hadjali, A., Yaghlane, B.B.: Fuzz-TIME: an intelligent system for managing fuzzy temporal information. Int. J. Intell. Comput. Cybern. **10**(2), 200–222 (2017)

12. Zadeh, L.A.: The concept of a linguistic variable and its application to approximate reasoning - II. Inf. Sci. **8**, 301–357 (1975)

13. http://cedric.cnam.fr/ ~ hamdif/upload/ICCS19/proofs.pdf

14. Bobillo, F., Straccia, U.: Fuzzy ontology representation using OWL 2. Int. J. Approx. Reason. **52**(7), 1073–1094 (2011)

15. Sirin, E., Parsia, B., Grau, B.C., Kalyanpur, A., Katz, Y.: Pellet: a practical OWL-DL reasoner. In: Web Semantics: Science, Services and Agents on the World Wide Web, pp. 51–53 (2007)

16. Bobillo, F., Straccia, U.: An expressive fuzzy description logic reasoner. In: FUZZ-IEEE 2008, pp. 923–930 (2008)

17. Métais, E., et al.: Memory prosthesis. Non-Pharmacol. Ther. Dement. **3**(2) (2015)

18. Herradi, N., Hamdi, F., Métais, E., Ghorbel, F., Soukane, A.: PersonLink: an ontology representing family relationships for the captain memo memory prosthesis. In: ER 2015 Workshops (2015)

Relevant Attributes in Formal Contexts

Tom Hanika[1,2], Maren Koyda[1,2(✉)], and Gerd Stumme[1,2]

[1] Knowledge and Data Engineering Group, University of Kassel, Kassel, Germany
{tom.hanika,koyda,stumme}@cs.uni-kassel.de
[2] Interdisciplinary Research Center for Information System Design,
University of Kassel, Kassel, Germany

Abstract. Computing conceptual structures, like formal concept lattices, is a challenging task in the age of massive data sets. There are various approaches to deal with this, e.g., random sampling, parallelization, or attribute extraction. A so far not investigated method in the realm of formal concept analysis is attribute selection, as done in machine learning. Building up on this we introduce a method for attribute selection in formal contexts. To this end, we propose the notion of relevant attributes which enables us to define a relative relevance function, reflecting both the order structure of the concept lattice as well as distribution of objects on it. Finally, we overcome computational challenges for computing the relative relevance through an approximation approach based on information entropy.

Keywords: Formal concept analysis · Relevant features ·
Attribute selection · Entropy · Label function

1 Introduction

The increasing number of features (attributes) in data sets poses a challenge for many procedures in the realm of knowledge discovery. In particular, methods employed in *formal concept analysis* (FCA) become less feasible for large numbers of attributes. Of peculiar interest is the construction, visualization and interpretation of *formal concept lattices*, algebraic structures usually represented through line or order diagrams.

The data structure used in FCA is a *formal context*, roughly a data table where every row represents an object associated with attributes described through columns. Contemporary such data sets consist of thousands of rows and columns. Since the computation of all formal concepts is at best possible with polynomial delay [1], thus sensitive to the output size, it is almost unattainable to be computed even for moderately large sized data sets. The problem for the computation of valid (attribute) implications is even more serious since enumerating them is not possible with polynomial delay [2] (in lexicographic order) and only few algorithms are known to compute them [3]. Furthermore, in many

---

Authors are given in alphabetical order. No priority in authorship is implied.

© Springer Nature Switzerland AG 2019
D. Endres et al. (Eds.): ICCS 2019, LNAI 11530, pp. 102–116, 2019.
https://doi.org/10.1007/978-3-030-23182-8_8

applications storage space is limited, e.g., mobile computing or decentralized embedded knowledge systems.

To overcome both the computational infeasibility as well as the storage limitation one is required to select a sub-context resembling the original data set most accurately. This can be done by selecting attributes, objects, or both. In this work we will focus on the identification of relevant attributes. This is, due to the duality of formal contexts, similar to the problem of selecting relevant objects. There are several comparable works, e.g., [4], where the author investigated the applicability of random projections. For supervised machine learning tasks there are even more sophisticated methods utilizing filter approaches, which are based on the distribution of labels [5]. Works more related to FCA resort, e.g., to concept sampling [6] and concept selection [7]. Both approaches, however, either need to compute the whole (possibly large) concept lattice or sample from it.

In this work we overcome this limitation and present a feasible approach for selecting relevant attributes from a formal context using information entropy. To this end we introduce the notion of *attribute relevance* to the realm of FCA, based on a seminal work by Blum and Langley [8]. In that work the authors address a comprehensible theory for selecting most relevant features in supervised machine learning settings. Building up on this we formalize a *relative relevance* measure in formal contexts in order to identify the most relevant attributes. However, this measure is still prone to the limitation for computing the concept lattice. Finally, we tackle this disadvantage by approximating the relative relevance measure through an information entropy approach. Choosing attributes based on this approximation leads to significantly more relevant selections than random sampling does, which we demonstrate in an empirical experiment.

As for the structure of this paper, in Sect. 2 we give a short overview over the previous works applied to relevant attribute selection. Subsequently we recall some basic notions from FCA followed by our definitions of relevance and relative relevance of attribute selections and its approximations. In Sect. 4 we illustrate and evaluate our notions through experiments showing the approximations are significantly superior to random sampling. We conclude our work and give an outlook in Sect. 5.

2   Related Work

In the field of supervised machine learning there are numerous approaches for feature set selection. The authors from [9] introduced a beneficial categorization for those in two categories: wrapper models and filters. The wrapper models evaluate feature subsets using the underlying learning algorithm. This allows to respond to redundant or correlated features. However, these models demand many computations and are prone to reproduce the procedural bias of the underlying learning algorithm. A representative for this model type is the class of selective Bayesian classifiers in Langley and Sage [10]. In that work the authors extended the Naive Bayes classifier by considering subsets of given feature sets only for predictions. The other category from [9] is filter models. Those work independently from the underlying learning algorithm. Instead these methods make use of general characteristics like the attribute distribution with respect to the labels in order to weigh an attribute's importance. Hence, they are more efficient but are likely to select redundant or futile features with respect to an underlying machine learning procedure. A well-known method representing this class is RELIEF [11], which evaluates the relevance of all features referring to the class label using a statistical method. An entropy based approach of a filter model was introduced by Koller et al. [12]. There the authors introduced selecting features based on the Kullback-Leibler-distance. All these methods incorporate an underlying notion of attribute relevance. This notion was captured and formalized in the seminal work by Blum and Langley in [8], on which we will base the notion of relevant attributes in formal contexts.

There are some approaches in FCA to face the attribute selection problem. In [4] a procedure based on random projection was developed. Less related are methods employed after computing the formal concept lattice, e.g., concept sampling [6] and concept selection [7]. Those could be compared to methods from [10], as they first compute the concept lattice. More related works originate from granular computing with FCA. A basic idea there is to find information granules based on entropy. To this end the authors of [13] introduced an (object) entropy function for formal contexts, which we will utilize in this work as well. Their approach used the principles of granulation as in [14], which is based on merging attributes to reduce the data set. Since our focus is on selecting attributes, we turn away from this notion in general.

3   Relevant Attributes

Before we start with our definition for relevant attributes of a formal context, we want to recall some basic notions from formal concept analysis. For a thorough introduction we refer the reader to [15]. A formal context is triple $\mathbb{K} := (G, M, I)$, where G and M are finite sets called *object set* and *attribute set*, respectively. Those are connected through a binary relation $I \subseteq G \times M$, called *incidence*. If $(g, m) \in I$ for an object $g \in G$ and an attribute $m \in M$, we write gIm and say "object g has attribute m". On the power set of the objects (power set of the attributes) we introduce two operators $\cdot' \colon \mathcal{P}(G) \to \mathcal{P}(M)$, where $A \mapsto A' := \{m \in M \mid \forall g \in A \colon (g, m) \in I\}$ and $\cdot' \colon \mathcal{P}(M) \to \mathcal{P}(G)$, where $B \mapsto B' := \{g \in G \mid \forall m \in B \colon (g, m) \in I\}$. A pair (A, B) with $A \subseteq G$ and $B \subseteq M$ is called *formal concept* of the context (G, M, I) iff $A' = B$ and $B' = A$. For a formal concept $c = (A, B)$ the set A is called the *extent* (ext(c)) and B the *intent* (int(c)). For two concepts (A_1, B_1) and (A_2, B_2) there is a natural partial order given through $(A_1, B_1) \leq (A_2, B_2)$ iff $A_1 \subseteq A_2$. The set of all formal concepts of some formal context $\mathbb{K}$, denoted by $\mathcal{B}(\mathbb{K})$, together with the just introduced partial order constitutes the *formal concept lattice* $\underline{B}(\mathbb{K}) := (\mathcal{B}(\mathbb{K}), \leq)$.

A severe computational problem in FCA is to compute the set of all formal concepts, which resembles the CLIQUE problem [1]. Furthermore, the number of formal concepts in a proper sized real-world data set tends to be very large, e.g., 238710 in the (small) mushroom data set, see Sect. 4.1. Hence, concept lattices for contemporary sized data sets are hard to grasp and hard to cope with through consecutive measures and metrics. Thus, a need for selecting sub-contexts from data sets or sub-lattices is self-evident. This selection can be conducted in the formal context as well as in the concept lattice. However, the computational feasible choice is to do this in the formal context. Considering an induced sub-context can be done in general in three different ways: One may consider only a subset $\hat{G} \subseteq G$, a subset $\hat{M} \subseteq M$, or a combination of those. Our goal for the rest of this work is to identify relevant attributes in a formal context. The notion of (attribute) relevance shall cover two aspects: the lattice structure and the distribution of objects on it. The task at hand is to choose the most relevant attributes which do both reflect a large part of the lattice structure as well as the distribution of the objects on the concepts. For this we will introduce in the next section a notion of *relevant attributes* in a formal context. Due to the duality in FCA this can easily be translated to object relevance.

3.1   Choosing Attributes

There is a plenitude of conceptions for describing the relevance of an attribute in a data set. Apparently, the relevance should depend on the particular machine learning or knowledge discovery procedure. One very influential work in this direction was done by Blum and Langley in [8], where the authors defined the *(weak/strong) relevance* of an attribute in the realm of labeled data. In particular, for some data set of examples D, described using features from some feature set F, where every $d \in D$ has the label (distribution) $\ell(d)$, the authors stated: A feature $x \in F$ is *relevant* to a target concept-label if there exists a pair of examples $a, b \in D$ such that a and b only differ in their assignment of x and $\ell(a) \neq \ell(b)$. They further expanded their notion calling some attribute x *weakly relevant* iff it is possible to remove a subset of the features (from a and b) such that x becomes relevant.

Since in the realm of formal concept analysis data is commonly unlabeled we may not directly adapt the above notion to formal contexts. However, we may motivate the following approach with it. We cope with the lack of a label function in the following way. First, we identify the data set D with a formal context (G, M, I), where the elements of G are the examples and M are the features describing the examples. Secondly, a formal concept lattice exhibits essentially two almost independent properties, the order structure and the distribution of objects (attributes) on it, cf. Example 3.1. Thus, a *conceptual label function* then shall reflect both the order structure as well as the distribution of objects in this structure. To achieve this we propose the following.

Definition 3.1 (Extent Label Function). Let $\mathbb{K} := (G, M, I)$ be a formal context and its concept lattice $\underline{\mathcal{B}}(\mathbb{K})$. The map $\ell_\mathbb{K} : G \to \mathbb{N}, g \mapsto |\{c \in \mathcal{B}(\mathbb{K}) \mid g \in \text{ext}(c)\}|$ is called *extent label function*.

	a	b	c	d	e	f	g	h	i
Leach	×	×					×		
Bream	×	×					×	×	
Frog	×	×	×				×	×	
Dog	×		×				×	×	×
Spike-weed	×	×		×		×			
Bean	×		×	×	×				

	a	b	c	d
Bream	×	×		
Frog	×	×	×	
Dog	×		×	
Spike-weed	×	×		×

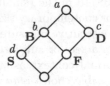

Fig. 1. Sub-contexts of "Living Beings and Water" [15]. The attributes are: a: needs water to live, b: lives in water, c: lives on land, d: needs chlorophyll to produce food, e: two seed leaves, f: one seed leaf, g: can move around, h: has limbs, i: suckles its offspring

One may define an *intent label function* analogously. Utilizing the just introduced label function we may now define the notion of relevant attributes in formal contexts.

Definition 3.2 (Relevance). Let $\mathbb{K} := (G, M, I)$ be a formal context. We say an attribute $m \in M$ is *relevant to* $g \in G$ if and only if $\ell_{\mathbb{K}_{\{m\}}}(g) < \ell_{\mathbb{K}}(g)$, where $\mathbb{K}_{\{m\}} := (G, M \setminus \{m\}, I \cap G \times (M \setminus \{m\}))$. Furthermore, m is *relevant to a subset* $A \subseteq G$ iff there is a $g \in A$ such that m is relevant to g. And, we say m is *relevant to the context* $\mathbb{K}$ iff m is relevant to G.

Example 3.1. Figure 1 (right) shows a formal context and its concept lattice. The objects from there are abbreviated by their first letter in the following. The extent label function of the objects can easily be read from the lattice and is given by $\ell_{\mathbb{K}}(B) = 2$, $\ell_{\mathbb{K}}(F) = 4$, $\ell_{\mathbb{K}}(D) = 2$, $\ell_{\mathbb{K}}(S) = 3$. Additionally, one can deduct the relevant attributes. E.g., for attribute b the equality $\ell_{\mathbb{K}_{\{b\}}}(D) = \ell_{\mathbb{K}}(D)$ holds. In contrast $\ell_{\mathbb{K}_{\{b\}}}(S) < \ell_{\mathbb{K}}(S)$, cf. Fig. 2. Hence, attribute b is not relevant to "Dog" but relevant to "Spike-weed". Thus, b is relevant to $\mathbb{K}$.

There are two structural approaches in FCA to identify admissible attributes, namely *attribute clarifying* and *reducibility*. Those are based purely on the lattice structure. A formal context $\mathbb{K} := (G, M, I)$ is called *attribute clarified* iff for all attributes $m, n \in M$ with $m' = n'$ follows that $m = n$. If there is furthermore no $m \in M$ and $X \subseteq M$ with $m' = X'$ the context is called *attribute reduced*. Analogously, the terms *object clarified* and *object reduced* can be determined. An attribute and object clarified (reduced) context is simply called *clarified* (*reduced*). The concept lattice of the clarified/reduced context is isomorphic to the concept lattice of the original context. If one of these properties does not hold for an attribute (or an object) the context can be clarified/reduced by eliminating all such attributes (objects). Obviously, the notion of relevant attributes is related to reducibility.

Lemma 3.3 (Irreducible). *For $m \in M$ in $\mathbb{K} = (G, M, I)$ holds*

$$m \text{ is relevant to } \mathbb{K} \iff m \text{ is irreducible.}$$

Proof. We first show ($\Rightarrow$) using a contraposition. We have to show that the following inequality holds: $|\{c \in \mathcal{B}(\mathbb{K}) \mid g \in \text{ext}(c)\}| \leq |\{c \in \mathcal{B}(\mathbb{K}_{\{m\}}) \mid g \in \text{ext}(c)\}|$ (assumed a reduceable attribute m). Since $g \in \text{ext}(c)$ and for any $c \in \mathcal{B}(\mathbb{K})$ exists a unique concept $\hat{c} \in \mathcal{B}(\mathbb{K}_{\{m\}})$ with $\text{int}(\hat{c}) \cup \{m\} = \text{int}(c)$, cf. [15, pg 24], we have that $g \in (\text{int}(\hat{c}) \cup \{m\})' \subseteq \text{int}(\hat{c})'$. We omitted the trivial case when $\text{int}(\hat{c}) = \text{int}(c)$. For ($\Leftarrow$) we employ [15, Prop. 30], i.e., there is a join preserving order embedding $(G, M \setminus m, I \cap (G \times (M \setminus \{m\}))) \rightarrow (G, M, I)$ with $(A, B) \mapsto (A, A')$. Hence, every extent in $\mathcal{B}(\mathbb{K}_{\{m\}})$ is also an extent in $\mathcal{B}(\mathbb{K})$ which implies for all $g \in G$ that $\ell_{\mathbb{K}_{\{m\}}}(g) \leq \ell_{\mathbb{K}}(g)$. Based on the relevance of attribute m there exists less concepts in $\mathcal{B}(\mathbb{K}_{\{m\}})$ than in $\mathcal{B}(\mathbb{K})$ so that $\ell_{\mathbb{K}_{\{m\}}}(g) < \ell_{\mathbb{K}}(g)$. □

The last lemma implies that no clarifiable attributes would be considered as relevant, even if the removal of all attributes that have the same closure would have a huge impact on the structure of the concept lattice. Therefore a meaningful identification of relevant attributes is equivalent to the identification of meaningful equivalence classes $[x]_{\mathbb{K}} := \{y \in M \mid x' = y'\}$ for all $y \in M$. Accordingly we consider in the following only clarified contexts. Transferring the relevance of an attribute $m \in M$ to its equivalence class is an easy task which can be executed if necessary.

So far we are only able to decide the relevance of an attribute but not discriminate attributes with respect to their relevance to the concept lattice. To overcome this limitation we introduce in the following a measure which is able to compare the relevancy of two given attributes in a clarified formal context. We consider the change in the object label distribution $\{(g, \ell_{\mathbb{K}}(g)) \mid g \in G\}$ going from $\mathbb{K}$ to $\mathbb{K}_{\{m\}}$ as characteristic to the relevance of a relevant attribute m. To examine this characteristic in more detail and to make it graspable via a numeric value we propose the following inequality: $\sum_{g \in G} \ell_{\mathbb{K}_{\{m\}}}(g) < \sum_{g \in G} \ell_{\mathbb{K}}(g)$. This approach does not only offer the possibility to verify the existence of a change in the object label distribution but also to measure the extent of this change. We may quantify this via $\sum_{g \in G} \ell_{\mathbb{K}_{\{m\}}}(g) / \sum_{g \in G} \ell_{\mathbb{K}}(g) =: t(m)$ whence $t(m) < 1$ for all attributes $m \in M$.

Definition 3.4 (Relative Relevance). Let $\mathbb{K} = (G, M, I)$ be a clarified formal context. The attribute $m \in M$ is *relative relevant* to $\mathbb{K}$ with

$$r(m) := 1 - \frac{\sum_{g \in G} |\{c \in \mathcal{B}(\mathbb{K}_{\{m\}}) \mid g \in \text{ext}(c)\}|}{\sum_{g \in G} |\{c \in \mathcal{B}(\mathbb{K}) \mid g \in \text{ext}(c)\}|} = 1 - t(m).$$

The values of $r(m)$ for an attribute are in $[0, 1)$. We say $m \in M$ is *more relevant* to $\mathbb{K}$ than $n \in M$ iff $r(n) < r(m)$. Double counting leads to the following proposition.

Proposition 3.5. *Let $\mathbb{K} = (G, M, I)$ be a formal context. For all $m \in M$ holds*

$$r(m) = 1 - \frac{\sum_{c \in \mathcal{B}(\mathbb{K}_{\{m\}})} |ext(c)|}{\sum_{c \in \mathcal{B}} |ext(c)|}$$

with $\mathcal{B}(\mathbb{K}_{\{m\}}) = \{c \in \mathcal{B} \mid (int(c) \setminus \{m\})' = ext(c)\}$.

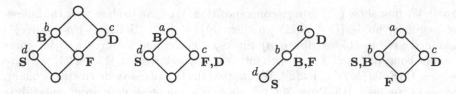

Fig. 2. Sub-lattices created through the removal of an attribute from Fig. 1 (right). From left to right: removing a,b,c, or d

This statement reveals an interesting property of the just defined relative relevance. In fact, an attribute $m \in M$ is more relevant to a formal context $\mathbb{K}$ if the join preserving sub-lattice, which one does obtain by removing m from $\mathbb{K}$, does exhibit a smaller sum of all extent sizes. This will enable us to find proper approximations to the relative relevance in Sect. 3.2.

Example 3.2. Excluding one attribute from the running example in Fig. 1 (right) results in the sub-lattices in Fig. 2. The relative relevance of the attributes to the original context is given by $r(a) = 0$, $r(b) = 4/11$, $r(c) = 3/11$, and $r(d) = 1/11$.

By means of $r(\cdot)$ it is also possible to measure the relative relevance of a set $N \subseteq M$. We simply lift Proposition 3.5 by $r(N) = 1 - \sum_{c \in \mathcal{B}(\mathbb{K}_N)} |\text{ext}(c)| / \sum_{c \in \mathcal{B}(\mathbb{K})} |\text{ext}(c)|$ with $\mathcal{B}(\mathbb{K}_N) = \{c \in \mathcal{B}(K) \mid (\text{int}(c) \setminus N)' = \text{ext}(c)\}$.

Lemma 3.6. *Let $\mathbb{K} = (G, M, I)$ be a formal context and $S, T \subseteq M$ attribute sets. Then*

i) $S \subseteq T \implies r(S) \leq r(T)$, and
ii) $r(S \cup T) \leq r(T) + r(S)$.

Proof. We prove (i) by showing $\sum_{c \in \mathcal{B}_S} |\text{ext}(c)| > \sum_{c \in \mathcal{B}_T} |\text{ext}(c)|$. Since $\forall c \in \mathcal{B}(\mathbb{K})$ we have $(\text{int}(c) \setminus T)' \supseteq (\text{int}(c) \setminus S)' \supseteq \text{ext}(c)$ we obtain $\mathcal{B}(\mathbb{K})_S \supseteq \mathcal{B}(\mathbb{K})_T$, as required.

For (ii) we will use the identity $(\star)$: $\mathcal{B}(\mathbb{K})_S \cap \mathcal{B}(\mathbb{K})_T = \mathcal{B}(\mathbb{K})_{S \cup T}$, which follows from $(\text{int}(c) \setminus S)' = \text{ext}(c) \wedge (\text{int}(c) \setminus T)' = \text{ext}(c) \iff (\text{int}(c) \setminus (S \cup T))' = \text{ext}(c)$ for all $c \in \mathcal{B}(\mathbb{K})$. This equivalence is true since $(\Rightarrow)$:

$$(\text{int}(c) \setminus (S \cup T))' = ((\text{int}(c) \setminus S) \cap (\text{int}(c) \setminus T))'$$
$$= (\text{int}(c) \setminus S)' \cup (\text{int}(c) \setminus T)' = \text{ext}(c) \cup \text{ext}(c) = \text{ext}(c)$$

$(\Leftarrow)$: From $(\text{int}(c) \setminus (S \cup T))' \supseteq (\text{int}(c) \setminus S)'$ and $(\text{int}(c) \setminus (S \cup T))' \supseteq (\text{int}(c) \setminus T)'$ we obtain with i) that $(\text{int}(c) \setminus S)' = \text{ext}(c)$. We now show ii) by proving the inequality $\sum_{\mathcal{B}(\mathbb{K})_S} |\text{ext}(c)| + \sum_{\mathcal{B}(\mathbb{K})_T} |\text{ext}(c)| \leq \sum_{\mathcal{B}(\mathbb{K})} |\text{ext}(c)| + \sum_{\mathcal{B}(\mathbb{K})_{S \cup T}} |\text{ext}(c)|$.

Using $\mathcal{B}(\mathbb{K})_S \setminus \mathcal{B}(\mathbb{K})_{S \cup T} \cup \mathcal{B}(\mathbb{K})_{S \cup T} = \mathcal{B}(\mathbb{K})_S$ where $\mathcal{B}(\mathbb{K})_S \setminus \mathcal{B}(\mathbb{K})_{S \cup T} \cap \mathcal{B}(\mathbb{K})_{S \cup T} = \emptyset$ we find an equivalent equation employing $(\star)$:

$$\sum_{\mathcal{B}_S \setminus \mathcal{B}_{S \cup T}} |\text{ext}(c)| + \sum_{\mathcal{B}_T \setminus \mathcal{B}_{S \cup T}} |\text{ext}(c)| + 2 \cdot \sum_{\mathcal{B}_{S \cup T}} |\text{ext}(c)| \leq \sum_{\mathcal{B}_S \setminus \mathcal{B}_{S \cup T}} |\text{ext}(c)| + \sum_{\mathcal{B}_T \setminus \mathcal{B}_{S \cup T}} |\text{ext}(c)| +$$

$$\sum_{\mathcal{B} \setminus (\mathcal{B}_S \cup \mathcal{B}_T)} |\text{ext}(c)| + 2 \cdot \sum_{\mathcal{B}_{S \cup T}} |\text{ext}(c)|$$

$$0 \leq \sum_{\mathcal{B} \setminus (\mathcal{B}_S \cup \mathcal{B}_T)} |\text{ext}(c)|$$

where $\mathcal{B}_X$ is short for $\mathcal{B}(\mathbb{K})_X$. $\qquad\qquad\qquad\qquad\qquad\qquad\qquad\qquad$ $\square$

Equipped with the notion of relative relevance and some basic observations we are ready to state the associated computational problem. We imagine that in real-world applications attribute selection is a task to identify a set $N \subseteq M$ of the most relevant attributes for a given cardinality $n \in \mathbb{N}$, i.e., an element from $\{N \subseteq M \mid |N| = n \wedge r(N) \text{ maximal}\}$. We call such a set N a *maximal relevant set*.

Problem 3.1 (Relative Relevance Problem (RRP)). Let $\mathbb{K} = (G, M, I)$ be a formal context and $n \in \mathbb{N}$ with $n < |M|$. Find a subset $N \subseteq M$ with $|N| = n$ such that $r(N) \geq r(X)$ for all $X \subseteq M$ where $|X| = n$.

Aiming to solve 3.1 in a straight forward manner evolves two difficulties. First, as n increases so does the number of possible subset combinations. The determination of a maximal relevant set requires the computation and comparison of $\binom{|M|}{|N|}$ different relative relevances, which presents itself infeasible. Secondly, the computation of the relative relevance does presume that the set of formal concepts is computed. This states also an intractable problem for large formal contexts, which are the focus of applications of the proposed relevance selection method. To overcome the first limitation we suggest an iterative approach. Instead of testings every subset of size n we construct $N \subseteq M$ by first considering all singleton sets $\{m\} \subseteq M$. Consecutively, in every step i where X is the so far constructed set we find $x \in M$ such that $r(X \cup \{x\}) \geq r(X \cup \{m\})$ for all $m \in M$. This approach requires the computation of only $\sum_{i=|M|-|n|+1}^{|M|} i$ different relative relevances and their comparisons, which is simplified $n \cdot |M| - (n-1) \cdot n/2$. We call a set obtained through this approach an *iterative maximal relevant set* IMRS. In fact the IMRS does not always correspond to the maximal relevant set. In (G, M, I) where $G = \{1, 2, 3, 4\}$, $M = \{a, b, c, d\}$ and $I = \{(1, a), (1, c), (1, d), (2, a), (2, b), (3, b), (3, c), (4, d)\}$ is b the most relevant attribute, i.e., $r(b) > r(x)$ for all $x \in M \setminus \{b\}$. However, we find $r(\{a, c\}) > r(\{b, x\})$ for all $x \in M \setminus \{b\}$. Hence, the relative relevance of an IMRS indicates a lower bound for the relative relevance of the maximal relevant set.

3.2   Approximating RRP

Motivated by the computational infeasibility of Problem 3.1 we investigate in this section the possibility of approximating RRP, more specifically the IMRS. Approaches for this approximation have to incorporate both aspects of the relative relevance the structure of the concept lattice and the distribution of the objects. Considering the former is not complicated due to [15, Proposition 30], which states that for any (G, M, I) $\mathcal{B}((G, N, I \cap (G \times N)))$ is join preserving order embeddable into $\mathcal{B}((G, M, I))$ for any $N \subseteq M$. Thus, this aspect can be represented through a quotient $|\mathcal{B}(\mathbb{K})_{M \setminus N}|/|\mathcal{B}(\mathbb{K})|$, which is a special case of the maximal common sub-graph distance, see [16]. Hence, whenever searching for the largest $\mathcal{B}((G, N, I \cap (G \times N)))$ the obvious choice is to optimize for large contranominal scales in sub-contexts of (G, M, I). For example, when selecting three attributes in Fig. 1 (left) the largest join preserving order embeddable lattice would be generated by the set $\{b, c, d\}$. However, the relative relevance of $\{b, c, g\}$ is significantly larger, in particular, $r(\{b, c, d\}) = 17/33$ and $r(\{b, c, g\}) = 19/33$.

Considering the second requirement, the distribution of the objects on the concept lattice, the sizes of the concept extents have to be incorporated. Since they are unknown, unless we compute the concept lattice, we need a proxy for estimating the influence of those. Accordingly, we want to reflect this with the quotient $E(\mathbb{K}_{M \setminus N})/E(\mathbb{K})$, which estimates the change of the object distribution on the concept lattices when selecting a set $N \subseteq M$. This quotient does employ a mapping $E : \mathcal{K} \to \mathbb{R}, \mathbb{K} \mapsto E(K)$, which is to be found. A natural candidate for this mapping would be information entropy, as introduced by Shannon in [17]. He defined the entropy of a discrete set of probabilities $p_1, \ldots, p_n$ as $H = -\sum_{i \in I} p_i \log p_i$. We adapt this formula to the realm of formal contexts as follows.

Definition 3.7. Let $\mathbb{K} = (G, M, I)$ be a formal context. Then the *Shannon object information entropy of* $\mathbb{K}$ is given as follows.

$$E_{SE}(\mathbb{K}) = \sum_{g \in G} -\frac{|g''|}{|G|} \, log_2 \left(\frac{|g''|}{|G|} \right)$$

For this entropy function we employ the quotient $|g''|/|G|$, which does reflect the extent sizes of the object concepts of $\mathbb{K}$. Obviously this choice does not consider all concept extents. However, since every extent in a concept lattice is either the extent of an object concept or the intersection of finitely many extents of object concepts we see that the Shannon object information entropy does relate to all extents to some degree. We found another candidate for E in the literature [13]. The authors there introduced an entropy function which is roughly speaking the mean distance of the extents of object concepts to the complete set objects.

Definition 3.8. Let $\mathbb{K} = (G, M, I)$ be a formal context. Then the *object information entropy of* $\mathbb{K}$ is given as follows.

$$E_{OE}(\mathbb{K}) = \frac{1}{|G|} \sum_{g \in G} \left(1 - \frac{|g''|}{|G|} \right)$$

We directly observe that this entropy decreases as the number of objects having similar attribute sets increases. Furthermore, we recognize an essential difference for E_{OE} compared to E_{SE}. The Shannon object information entropy reflects on the number of necessary bits to encode the formal context. In contrary the object information entropy reflects on the average number of bits to encode an object from the formal context. To enhance the first grasp of the just introduced functions as well as the relative relevance defined in Definition 3.4 we want to investigate them on well known contextual scales. In particular, the *ordinal scale* $\mathbb{O}_n := ([n], [n], \leq)$, the *nominal scale* $\mathbb{N}_n := ([n], [n], =)$, and the *contranominal scale* $\mathbb{C}_n := ([n], [n], \neq)$, where $[n] := \{1, \ldots, n\}$. Since there is a bijection between the set $\{1, \ldots, n\}$ to the extent sizes $|g''|$ in an ordinal scale we obtain that $E_{SE}(\mathbb{O}_n) = -\sum_{i=1}^{n} \frac{i}{n} log_2\left(\frac{i}{n}\right)$ and $E_{OE}(\mathbb{O}_n) = \frac{1}{n} \sum_{i=1}^{n}\left(1 - \frac{i}{n}\right) = \frac{1}{n} \frac{n(n+1)}{2n} = \frac{n+1}{2n}$. The former diverges to ∞ whereas the latter converges to $1/2$. Based on the linear structure of $\underline{\mathcal{B}}(\mathbb{O}_n)$ we conclude that the set $\mathcal{B}(\mathbb{K})\backslash\mathcal{B}(\mathbb{K})_{\{m\}} = \{(m', m'')\}$ for all $m \in M$. So the relative relevance of the attribute $m \in M$ amounts to $r(m) = 1 - \left(\sum_{i=1}^{n} i - |m''|\right) / \sum_{i=1}^{n} i = 2|m''|/(n \cdot (n+1))$.

Both the nominal scale as well as the contranominal scale satisfy $g'' = g$ for all $g \in G$ for different reasons. We conclude that E_{SE} and E_{OE} evaluate respectively equally for $\mathbb{N}_n$ and $\mathbb{C}_n$. In detail, $E_{SE}(\mathbb{N}_n) = E_{SE}(\mathbb{C}_n) = -\sum_{g \in G} \frac{1}{n} log_2\left(\frac{1}{n}\right) = log_2(n)$ and $E_{OE}(\mathbb{N}) = E_{OE}(\mathbb{C}) = \frac{1}{n} \sum_{g \in G}\left(1 - \frac{1}{n}\right) = \frac{n-1}{n}$. For the relative relevance we observe that $r(m) = r(n)$ for all $m, n \in M$ in the case of the nominal/contranominal scale. This is due to the fact that every attribute is part of the same number of concepts. For the nominal scale holds $r(m) = 1 - \frac{2n-1}{2n}$ for all $m \in M$. Hence, as the number of attributes increases does the relevance of a single attribute converge to zero. The relative relevance of an objects in the case of the contranominal scale is $r(m) = 1 - \frac{\sum_{k=0}^{n} \binom{n}{k}(n-k) - \sum_{k=0}^{n-1} \binom{n-1}{k}(n-1-k)}{\sum_{k=0}^{n} \binom{n}{k}(n-k)}$ for all $m \in M$.

Example 3.3. Revisiting our running example Fig. 1 (right). This context has four objects with $\{B\}'' = \{B, F, S\}$, $\{F\}'' = \{F\}$, $\{D\}'' = \{F, D\}$ and $\{S\}'' = \{S\}$. Its entropies are given by $E_{OE}(\mathbb{K}) = \frac{1}{4} \sum_{g \in G}\left(1 - \frac{|g''|}{4}\right) \approx 0.56$ and $E_{SE}(\mathbb{K}) \approx 0.45$.

Considering both aspects discussed in this section we now want to introduce a function which shall be capable of approximating RRP.

Definition 3.9. Let $\mathbb{K} = (G, M, I)$ and $\mathbb{K}_{\overline{N}} := (G, N, I \cap (G \times N))$ be formal contexts with $N \subseteq M$. The *entropic relevance approximation (ERA)* of N is defined as

$$ERA(N) := \frac{|\mathcal{B}(\mathbb{K}_{\overline{N}})|}{|\mathcal{B}(\mathbb{K})|} \cdot \frac{E(\mathbb{K}_{\overline{N}})}{E(\mathbb{K})}.$$

First, the ERA compares the number of concepts in a given formal context to the number of concepts in a sub-context on $N \subseteq M$. This reflects the structural impact when restricting the attribute set. Secondly, a quotient is evaluated where the entropy of $\mathbb{K}_{\overline{N}}$ is compared to the entropy of $\mathbb{K}$. When using Definition 3.9 for finding a subset $N \subseteq M$ with maximal (entropic) relevance it suffices to compute N such that $\mathcal{B}(\mathbb{K}_{\overline{N}}) \cdot E(\mathbb{K}_{\overline{N}})$ is minimal. This task is essentially less complicated since we only have to compute $\mathcal{B}(\mathbb{K}_{\overline{N}})$ and $E(\mathbb{K}_{\overline{N}})$ for some comparable small formal context $\mathbb{K}_{\overline{N}}$.

4   Experiments

To assess the ability for approximating relative relevance through Definition 3.9 we carried out several experiments in the following fashion. For all data sets we computed the iterative maximal relevant subsets of M of sizes one to seven (or ten) in the obvious manner. We decided for those fixed numbers for two reasons. First, using a relative number, e.g., 10% of all attributes, would still lead to an infeasible computation when the initial formal context is very large. Secondly, formal contexts with up to ten attributes permit a plenitude of research methods that are impracticable for larger contexts, in particular, human evaluation.

Then we computed subsets of M using ERA, for which we used both introduced entropy functions, and their relative relevance. Finally, we sampled subsets of M randomly at least $|M| \cdot 10$ many times and computed their average relative relevance as well as the standard deviation in relative relevance.

4.1   Data Set Description

A total of 2678 formal contexts were considered in this experimental study. From those 2674 contexts were excerpts from the BibSonomy platform[1] as described in [18]. All those contexts are equipped with an attribute set of twelve elements and a varying number of objects. The particular extraction method is described in detail in [19]. For the rest we revisited three data sets well known in the realm of formal concept analysis, i.e., *mushroom, zoo, water* [15,20], and additionally a data set *wiki44k* introduced in [21], which is based on a 2014 Wikidata[2] database dump. The well-known *mushroom* data set is a collection of 8124 mushrooms described by 119 (scaled) attributes and exhibits 238710 formal concepts. The *zoo* data set possesses 101 animal descriptions using 43 (scaled) attributes and exhibits 4579 formal concepts. The *water* data set, more formally "Living beings and water", has eight objects and nine attributes and exhibits 19 formal concepts. Finally, the *wiki44k* has 45021 objects and 101 attribute exhibiting 21923 formal concepts.

4.2   Results

In Figs. 3, 4 and 5 we depicted the results of our computations. We observe in all experiments that the relative relevances of the subsets found through the iterative approach are an upper bound for the relative relevance of all subsets computed through entropic relevance approximation or random selection, with

---

[1] https://www.kde.cs.uni-kassel.de/wp-content/uploads/bibsonomy/.
[2] https://www.wikidata.org.

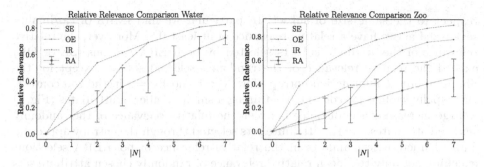

Fig. 3. Relevance of attribute selections through entropy (SE, OE), IMRS (IR), and random selection (RA) for the "Living beings in water" (left) and the zoo context (right)

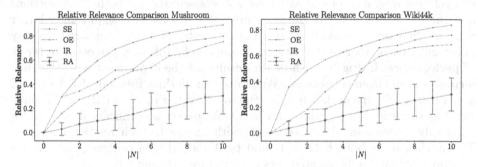

Fig. 4. Relevance of attribute selections through entropy (SE, OE), IMRS (IR), and random selection (RA) for the mushroom (left) and the wiki44k context (right).

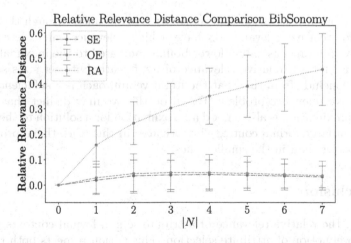

Fig. 5. Average distance and standard deviation to IMRS for entropy and random based selections of $|N|$ attributes for 2674 formal contexts from BibSonomy

respect to the same size of subset. In particular we find IMRS of cardinality seven and above have a relative relevance of at least 0.8. Moreover, the relative relevance of the attribute subsets selected by both ERA versions (SE or OE) exceed the relative relevance of the randomly selected subsets except for the Shannon object information entropy for $|N| = 1$ and $|N| = 2$ in the zoo context. Principally we find for contexts containing a small number of attributes (Fig. 3) a large increase of the distance between the relative relevance of the randomly selected attributes and the attribute sets selected through the entropy approach. This characteristic manifests in the relative relevance of both ERA selections excelling not only the mean relative relevance of randomly chosen attribute sets but also the standard deviation for subset sizes of $|N| = 4$ and above. In the case of contexts containing a huge number of attributes this observation can be made for selections with $|N| = 1$, already. Furthermore, the interval between the relative relevance of the attribute subsets selected by both ERA versions and the relative relevance of the randomly selected subsets is significantly larger than in the case of contexts with small attribute set sizes. In general we may point out that neither of the entropies seems preferable over the other in terms of performance. In Fig. 5 we show the results for the experiment with the 2674 formal contexts from BibSonomy. We plotted for all three methods, ERA-OE/SE and random, the mean distance in relative relevance to the IMRS of the same size together with the standard deviation. We detect a significant difference for randomly chosen and ERA chosen sets with respect to their relative relevance. The deviation for both ERA is bound by 0 and 0.12. In contrast, the relative relevance for randomly selected sets is bound by 0.09 and 0.6.

4.3 Discussion

We found in our investigation that attribute sets obtained through the iterative approach for relative relevance do have a high relevance value. Even though their relative relevance is only a lower bound compared to the maximal relevant set they do exhibit a relative relevance of 0.8 for attribute set sizes seven and above. We conclude from this that the iterative approach is a sufficient solution to the relative relevance problem. Based on this we may deduct that entropic relative approximation is also a good approximation for a solution to the RRP. In particular, in large formal contexts investigated in this work the approximation was even better than in the smaller ones.

5   Conclusion

By defining the relative relevance of attribute sets in formal contexts we introduced a novel notion of attribute selection. This notion respects both the structure of the concept lattice and the distribution of the objects on it. To overcome computational limitations, which arised from the notion of relative relevance, we introduced an approximation based on two different entropy functions adapted to formal contexts. For this we used a combination of two factors. The change in the number of concepts and the change in entropy that arise by the selection of an attribute subset. The experimental evaluation for relative relevance as well as the entropic approximation seem to comply with the theoretical modeling.

We conclude our work with two open questions. First, even though IMRS seems a good choice for relevant attributes we suspect that computing the maximal relevant set, with respect to RRP, can be achieved more feasible. Secondly, so far our justification for RRP is based on theoretical assumptions and a basic experimental study. We imagine, and are curious, if maximal relevant attribute sets are also employable in supervised machine learning setups. For example, one may perceive the task of adding a new object to a given formal context as instance of such a setup. The question is, how capable is the context to add this object to an already existing concept.

References

1. Johnson, D.S., Yannakakis, M., Papadimitriou, C.H.: On generating all maximal independent sets. Inf. Process. Lett. **27**(3), 119–123 (1988)
2. Distel, F., Sertkaya, B.: On the complexity of enumerating pseudointents. Discrete Appl. Math. **159**(6), 450–466 (2011)
3. Obiedkov, S., Duquenne, V.: Attribute-incremental construction of the canonical implication basis. Ann. Math. Artif. Intell. **49**(1–4), 77–99 (2007)
4. Kumar, C.: Knowledge Discovery in Data Using Formal Concept Analysis and Random Projections. Int. J. Appl. Math. Comput. Sci. **21**(4), 745–756 (2011)
5. Yu, L., Liu, H.: Feature selection for high-dimensional data: a fast correlation-based filter solution. In: Proceedings of the 20th international conference on machine learning (ICML-03), pp. 856–863 (2003)
6. Boley, M., Gärtner, T., Grosskreutz, H.: Formal concept sampling for counting and threshold-free local pattern mining. In: Proceedings of the 2010 SIAM International Conference on Data Mining, pp. 177–188 (2010)
7. Klimushkin, M., Obiedkov, S., Roth, C.: Approaches to the selection of relevant concepts in the case of noisy data. In: Kwuida, L., Sertkaya, B. (eds.) ICFCA 2010. LNCS (LNAI), vol. 5986, pp. 255–266. Springer, Heidelberg (2010). https://doi.org/10.1007/978-3-642-11928-6_18
8. Blum, A.L., Langley, P.: Selection of relevant features and examples in machine learning. Artif. Intell. **97**(1), 245–271 (1997)
9. John, G., Kohavi, R., Pfleger, K.: irrelevant features and the subset selection problem. In: Cohen, W., Hirsh, H. (eds.) Machine Learning Proceedings 1994, pp. 121–129. Morgan Kaufmann, San Francisco (1994)
10. Langley , P., Sage, S.: Induction of selective Bayesian classifiers. In: Proceedings of the 10th International Conference on Uncertainty in Artificial Intelligence. UAI 1994, pp. 399–406. Morgan Kaufmann Publishers Inc., San Francisco (1994)
11. Kira, K., Rendell, L.: The feature selection problem: traditional methods and a new algorithm, pp. 129–134. In: Proceedings of the 10th National Conference on Artificial Intelligence. AAAI 1992. AAAI Press (1992)
12. Koller, D., Sahami, M.: Toward optimal feature selection. In: Proceedings of the 13th International Conference on International Conference on Machine Learning. ICML 1996, pp. 284–292. Morgan Kaufmann Publishers Inc., Bari (1996)

13. Loia, V., Orciuoli, F., Pedrycz, W.: Towards a granular computing approach based on formal concept analysis for discovering periodicities in data. Knowl. Based Syst. **146**, 1–11 (2018)
14. Zadeh, L.A.: Toward a theory of fuzzy information granulation and its centrality in human reasoning and fuzzy logic. Fuzzy Sets Syst. **90**(2), 111–127 (1997)
15. Ganter, B., Wille, R.: Formal Concept Analysis: Mathematical Foundations, p. x+284. Springer-Verlag, Berlin (1999). https://doi.org/10.1007/978-3-642-59830-2
16. Bunke, H., Shearer, K.: A graph distance metric based on the maximal common subgraph. Pattern Recogn. Lett. **19**(3), 255–259 (1998)
17. Shannon, C.E.: A mathematical theory of communication. Bell Syst. Techn. J. **27**(3), 379–423 (1948)
18. Benz, D., et al.: The social bookmark and publication management system BibSonomy. VLDB J. **19**(6), 849–875 (2010)
19. Borchmann, D., Hanika, T.: Some experimental results on randomly generating formal contexts. In: Huchard, M., Kuznetsov, S. (ed.) CLA. CEUR Proceedings. CEUR-WS.org, vol. 1624, pp. 57–69 (2016)
20. Dheeru, D., Karra Taniskidou, E.: UCI Machine Learning Repos (2017)
21. Ho, V.T., Stepanova, D., Gad-Elrab, M.H., Kharlamov, E., Weikum, G.: Rule learning from knowledge graphs guided by embedding models. In: Vrandečić, D., et al. (eds.) ISWC 2018. LNCS, vol. 11136, pp. 72–90. Springer, Cham (2018). https://doi.org/10.1007/978-3-030-00671-6_5

Adaptive Collaborative Filtering for Recommender System

An La$^{(\boxtimes)}$, Phuong Vo$^{(\boxtimes)}$, and Tu Vu

Big Data Department, FPT Telecom Vietnam, Ho Chi Minh City, Vietnam
{AnLNT2,PhuongVTH,TuVA}@fpt.com.vn

Abstract. On online websites or e-commerce services, the explosive growth of resource makes the problem of content exploring increasingly challenging. The recommender system is a powerful information filtering tool to support user interaction and promote products. Dealing with determining customer interests, graph-based collaborative filtering is recently the most popular technique. Its only drawback is high computing cost, leads to bad scalability and infeasibility for large size network. Moreover, most previous studies concentrate solely on the accuracy of user preference prediction, while the efficiency of recommendation methods should be considered in many characteristics with complicated relationships, depending on particular systems: popularity, diversity, coverage, congestion. Attempt to conquer these challenges, we propose Adaptive Weighted Conduction formula handling multiple metrics, then construct a scalable model with small complexity, named Adaptive Collaborative Filtering. Experiments are conducted on Movielens, a public dataset, and FPT PLAY, a dataset of our media service. We have an increase of 6% on precision and get close to the best of previous methods on diversity, coverage and congestion. This result shows that the proposed model automatically reveals and adapts to varied requirements of recommender systems, reaches high accuracy and still balances other evaluation aspects.

Keywords: E-commerce service · Recommender system ·
Graph-based collaborative filtering · Scalability · Evaluation metrics

1 Introduction

Half of the world population is now online [11] and e-commerce retail continues to grow at accelerated rate [1]. Accordingly, the most essential question of both research and business is how to improve the interaction of customers and bring suitable products to them. Since the rapid increase in the number of products, this issue is more awkward. Users are overwhelmed by a vast amount of options and often expect a systematical process that helps them in making decisions. Supporting users to cope with content overloading is the key challenge of information filtering techniques. While other tools like search engine typically require

© Springer Nature Switzerland AG 2019
D. Endres et al. (Eds.): ICCS 2019, LNAI 11530, pp. 117–130, 2019.
https://doi.org/10.1007/978-3-030-23182-8_9

users to determine in advance what they need, a recommender system proactively gives various suggestions based on currently watching or historical items. It also dynamically controls product display, plays a vital role in the activities of online services.

Many recommendation algorithms have been proposed [13]. Mining what user selected in the past, collaborative filtering is the most ubiquitous technique [21]. Without the need of explicit item information, it automatically figures out implicit relations between objects (users or items) and captures up-to-date interests of customers. For visual representation and analysis, recent studies build Bipartite Network simulating user history then make recommendation on this structure, forming graph-based approach [4, 6, 20, 22]. However, comparing all pairs of users has expensive computing cost, while user profiles usually update very fast and the entire system has to be rebuilt. Speed up can be attained by pre-constructing graph, but with some applications, large numbers of users and items make them impractical and badly scalable.

Another factor for the success of a recommender system is evaluation: how do we know suggestion is good or not? Customer interests change quickly, especially on systems with heated activity. The intervention of recommendation, affecting to vision and emotion of users, causes the alteration also. Thus, it is difficult to precisely foretell their next choices. Moreover, concentrating solely on accuracy may not make realistic effects. Being accurate is sometimes not useful to users, even hurts the system [17]. In addition, to validate whether items which are incorrect in the testing set could attract users, offline evaluating is insufficient. Meanwhile, with the ability of dynamical controlling visibility of products, a few studies solve other characteristics of e-commerce services, such as item coverage [14, 20], diversity and novelty [15, 16], diversity-accuracy dilemma [2, 3, 19]. Therefore, not purely precision, a recommendation algorithm should be considered in multiple properties, reflected by corresponding metrics. However, the correlation between them is complicated and their priorities are inconsistent, depending on a specific system. It is necessary to have a general way that allows us to understand the user-item distribution and foresee the importance of these properties.

In making the effort of overcoming these limitations, we propose Adaptive Weighted Conduction (AWC), a hybrid formula of existing studies dealing problems of evaluation, and figure out how our model can adapt with varied requirements on recommendation properties. We also remedy the bad scalability for the class of methods using graph. For multi-purpose adaptability, our proposal is called Adaptive Collaborative Filtering (ACF).

The rest of this paper is organized as follows. In Sect. 2, we discuss related works solving evaluation problems and current solutions of scalability issue. Detail of our proposal and proof complexity of ACF are described in Sect. 3. Section 4 includes description of evaluation metrics, experimental results and analysis on Movielens and FPT Play in order to illustrate the ability of AWC. Finally, Sect. 5 presents our conclusion.

2 Related Work

Evaluation is the essential challenge demonstrating the performance of recommendation methods. Besides accuracy, multiple properties in complicated relationships need to be considered. A few studies achieved in directly using item characteristics to control all metrics, although each of them has its own disadvantages. ProbS [19] mainly outputs trending products, which is a safe suggestion for most customers, has a limited visible product size and lack of diversity. HeatS [19] assumes that new items are selected by just a small number of users, prioritizes unpopular items to grow novelty and personalization capability. Hybrid of ProbS and HeatS [19] is a successful method in balancing between accuracy and diversity. DWC [20] raises and solves congestion problem in recommender systems, also reaches remarkable performance on both diversity and coverage. Nevertheless, it strictly gives more priority to less popular items as HeatS, which makes their precision worse.

Another common drawback of four methods is high complexity. In general, it is the limitation of almost graph-based collaborative filtering methods, caused by constructing Bipartite Network and matching all pairs of users [6]. Besides that, inspired by "people who buy x also buy y", item-based approach calculates similarities between items instead of users to overcome both data sparsity and scalability problem [10]. Utilizing this advantage, a few previous works build a graph representing item-item matrix [4,5,7,12,18], unfold an approach which has several strengths: fast computational time [7], ability to capitalize on graphical meaning and outperform standard item-based methods [12,18].

In this paper, we propose a hybrid of ProbS, HeatS, the Hybrid and DWC in order to exploit their strategies dealing with evaluation challenge, called Adaptive Weighted Conduction (AWC). After that, ACF is formed by presenting AWC as an item-item network to make sure high scalability. The detail of our proposal is described in the next section.

3 The Model

3.1 Previous Methods

Bipartite Network provides a clear way to visualize activities of users. It is denoted as $G(U, I, E)$, where U, I is respectively set of users and set of items, E includes connections of one vertex in U to one vertex in I. User set has size $m = |U|$ and item set has size $n = |I|$. We use Greek letters (α, β) to indicate items and italic letters (i, j) to indicate users.

Let the adjacency matrix $A_{m \times n}$ describe E. If a user i selected item α, (i, α) is an edge in E and $a_{i\alpha} = 1$, $a_{i\alpha} = 0$ otherwise. The degree of item α is the total number of users selected it, denoted as k_α. Similarly, the degree of user i is history length of user i, denoted as k_i. For each user i, ProbS, HeatS, the Hybrid and DWC process two steps below:

Step 1 - Diffusion from user side to item side: Calculate relation score for every neighbor j to user i, denoted by g_{ij}.

Step 2 - Diffusion from item side to user side: Compute preference score of user i for item α, denoted by $f_{i\alpha}$.

Following these steps, each method has a specific formula.

Hybrid of ProbS and HeatS (the Hybrid). Solving diversity-accuracy dilemma, [19] proposed a hybrid of ProbS and HeatS:

$$g_{ij} = \sum_\alpha \frac{a_{i\alpha}a_{j\alpha}}{k_\alpha^\lambda k_j^{1-\lambda}} \tag{1}$$

$$f_{i\alpha} = \sum_j \frac{a_{j\alpha}g_j}{k_\alpha^{1-\lambda}k_j^\lambda} \tag{2}$$

where λ is tunable parameter in range $[0,1]$. When $\lambda = 1$, it becomes ProbS that mostly recommends trending products. When $\lambda = 0$, the Eqs. (1) and (2) turn to be HeatS and just outcomes unpopular items.

In addition, [19] rewrote these formulas as dot product: $f_i = Wa_i$, where a_i and f_i is respectively a vector denoting historical and recommended items of user i. The combination of ProbS and HeatS is archived in a transition matrix $W_{n \times n}$:

$$w_{\alpha\beta} = \frac{1}{k_\alpha^{1-\lambda}k_\beta^\lambda} \sum_{j=1}^m \frac{a_{j\alpha}a_{j\beta}}{k_j} \tag{3}$$

Directed Weighted Conduction (DWC). [20] keeps $f_{i\alpha}$ as HeatS and just modifies how to match two people:

$$g_{ij} = \frac{\sum_\alpha h_{j\alpha}a_{j\alpha}a_{i\alpha}}{\sum_\alpha h_{j\alpha}a_{j\alpha}} \tag{4}$$

where $h_{j\alpha} = (k_j k_\alpha)^\gamma$. By experiment on particular datasets, authors suppose not to use $\gamma > 0$.

3.2   Adaptive Weighted Conduction (AWC)

Despite different strategies, previous studies use the same mechanism of diffusion on Bipartite Graph. The node degree has important information, uncovers characteristics of objects, such as how active a user is or popularity of an item. Both ProbS, HeatS, the Hybrid and DWC exploit this value in matching tastes of people and recommending items for users. Since the relation between popularity and diversity, coverage, congestion, they also succeed in considering product display. However, confusing that novelty is small popularity, they strive to minimize popularity to enhance the quality of suggestions. We suppose that only counting number is inadequate to discriminate between new items and items which have unconcern of users. Generally, relying on a specific system, the homology between novelty and popularity is uncertain. More product information, such as rating or release date, should be examined. In this paper, this metric is called popularity. Instead of optimizing it, popularity becomes an indicator for all product display aspects due to its relation to others. Rather than investigating each metric individually or facing their dilemma relationships, our target is to acquire higher precision and balance all display metrics at the same time.

We process two diffusion steps and drive degrees of nodes as previous methods, but aim to bring precisely both popular and unpopular items to particular users.

At the first diffusion step, identifying how similar between people is a difficult mission. Addressing this challenge, DWC changes weights of common items according to their counting values rather than treats them equally as the Hybrid. We generalize the idea of DWC and say that the node degree reflects the role of an item in determining user interests, not exclusively in comparing tastes of customers. This comparable information is expressed by:

$$t_{j\alpha} = \frac{a_{j\alpha}k_\alpha^\gamma}{\sum_\beta a_{j\beta}k_\beta^\gamma} \tag{5}$$

When $\gamma > 0$, the weight increases as the degree goes up. That means popular items contribute more to the relation score of two users than unpopular items. On the contrary, when $\gamma < 0$, the weight increases as the degree goes down, unpopular items have a higher contribution. In practice, not widely-known items demonstrate the stronger relationship between users so that we suggest not using $\gamma > 0$, which is the same as the conclusion by experiments of DWC.

The second step of each method is harnessing counting values to go straight to the target. ProbS primarily gives trending products for accuracy. HeatS concentrates on unpopular items for novelty and diversity. Directly combining two opposite strategies, the Hybrid balances them by a tunable parameter λ, solves the diversity-accuracy dilemma. We leverage the second step of the Hybrid, keep $f_{i\alpha}$ as Eq. (2), so that our model could balance accuracy and diversity, but use the idea of DWC when matching user interest in order to increase its accuracy. The relation score between users of AWC is:

$$g_{ij} = \sum_\alpha \frac{a_{i\alpha}a_{j\alpha}t_{j\alpha}}{k_\alpha^\lambda k_j^{1-\lambda}} \tag{6}$$

Replace g_{ij} in (2) by (6), expansion of preference score in AWC:

$$f_{i\alpha} = \sum_j \frac{a_{j\alpha}}{k_\alpha^{1-\lambda}} \sum_\beta \frac{a_{i\beta}a_{j\beta}t_{j\beta}}{k_\beta^\lambda} \tag{7}$$

When $\gamma = 0$, AWC is the Hybrid with λ is the tunable parameter. Rewriting $f_{i\alpha}$ of the Hybrid by expanding g_{ij} from (1), we have:

$$f_{i\alpha} = \sum_j \frac{a_{j\alpha}g_{ij}}{k_\alpha^{1-\lambda}k_j^\lambda} = \sum_j \frac{a_{j\alpha}}{k_\alpha^{1-\lambda}} \sum_\beta \frac{a_{i\beta}a_{j\beta}}{k_\beta^\lambda k_j} \tag{8}$$

In case of $\gamma = 0$, $t_{j\beta} = \dfrac{1}{k_j}$, so that (8) is equal to (7).

When $\lambda = 0$, AWC is DWC with γ is the tunable parameter. Express g_{ij} of DWC in Eq. (4) by $t_{j\alpha}$ in Eq. (5), we obtain:

$$g_{ij} = \sum_\alpha a_{i\alpha} a_{j\alpha} t_{j\alpha} \tag{9}$$

Replacing g_{ij} in $f_{i\alpha}$ by (9), expansion of DWC:

$$f_{i\alpha} = \sum_j \frac{a_{j\alpha} g_{ij}}{k_\alpha} = \sum_j \frac{a_{j\alpha}}{k_\alpha} \sum_\beta a_{i\beta} a_{j\beta} t_{j\beta} \tag{10}$$

Obviously, in case $\lambda = 0$, Eq. (10) is equal to (7).

Using dual parameters in the first step only unfolds the space for exploring the problem of capturing user interests. Although it is able to increase the accuracy, reaching the best performance on all evaluation metrics is the other challenge. We still keep balancing state between product display aspects when getting the possible highest precision. Due to inheriting Hybrid of ProbS and HeatS, solving the accuracy-diversity dilemma, AWC could remedy the low diversity while optimizing precision, which means the model found a global or local optimal point that efficiently recommends both popular and unpopular items to users correctly. Naturally, using a wide range of popularity, coverage is enlarged, and the congestion problem, caused by suggesting solely a small set of items, is reduced.

Therefore, bringing precisely both popular and unpopular items to particular users subsequently balance all other metrics.

3.3 Adaptive Collaborative Filtering (ACF)

Both ProbS, HeatS, the Hybrid and DWC go through two steps of diffusion, each step has to consider all pairs of users and all common items of them, which has high computing cost. Meanwhile, item-based methods calculate similarities between items instead of users, extremely reduce the complexity. We embed AWC formula into an item-item matrix, then construct an item graph to speed up our method.

Item-Based Recommendation. [19] rewrote two-step diffusion as $f_i = W a_i$, with $W_{n \times n}$ is a hybridization matrix of ProbS and HeatS. Inspired by this idea, from (7) we extract the hybridization matrix for AWC:

$$w_{\alpha\beta} = \frac{1}{k_\alpha^{1-\lambda} k_\beta^\lambda} \sum_j a_{j\alpha} a_{j\beta} t_{j\beta} \tag{11}$$

The recommended matrix $F_{m \times n}$ is result of multiplication between history matrix $A_{m \times n}$ and item-item matrix $W_{n \times n}$: $F = AW^\top$.

Item-Graph Recommendation. Let call $G^I(I, E^I)$ is a Weighted Directed Graph expressing $W_{n \times n}$, where I is item set and E^I is all available connections between items. Because $W_{n \times n}$ is not symmetric, (α, β) and (β, α) has different weights. In detail, if (β, α) is an edge in E, its weight is equal to $w_{\alpha\beta}$. Any pair of items with zero-weight in $W_{n \times n}$ does not have any edge in E.

When two items α and β both appear in the history of a user j, they are connected to each other, two edges (α, β) and (β, α) are established. For more convenient in computing, let call:

$$s_j = \sum_\alpha a_{j\alpha} k_\alpha^\gamma \tag{12}$$

so that $t_{j\beta} = \dfrac{a_{j\beta} k_\beta^\gamma}{s_j}$ and Eq. (11) becomes:

$$w_{\alpha\beta} = k_\alpha^{\lambda-1} k_\beta^{\gamma-\lambda} \sum_j \frac{a_{j\alpha} a_{j\beta}}{s_j} \tag{13}$$

Obviously, for every user j selected both α and β, weight of edge (β, α) is computed by:

$$\sum_j \frac{k_\alpha^{\lambda-1} k_\beta^{\gamma-\lambda}}{s_j} \tag{14}$$

Two steps to construct the $G^I(I, E^I)$:

Step 1 - Prepare features of users and items: Read all user history and calculate k_α for every items, k_i and s_i for every user i.

Step 2 - Establish edges of item graph: Visit history of all users again. For every pair of α and β both appear in the history of user j, connect them in $G^I(I, E^I)$ with weight computed by Eq. (14).

To recommend for user i on graph, preference score of item α is equal to sum of all edge weights from historical item β of i to α: $f_{i\alpha} = \sum_\beta w_{\alpha\beta} a_{i\beta}$.

Complexity. Let d is the number of ratings or user selections in history, or $d = \sum_m k_i$. Let s reflects sparsity of graph, is calculated by $\dfrac{d}{m * n}$, which means the portion of the actual edges in maximum possible edges. Averaging the number of items selected by a user, denoted by K, is equal to $\overline{k_i} = \dfrac{d}{m} = s * n$. It is clearly to see that $K \leq n$. $K = n$ occurs only when the graph is fully connected, or every item connects to each other. As usual, because of data sparsity, $K \ll n$.

When implementing the pure formula of the Hybrid or DWC, we visit all pairs of users and match them by all items, spend $\mathcal{O}(m^2 n)$ to compute g and f. Using the definition of Bipartite Network and just considering items in common, the computational cost is reduced to $\mathcal{O}(m^2 K)$.

Obviously, item-based version of ACF has $\mathcal{O}(mK^2)$ to measure item-item matrix. With a simple matrix multiplication algorithm, it takes $\mathcal{O}(mn^2)$ for

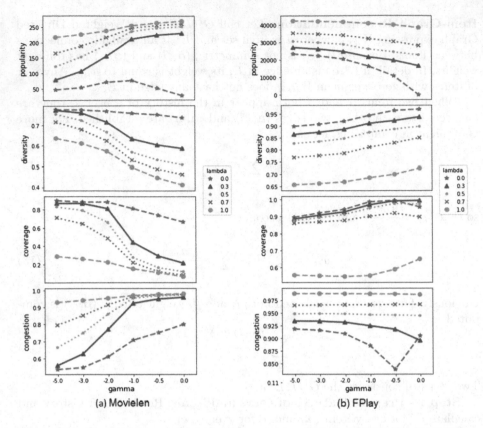

Fig. 1. The change of four properties on testing data of Movielens (left) and FPT Play (right). To visualize, we select the same sets of parameters for all datasets, in which $\lambda = 0.3$ is the optimal line (solid line), subjecting to the precision. Via γ (horizontal axis) and the fixed order of λ, the decrease of popularity causes better tendencies other properties.

making recommendation. In comparison to using Bipartite Network, this way is slower only when the number of users is less than the number of items, not a popular case in recommender systems.

With the item-graphversion of ACF, to construct the graph, the first step requires $\mathcal{O}(mK)$ to read all user history, the second step takes $\mathcal{O}(mK^2)$ to generate all pairs of items within the history of each user. Suppose that each historical item β connects to T recommended items α on average, making recommendation for all users needs $\mathcal{O}(mTK)$. Therefore, the complexity is $\mathcal{O}(mK^2)$ to pre-construct the network and $\mathcal{O}(mTK)$ in total. In case of fully connected graph, $T = n$, otherwise $T < n$, so that item-net model has extremely reduced complexity.

Table 1. Statistical properties of Movielens and FPT Play dataset. Sparsity is the rate of connections between nodes on graph. FPT Play has larger numbers of users and items and a sparser network.

Movielens	Users	Items	Links	Sparsity
Total	943	1,682	100,000	6.82×10^{-2}
Train	617	1,515	62,414	6.68×10^{-2}
Test	134	1,040	4,910	
FPT Play	Users	Items	Links	Sparsity
Total	1,377,579	19,371	13,741,845	0.05×10^{-2}
Train	1,252,058	18,615	10,757,016	0.05×10^{-2}
Test	476,385	14,774	2,445,341	

Table 2. Performances of different methods on testing data of Movielens (top) and FPT Play (bottom). For parameter-dependent algorithms, the results are obtained by the optimal set of parameters, which is label in brackets. In AWC, the first one is λ, the next is γ. We do not judge methods by popularity directly. For remaining metrics, except the congestion, the higher is the better. The first and second best results are emphasized.

Movielens	Popularity	Diversity	Coverage	Congestion	Precision	Rating
ProbS	270	0.4112	0.0695	0.9808	0.0884	3.0385
HeatS	26	0.7351	0.6642	0.8005	0.0470	1.7143
Hybrid (0.2)	202	0.6483	0.3284	0.9366	0.0821	**3.1739**
DWC (−5.0)	46	**0.7762**	**0.8960**	**0.5340**	0.0981	2.8675
AWC (0.3, −5.0)	78	**0.7730**	**0.8665**	**0.5569**	**0.1037**	**3.1605**
FPT Play	Popularity	Diversity	Coverage	Congestion	Precision	
ProbS	38481	0.7243	0.6507	0.9860	**0.1021**	
HeatS	59	**0.9689**	0.9557	0.9050	0.0709	
Hybrid (0.1)	3234	**0.9769**	0.9877	**0.8676**	0.0967	
DWC (−0.5)	10868	0.9634	**0.9936**	**0.8386**	0.0978	
AWC (0.3, −0.5)	19811	0.9212	**0.9915**	0.9176	**0.1078**	

Table 3. The improvement of AWC in comparison to other methods. It is computed by $\dfrac{r_1 - r_0}{r_0}$, where r_0, r_1 is respectively value of AWC and the best of previous method targeting the precision. Except for the congestion, the more positive is the better. Outperformed values of AWC are emphasized.

	Diversity	Coverage	Congestion	Precision	Rating
Movielens	−0.41%	−3.29%	4.29%	**5.70%**	**10.22%**
FPT Play	**27.19%**	**52.37%**	**−6.94%**	**5.58%**	

4   Experiments and Results

In this section, we focus only on demonstrating the ability of AWC in dealing with multiple evaluation metrics. We separate each dataset into two parts: training and testing. The graph is constructed from training data, then predicts L items for each user and compares to testing data. We experiment with many values of L and take $L = 20$ for example and visualization. Characteristics of an algorithm are evaluated based on its outcome through four metrics: popularity, diversity, coverage and congestion. Comparing lists of L recommended items and testing data figures out the precision. Rating is considered on Movielens in order to check the quality of results. Details of datasets, evaluation metrics and results are presented below.

4.1   Datasets and Evaluation Metrics

Datasets. Statistical properties of datasets are described in Table 1.
Movielens. A movie rating dataset of the GroupLens project at the University of Minnesota [8]. It can be downloaded from www.grouplens.org. Each row includes the id of a user, the id of an item and rating on range $[1, 5]$. Training and testing part are extracted with ratio $0.95 : 0.05$, then we filter the testing by removing ratings which have strange user or item to the training.

FPT PLAY. This is taken from history of users on fptplay.vn [9], our online service that allows customers to watch a wide variety of movies, TV shows and more. We use 40-day history, where the testing part is consists of the last 10-day activities of all users on the system and applied the filtering as on Movielens testing part.

Evaluation Metrics
Popularity. This reflects how popular items are on result lists. In DWC, assuming that new items have low counting values, this metric is called as novelty and minimized by algorithms. We suppose that low popularity and novelty are not the same and do not optimize this value. To calculate, for a target user i and list of L recommended items α, his or her popularity is: $N_i(L) = \dfrac{1}{L} \sum_\alpha k_\alpha$. The popularity of an algorithm is taking average N_i of all users.

Diversity. Diversity shows how different the suggesting outcomes are between users. The higher value, the more personalized. It is also related to popularity and accuracy. Bringing mostly popular items is a safe strategy for fitting customer interest, but leads to low difference between users. In contrast, using more unpopular products enhances personalization capability but has a high risk of satisfying customers.

Let call D_{ij} is the number of distinct objects between results of user i and j. Diversity is computed by averaging D_{ij} of all pairs of users.

Coverage. This metric demonstrates the efficiency of resource usage by a recommendation algorithm. It is equal to the rate of items which are recommended to at least one user on the total resource (Table 4).

Table 4. Statistical properties of Item Graphs

	Nodes	Edges	Sparsity
Movielens	1,515	1,414,988	0.61
FPT Play	18,615	35,264,316	0.10

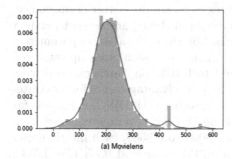
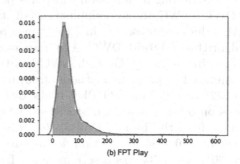

(a) Movielens   (b) FPT Play

Fig. 2. Distribution of items by averaging degrees their users on Movielens (top) and FPT Play (bottom). On Movielens, the shape is normal distribution, while on FPT Play is extremely right skewed.

Congestion. [20] introduced the congestion problem and proposed this metric. Congestion occurs when a few distinct items are in suggesting lists of numerous users. Therefore, the lower is the better. It can be seen as hard version of coverage. Coverage just checks whether an item is in result of any user, while congestion compares the number of times it is recommended.

Precision. Precision is one of accuracy metrics, which are always the first priority. If a method has bad accuracy, no need to consider other properties. It is taken by counting the number of items that are correctly given to a user, then getting average of these values of all users.

Rating. Rating is a score pointing out how users are satisfied with content of items. In this paper, together with precision, rating is another accuracy metric, while other methods use it as a feature. Our purpose is to validate whether the model exploits low-degree items but distinguishes between novelty and bad quality. It is measured by averaging scores of all items recommended for each user first, then taking average these values of all users.

4.2 Results

Complicated relationships between properties of recommendation come from practical requirements. To balance all product display aspects, we use a wide range of objects, from trending to unpopular. Figure 1 visualizes this ability of AWC. Regardless of the change of duel parameters γ and λ, relationships of metrics are always a unified pattern: diversity, coverage, and congestion are followed by popularity. By γ, the popularity decreases and the other properties tend to be better: diversity, coverage goes up and congestion falls. Following λ, the order of lines stays the same on every characteristic: the lower λ, the lower popularity and congestion, the higher diversity and coverage. Due to this pattern, AWC drives popularity and thus indirectly manages other metrics. Therefore, it allows us to understand and control all evaluation aspects of recommender systems.

Discovering a dimension which has boundaries $\gamma = 0$ (the Hybrid) and $\lambda = 0$ (DWC), AWC unfolds combinations of strategies to acquire better performance. All values are presented in Table 2, where results of three parameter-dependent algorithms (Hybrid, DWC, AWC) are obtained by the optimal set of parameters targeting accuracy. Overall, AWC has the highest precision, goes up by $\approx 6\%$ compared to previous methods, from 0.0981 to 0.1037 on Movielens and from 0.1021 to 0.1087 on FPT Play. It also overcomes disadvantages of different strategies on other metrics. On Movielens dataset, together with DWC, it exceeds far away from the best of ProbS, HeatS and the Hybrid: coverage enlarges from 0.6642 to 0.8665, congestion declines from 0.8005 to 0.5569, each metric grows $\approx 30\%$; diversity has a soft increase, from 0.7351 to around 0.77. Like DWC, small popularity means recommending mostly unpopular items, but the rating of our model is 10.22% higher and very close to the value of the Hybrid, which takes the first rank. This contributes to illustrating the insufficiency of elevating novelty by minimizing popularity; simultaneously, showing the capability of AWC to excommunicate low-quality items. We conclude that on Movielens, AWC has the greatest precision and approximates to the best values on other metrics. On FPT Play, within previous methods, focusing on popular items but still holding 65% coverage and 0.7243 diversity, ProbS is the most suitable strategy. That means users should be recommended by trending products, fitting their interests by unpopular items is precarious. Obviously, the Hybrid and DWC compromise their accuracy. Nevertheless, our proposal succeeds in selecting more unpopular objects. Not exclusively rise the precision, AWC exceeds ProbS and reaches close to other methods on remaining metrics. Diversity extends 27%, from 0.7243 to 0.9212. Coverage dramatically spreads 52%, from 0.6507 to 0.9915 and very close the best value, which is 0.9936 of DWC. Congestion has a 7% reduction, from 0.9860 to 0.9176. Therefore, AWC has a dramatic growth from ProbS and a competitive performance on FPT Play dataset.

To clarify the distinction between FPT Play and Movielens that leads to the difference in strategies applied, we present simple analysis of two graphs. Averaging length of user history, Movielens is around 100 and FPT Play approximates 10. Figure 2 shows that while Movielens has a normal user-item distribution, almost FPT Play items are selected by low-degree users. A too short history and a large number of items cause sparsity of graph: a few edges are established with low reliability, items have a small number of connections, especially unpopular ones. In this circumstance, recommending not widely-known products has a very high risk. This explicates the poor precision of HeatS, the Hybrid and DWC on FPT Play. Meanwhile, Movielens faces another problem. Regardless dense or sparse graph, trending objects attract more connections, dominate other products. The repeat of recommending mostly popular items is the root of the congestion problem. Solving this challenge, DWC outperforms previous methods. Instead of examining user-item distribution likes this, tuning parameters of AWC reveals and adapts to characteristics of two graph types, reaches better performance on both datasets.

5   Conclusion

The recommender system is a powerful information filtering technique which has two important roles: bring suitable products to user and control product display. User satisfaction is difficult to be offline evaluated and focusing solely on the accuracy of predicting user selection may not make realistic effects. Meanwhile, item visibility can be judged directly via diversity, coverage and congestion. ProbS, HeatS, the Hybrid and DWC have their own strategies and targeting metrics when dealing with these metrics. We propose a hybrid formula, called Adaptive Weighted Conduction (AWC), combining strengths of those methods for better capturing user interests. Improving the Hybrid by similarity computing of DWC, our model is able to balance all remaining metrics. We also overcome the issue of high computing cost, which leads to bad scalability, by forming Adaptive Collaborative Filtering (ACF) model from AWC. Experiments on Movielens and FPT Play show that our scalable model automatically reveals and adapts to varied requirements of recommender systems, not only outperforms on precision, but also has competitive results on other aspects.

When solving evaluation and scalability problems of recommender systems, this study provides three main contributions. Firstly, we present the insight into the evaluation: the difference between novelty and popularity. Instead of minimizing novelty or solving dilemma relationships of metrics as previous works, utilizing relation of popularity to remaining properties, we harness counting values to control all product display aspects. The second is the success of AWC formula in exploiting strengths of previous methods to acquire better precision and balance other metrics. Moreover, due to the combining of different strategies, AWC uncovers varied traits of particular systems when tunning dual parameters. The final contribution is the scalability of ACF model. It provides evidence for the power of item-graph based approach.

In conclusion, with multi-purpose adaptability, handling from evaluation challenge to scalability issue, our proposal is a practical model for recommender systems.

References

1. 2018 internet trends report. www.recode.net/2018/5/30/17385116. Accessed 13 Jan 2019
2. Gogna, A., Majumdar, A.: Balancing accuracy and diversity in recommendations using matrix completion framework. Knowl. Based Syst. **125**, 83–95 (2017)

3. Javari, A., Jalili, M.: A probabilistic model to resolve diversity-accuracy challenge of recommendation systems. Knowl. Inf. Syst. **44**(3), 609–627 (2015)
4. Putra, A.A., Mahendra, R., Budi, I., Munajat, Q.: Two-steps graph-based collaborative filtering using user and item similarities: case study of E-commerce recommender systems. In: International Conference on Data and Software Engineering, pp. 1–6. IEEE, Indonesia (2017)
5. Rostami, B., Cremonesi, P., Malucelli, F.: A graph optimization approach to item-based collaborative filtering. In: Fidanova, S. (ed.) Recent Advances in Computational Optimization. Studies in Computational Intelligence, vol. 470, pp. 15–30. Springer, Heidelberg (2013). https://doi.org/10.1007/978-3-319-00410-5_2
6. Shams, B., Haratizadeh, S.: Graph-based collaborative ranking. Expert. Syst. Appl. **67**, 59–70 (2017)
7. Wang, F., Ma, S., Yang, L., Li, T.: Recommendation on item graphs. In: ICDM 2006 the sixth International Conference, pp. 1119–1123. IEEE, Hong Kong (2006)
8. Harper, F.M., Konstan, J.A.: The movielens datasets: history and context. ACM Trans. Interact. Intell. Syst. (TIIS) **5**(4), 19 (2016)
9. FPT Play. http://fptplay.vn. Accessed 13 Jan 2019
10. Linden, G., Smith, B., York, J.: Amazon.com recommendations: item-to-item collaborative filtering. IEEE Internet Comput. **1**, 76–80 (2003)
11. Internet World Stats. https://www.internetworldstats.com/stats.htm. Accessed 13 Jan 2019
12. Item Graph Based Recommendation System for Bookopolis of Stanford Course. http://snap.stanford.edu/class/cs224w-2014/projects2014/cs224w-84-final.pdf. Accessed 13 Jan 2019
13. Bobadilla, J., Ortega, F., Hernando, A., Gutirrez, A.: Recommender systems survey. Knowl. Based Syst. **46**, 109–132 (2013)
14. Ge, M., Delgado-Battenfeld, C., Jannach, D.: Beyond accuracy: evaluating recommender systems by coverage and serendipity. In: The Fourth ACM Conference on Recommender Systems, pp. 257–260. ACM, New York (2010)
15. Castells, P., Vargas, S., Wang, J.: Novelty and diversity metrics for recommender systems: choice, discovery and relevance. In: International Workshop on Diversity in Document Retrieval (DDR). ACM, New York (2011)
16. Vargas, S., Castells, P.: Rank and relevance in novelty and diversity metrics for recommender systems. In: The Fifth ACM Conference on Recommender Systems, pp. 109–116. ACM, Chicago (2011)
17. McNee, S.M., Riedl, J., Konstan, J.A.: Being accurate is not enough: how accuracy metrics have hurt recommender systems. In: CHI 2006 Extended Abstracts on Human Factors in Computing Systems, pp. 1097–1101. ACM, Montral (2006)
18. Ha, T., Lee, S.: Item-network-based collaborative filtering: a personalized recommendation method based on a user's item network. Inf. Process. Manag. **53**(5), 1171–1184 (2017)
19. Zhou, T., Kuscsik, Z., Liu, J.G., Medo, M., Wakeling, J.R., Zhang, Y.C.: Solving the apparent diversity-accuracy dilemma of recommender systems. In: the National Academy of Sciences, USA, pp. 4511–4515 (2010)
20. Ren, X., Lü, L., Liu, R., Zhang, J.: Avoiding congestion in recommender systems. New J. Phys. **16**(6), 063057 (2016)
21. Yang, X., Guo, Y., Liu, Y., Steck, H.: A survey of collaborative filtering based social recommender systems. Comput. Commun. **41**, 1–10 (2014)
22. Xu, Y., Ma, J., Sun, Y., Hao, J., Sun, Y., Zhao, Y.: Using social network analysis as a strategy for e-commerce recommendation. In: The Thirteenth Pacific Asia Conference on Information Systems, pp. 106. AIS, Hyderabad (2009)

Exploring and Conceptualising Attestation

Ian Oliver[1]®, John Howse[2(✉)]®, Gem Stapleton[2]®, Zohreh Shams[3]®,
and Mateja Jamnik[3]®

[1] Nokia Bell Labs, Espoo, Finland
ian.oliver@nokia-bell-labs.com
[2] Centre for Secure, Intelligent and Usable Systems,
University of Brighton, Brighton, UK
{John.Howse,g.e.stapleton}@brighton.ac.uk
[3] University of Cambridge, Cambridge, UK
{zs315,Mateja.Jamnik}@cam.ac.uk

Abstract. When formalising the rules of trust in the remote attestation of TPM-based computer systems it is paramount that the rules are precisely understood, supporting unambiguous communication of information about system requirements between engineers. We present a diagrammatic approach to modelling rules of trust using an extended version of concept diagrams. Within the context of our proof-of-concept Network Function Virtualisation and Attestation environment, these rules allow different level of trust to be explored and, importantly, allow us to identify when a computer system should not be trusted. To ensure that the modelling approach can be applied to general systems, we include generic patterns for extending our domain model and rules of trust. Consequently, through the use of a formal, yet accessible, diagrammatic notation, domain experts can define rules of trust for their systems.

Keywords: Attestation · Trust · Networks · Specification · Diagrams

1 Introduction

A major problem in the security of critical telecommunications infrastructure is knowing when it is appropriate to trust an element: a server machine, an edge node (e.g., base station) and more commonly IoT and UE (user equipment, e.g., mobile phones) devices. This paper presents a formal, diagrammatic approach to modelling the data structure related to trust in systems, allowing rules to be defined that capture system integrity. In particular, the rules, based upon

Stapleton, Shams, and Jamnik were funded by a Leverhulme Trust Research Project Grant (RPG- 2016-082) for the project entitled Accessible Reasoning with Diagrams. Oliver was supported by the EU-funded SCOTT and Secredas projects.

© Springer Nature Switzerland AG 2019
D. Endres et al. (Eds.): ICCS 2019, LNAI 11530, pp. 131–145, 2019.
https://doi.org/10.1007/978-3-030-23182-8_10

the Trusted Computing Group's[1] Trusted Processor Module (TPM) Technology, allow machines to be remotely attested so establishing whether a given system is trusted [17]. Attestation is a method for authenticating trustworthiness of your system to a remote party. Of course, the idea of using models, and in particular diagrammatic representations of those models, is not new, UML being a canonical example. But, the use of diagrammatic models to represent constraints of the complexity that arise in the attestation of machines in networks is not common, with B [1] or Z [14] sometimes being notations of choice. The reason for the lack of diagrammatic models arises due to expressiveness limitations that are considered inherent in diagrammatic languages [4]. However, recent research has pushed the boundaries of what can be expressed diagrammatically [8] in ways effective for humans to understand [2,7,10–12].

In this paper we present a diagrammatic method for formally defining the data structure over which rules are used to test the integrity of systems, using trusted computing principles. Our focus is the particular application area of the remote attestation of telecommunications cloud infrastructures known as Network Function Virtualisation (NFV) [5,9], as has been defined by the European Telecommunications Standards Institute (ETSI). The contributions made in this paper are as follows:

1. We diagrammatically define specific rules of trust, considering the system to be static, allowing the integrity of systems to be established at the level of individual rules. We present patterns so that rules for additional kinds of data associated with machines can be included in the attestation framework.
2. We explore how sets of rules of trust can be considered in combination to define different levels of trust, allowing us to attest elements. The attestation rules are partially ordered, thus network routing provision can select a more trusted environment for running sensitive and critical workloads.
3. We argue, by appealing to known results, that our diagrammatic approach to modelling is more effective than competing textual and symbolic methods. This suggests that people are likely to produce more understandable and, thus, fit-for-purpose, rules of trust. This, in turn, will lead to more robust network provision.

Our diagrammatic approach to modelling the rules of trust can also be considered desirable as compared to existing approaches, such as database access, which hide the actual functioning of the rules themselves. Given a formal specification of the rules, such as those we propose in this paper, an implementation of them in a network can be provided. We conclude the paper by discussing how one might extend this approach to define trust in the temporal case, where information known by machines changes over time.

2   Context: Trusted Computing in NFV

Based around a hardware root of trust, trusted computing provides a mechanism for measuring, cryptographically, critical system components which include

---

[1] https://trustedcomputinggroup.org.

BIOS, Operating System, critical system files and so forth. These measurements can be provided, in a secure manner, to an external remote attestation server. Once the measurements are provided, they can be used to determine whether the machine that provided the measurements can, for example, be trusted for use or workload placement.

This process – of remotely providing measurements and checking them against expected values – is used as a security mechanism to ensure that systems providing telecommunication services remain in a known (trusted) state. When measurements do not match, changes can be monitored and acted upon. The integrity of systems, using this approach, can be provided by utilising the Trusted Platform Module (TPM) and remote attestation in a novel manner by reasoning over the latest data as well as historical records in the context of system events such as restarting a machine or patching. Identifying system integrity in telecommunication systems is clearly important in both the static and temporal cases. The primary focus of this paper is on the static case, with the temporal case left as future work.

2.1   Network Function Virtualisation

Telecommunications infrastructure is increasingly being virtualised – this is known as Network Function Virtualisation (NFV). Such an environment consists of a set of elements – servers, IoT, Edge, UE elements. Server machines are generally known as the NFV Infrastructure (NFVI) and run the core telecommunications workloads. This workload is in the form of Virtualised Network Functions (VNFs) which communicate amongst themselves and with the Edge elements. Ensuring the integrity by knowing what exactly is running in terms of whether system components are exactly as expected (i.e., non-tampered, no rootkits, known BIOS/firmware/kernel/VNF configurations, etc.) is critical to the security of such a system.

We are constructing an attestation environment that encompasses the NFVI, VNFs and ultimately Edge, IoT and UE elements. This environment monitors, attests and stores known good configurations and acts as arbiter to other infrastructure components in questions of whether elements or structures of elements are trusted. Failure of trust can have significant consequences for overall network integrity, workload placement, and data integrity, for example.

Traditional attestation tends to focus on whether an element is trusted or not against a single policy. NFV is a much more complex and dynamic environment where the trust decision can vary depending upon circumstances, for example, not all elements have the same notion of trust. In this respect we break the monolithic trust decision into a larger number of simpler rules which can be combined with varying policies. This allows finer grained analysis and trust history to be combined to provide a more context-specific answer to whether a given element is trusted.

2.2 Integrity Measurements and Attestation

An important question arises from the prior discussions: how do we know whether the measurements we obtain from elements are correct and, thus, the element is trustworthy. We can make an *integrity measurement* by requesting a *quote* from a given (element of) a machine for a given kind of measure. As one example, we might ask a machine to quote its core root of trust and BIOS measurement as well as its operating system kernel configuration. In this case, a TPM device will send a reply comprising a data structure with these measurements alongside a signature and some meta-data which is based on the TPM's attestation key; this key is unique to each TPM device.

We now include an example to illustrate modelling trust in networks. Suppose that we have a quote for a machine which includes its CRTM, BIOS configuration and DRTM measurement as stored in the TPM's SHA-256 PCR bank. Additionally, we can supply the handle in the TPM of a signing key, such as the attestation key, as well as a hashing algorithm for the quote. Thus, the quote itself is returned and the quote taken against the attestation private key, which (using significantly truncated values) may look something like:

```
tpm2 quote -k 0x81010003 -L sha256:0,1,2,3,17
quoted: ff544347801...eca71a signature: 1400...6334
```

Importantly, the quoted value is constructed from a number of data items: the hash of the requested PCR, the attested value, the TPM's clock, the firmware version, the reset and restart counts (which correspond to the number of boot and suspend events associated with the machine), as well as clock integrity measures and a TCG-defined type and a magic number. These quoted values must be compared to the expected values. The attested value itself *must* match the given known expected value. By comparing the other items of meta-data along with signature verification, using the attestation public key, we are able to reach a decision on the machine's integrity status. If expected values do not match actual values the integrity of the machine is uncertain and it should not be trusted.

With TPM a number of concepts of trust are defined (at least on x86 platforms): CRTM – the core root of trust measurement for a system, the SRTM – a measurement over BIOS and initial boot loader configurations (with other aspects as necessary), DRTM – a measurement relying upon certain sandboxing features of x86 processors to measure operating system components prior to launch. We can continue to build policies over measurements to be taken over the file system at run-time (e.g., Linux IMA and EMA). Furthermore the TPM specification is open to further measures such as geographical trust.

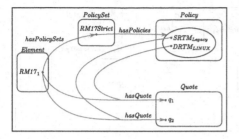

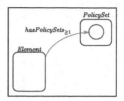

Fig. 1. An example situation depicted using an extended concept diagram.

Fig. 2. Elements and their policy sets.

3 Modelling the Data Structure

We will now propose a formal model of the data structure discussed in the previous section. To reiterate, the decision to trust a given system depends on the latest quote for a given NFVI element (machine) matching certain properties which are expressed as a policy. In the data structure, there are four main classes: *Element*, *Quote*, *Policy*, and *PolicySet*. Elements and quotes have been defined earlier. A policy, however, is a combination of measures. For example, a policy might be for a given CRTM, partial SRTM measures, a DRTM measure, or user defined measures, say. A policy set groups these policies into logical sets which enable ease of measurement management as machines/elements are updated or need to comply with varying situations. One novelty in our approach is moving away from static, monolithic measurement to finer grained policies; for example, it is perfectly possible to have two machines with the same CRTM/SRTM measures and different DRTM; an example is two different Linux kernels on the same hardware and the same configuration. We want to capture the following information:

1. Every element is associated with at least one policy set.
2. A policy set is (essentially) a non-empty set of policies.
3. Given an element and one of its associated policies, there is exactly one quote. Thus, given an element and policy pair, there is either no quote (when the policy is not associated with the element) or exactly one quote (when the policy is associated with the element).

We assume that Element, Policy, PolicySet and Quote are pairwise disjoint.

Our approach to defining this data structure is to use an extended version of a diagrammatic logic, called *concept diagrams* [8], which has a formal syntax and semantics and they form a second-order dyadic logic [15]. Concept diagrams have been empirically evaluated against both a stylised textual notation (Manchester OWL Syntax) and a symbolic notation (description logic [3]), with the results suggesting that people can interpret concept diagrams significantly more effectively (measured via accuracy and time performance) [2]. In addition, they form a richly expressive diagrammatic logic, capable of expressing a wide

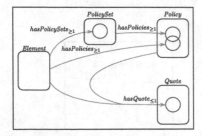

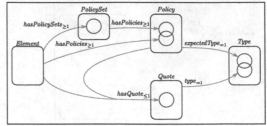

Fig. 3. The basic structure.   **Fig. 4.** Adding in information about types.

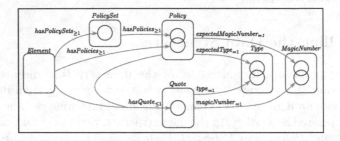

Fig. 5. Adding in information about magic numbers.

range of constraints including, with some minor extensions to allow the expression of ternary relations, the rules that are needed to identify whether we can trust elements [16].

An example of what this data structure looks like can be seen in the extended concept diagram in Fig. 1. The four classes are represented by four rectangles. We can see that $RM17_1$ is an *Element*. In addition, $RM17_1$ is associated with one policy set called *RM17Strict*. In turn, we can see that this policy set includes two policies, $SRTM_{Legacy}$ and $DRTM_{Linux}$. We can see that $RM17_1$ along with the policy $SRTM_{Legacy}$ returns the quote q_2 and, with the policy $DRTM_{Linux}$ returns the quote q_1. Note that concept diagrams as in [8] do not include arrows with two sources. Here, these are used to represent ternary relations.

In Fig. 2, the classes *Element* and *PolicySet* are (again) represented by non-overlapping rectangles; their non-overlapping nature asserts that no two things can be in both classes – they are disjoint. Now, the fact that elements are associated with at least one policy set is expressed by the arrow. Here, the arrow, labelled *hasPolicySets*, shows that there is an association (binary relation) between *Element* and *PolicySet*. The annotation $_{\geq 1}$ tells us that every element is associated, under the *hasPolicySet* relation, to at least one policy set.

Figure 2 is extended in Fig. 3 to express further constraints. For instance, the arrow from *PolicySet* to *Policy* also has the annotation $_{\geq 1}$, which informs us that policy sets are associated with at least one policy under the *hasPolicies* relation. It is helpful to define a further relation, that allows us to navigate directly from elements to policies, indicated here by the *hasPolicies* arrow sourced on

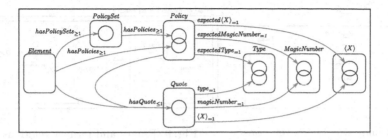

Fig. 6. Extending the model using patterns.

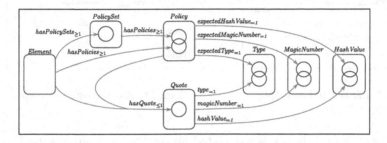

Fig. 7. Extending the model to include additional classes for measures.

Element and targeting *Policy*. There is also an arrow, labelled *hasQuote*, which is sourced on *Element* and *Policy* and targets an anonymous subset of *Quote*. This expresses that given an element and a policy, we 'return' a set of quotes. The arrow annotation, $_{\leq 1}$, tells us that the returned set of quotes contains at most one quote. There is a required constraint that this diagram does not capture: the *hasPolicies* relation from element to quote is the composition of the relations *hasPoliciesSet*, from elements to policy sets, and *hasPolicies*, from policy sets to policies. We will return to this missing constraint later.

Our task now is to capture information about the values that policies expect to obtain from quotes. We will define two cases, from which we will extract a basic pattern that can be used to extend our model when policies expect other kinds of values, as well as the two we consider, namely: *Type* and *MagicNumber*. *Type* and *MagicNumber* are defined by the TCG and are present in the whole quote structure. In this case *Type* is a value which encodes the type of the datastructure, that is, a TPM2 Quote, and magic number is a fixed value stating that the quote is from a TPM. We will then show how the pattern can be applied to a third case, *HashValue*, which is a single value calculated from recursive extension of the individual hash values of a PCR in a policy.

Figure 4 shows how to extend the basic data structure in Fig. 3 to include the class *Type* and the two new binary relations, *expectedType* and *type*. We ultimately want to check that the value expected by a policy, given an element and a quote, matches the value provided by the quote for a type. Each policy expects a unique value for *Type*. In Fig. 4, we have an arrow from *Policy* to *Type*,

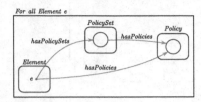

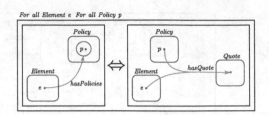

Fig. 8. Composing binary relations.   **Fig. 9.** Binary and ternary relations.

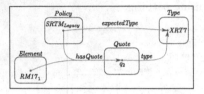

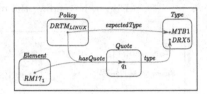

Fig. 10. A trusted element.   **Fig. 11.** An untrusted element.

indicating that each policy is associated, under the relation *expectedType*, to a unique *Type* (indicated by the $_{=1}$ annotation). Similarly, each quote is associated with a unique thing in the class *Type*. When modelling rules that capture trust, we will require that the expected type for the policy matches the (actual) type for the quote in order for an element to be trusted.

Information about magic numbers is added to the model in Fig. 5, extending Fig. 4. We can see that the extension has a very similar structure to the previous case: add a new rectangle for the new class, with two further arrows, one from *Policy* and one from *Quote*. We adopt the naming convention that the arrow from *Quote* to the new rectangle, *MagicNumber* is labelled *magicNumber*. The other new arrow has the same label, but with a leading capital letter and then prefixed with *expected*, giving the label *expectedMagicNumber*. This leads to a general pattern for extending the basic data structure to include new kinds of classes for which measurements can be obtained for quotes, shown in Fig. 6. The extension of Fig. 5 to include *HashValue*, shown in Fig. 7, is then straightforward.

Returning now to the missing constraint identified above, we show how to define the composition with reference to Fig. 8. We want to express that, for each element, the set of policies it 'has direct access to' under the *hasPolicy* relation are exactly those associated with its policy sets. Since we need to talk about all elements, the diagram in Fig. 8 includes a *quantification expression* above the bounding box. In the diagram, we can then see that if we navigate from (any element) *e* to its set of policies via *PolicySet*, under first the *hasPolicySets* relation and then the *hasPolicies* relation, we get to exactly the same set of policies if we go directly from *e* to policies under the *hasPolicies* relation.

To conclude this section, we now focus on the relationship between the *hasPolicy* and *hasQuote* relations, shown in Fig. 9. This diagram also uses a

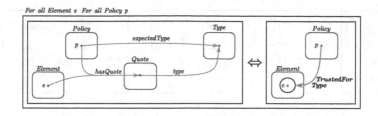

For all Element e For all Policy p

Fig. 12. Defining a rule of trust for the *Type* class.

quantification expression, allowing us to talk about all elements and all policies. In addition, it incorporates a standard logical connective, $\Leftrightarrow$, to represent bi-implication. Reading the diagram, inside the bounding rectangles, we see:

1. if e is an element, p is a policy and e *hasPolicy* p then there is a unique quote (here represented by the unlabelled dot) where element e and policy p have the quote.
2. if e is an element, p is a policy and there is some unique quote where e and p have that quote then element e has policy p.

Using this data structure and its associated constraints, we can now proceed to define rules of trust.

4   Rules over Elements and Policies

Intuitively, we want expected measures to be the same as actual measures in order to trust an element. Looking at the data structure visualised in Fig. 7, we can see that we must navigate from elements and policies to quotes in order to get access to (actual) measures for particular classes, such as *Type*. Essentially, rules of trust are binary relations, from policies to elements: given any policy, it can either trust an element or not.

Figure 10 shows an instance where the element $RM17_1$ is trusted by policy $SRTM_{Legacy}$. The quote provided is associated with type $XRT7$ which is the value expected by $SRTM_{Legacy}$. By contrast, Fig. 11 shows an example where a different policy does not trust $RM17_1$. Here, $RM17_1$'s quote, given the policy $DRTM_{Linux}$, is q_1, which returns $DRX5$ as the type. But, the policy $DRTM_{Linux}$ expects the value $MTB1$. These values for *Type* do not match, so $DRTM_{Linux}$ does not trust $RM17_1$. This example illustrates that some policies can trust an element whilst other do not.

We define our first rule of trust, in Fig. 12, for the *Type* class. Again, this diagram uses a quantification expression: we need access to all elements, e, and all policies, p. Figure 9, expresses that if e has the policy p then there is a unique quote, q, for that element and policy pair. Whenever we have a (unique) quote, q, we can get access to q via the *hasQuote* relation. At that point, we can obtain both the expected value, t_1, of *Type* for the policy *and* the actual value t_2, of

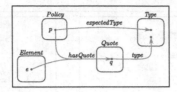
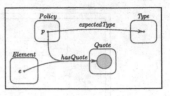

Fig. 13. A policy does not trust an element.

Fig. 14. Measures do not match.

Fig. 15. There is no quote.

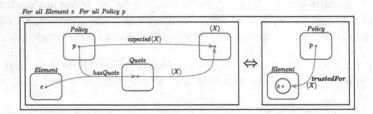

Fig. 16. Pattern for defining a rule of trust.

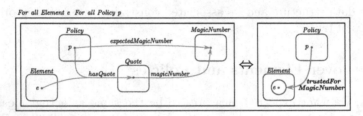

Fig. 17. Defining a rule of trust for the *MagicNumber* class.

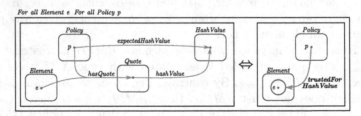

Fig. 18. Defining a rule of trust over the *HashValue* class.

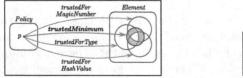

Fig. 19. A minimum level of trust.   **Fig. 20.** A minimum level of trust does not hold.

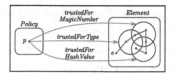
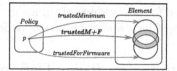

Fig. 21. A non-trusted element.   **Fig. 22.** A higher level of trust.

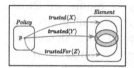
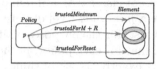
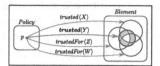

Fig. 23. A simple attestation rule pattern: adding one rule of trust.

Fig. 24. Extending *trustedMinimum* to include *Reset.*

Fig. 25. A more complex attestation rule pattern: adding two rules of trust.

Type for the quote. Only when $t_1 = t_2$ does p trust e for the *Type* class. In the diagram of Fig. 12, the left-hand rectangle constructs the relationships between e, p, and their quote: the two arrows *expectedType* and *type* hit the same dot (which represents an anonymous individual), expressing that the expected and actual measures are the same. The policy p *trusts* e given the expected and actual measures for the class *Type*. Likewise, if p trusts e for *Type* then the expected and actual measures for *Type* must match. Essentially, the diagram in Fig. 12 is defining the relation *trustedForType*: given p, the set of elements p is related to under *trustedForType* is precisely the set of things that p trusts for *Type*.

Having defined what it means to be trusted by a policy for the class *Type*, we can readily deduce what it means to not be trusted. Suppose that policy p does not trust element e, as shown in Fig. 13. This figure depicts that e is not trusted by p since it is outside the (curve that represents) the set of things that p trusts for *Type*. How can this situation arise? Well, the obvious case is shown in Fig. 14, where the expected value for the policy does not match that given by the quote. Perhaps a less obvious case is covered in Fig. 15, where there is no quote for e and p. The construction here builds the set of quote for p and q using an unlabelled curve. The shading inside the curve is used to denote the emptiness of the corresponding set: there are no quotes for e and p. Given the data structure in Fig. 4 along with Figs. 8 and 9, we can deduce that p is not a policy of q in this case. So, the only way that an element can fail to be trusted *for one of its policies* is when the measures do not match.

Returning our attention to defining rules of trust, we can readily extract a pattern from Fig. 12. For any given rule, we want the expected measures and actual measures to have the same value, for a given class; the generic pattern is shown in Fig. 16. This pattern is used to create Figs. 17 and 18, defining rules of trust over the *MagicNumber* and *HashValue* classes. Many more rules of trust can be defined for other kinds of things in the TPM quote field. These things include Firmware, Clock and Safe (which denotes clock integrity), amongst others.

5   Attestation Rules Defined from Rules of Trust

We can use individual rules of trust to define different levels of trust, giving rise to attestation rules over sets of classes. As a minimum, we require all three rules of trust to pass to provide a *minimum* level of trust for an element given a policy. This minimum level of trust, for the purposes of attestation, is defined in Fig. 19. The diagram expresses that for each policy, p, the set of things in which p has a minimum level of trust is exactly the set of things that p trusts under the three previously defined rules of trust. Notice the use of shading here: the region inside the target of the *trustedMinimum* arrow that is not inside the targets of *all* the other arrows is shaded, so no elements can be in (the set represented by) that region. Given *trustedMinimum*, elements are attestable by policies.

Suppose, for a given element e and policy p we have the situation shown in Fig. 20: p does not have a minimum level of trust in e. This can arise when p fails to trust e for at least one of the rules of trust used to define *trustedMinimum*. There are seven ways in which this can happen, illustrated in Fig. 21: e must lie in one of the regions that contain a node of the tree labelled e. The tree thus represents disjunctive information, showing that e fails all of the rules of trust (represented the node outside the three unlabelled curves), or exactly one of the rules of trust (represented by the three nodes each inside exactly one unlabelled curve), or any pair of the rules of trust (represented by the other three nodes). It is possible to prove (using sound diagrammatic inference rules) that these are the possibilities for e given the lack of trust by p.

Further attestation rules can be defined, exploiting different sets of rules of trust, to give stronger levels of trust. This is useful since, in some situations, having a basic level of trust in an element is sufficient for the purposes of attestation, yet at other times a stronger level of trust is required. To illustrate, TPM includes Firmware as one of its quote fields. Assuming the pattern in Fig. 16 is used to define the *trustedForFirmware* rule of trust, we can define a higher level of trust, which we call *trustedM+F*. This is shown in Fig. 22, where we can see that the set of elements that policies trust under *trustedM+F* is exactly the set of elements trusted under both *trustedMinimum* and *trustedForFirmware*.

From this, we can readily extract a pattern, given in Fig. 23, for defining higher levels of attestation rules of trust. This pattern takes one attestation rule and extends it using one rule of trust. Suitable names should be substituted for $\langle X \rangle$, $\langle Y \rangle$ and $\langle Z \rangle$, as in Fig. 24 which defines an attestation rule, *trustedForM+R*, for the *Reset* TPM quote field, assuming that *trustedForReset* has been defined. The pattern readily generalises to allow attestation rules to be extended by two or more rules of trust at the same time. The pattern for extending by two rules of trust is given in Fig. 25. It is easy to see that by defining attestation rules in this way, a partial order over them is derivable. This partial order allows the level of trust for an element, given a policy, to be ascertained.

6   Human Cognition and the Benefits of Diagrams

A major motivation for using diagrams to model systems, in our case rules of trust in the context of attestation, is the potential benefits they bring from the perspective of human cognition. It is important for models to be properly understood by all stakeholders. Focusing specifically on concept diagrams, there is empirical evidence to suggest that they are superior modes of communication compared to symbolic notations (specifically description logic) and textual notations (specifically the Manchester OWL syntax (MOS)) [2,7]. Here we give some explanation as to why these diagrams have cognitive benefits by appealing to *well-matchedness* [6].

A notation is said to be well-matched when its syntactic relations, that convey semantics, 'match' the semantic concepts being conveyed. In concept diagrams, spatial properties, such as the disjointness of the interiors of closed curves, are used to express information. Disjoint curve interiors assert that the sets are disjoint, for example: this is a well-matched feature. Likewise, the region inside the overlap of curves represents the intersection of the represented sets and so on. Arrows are directed and are used to express directed relationships. Hence, concept diagrams are generally well-matched to their semantics.

Well-matched diagrams often have *free rides* which correspond to information that can readily be extracted from the diagram but which needs to be inferred from symbolic or textual representations [13]. For instance, from Fig. 21, by expressing that p is a policy, e is an element and the sets policy and element are disjoint, we can read off the diagram that p and e are distinct. An equivalent MOS representation of the information just described comprises the statements

```
ClassAssertion( Policy p ),
ClassAssertion( Element e ), and
DisjointClasses( Policy Element )
```

from which one needs to deduce that p and e are distinct individuals. The diagram possesses other free rides also, such as directly expressing the fact that all of the individuals to which p is related under *trustedForType* are not policies; this free ride follows from the containment of the unlabelled curve targeted by the arrow labelled *trustedForType* being inside the *Element* curve which, in turn, is disjoint from the *Policy* curve.

7   Conclusion and Future Work

We have presented a diagrammatic approach to modelling rules of trust, over a specified data structure, specifically for use in the context of the remote attestation of TPM-based computer systems. Using rules of trust, which determine the trustworthiness of system elements for given policies and specific classes, we were able to define attestation rules to decide on the trustworthiness of elements over sets of classes. If we detect a failure of trust, for a particular attestation rule, we know that one or more of the rules of trust have failed. Once a failure has been recognised, the next stage is to understand the root cause, with the attestation rules thus contributing to system diagnosis and forensics. The partial order over the attestation rules further permits the network routing provision to select a more trusted environment for running sensitive and critical workload.

The data structure, rules of trust, and attestation rules that we have provided, along with patterns that allow their extension to more complex environments, are suitable for a static view of trustworthiness. It is important to define rules of trust for the temporal case, which can include pairs of policies with expected values that change over time. Currently, there is no diagrammatic logic that is capable of formalising temporal constraints over the rich data structures, and corresponding rules that arise in the trust and attestation requirements of TPM-based computer systems, which has been shown to be more effective for people to use than competing symbolic and textual notations. This is an interesting avenue of future work, since it is desirable to exploit the established usability benefits of diagrams in the temporal case. As a result, we would expect a deeper, more accurate, understanding of the individual rules of trust and attestation to be gained by the designers of networks and systems in which these temporal rules are needed.

References

1. Abrial, J.: The B-Book: Assigning Programs to Meanings. CUP, Cambridge (1996)
2. Alharbi, E., Howse, J., Stapleton, G., Hamie, A., Touloumis, A.: Visual logics help people: an evaluation of diagrammatic, textual and symbolic notations. In: Visual Languages and Human-Centric Computing, pp. 255–259. IEEE (2017)
3. Baader, F., Horrocks, I., Sattler, U.: Description logics as ontology languages for the semantic web. In: Hutter, D., Stephan, W. (eds.) Mechanizing Mathematical Reasoning. LNCS (LNAI), vol. 2605, pp. 228–248. Springer, Heidelberg (2005). https://doi.org/10.1007/978-3-540-32254-2_14
4. Chapman, P., Stapleton, G., Howse, J., Oliver, I.: Deriving sound inference rules for concept diagrams. In: IEEE Symposium on Visual Languages and Human-Centric Computing, pp. 87–94. IEEE (2011)
5. Dai, W., et al.: TEE: a virtual DRTM based execution environment for secure cloud-end computing. Future Gener. Comput. Syst. **49**, 47–57 (2015)
6. Gurr, C.: Effective diagrammatic communication: syntactic, semantic and pragmatic issues. J. Vis. Lang. Comput. **10**(4), 317–342 (1999)
7. Hou, T., Chapman, P., Blake, A.: Antipattern comprehension: an empirical evaluation. In: Formal Ontology in Information Systems. Frontiers in Artificial Intelligence, vol. 283, pp. 211–224. IOS Press (2016)
8. Howse, J., Stapleton, G., Taylor, K., Chapman, P.: Visualizing ontologies: a case study. In: Aroyo, L., Welty, C., Alani, H., Taylor, J., Bernstein, A., Kagal, L., Noy, N., Blomqvist, E. (eds.) ISWC 2011. LNCS, vol. 7031, pp. 257–272. Springer, Heidelberg (2011). https://doi.org/10.1007/978-3-642-25073-6_17
9. Oliver, I., Holtmanns, S., Miche, Y., Lal, S., Hippeläinen, L., Kalliola, A., Ravidas, S.: Experiences in trusted cloud computing. In: Yan, Z., Molva, R., Mazurczyk, W., Kantola, R. (eds.) NSS 2017. LNCS, vol. 10394, pp. 19–30. Springer, Cham (2017). https://doi.org/10.1007/978-3-319-64701-2_2

10. Sato, Y., Masuda, S., Someya, Y., Tsujii, T., Watanabe, S.: An fMRI analysis of the efficacy of Euler diagrams in logical reasoning. In: IEEE Symposium on Visual Languages and Human-Centric Computing, pp. 143–151. IEEE (2015)
11. Sato, Y., Mineshima, K.: How diagrams can support syllogistic reasoning: an experimental study. J. Log. Lang. Inf. **24**, 409–455 (2015)
12. Shams, Z., Sato, Y., Jamnik, M., Stapleton, G.: Accessible reasoning with diagrams: from cognition to automation. In: Chapman, P., Stapleton, G., Moktefi, A., Perez-Kriz, S., Bellucci, F. (eds.) Diagrams 2018. LNCS (LNAI), vol. 10871, pp. 247–263. Springer, Cham (2018). https://doi.org/10.1007/978-3-319-91376-6_25
13. Shimojima, A.: Semantic Properties of Diagrams and Their Cognitive Potentials. CSLI Publications, Stanford (2015)
14. Spivey, J.: The Z Notation: A Reference Manual. Prentice Hall, New York (1989)
15. Stapleton, G., Howse, J., Chapman, P., Delaney, A., Burton, J., Oliver, I.: Formalizing concept diagrams. In: 19th International Conference on Distributed Multimedia Systems, pp. 182–187. Knowledge Systems Institute (2013)
16. Yang, Y., Shiwei, X., Hunguo, Z., Fan, Z.: Using first order logic to reason about TCG's TPM specification. In: International Forum on Information Technology and Applications, pp. 259–263. IEEE (2009)
17. Zimmer, V., Dasari, R., Brogan, S.: TCG-based firmware: white paper by Intel Corporation and IBM Corporation Trusted Platforms (2009). https://people.eecs.berkeley.edu/kubitron/cs194-24/hand-outs/SF09_EFIS001_UEFI_PI_TCG_White_Paper.pdf. Accessed May 2018

Enhancing Layered Enterprise Architecture Development Through Conceptual Structures

Simon Polovina[1]([⊠]), Mark von Rosing[2], Wim Laurier[3], and Georg Etzel[4]

[1] Conceptual Structures Research Group, Sheffield Hallam University, Sheffield, UK
S.Polovina@shu.ac.uk
[2] Global University Alliance, Chateau Du Grand Perray, La Bruere Sur Loir, France
mvr@globaluniversityalliance.org
[3] Université Saint-Louis – Bruxelles, Brussels, Belgium
wim.laurier@usaintlouis.be
[4] LEADing Practice ApS, 86157 Augsburg, Germany
ge@leadingpractice.com

Abstract. Enterprise Architecture (EA) enables organisations to align their information technology with their business needs. Layered EA Development (LEAD) enhances EA by using meta-models made up of layered meta-objects, interconnected by semantic relations. Organisations can use these meta-models to benefit from a novel, ontology-based, object-oriented way of EA thinking and working. Furthermore, the meta-models are directed graphs that can be read linearly from a Top Down View (TDV) or a Bottom Up View (BUV) perspective. Conceptual Structures through *CG-FCA* (where *CG* refers to Conceptual Graph and *FCA* to Formal Concept Analysis) is thus used to traverse the TDV and BUV directions using the LEAD Industry 4.0 meta-model as an illustration. The motivation for *CG-FCA* is stated. It is discovered that *CG-FCA*: (a) identifies any unwanted cycles in the 'top-down' or 'bottom-up' directions, and (b) conveniently arranges the many pathways by which the meta-models can be traversed and understood in a Formal Concept Lattice. Through the LEAD meta-model exemplar, the wider appeal of *CG-FCA* and directed graphs are also identified.

1 Introduction

Enterprise Architecture (EA) enables organisations to align their information technology with their business needs. In common with certain other Enterprise Architecture (EA) frameworks, models or approaches (e.g. The Open Group Architecture Framework, TOGAF [6]), Layered Enterprise Architecture Development (LEAD) has developed meta-models that formally depict best current and future business practices as reusable patterns by organisations. By reusing what is already known, organisations avoid reinventing the wheel thus freeing them to concentrate their limited resources on best serving their clients rather than incurring unnecessary costs and risks. LEAD is a layered EA because

© Springer Nature Switzerland AG 2019
D. Endres et al. (Eds.): ICCS 2019, LNAI 11530, pp. 146–159, 2019.
https://doi.org/10.1007/978-3-030-23182-8_11

it articulates an organisation's business, information and technology domains according to 87 elements or 'meta-objects' in layers and sub-layers[1]. The 87 meta-objects are interconnected by semantic relations that collectively make up the meta-models provided by LEAD. Through the LEAD practitioners' body LEADing Practice and the non-profit Global University Alliance (GUA) academic and research community, organisations and academia benefit from a novel, ontology-based and object-oriented way of EA thinking and working [11,14].

The rest of the paper is structured as follows. Section 2 introduces the LEAD meta-model and how it was formalised and analysed. Section 3—the method section—explains why CG-FCA (where CG refers to Conceptual Graph and FCA to Formal Concept Analysis) was applied to this meta-model. Section 4 shows the resulting Formal Concept Lattice (FCL). Section 5 provides further discussion about the cycles that may emerge during this process, as well as related and future research. Section 6 concludes the paper.

2   The Meta-Model Diagram

Like TOGAF and others, the LEAD meta-models are visualised as UML Class Diagrams with one compartment for the meta-object's name as the class type with two-way directed associations called semantic relations that run to-and-from each meta-object. As such, each semantic relation describes how a given meta-object can be viewed from its associated meta-object, and vice versa. The meta-models are thus two-way directed graphs that can be read linearly from top to bottom (i.e. 'top-down') or bottom to top ('bottom-up') depending on the meta-object's position in the meta-model.

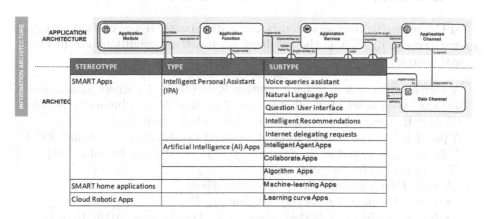

Fig. 1. LEAD Industry 4.0 meta-model, illustrated with levels

Figure 1 is an extract of the LEAD meta-model for Industry 4.0 that is not shown here due to lack of space. It also needs to be viewed as an enlarged, readable version that's bigger than the page size of the paper. The whole meta-model can thus be retrieved from: www.polovina.me.uk/publications/iccs2019.

---

[1] www.polovina.me.uk/publications/iccs2019 has a 'periodic table' of the 87 elements.

It consists of a layered meta-model composed of a subset of the 87 meta-objects i.e. 33 meta-objects, and 54 semantic relations. Its layers are: Business Architecture, Information Architecture (shown in Fig. 1) and Technology Architecture.

Each layer has a sub-layer e.g. Information Architecture has 'Application Architecture' as its sub-layer. Figure 1 illustrates this layer and sub-layer. It also shows the levels within the layers of the Industry 4.0 meta-model. These levels (as opposed to layers) are stereotype (level 2), type (level 3), and sub-type (level 4). As these lower levels are subclasses or instances of level 1—the meta-object—they can substitute the meta-object and inherit its semantic relations with other meta-objects. Similar substitutions for populating a model from a meta-model have also been demonstrated in CGs [5]. They follow Liskov's substitution principle, thereby bringing the polymorphism that object-orientation offers into the meta-model [8].

The focus of this paper is however on the meta-objects (level 1). Consequently, the levels in Fig. 1 were included to illustrate how a meta-object might be populated with objects having more specific content. These subclasses and instances are nonetheless dependent on the meta-object (again after Liskov). It is also important that the meta-model is useful, after Box's remark that "All Models are Wrong, but Some are Useful" [4]. The aim therefore is for the meta-models to be as expressive and useful as possible rather than perfect. They must still avoid being useless or harmful; inaccuracies may have an adverse impact on the organisation as it populates the model with its subclasses or instances of the meta-objects.

3   Analysing the Meta-Model with CG-FCA

CG-FCA brings to the meta-models the mathematical rigour of FCA [3,12]. A formal concept in FCA is the result of when certain conditions are met in a formal context:

- A formal context is a ternary relation $\mathbb{K} = (G, M, I)$, where G is a set of objects, M is a set of attributes, and $I \subseteq G \times M$ is a binary (true/false) relation that expresses which objects have which attributes.
- A pair (A, B) is a formal concept of a context (G, M, I) provided that $A \subseteq G$, $B \subseteq M$, $A' = B$, and $B' = A$, where $A' = \{m \in M \mid gIm \text{ for all } g \in A\}$, and $B' = \{g \in G \mid gIm \text{ for all } m \in B\}$.
- (A, B) is thus a formal concept precisely when:
  - every object in A has every attribute in B,
  - for every object in G that is not in A, there is some attribute in B that the object does not have,
  - for every attribute in M that is not in B, there is some object in A that does not have that attribute.

The formal concepts can then be presented in a lattice, namely a Formal Concept Lattice (FCL), as will be demonstrated in Sect. 4. CG-FCA allows FCA to be applied to the meta-models through the *CGtoFCA* ternary relation-to-binary relation algorithm and its implementation in the CG-FCA software[2]. The motivation for this approach will be elaborated as part of the related research discussion in Subsect. 5.2 of Sect. 5 below. Whereas CG-FCA formerly converted Conceptual Graphs (CGs) only, it can now read 3-column CSV files thereby (primitively) allowing any form of ternary relations to benefit from CG-FCA [3].

3.1 Discovering Pathways

The purpose of stating the meta-model as directed graphs is to discover the pathways from one meta-object to all other meta-objects that it is semantically associated with through the semantic relations. These semantic associations can both be direct (i.e. *Meta-Object, semantic relation, Meta-Object*) and indirect (i.e. *Meta-Object, semantic relation, ...*[3], *semantic relation, Meta-Object*). These pathways allow us to define a meta-object's **view**, which is the set of all meta-objects that can be associated with the meta-object defining the view through direct and indirect associations in a single direction (i.e. top-down or bottom-up).

Each view represents how that meta-object views itself in relation to its associated meta-objects. For example, reading from top to bottom: `Data Component, implemented by, Application Function` states that from the Data Component's point of view it sees itself as being implemented by an Application Function[4], and reading from bottom-to-top, `Application Function, implements, Data Component` states the association from Application Function's point of view (i.e. an Application Function views itself as implementing a Data Component). The two views are thus complementary to each other. For convenience, we shall refer to these linear directions as the (a) Top-Down View (TDV) and (b) Bottom-Up View (BUV).

3.2 Managing Cycles

However if we navigate from both points of view (i.e. TDV *and* BUV), then we end up in an immediate cycle whereby the meta-objects cycle with each other rather than traverse the whole meta-model linearly. Figure 2 illustrates the evident cycle for the `Application Function, implements, Data Component, implemented by, Application Function` example above. As the dotted line in CGs represent co-referent links thereby meaning that the CG concepts (meta-objects) are identical, Fig. 2 shows the actual CG join on the right-hand CG hence the cycle. Consequently, we must navigate from one view being either

---

[2] https://sourceforge.net/projects/cgfca/.

[3] These dots can either be replaced a Meta-Object or by a chain of any number of *Meta-Object, semantic relation, Meta-Object* triples.

[4] Note the reference to 'a' and 'an' in this statement; as will be elucidated by CGs shortly we refer to instances (called 'referents' in CGs terminology) stating that we are referring to the objects instantiated by the meta-objects, even when a meta-object points to itself, which is also described in Subsect. 5.1 of Sect. 5.

TDV or BUV, *not* both. Incidentally, we call these 'top-down' or 'bottom-up' as a convenient term to suggest the initial direction of the view traversal. Typically therefore, going 'top-down' (TDV) suggests choosing a starting (or source) meta-object that is somehow seen as higher up in the layers (and vice versa for 'bottom-up', BUV). This can easily be subjective, as for example with meta-objects next to each other in the same sub-layer which one of them may be the 'higher'? Furthermore, semantic relations that initially start top-down may turn bottom-up as associated meta-objects are navigated in turn. Our reference to top-down or bottom-up is thus a working definition rather than a perfect one, especially for our models to be useful [4].

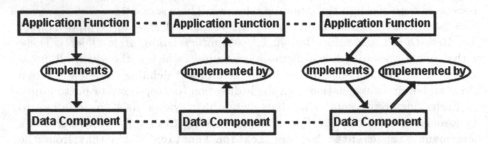

Fig. 2. CG views of data component and application function

3.3   Applying CG-FCA to the Exemplar

Going back to the complete version of Fig. 1 as our industrial exemplar of a meta-model with bidirectional associations, CG-FCA is applied to the ternary relations that make up directed graphs thereby turning them into binary relations. The *meta-object → semantic relation → meta-object* ternary relations that make up the complete version of Fig. 1 are saved in a simple CSV file. This file has as its the first column the (source) meta-object, the second the semantic relations, and third the (target) meta-object. For example, reading from top to bottom: `Data Component, implemented by, Application Function` and from bottom to top: `Application Function, implements, Data Component`.

These ternary relations are amongst the ternary relations that, when joined together, make up the complete version of Fig. 1 and, incidentally, reveal the two-way nature of the semantic relations. Each ternary relation forms a new row in the CSV file. All the ternary relations can then in turn be read by the CG-FCA software converting it to *meta-object⌒semantic relation → meta-object* binary relations. For example the ternary relation: `Data Component, implemented by, Application Function` becomes the binary: `Data Component⌒implemented by → Application Function`. The binary relations are subsequently re-joined in an FCL as illustrated in Sect. 4. From the reports generated by CG-FCA, applying CG-FCA to the meta-model allowed for identifying any bi-directional relation cycles between two related meta-objects with unwanted cycles.

3.4   More Cycles

All legitimate cycles originating in the bidirectional nature of the associations should be eliminated by separating the directed graphs into TDV and BUV. CG-FCA still however identifies the following cycles in the complete version of Fig. 1's TDV and BUV respectively:

TDV
```
Cycle: Business Service - contributes value in support of -
Mission - threatened by - Risk - mitigated by - Security -
protects - Business Service
Cycle: Business Service - contributes value in support of -
Mission - threatened by - Risk - mitigated by - Security -
protects - Location - delivers - Business Service
Cycle: Business Service - contributes value in support of -
Mission - threatened by - Risk - influences the design of -
Business Channel - serves - Business Service
```

BUV
```
Cycle: Mission - supported by - Business Service - protected by -
Security - mitigates - Risk - threatens - Mission
Cycle: Mission - supported by - Business Service - delivered at -
Location - protected by - Security - mitigates - Risk - threatens
- Mission
Cycle: Mission - supported by - Business Service - served by -
Business Channel - design influenced by - Risk - threatens -
Mission
```

At this point it is worth reiterating that putting EA meta-models together is a manual activity. The risk of the human modeller making mistakes in producing the meta-model is always present. This likelihood was demonstrated for CG-based models so could equally happen to the LEAD meta-model [3]. Recognising this possibility is one of the key motivators for using CG-FCA's automated capacities to capture manual errors in the LEAD meta-models.

The cycles above highlight this issue: The TDV and BUV semantic relations between the Mission and Risk meta-objects could be under the wrong view and simply need to be swapped over. The modeller (e.g. an Enterprise Architect or Business Analyst) could also have chosen other candidates to swap instead, such as the semantic relations between Business Service and Mission but from the feedback given by CG-FCA's report decides on Mission and Risk. In practice the modeller may want to explore the other candidates, further informed by the FCL in Sect. 4. CG-FCA and the FCL thus augments the expertise of the modeller through these subsequent iterations towards a more useful meta-model [4].

Remaining with the modeller's at least initial choice, the TDV 'threatened by' semantic relation from Mission to Risk is thus changed to a BUV, and

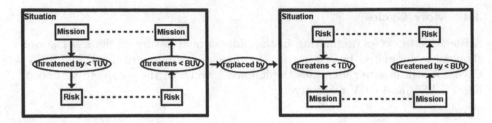

Fig. 3. CG changing the order of TDV and BUV semantic relations

the corresponding BUV 'threatens' semantic relation is changed to a TDV. Figure 3 formally describes this swap in CGs by re-depicting 'threatens' as a TDV sub-relation, 'threatened by' as a BUV sub-relation and vice versa. When CG-FCA is re-run on the corrected TDV of the meta-model and the corrected BUV of the meta-model, the cycles disappear.

Another Cycle: Well, almost. In the BUV report there were other cycles:
Cycle: Platform Device - hosts - Application Service - specializes as - Platform Service - instantiates - Platform Device
Cycle: Platform Service - hosts - Application Service - specializes as - Platform Service
    As there are no 'complementary' cycles in the TDV report that would suggest a TDV would need to be swapped with a BUV, this finding was suspect. It emerges that there was a classic human error—i.e. a typo—in the CSV file i.e.: Application Service, specializes, Platform Service. By correcting it to: Infrastructure Service, specializes as, Platform Service those remaining rogue cycles were gone. We are of the view that legitimate cycles in the meta-models though conceivable would be exceptional. They would always require special investigation rather than simply accepting them, as the later Subsect. 5.1 in Sect. 5 further highlights.

4   Visualising the Complex Pathways in the FCL

We now explore and interpret the FCL from the FCA formal context that was generated by CG-FCA as first described in Sect. 3. To do so, the FCA formal context file (.cxt) file produced by CG-FCA is read into Concept Explorer (https://sourceforge.net/projects/conexp/) from which the FCL can be generated. Figure 4 visualises the result for the TDV of the meta-model. It is one of the linear views; there is also an FCL for the BUV view going in the opposite direction but that is not shown due to space limitations in this paper. However as it is complementary to the TDV (i.e. simply going in the other direction), we can refer to the TDV FCL for demonstrating the BUV FCL as well[5].

---

[5] www.polovina.me.uk/publications/iccs2019 has the BUV FCL.

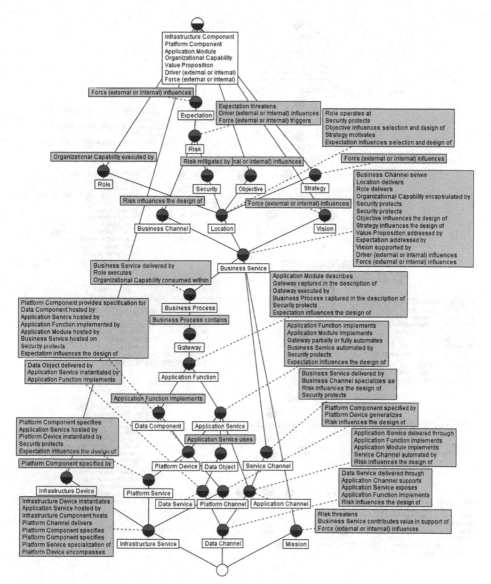

Fig. 4. TDV FCL

Figure 4 formalises the UML-based LEAD Industry 4.0 meta-model diagram (of which Fig. 1 is an extract) as a TDV lattice with one formal concept at the top, called the *top-most* concept and one formal concept as the bottom, called the *bottom-most* concept. The top-most concept has the `Infrastructure Component`, `Platform Component`, `Application Module`, `Organisational Capability`, `Value Proposition`, `Driver` and `Force` meta-objects as part of its extent.

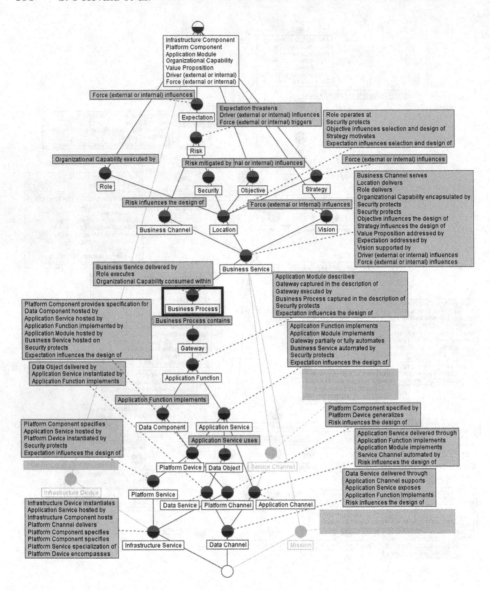

Fig. 5. TDV FCL showing extent and intent of Business Process

Traversing down the lattice, the meta-objects relative dependencies are revealed. For example, Business Process, which is highlighted in Fig. 5. All the meta-objects in the pathways *below* the formal concept for the meta-object Business Process are dependent on it. They are said to be in the *extent* of the Business Process meta-object. The bottom-most formal concept (at the very bottom of the lattice) has no meta-objects attached to it (i.e. an empty extent).

We can also refer to the *intent* of a formal concept, based on the attributes of the formal context that was set out in the definition of a formal concept at the beginning of Sect. 3 earlier. (The extent refers to the objects in that definition.) For example the intent of the `Business Process` meta-object are *all* the attributes *above* it in the lattice. Hence, the `Business Process` meta-object depends on the entire *meta-object⌒semantic relation* set of attributes above it. The dimmed component parts in Fig. 5 show those meta-objects and semantic relations that are not in the extent and intent of `Business Process`. The top-most formal concept has no attributes attached to it (i.e. an empty intent).

All in all by elucidating the pathways, intents and extents the FCL elicits information that: (a) is not evident in the UML-based meta-model diagram, (b) empowers our understanding of the meta-models and their usefulness, and (c) empowers the organisation's EA through this deeper understanding.

5 Discussion

5.1 Cycles to the Same Meta-Object

Returning to cycles, the semantic relation `'composed of or contained within'` isn't in the Industry 4.0 meta-model illustration. It does however appear in another LEAD meta-model from which this semantic relation is taken. It is explicitly referred to here as it reveals another form of cycle to which this semantic relation is applied—i.e. one than can point to the same meta-object. In fact, although they have the same meta-object name they aren't the same instance. They are *different* business processes[6]. In CGs this distinction is conveniently made. Figure 6 shows this directed ternary relation (view) in CGs, which are based on existential logic that assumes a different referent (instance) unless told otherwise [10]. In CGs to make them the same we have to express them as having the same referent—i.e. co-referent—as illustrated by the variable '*a' in Fig. 7's CG[7]. The onus is thus to override the default behaviour of CGs, thereby feeding back to us to check cycles rather than accept them at the outset.

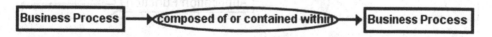

Fig. 6. CG of Business Process

---

[6] Differentiated by the names given at levels 1 to 4, akin to the example of Fig. 1.
[7] Equivalent to the dotted lines denoting co-referents in Figs. 2 and 3.

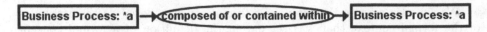

Fig. 7. CG of Business Process that is a cycle

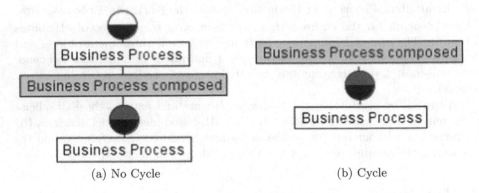

(a) No Cycle   (b) Cycle

Fig. 8. FCL for Business Process

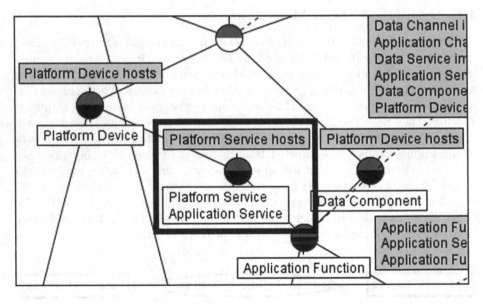

Fig. 9. CG of Business Process that is a cycle

Figure 8 highlights how Figs. 6 and 7 are thereby respectively displayed as a FCL[8]. In an FCL, the circles are the formal concepts. Notably, in the cycle FCL

---

[8] The CGs in this paper were drawn in CharGer (http://charger.sourceforge.net/) then for these Figs. converted to CGIF (Conceptual Graphs Interchange Format), which is part of the ISO/IEC 24707:2007 Common Logic Standard. The CGIF file is then read in by CG-FCA, which generates the formal context (.cxt) file that can be turned into an FCL.

it doesn't point to another formal concept—i.e. the second Business Process. Rather, CG-FCA expresses the cycle by simply denoting it in the same formal concept. (The semantic relation in the Fig. is shortened from 'composed of or contained within' to 'composed' for convenience.)

For comparison, to show cycles generally in an FCL from CG-FCA the Fig. 9 shows an extract from a larger FCL with the earlier ternary relation that was described under '**Another Cycle**' in Sect. 3.4 of Sect. 3—i.e. Application Service, specializes, Platform Service before it was corrected to: Infrastructure Service, specializes as, Platform Service. It caused Platform Service to have a cycle that, in this case, was unwanted due to it being a typo.

5.2 Related Research

Earlier we remarked on the motivation for *CGtoFCA* and CG-FCA. Interrelating CGs and FCA has been a subject of much interest e.g. [9]. *CGtoFCA* arose from Wille's (and others') long-standing work on Concept Graphs, and identifying certain shortcomings with Concept Graphs—which Wille distinguished from CG (Concept*ual* Graphs)—and how they are overcome with *CGtoFCA* [2,15]. To test its value, *CGtoFCA* was implemented in computer software i.e. CG-FCA[9] and its use and benefits published (e.g. [3,5,11]).

Similar work was also investigated. Relational Concept Analysis (RCA) explores the attributes found in three compartment UML class diagrams [13]. *CGtoFCA* however works with single component UML class diagrams where the class name (the meta-object in our case) alone is of interest. This also reflects that *CGtoFCA* is more in-keeping with Concept Graphs, from which it derives. The approach applied (in our case to cycles) in Subsect. 3.4 of Sect. 3 also touches upon similar work on ontological patterns, anti-patterns and pattern languages for conceptual modelling [7].

5.3 Future Research

In our ongoing research, we need to understand what else FCA (through CG-FCA and the FCL) may be telling us. We are in the process of streamlining the process by integrating CG-FCA and the FCL into the Enterprise Modelling tool *Enterprise Plus* (*E+*, www.enterpriseplus.tools). Whereas we only remained with the modeller's initial choices (e.g. in rectifying the unintended cycles), such a streamlined process would allow the efficient explorations of alternatives only indicated in this paper.

Another area of interest is whether the bottom-most formal concept should have its own object. In previous work, populating this formal concept with a meta-object was presented as pertinent to the validity of the meta-model [11].

---

[9] https://sourceforge.net/projects/cgfca/.

But as we are currently evaluating the validity of such a claim, that assertion is not made in this paper.

The information gathered by CG-FCA and the FCL of the meta-model complements lucidly the UML-based meta-model diagram, serving our present purposes. There may however be even more lucid ways of visualising the CG-FCA results. The validity of our approach may spur others to research such visualisations. As one alternative, we are evaluating formal concept trees [1]. Given its proximity to *CGtoFCA*, we also maintain an interest in RCA and to explore it in more depth.

As CG-FCA can be applied to any directed graph beyond the meta-models that we've described here, there is potentially a wider remit for its use in the real-world. Previously it was applied to Conceptual Graphs (CGs), and now to single compartment UML class diagrams with directed associations. RDF, RDF(S), OWL are examples of future candidates. Further research in these and other hitherto unidentified areas would be of interest. Meanwhile our work remains focussed in LEAD and the usefulness of EA meta-models for organisations and their clients, given there is more to discover in this focussed area of our research.

6   Conclusion

By applying CG-FCA to LEAD, we have shown how directed graphs can contribute to a better understanding of LEAD (and other EA) thus lead to a more meaningful EA for organisations. LEAD articulates how the classes—i.e. meta-objects—and two-way associations—i.e. semantic relations—can best be identified and related, and LEADing Practice including its association with the GUA has built a comprehensive set of reusable reference content based on it. CG-FCA thus helps to: (a) deepen our understanding of this content, (b) check human error given that meta-model development is a manual process hence inherently error prone, (c) unpick the complexity in the meta-models, and (d) relate it back to our human understanding through the FCL.

References

1. Andrews, S., Hirsch, L.: A tool for creating and visualising formal concept trees. In: CEUR Workshop Proceedings, vol. 1637, pp. 1–9 (2016)
2. Andrews, S., Polovina, S.: A mapping from conceptual graphs to formal concept analysis. In: Andrews, S., Polovina, S., Hill, R., Akhgar, B. (eds.) ICCS 2011. LNCS (LNAI), vol. 6828, pp. 63–76. Springer, Heidelberg (2011). https://doi.org/10.1007/978-3-642-22688-5_5
3. Andrews, S., Polovina, S.: Exploring, reasoning with and validating directed graphs by applying formal concept analysis to conceptual graphs. In: Croitoru, M., Marquis, P., Rudolph, S., Stapleton, G. (eds.) GKR 2017. LNCS (LNAI), vol. 10775, pp. 3–28. Springer, Cham (2018). https://doi.org/10.1007/978-3-319-78102-0_1
4. Box, G.E.P., Draper, N.R.: Empirical Model-building and Response Surfaces. Wiley, Hoboken (1987)

5. Caine, J., Polovina, S.: From enterprise concepts to formal concepts: a university case study. In: Croitoru, M., Marquis, P., Rudolph, S., Stapleton, G. (eds.) GKR 2017. LNCS (LNAI), vol. 10775, pp. 84–96. Springer, Cham (2018). https://doi.org/10.1007/978-3-319-78102-0_5
6. The Open Group. 30. Content Metamodel (2018). http://pubs.opengroup.org/architecture/togaf92-doc/arch/chap30.html
7. Guizzardi, G.: Ontological patterns, anti-patterns and pattern languages for next-generation conceptual modeling. In: Yu, E., Dobbie, G., Jarke, M., Purao, S. (eds.) ER 2014. LNCS, vol. 8824, pp. 13–27. Springer, Cham (2014). https://doi.org/10.1007/978-3-319-12206-9_2
8. Liskov, B.H., Wing, J.M.: A behavioral notion of subtyping. ACM Trans. Program. Lang. Syst. **16**(6), 1811–1841 (1994)
9. Mineau, G., Stumme, G., Wille, R.: Conceptual structures represented by conceptual graphs and formal concept analysis. In: Tepfenhart, W.M., Cyre, W. (eds.) ICCS-ConceptStruct 1999. LNCS (LNAI), vol. 1640, pp. 423–441. Springer, Heidelberg (1999). https://doi.org/10.1007/3-540-48659-3_27
10. Polovina, S.: An introduction to conceptual graphs. In: Priss, U., Polovina, S., Hill, R. (eds.) ICCS-ConceptStruct 2007. LNCS (LNAI), vol. 4604, pp. 1–14. Springer, Heidelberg (2007). https://doi.org/10.1007/978-3-540-73681-3_1
11. Polovina, S., von Rosing, M.: Using conceptual structures in enterprise architecture to develop a new way of thinking and working for organisations. In: Chapman, P., Endres, D., Pernelle, N. (eds.) ICCS 2018. LNCS (LNAI), vol. 10872, pp. 176–190. Springer, Cham (2018). https://doi.org/10.1007/978-3-319-91379-7_14
12. Priss, U.: Formal concept analysis in information science. Annu. Rev. Info. Sci. Technol. **40**(1), 521–543 (2006)
13. Rouane-Hacene, M., Huchard, M., Napoli, A., Valtchev, P.: Relational concept analysis: mining concept lattices from multi-relational data. Ann. Math. Artif. Intell. **67**, 81–108 (2013)
14. von Rosing, M., Laurier, W.: An introduction to the business ontology. Int. J. Concept. Struct. Smart Appl. (IJCSSA) **3**(1), 20–41 (2015)
15. Wille, R.: Conceptual graphs and formal concept analysis. In: Lukose, D., Delugach, H., Keeler, M., Searle, L., Sowa, J. (eds.) ICCS-ConceptStruct 1997. LNCS, vol. 1257, pp. 290–303. Springer, Heidelberg (1997). https://doi.org/10.1007/BFb0027878

Ontology-Informed Lattice Reduction Using the Discrimination Power Index

Qudamah Quboa[1(✉)], Ali Behnaz[2], Nikolay Mehandjiev[1], and Fethi Rabhi[2]

[1] Alliance Manchester Business School,
University of Manchester, Manchester, UK
{qudamah.quboa,n.mehandjiev}@manchester.ac.uk
[2] School of Computer Science and Engineering,
University of New South Wales, Sydney, Australia
{ali.behnaz,f.rabhi}@unsw.edu.au

Abstract. The increasing reliance on data for decision making has led to a number of techniques for automatic knowledge acquisition such as Formal Concept Analysis (FCA). FCA creates a lattice comprising partial order relationships between sets of object instances in a domain (extent) and their properties (intent). This is mapped onto a semantic knowledge structure comprising domain concepts with their instances and properties. However, this automatic extraction of structure from a large number of instances usually leads to a lattice which is too complex for practical use. Algorithms to reduce the lattice exist. However, these mainly rely on the lattice structure and are agnostic about any prior knowledge about the domain. In contrast, this paper uses existing domain knowledge encoded in a semantic ontology and a novel relevance index to inform the reduction process. We demonstrate the utility of the proposed approach, achieving a significant reduction of lattice nodes, even when the ontology only provides partial coverage of the domain of interest.

Keywords: FCA · Semantic structures · Lattice reduction

1 Introduction

Three main factors underpin the growth of data gathered by organizations today: the low costs of storage, the increasing role of ICT in business and the reliance on data for decision making at all organizational levels. Only a small percentage of the data gathered is ever used, though, because of the difficulties in automatically analyzing the meaning (semantics) of the data. The problem of knowledge acquisition [1] includes processing voluminous data [2], understanding its meaning and relationships [3], and then presenting the results using simplified and relevant models [4].

Manual semantic tagging of data for the purpose of knowledge acquisition is too labor intensive for practical use, and researchers are trying to automate this. One such technique is Formal Concept Analysis (FCA). FCA takes a table of incidence relations between sampled data instances and their properties, called a formal context, and constructs a lattice of partial order relationships between the instance sets and between

© Springer Nature Switzerland AG 2019
D. Endres et al. (Eds.): ICCS 2019, LNAI 11530, pp. 160–174, 2019.
https://doi.org/10.1007/978-3-030-23182-8_12

the property sets. However the lattices generated by FCA are too complex for practical semantic analysis of real-world datasets. Existing approaches to reduce these lattices are based on mathematical measurements of relevancy [4] and do not consider existing knowledge of the targeted domain, even when it is formalized and represented in a semantic structure or an ontology.

The similarities between FCA and ontology-based semantic representations have inspired a number of approaches drawing on both, such as merging different ontologies [5, 6], ontology modelling and attribute exploration [7, 8]. However, the use of existing semantic knowledge encoded as ontology to support the lattice reduction has not been explored until now. Our main research question is thus:

How can we use domain ontology to support attaching semantics to further instances in the domain through FCA?

In this paper, we present an approach which answers these questions by using prior domain knowledge (encoded in semantic ontology format) to classify and guide the reduction process of a sampled formal context where not all instances are in the ontology. The approach extracts semantic structures from the ontology, transforms them into a formal context and aligns the two formal contexts using two main activities (1) basic mapping using known instances which exist in both the ontology and the sampled formal context; and (2) advanced alignment combining similarity measurements that use both instances and properties of the sampled formal context plus the concepts added from the ontology. Finally, the proposed approach uses the ontology generated one to reduce the sampled one, resulting in a lattice output of FCA which we show to be significantly simpler than the lattice produced without the approach, and where concepts in the lattice are aligned with ontology concepts from the targeted ontology, thus classifying previously unclassified instances from the sample domain. The approach relies on a new concept relevancy metric called Discrimination Power Index (*DPI*).

The proposed approach enables the construction of intelligent analysis tools that could be integrated within information retrieval and knowledge processing systems, by addressing the problem of large lattices produced when applying FCA to real-world data. We present results from a realistic case study which confirm the feasibility and the validity of the proposed approach.

The remainder of this paper is structured as follows: Sect. 2 describes the background of the work. Sections 3 and 4 describe the proposal and define the proposed similarity and reduction indices and mechanisms. Section 5 provides a case study to evaluate the proposed approach and Sect. 6 concludes the paper.

2 Background

2.1 Formal Concept Analysis (FCA)

Formal Concept Analysis (FCA) is a mathematical mechanism to automatically analyze the structure of a target domain [2, 9] and create a lattice representing partial order relationships between sets of observed (sampled) object instances in a domain of interest and between sets of their properties constructed from a matrix of incidence relationships. The resultant lattice is used to reason with these relationships and map them onto a semantic knowledge structure representing concepts in the domain with their instances, properties and specialization relationships [2].

Definition 1 (*Formal Context*). A formal context is a triple $K := (G, M, I)$, where G and M are two sets of instances and properties respectively and I is a set of relations between instances of G and properties of M, $I \subseteq G x M$ $I \subseteq G x M$.

Definition 2 (*Formal Concept*). A formal concept is a pair (A, B), such that $A \subseteq G$, $B \subseteq M$, where $A = B'(B' = \{g \in G | \forall m \in B : (g, m) \in I\})$ $A = B'(B' = \{g \in G | \forall m \in B : (g, m) \in I\})$ and $B = A'(A' = \{m \in M | \forall g \in A : (g, m) \in I\})$.

The set of instances A represents the extension of the formal concept (extent) and the set of properties B represents the intent of the formal concept (intent).

Definition 3 (*Subconcept and Superconcept*). The partial ordering relationship ($\leq$) for context K may exist among each of the formal concepts. It is defined by a subset relation between the concepts' extents or the superset relation between the concepts' intents. That is $(A_1, B_1) \leq (A_2, B_2) \Leftrightarrow A_1 \subseteq A_2 (\Leftrightarrow B_2 \subseteq B_1)$ where the concept (A_1, B_1) is considered a more specific concept, a subconcept of (A_2, B_2), compared to (A_2, B_2), which is a superconcept of (A_1, B_1).

Definition 4 (*Concept Lattice*). A concept lattice (Λ) is the set of all formal concepts ordered by their partial ordering relationship ($\leq$) of the context K and formulated as $\Lambda = (K, \leq)$.

2.2 Semantic Web Ontology

Ontology is defined as an explicit representation of a formal conceptualization of a specific domain where the semantics of information is specified using human-readable text formulated using a machine-readable language [10, 11] such as the *Web Ontology Language* (OWL).

Domain experts have developed standardised and general-purpose ontologies to capture knowledge and share information in multiple disciplines such as the National Center for Biomedical Ontology [12], the Financial Industry Business Ontology (FIBO) [13], and the Institutional ontology [14]. Most often, domain ontologies are designed to determine a set of data and its structure for the use of other programs. Ontology can be used as a data sharing mechanism between different software agents or applications such as the use of the ontology as a data interchange format [15] and as a data integration mechanism [16].

2.3 Existing Lattice Reduction Techniques

A major issue with FCA is the large size of lattices generated from realistic data sets because of exceptions and noise [2, 17]. A number of algorithms have been developed to reduce the lattice based on the structure of the lattice itself. These are based on redundant information removal, simplification or selection [4].

Redundant information removal techniques aim to remove instances and/or properties without affecting the general lattice structure. Examples include incomplete decision contexts reduction [18] and attribute reduction by deletion transformations [19].

Simplification reduction is any technique that focuses on creating a high-level abstraction of the formal concept lattice, which only keeps the main key aspects. Examples are "junction based on instances similarity" (JBOS) reduction [20], and Fuzzy K-Means clustering reduction [21].

Selection reduction represents any technique that focuses on choosing specific instances, properties and/or concepts according to their relevancy measurements (a set of constraints that needs to be satisfied). Selection reduction can be based on different factors, such as weight (frequent weighted concept reduction [22]), logic (based on user's attributes priorities [23]), or hierarchies (based on hierarchically ordered attributes [24]). This type of reduction is applied after the construction of the formal context has been completed [4].

All these techniques share a common shortfall by failing to consider existing domain knowledge, making the results more vulnerable to systemic noise in the data.

2.4 Integrating FCA and Ontologies

The definitions of FCA and ontology-based domain modelling may create a wrong impression that both approaches are similar, whereas the FCA approach is quite different from the ontology approach in terms of core perspectives and language representations. Indeed, FCA follows an "inductive" approach, which is focused on constructing concepts from individuals (extensional description of the domain), and represents intents and extents by atomic level of representation. Ontologies follow the opposite "deductive" approach, which is focused on inferring and reasoning relations between concepts starting from the concepts themselves (intensional definition of concepts), and representing them using a richer expression representation language [3, 25]. Therefore, Ontologies and FCA could complement each other allowing better understanding of, and dealing with the complexity of data and knowledge [3].

This complementarity has motivated research proposals for integrating these techniques. An example is the use of FCA to merge different ontologies based on a bottom-up approach with the help of natural language processing (NLP) and selective documents from the domain of interest [5, 6]. Another example is the use of an FCA approach in ontology modelling and the exploration of properties to discover implications over the target context [7, 8]. Yet, none of the proposed approaches uses domain knowledge (represented in a semantic ontology) in the reduction process of the FCA.

2.5 Similarity Measurements

We use three similarity measurements to align the two different formal contexts (ontology-derived and sampled) and integrate them. The first two are well-known:

Jaccard Similarity Coefficient Index. This well-known similarity measurement [26] is based on the following formula:

$$S_{Jac} = \frac{|B_1 \cap B_2|}{|B_1 \cup B_2|} \tag{1}$$

The Jaccard index of any two instances is the ratio of the number of common properties divided by the number of all properties that belong to at least one instance.

Hamming Distance Index. This is also a well-known similarity measurement [27] and is based on the following formula:

$$D_{hamming} = b + c \tag{2}$$

where b represents the number of properties that do not belong to the concept 1 but exist in the concept 2, while c represents the number of properties that belong to the concept 1 and do not exist in the concept 2.

Both indices treat all properties as of equal importance whilst our observations demonstrate that some properties have a higher discriminatory power than others. We thus introduce a new complementary index called Discrimination Power Index (*DPI*), described below.

3 Ontology-Informed Lattice Reduction Approach

Our approach uses existing knowledge about the domain to simplify the lattice Λ when extracting structure from sampled data represented in a formal context K. We assume that the existing knowledge is in the ontology Ω and is encoded in OWL.

The proposed approach for the FCA reduction could be divided into four main steps (shown in Fig. 1): (a) *Data Extraction:* extracting relevant portion from the ontology-based knowledge base; (b) *Data Transformation:* transforming the ontology data and structure into a formal context format; (c) *Data Alignment:* aligning it with the sampled formal context; and (d) *Data Reduction:* reducing the unnecessary complexity of the formal context through the ontology concepts using a combination of measurements that allows a simplified and more stable FCA lattice to be produced.

During the initial processing steps (a) and (b) of the proposed approach, data from the semantic ontology source is extracted (using SPARQL queries) and transformed into an acceptable formal context format (matrix of incidence). This creates the baseline for the integration between the ontology data and the targeted FCA lattice. It allows the alignment to be carried out as well as the enrichment of the targeted FCA lattice with high-level structural concepts (from the ontology).

The Data Alignment step (c) starts by basic mapping - identifying the set of instances G that exist in both Ω and in K, using them to identify and mark their

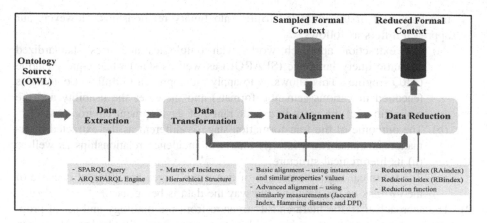

Fig. 1. The general outline of the ontology-informed lattice reduction approach.

corresponding ontology concepts from Ω in K, adding the properties from these ontology concepts to G, thus extending the current K into K_e. The approach then automatically associates the remaining instances $G_R = G \backslash G$ that exist only in K to ontology concepts from K_e using:

(1) The properties they have in common with the shared instances G using the Jaccard Similarity index and Hamming Distance index (see Sect. 2.5), and
(2) The discrimination power of their properties using *DPI* (see Sect. 4.1).

The approach is thus an example of the selection reduction techniques according to Dias and Vieira [4].

This is followed by step (d) where K_e is reduced using two reduction measurements (*RAindex* and *RBindex*) with their evaluation functions and the reduction function (see Sect. 4.2). *RAindex* aims to keep any property that is essential to a specific ontology concept from the used ontology and flag any property that has an uncertainty in the decision. *RBindex* is a complementary measurement to ensure the right reduction decision is applied for the properties flagged as uncertain by *RAindex*. Finally, reduction function is applied to the flagged incidence relationships (resulted from applying *RAindex* and *RBindex*).

The resultant formal context K_R has three notable features:

• It is smaller than the original context and has a simpler lattice.
• It depends on the existing domain knowledge as captured in the ontology Ω. This is unique amongst the existing alternative reduction approaches.
• The reduced lattice Λ is similar to, but not identical to the structure of the ontology Ω due to the existence of extra properties and instances.

It is worth mentioning that

(1) The idea behind the Data Extraction and the Data Transformation are indeed similar to the work presented by Andrews and Polovina [28] specifically in the

transformation of the extracted triples into binary relationships. However, our approach differs as follows:

(a) Our extraction approach works with ontologies and uses standardized semantic query language (SPARQL) as well as standardized query engine (ARQ Engine). This allows us to apply the approach to different ontologies (encoded in various semantic formats) and increases the usability and the replications of the work in a wide range of development environments.

(b) The outcome of the transformation stage is different as the extracted information is transformed into (i) matrix of incidence relationships as well as (ii) its hierarchical structure.

(c) The technical implementations of those two stages are different because of the formats of the data and the way the data is being used.

(2) The approach uses the hierarchical structure from the ontology and set of properties and incidence relationships' values to align and simplify the formal context. This is specifically applied to all the proposed measurements of the approach (*DPI*, *RAindex* and *RBindex*).

4   Formal Description of Data Alignment and Reduction

4.1   Data Alignment

To assign an instance from the sampled formal context to one of the existing ontology concepts, a combination of different similarity indices is used to evaluate and align concepts from both contexts based on their intents and extents. In this step, a Jaccard similarity coefficient index is first used. If this fails to produce a single "best match", the Hamming distance is used, and if that is still inconclusive with several candidate concepts for best match, we use our proposed index *DPI*.

DPI is thus a complementary metric. It selects one of the candidate ontology concepts based on the discrimination power of their properties. The fewer the instances that share a certain property, the higher the discrimination power of this property:

$$DPI = \frac{|\{\forall g \in G | b \in B_1 \cap B_2 : (g, b) \in I\}|}{|G|} \tag{3}$$

In this equation, B_1 is the set of properties of the evaluated unclassified instance, and B_2 is the set of properties filtered by previous similarity indices for the same instance (defining the intent of candidate ontology concepts). *DPI* then is the ratio of the number of all instances that have incidence relationships with both B_1 and B_2 and the complete set of instances. This index relies on the sampled formal context K (using both G and M) to avoid misclassifying or choosing the wrong ontology concept during the transform and align steps of the approach in an attempt to consider the big picture during the calculation.

The assessment of different instances during the alignment process is always comparing any unknown instance with already assigned instances (aligned with the concepts from the used ontology) and this applies to all the used indices in this step. The result of this step is an extended formal context incorporating both the sampled data and the data extracted from the knowledge base.

4.2 Data Reduction

During this step, the extended formal context $(K_{new}: = (G_{new}, M_{new}, I_{new}))$, which results from the alignment process above, is passed to the reduction process where two indices are applied before applying the reduction function. These indices identify the noise and the complexity that can be removed without affecting the stability of the sampled formal context by utilizing the knowledge from the hierarchical structure of the ontology and the formal context derived from it. The ontology guides the reduction procedure and works as a reference point at all times.

The first index (*RAindex*): this is proposed to evaluate the value of each property regarding each one of the concepts from the domain ontology. This is to provide an indication whether a property is essential to a specific concept from the ontology or if there is an uncertainty in the decision.

To do that, we scan every property from the extended formal context to check (1) whether all its instances have the evaluated classification concept from the ontology (meaning it is essential) or (2) whether none of its instances have the evaluated classification ontology concept (meaning it can be removed). This process is applied for each one of the ontology concepts and is formally represented as follows:

$$RAindex = \frac{|\{\forall g \in G_{new} | \exists m \in M_{new} \cap M \wedge c \in M_{new} \cap M_{Ontology} : (g,m) \in I_{new} \cap (g,c) \in I_{new}\}|}{|\{\forall g \in G_{new} | \exists m \in M_{new} \cap M : (g,m) \in I_{new}\}|}$$

(4)

$$f(RAindex) = \begin{cases} Stop & if(RAindex) = 0\, or\, 1 \\ RBindex & otherwise \end{cases}$$

(5)

Equation (4) takes the number of all instances that have incidence relationships with both the target concept (the evaluated classification concept from the ontology) and a property that exists in both the initial formal context and the new extended formal context. This is divided by the number of the instances that have an incidence relation with the current evaluated property (regardless of their classification concepts from the ontology). The calculation of *RAindex* starts from the most abstracted concept of the ontology (the top level of the extracted hierarchical structure of the used ontology) to the most specialized concepts (the bottom level of the hierarchical structure).

Then the ratio of these two parts (*RAindex*) is evaluated based on its value (5). If the *RAindex* value is 1, this means the evaluated property is a key property of the ontology concept or if the value is 0 then there are no incidence relationships connecting the evaluated property and the ontology concept. In both cases, there is no need for any reduction to apply. Otherwise, the second reduction index (*RBindex*) is applied to make the right judgment.

The second reduction index (*RBindex*). This is a complementary index to ensure that the right action is applied, which allows the reduction process to be completed. It provides an indication where the reduction is necessary by flagging both the property and the ontology's concept that needs the reduction. This is based on a specific reduction percentage (provided by the user of the system).

To do so, we evaluate the instances of the selected property (received from *RAindex*) that share the targeted concept from the ontology with all the instances of the same ontology concept and check whether the ratio passes the reduction threshold or not. If the case is the latter, then this is finished by flagging the unnecessary incidence relationships within the selected property (which will be removed without damaging the stability of the formal context). This is formally defined as follows:

$$RBindex = \frac{|\{\forall g \in G_{new} | \exists m \in M_{new} \cap M \bigwedge c \in M_{new} \cap M_{Ontology} : (g,m) \in I_{new} \cap (g,c) \in I_{new}\}|}{|\{\forall g \in G_{new} | c \in M_{new} \cap M_{Ontology} : (g,c) \in I_{new}\}|}. \tag{6}$$

$$f(RBindex) = \begin{cases} Trim(m,c) & if(RBindex) < ReductionPercentage \\ Stop & otherwise \end{cases}. \tag{7}$$

Equation 6 presents the second reduction index as the ratio of the dividend part of (4) (the same translation provided in *RAindex* section) and the total number of instances which have incidence relationships with the evaluated ontology's concept (regardless of their evaluated property from the formal context). If the ratio of the index (7) is over the reduction threshold then the evaluated property is an important property and should not be reduced. Otherwise, this indicates that the evaluated property related to the current ontology concept can be removed.

Based on the results of both *RAindex* and *RBindex*, the reduction function is applied when needed. Its function is to remove the incidence relationships between the instances and the evaluated property related to the used ontology concept. This is done by scanning the extended formal context for any flagged incident relationship (resulted from *RAindex* and *RBindex*) and removing them from there. The formula of this function is as follows:

$$Reduction(m,c) = \forall g \in G_{new} | m \in M_{new} \cap M \bigwedge c \in M_{new} \cap$$
$$M_{Ontology} \bigwedge (g,m) \in I_{new} \bigwedge (g,c) \in I_{new} \Rightarrow (g,m) = 0 \tag{8}$$

It is worth mentioning that (1) the sequence of selecting the ontology's concepts to apply the reduction indices is based on the level of the concepts in the original ontology. The reduction procedure is starting from level 0 which is the most general ontology concept, moving down level by level towards the most specific ontology concepts. (2) Both indices are relying on the intents and extents of the new formal context, the ontology structure and incidence relationships to apply the right reduction at right places and avoid causing instability in the evaluated context. (3) The reduction is not a blind reduction and provides enough precautions and considerations before removing any incidence relationships between the evaluated property and its instances that could cause instability to the whole process. (4) The result is resistant to wide-spread (systematic) noise as reduction indices rely on existing domain ontology to guide the reduction.

5 Applying the Approach to Machine Learning Ontology and Formal Context

This section tests the effectiveness of the approach by applying it to a case study of machine learning. Indeed, machine learning and predictive analytics techniques have become increasingly popular with the proliferation of data, enabling value to be extracted from data which is too plentiful for human analysis.

Designing and implementing a predictive analytics study is a complex process requiring business understanding, data understanding, data preparation, modelling, evaluation and deployment [29]. Modelling focuses on selecting the appropriate machine learning technique and adjusting parameters to generate correct results. The decision to use a specific technique is driven by the characteristics of the data and the objectives of the study. However, even an experienced data scientist can lack the holistic knowledge about all possible modelling techniques, and no single modelling technique has absolute merit over others [30].

In this case study, we use semantic technology to capture and represent the knowledge related to machine learning techniques [31, 32] to support model selection. The knowledge is extracted and represented in an ontology covering a set of popular machine learning techniques, built into Microsoft Azure Machine Learning. This is an integrated analytics solution which enables a data scientist to select and deploy machine learning techniques on the cloud [33]. We have adopted the selection logic suggested by Azure Machine Learning to determine the appropriate machine learning techniques for different situations, and to construct our ontology (see Fig. 2).

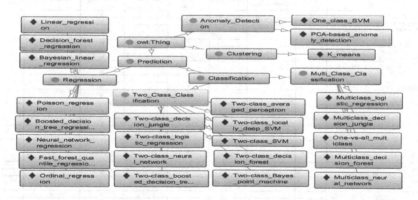

Fig. 2. The machine learning techniques ontology (adapted from [33]).

To illustrate the workings of the approach given the space constraints of this paper, we first use a simplified set of sampled data as in the formal context presented in Table 1. We then apply the proposed approach. Figure 3 shows the lattice of the extended formal context resulting from aligning the ontology with the sampled data (Data Alignment step). Then Fig. 4 shows the reduced lattice based on the reduced formal context (Data reduction step).

Some properties in Table 1 such as 'Fast training time' and 'Unsupervised learning' are evidently not essential for the majority of the techniques. Our approach has detected that and applied the reduction process to these properties. Other properties, such as 'Find unusual occurrences' and 'Discover structure' are not popular in the formal context (only appear in a couple of techniques), but are important for differentiating their instances, as they refer to two main machine learning categories: anomaly detection and clustering respectively (see Fig. 4), and should not be reduced (and the system has identified that).

In the smaller example from the first phase, the calculated similarity is 100%. This is a very good indication as it reflects how the properties of the resultant lattice are related to the concepts from the ontology. When we apply the same calculation to the larger dataset in the second phase, the similarity is some 85%. This is expected since many properties and instances of the sampled formal context are not found in the ontology.

Furthermore, the pre-reduction lattice has 18 unique nodes of which only 10 are left after applying the reduction approach, a reduction of 44.44%. This result is with an *RBindex* threshold of 40%. Different thresholds were tested, for example at 30% the reduction was 16.66%, while increasing the threshold above 40% did not achieve significant improvement of the reduction effect so 40% seems optimal here.

Table 1. The machine learning techniques formal context (adapted from [33]).

	Predict values	Find unusual occurrences	Discover structure	Predict between two categories	Predict between several categories	Supervised learning	Unsupervised learning	Fast training time
Ordinal_regression	X					X		
Poisson_regression	X					X		
Fast_forest_quantile_regression	X					X		
Linear_regression	X					X		X
Bayesian_linear_regression	X					X		
Neural_network_regression	X					X	X	
Decision_forest_regression	X					X		X
One_class_SVM		X				X		
K_means			X				X	
Two-class_SVM				X		X		
Two-class_averaged_perceptron				X		X		
Two-class_Bayes_point_machine				X		X		
Two-class_decision_forest				X		X		X
Two-class_logistic_regression				X		X		X
Two-class_boosted_decision_tree				X		X		X
Two-class_decision_jungle				X		X		
Two-class_neural_network				X		X	X	
Multiclass_logistic_regression					X	X		X
Multiclass_neural_network					X	X	X	
Multiclass_decision_jungle					X	X		
One-vs-all_multiclass					X	X		
Boosted_decision_tree_regression	X					X		X
PCA-based_anomaly_detection		X				X		X
Two-class_locally_deep_SVM				X		X		
Multiclass_decision_forest					X	X		X

As a second phase of validation, we run the approach using a bigger sampled dataset of 207 unique nodes and 95 instances against the same ontology. The application of the proposed approach achieves a maximum reduction of 70% lattice nodes, when *RBindex* threshold is 40%. It is worth noting that the threshold is not the only reduction factor since *RBindex* will only be used when the first proposed reduction index (*RAindex*) cannot produce an unequivocal decision.

As we are simplifying the lattice, part of the information is lost during the reduction stage. A very small dataset is more prone to lose crucial information yet this risk is reduced for realistic datasets with bigger sizes.

In this specific case, the sampled dataset did not have enough support to keep the general ontology concept ("prediction") in its position during the reduction process which caused the movement of this general concept to represent a more specialised concept in the resulted lattice ("Regression"/"Predict Values") (shown in Fig. 4). However, when we did the same experiment using a larger sampled dataset, the same ontology concept kept in its position representing the general high-level ontology concept (even with a 90% reduction threshold).

As the ontology is manually created to capture knowledge about the domain whilst the sampled context is generated from real data that likely contains a wider range of properties and instances, the simplified lattice produced by our approach is expected to be similar but not necessarily identical to the domain ontology. One measure of the quality of the approach then would be to measure similarity - the percentage of the

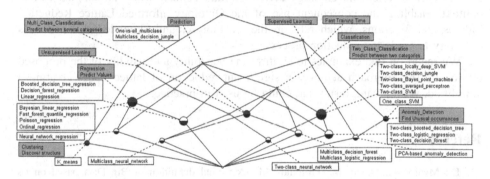

Fig. 3. The visualization of the extended FCA lattice resulted from the data alignment step.

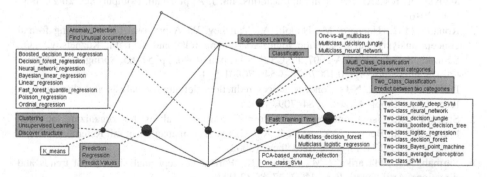

Fig. 4. The machine learning techniques lattice after applying the proposed approach (*RBindex* threshold of 40%).

concepts from the ontology which appear in the final lattice. We would only consider ontology concepts which have instances represented in the formal context because the ontology could be much larger than the domain represented in the formal context.

6 Conclusion

The proliferation of data and its importance for decision-making motivates the development of automatic ways of extracting information about relationships between data instances. Using Formal concept analysis (FCA) to achieve this does not yield simple enough lattices and requires a reduction step to generate structures which are simple to understand whilst preserving key information about the domain. Existing reduction algorithms are agnostic about any existing domain knowledge and this creates an opportunity to develop a new approach, which relies on the use of an existing domain knowledge encoded in a semantic ontology to inform the process of reducing the formal context and remove noisy data. Such an approach can enable the automatic processing of large data sets and thus support the construction of intelligent information systems. Our contribution to knowledge comprises an overall approach for ontology-driven lattice reduction and a novel index called the Discrimination Power Index (*DPI*). *DPI* is used to align the ontology-derived formal context with the sampled formal context, enabling the consequent use of the Ontology-informed Lattice Reduction indices and functions, which rely on the existing semantic knowledge encoded as ontology to guide the reduction process.

We report on two examples to confirm the feasibility and validity of the proposed approach. The approach achieves a significant reduction of lattice nodes creating a simplified, yet relevant, result that could be used in practice.

References

1. De Mauro, A., Greco, M., Grimaldi, M.: A formal definition of Big Data based on its essential features. Libr. Rev. **65**(3), 122–135 (2016)
2. Singh, P.K., Aswani Kumar, C., Gani, A.: A comprehensive survey on formal concept analysis, its research trends and applications. Int. J. Appl. Math. Comput. Sci. **26**(2), 495–516 (2016)
3. Rouane, M.H., Huchard, M., Napoli, A., Valtchev, P.: A proposal for combining formal concept analysis and description logics for mining relational data. In: Kuznetsov, S.O., Schmidt, S. (eds.) ICFCA 2007. LNCS (LNAI), vol. 4390, pp. 51–65. Springer, Heidelberg (2007). https://doi.org/10.1007/978-3-540-70901-5_4
4. Dias, S.M., Vieira, N.J.: Concept lattices reduction: definition, analysis and classification. Expert Syst. Appl. **42**(20), 7084–7097 (2015)
5. Stumme, G.: Using ontologies and formal concept analysis for organizing business knowledge. In: Becker, J., Knackstedt, R. (eds.) Wissensmanagement mit Referenzmodellen 2002, pp. 163–174. Physica, Heidelberg (2002)
6. Sarmah, A.K., Hazarika, S.M., Sinha, S.K.: Formal concept analysis: current trends and directions. Artif. Intell. Rev. **44**(1), 47–86 (2015)

7. Ignatov, D.I.: Introduction to formal concept analysis and its applications in information retrieval and related fields. In: Braslavski, P., Karpov, N., Worring, M., Volkovich, Y., Ignatov, D. (eds.) Information Retrieval, vol. 505, pp. 42–141. Springer, Cham (2014)
8. Baader, F., Ganter, B., Sertkaya, B., Sattler, U.: Completing description logic knowledge bases using formal concept analysis. In: Proceedings of the 20th International Joint Conference on Artificial Intelligence (IJCAI), pp. 230–235, Hyderabad, India (2007)
9. Ganter, B., Wille, R.: Formal Concept Analysis. Springer, Heidelberg (1999). https://doi.org/10.1007/978-3-642-59830-2
10. Gruber, T.R.: A translation approach to portable ontology specification. Knowl. Acquisition 5, 199–220 (1993)
11. Lecue, F., Mehandjiev, N.: Seeking quality of web service composition in a semantic dimension. IEEE Trans. Knowl. Data Eng. 23(6), 942–959 (2011)
12. Musen, M.A., et al.: The national center for biomedical ontology. J. American Medical Informatics Association 19(2), 190–195 (2011)
13. Bennett, M.: The financial industry business ontology: Best practice for big data. Journal of Banking Regulation 14(3–4), 255–268 (2013)
14. Eriksson, O., Johannesson, P., Bergholtz, M.: Institutional ontology for conceptual modeling. J. Inf. Technol. 33(2), 105–123 (2018)
15. Shah, T., Rabhi, F., Ray, P.: Investigating an ontology-based approach for Big Data analysis of inter-dependent medical and oral health conditions. Cluster Comput. 18(1), 351–367 (2015)
16. De Giacomo, G., Lembo, D., Lenzerini, M., Poggi, A., Rosati, R.: Using ontologies for semantic data integration. In: Flesca, S., Greco, S., Masciari, E., Saccà, D. (eds.) A Comprehensive Guide Through the Italian Database Research Over the Last 25 Years. SBD, vol. 31, pp. 187–202. Springer, Cham (2018). https://doi.org/10.1007/978-3-319-61893-7_11
17. Singh, P.K., Kumar, C.A.: Concept lattice reduction using different subset of attributes as information granules. Granular Comput. 2(3), 159–173 (2017)
18. Li, J., Mei, C., Lv, Y.: Incomplete decision contexts: approximate concept construction, rule acquisition and knowledge reduction. Int. J. Approximate Reasoning 54(1), 149–165 (2013)
19. Wang, X., Zhang, W.: Attribute reduction in concept lattices based on deletion transformations. In: 6th International Conference on Natural Computation (ICNC), pp. 2065–2069. IEEE, Yantai (2010)
20. Dias, S.M., Vieira, N.J.: Applying the JBOS reduction method for relevant knowledge extraction. Expert Syst. Appl. 40(5), 1880–1887 (2013)
21. Kumar, C.A.: Fuzzy clustering-based formal concept analysis for association rules mining. Appl. Artif. Intell. 26(3), 274–301 (2012)
22. Zhang, S., Guo, P., Zhang, J., Wang, X., Pedrycz, W.: A completeness analysis of frequent weighted concept lattices and their algebraic properties. Data Knowl. Eng. 81, 104–117 (2012)
23. Belohlavek, R., Vychodil, V.: Formal concept analysis with background knowledge: attribute priorities. IEEE Trans. Syst. Man Cybern. Part C (Appl. Rev.) 39(4), 399–409 (2009)
24. Bělohlávek, R., Sklenář, V., Zacpal, J.: Formal concept analysis with hierarchically ordered attributes. Int. J. Gen Syst 33(4), 383–394 (2004)
25. Sertkaya, B.: A survey on how description logic ontologies benefit from formal concept analysis. In: Proceedings of the 7th International Conference on Concept Lattices and Their Applications, (CLA 2010), pp. 2–21, Sevilla, Spain (2010)

26. Domenach, F., Portides, G.: Similarity measures on concept lattices. In: Wilhelm, Adalbert F.X., Kestler, Hans A. (eds.) Analysis of Large and Complex Data. SCDAKO, pp. 159–169. Springer, Cham (2016). https://doi.org/10.1007/978-3-319-25226-1_14

27. Choi, S.S., Cha, S.H., Tappert, C.C.: A survey of binary similarity and distance measures. J. Syst. Cybernet. Inf. **8**(1), 43–48 (2010)

28. Andrews, S., Polovina, S.: Exploring, reasoning with and validating directed graphs by applying formal concept analysis to conceptual graphs. In: Croitoru, M., Marquis, P., Rudolph, S., Stapleton, G. (eds.) GKR 2017. LNCS (LNAI), vol. 10775, pp. 3–28. Springer, Cham (2018). https://doi.org/10.1007/978-3-319-78102-0_1

29. Wirth, R. Hipp, J.: CRISP-DM: Towards a standard process model for data mining. In: Proceedings of the 4th International Conference on the Practical Applications of Knowledge Discovery and Data Mining, Manchester, UK, pp. 29–39 (2000)

30. Wolpert, D.H.: The supervised learning no-free-lunch theorems. In: Roy, R., Köppen, M., Ovaska, S., Furuhashi, T., Hoffmann, F. (eds.) Soft Computing and Industry, pp. 25–42. Springer, London (2002). https://doi.org/10.1007/978-1-4471-0123-9_3

31. Nural, M.V., Cotterell, M.E., Miller, J.A.: Using semantics in predictive big data analytics. In: IEEE International Congress on Big Data (BigData Congress), pp. 254–261. IEEE, New York (2015)

32. Lin, M.S., Zhang, H., Yu, Z.G.: An ontology for supporting data mining process. In: IMACS Multi-Conference on Computational Engineering in Systems Applications, pp. 2074–2077. IEEE, Beijing (2006)

33. Azure Machine Learning. https://docs.microsoft.com/en-us/azure/machine-learning/studio/algorithm-choice

Redescription Mining for Learning Definitions and Disjointness Axioms in Linked Open Data

Justine Reynaud[(⊠)], Yannick Toussaint, and Amedeo Napoli

Université de Lorraine, CNRS, Inria, LORIA, 54000 Nancy, France
{justine.reynaud,yannick.toussaint,amedeo.napoli}@loria.fr

Abstract. In this article, we present an original use of Redescription Mining (RM) for discovering definitions of classes and incompatibility (disjointness) axioms between classes of individuals in the web of data. RM is aimed at mining alternate descriptions from two datasets related to the same set of individuals. We reuse this process for providing definitions in terms of necessary and sufficient conditions to categories in DBpedia. Firstly, we recall the basics of redescription mining and make precise the principles of our definitional process. Then we detail experiments carried out on datasets extracted from DBpedia. Based on the output of the experiments, we discuss the strengths and the possible extensions of our approach.

Keywords: Redescription mining · Linked Open Data ·
Definition of categories · Disjointness axioms ·
Formal Concept Analysis

1 Introduction

The Linked Open Data (LOD) cloud has become a very large reservoir of data over the last fifteen years. This data cloud is based on elementary triples (subject, predicate, object), denoted by $\langle s, p, o \rangle$, where s, p and o denote resources. These triples can be related to form a (huge) directed graph $G = (V, E)$ where vertices in V correspond to resources –or individuals–, and edges in E correspond to relations or predicate linking resources. Besides the graph structure, individuals can be grouped using the Resource Description Framework (RDF) thanks to the special predicate rdf:type in a class, and then individuals are "instances" of this class. In turn, using RDF Schema (RDFS), the set of classes can be organized within a poset thanks to the partial ordering rdfs:subClassOf.

A class can be defined through an *extension* by enumeration of all individuals composing this extension. For example, the extension of the Smartphone class would include the set of all "known" smartphones in a given universe.

Supported by "Région Lorraine" and "Délégation Générale de l'Armement".

© Springer Nature Switzerland AG 2019
D. Endres et al. (Eds.): ICCS 2019, LNAI 11530, pp. 175–189, 2019.
https://doi.org/10.1007/978-3-030-23182-8_13

Dually, a class may also be defined through an *intension* by enumeration of all characteristics common to individuals in the class. For example, the intension of the `Smartphone` class could be described as "a small computer equipped with a cellular antenna".

A standard classification problem is to provide a suitable definition to a class of individuals, i.e. a description based on a set of characteristics which are common to all individuals. This problem arises whenever there is a need for building classes for an ontology or a knowledge base related to a particular domain. Actually, such a classification process is related to clustering and to concept lattices in Formal Concept Analysis (FCA [8]).

Going back to the LOD cloud, there are classes defined by an extension but usually without any corresponding intension. More concretely, we may consider individuals as subjects s whose description is composed of the set of available pairs (p, o). A direct application of this classification problem is the mining of definitions of DBpedia categories, in the line of the work in [1]. Actually, DBpedia categories are automatically extracted from Wikipedia. In Wikipedia, a category is a specific page which lists all the pages related to itself, as is the case for example for the page `Category:Smartphones`[1]. In DBpedia, a category is a resource appearing in the range of the predicate `dct:subject`, thanks to the Dublin Core Metadata terms (DCT). Moreover, categories are widespread as there are more than one million of categories but, most of the time, a category does not have any "processable" description and there does not exist any ordering or structure among categories.

Accordingly, we can formulate our classification problem as follows: given a class defined by a set of instances, is it possible to find a corresponding definition in terms of a description made of set of characteristics or properties related to all these instances. Then, the class could be defined in terms of necessary and sufficient conditions for an individual to be a member of the class. The necessary condition means that all instances share the characteristics of the description while the sufficient condition means that any individual having those characteristics should be an instance of the class. In this work, we aim at defining the classes in two complementary ways: (i) by building a description shared by all the instances of a given class, (ii) by finding potential incompatible classes, i.e. classes which do not share any instance.

Actually, the present work is a continuation of a work initiated in [1] and in [12]. In [1], authors rely on FCA [8] and implication between concepts for discovering definitions in LOD. These definitions are based on pairs of implications, i.e. $C \implies D$ and $D \implies C$, which stand for necessary and sufficient conditions. A double implication is considered as a definition $C \equiv D$, but most of the time $C \implies D$ is an implication (i.e. the confidence is 1) while $D \longrightarrow C$ is an association rule whose confidence is less than 1, meaning that the data at hand are incomplete but that the definition is plausible. In [12], we ran a preliminary comparison between several approaches for mining definitions in LOD, based on FCA, redescription mining and translation rule mining.

---

[1] https://en.wikipedia.org/wiki/Category:SmartPhones.

In the present paper, we focus on Redescription Mining (RM) [5,6]. RM aims at discovering alternate characterizations of a set of individuals from two sets of characteristics. The characterizations can be expressed thanks to Boolean connectors within propositional logic formulas. Thus, it appears that RM is a valuable and challenging candidate approach for discovering definitions in LOD. This research work is original and one of the first attempts to reuse redescription mining for mining definitions in LOD. Moreover, the fact that negation can be taken into account allows us to extend the FCA-based approach and to mine not only definitions but also disjointness axioms, as we have in a notation borrowed from Description Logics[2] [2]: $C \equiv D \Longleftrightarrow C \sqsubseteq D$ and $D \sqsubseteq C$ and $C \sqcap D \equiv \bot \Longleftrightarrow C \sqsubseteq \neg D$ or $D \sqsubseteq \neg C$. This approach was applied on various datasets from DBpedia [10] running the so-called ReReMi algorithm [5], and has shown a very good practical behavior.

The paper is organized as follows. Section 2 presents the problem statement while Redescription Mining is introduced in Sect. 3. Section 4 is related to experiments which are conducted to evaluate the approach, and a discussion on the quality of the results and the possible improvements. Finally, Sect. 5 includes related work preceding Sect. 6 with future work and conclusions.

2 Problem Statement in FCA

2.1 Basics of FCA and Implications

Formal Concept Analysis (FCA) is a mathematical framework mainly used for classification and knowledge discovery [8]. FCA starts with a formal context (G, M, I) where G is a set of objects, M a set of attributes, and $I \subseteq G \times M$ a binary relation, with gIm meaning that object g has attribute m. Two dual derivation operators, denoted by $'$, are defined as follows:

$$A' = \{m \in M / \forall g \in A, gIm\} \text{ for } A \subseteq G \text{ and}$$
$$B' = \{g \in G / \forall m \in B, gIm\} \text{ for } B \subseteq M$$

The two compositions of the both derivation operators, denoted by $''$, are closure operators. In particular, for $A \subseteq G$ and $B \subseteq M$, we have $A \subseteq A''$ and $B \subseteq B''$. Then A and B are closed sets when $A = A''$ and $B = B''$ respectively. Moreover, a pair (A, B) is a "concept" whenever $A' = B$ and $B' = A$, where A is closed and called the "extent" of (A, B), and B is closed and is called the intent of (A, B). The set of concepts is organized within a "concept lattice" thanks to the partial ordering defined by $(A_1, B_1) \leq (A_2, B_2)$ when $A_1 \subseteq A_2$ or dually $B_2 \subseteq B_1$.

Two types of rules can be extracted from concepts, namely "association rules" and "implications". An implication $B_1 \Longrightarrow B_2$ states that all objects having all attributes in B_1 have all attributes in B_2, i.e. $B_1' \subseteq B_2'$. The implication $B_1 \Longrightarrow B_2$ has a *support* defined as the cardinality of the set $B_1' \cap B_2'/G$, and a

---

[2] We adopt this formalism for the readers of this paper. Finding the good representation of the rules for domain experts is out of the scope of this paper.

confidence defined as the cardinality of the set $B_1' \cap B_2'/B_1'$. The confidence can be interpreted as a conditional probability:

$$\text{support}(B_1 \Longrightarrow B_2) = \frac{|B_1' \cap B_2'|}{|G|} \quad \text{and} \quad \text{conf}(B_1 \Longrightarrow B_2) = \frac{|B_1' \cap B_2'|}{|B_2'|}.$$

The confidence is used for measuring the quality of a rule. The confidence of an implication is always 1, and which is not the case for an "association rule" $B_1 \longrightarrow B_2$. Then, an association rule is "valid" if its confidence is above a given threshold θ.

Finally, if both $B_1 \Longrightarrow B_2$ and $B_2 \Longrightarrow B_1$, then the definition $B_1 \equiv B_2$ or $B_1' = B_2'$ can be inferred.

2.2 Defining Categories in DBpedia

The content of *DBpedia* is built with information extracted from *Wikipedia*, an online encyclopedia. In *Wikipedia*, a category say X is a specific kind of Wikipedia page listing all pages related to X (see page `Category:Smartphones`[3] for example). In *DBpedia*, a category appears in RDF triples in the range of the relation `dct:subject`. For example, the triple $\langle$x, dct : subject, Smartphones$\rangle$ states that the x subject belongs to the `Smartphones` "category".

Moreover, speaking in terms of knowledge representation and reasoning, the name of a category is a purely syntactic expression, and thus a category does not have any formal definition as one could expect (see discussion in [1] on this aspect). Then it is impossible to perform any classification within the set of categories as the latter are not defined in terms of necessary and sufficient conditions. This is precisely what we want to deal with, i.e. providing a definition to a category. This amounts to finding pairs of the form $(C, \{d_1, \ldots, d_n\})$ where C denotes a category, such as `Nokia_Mobile_Phone` for example, and d_i denotes a pair (p, o), such as (manufacturer, Nokia) for example. Then the whole set of d_i will stand for a possible description of C. A parallel can be drawn with concept definitions in Description Logics [2], where a form of definition is given by $C \equiv d_1 \sqcap \cdots \sqcap d_n$, such as:

$$\text{Nokia\_Mobile\_Phone} \equiv \text{Phone} \sqcap \exists \text{manufacturer.Nokia}$$

Following the same line, we aim also at finding "incompatible categories", i.e. pairs of categories (C_i, C_j) such as there does not exist any subject s verifying both $\langle$s, dct : subject, C$_i\rangle$ and $\langle$s, dct : subject, C$_j\rangle$. In terms of Description Logics, this is written as $C_i \sqcap C_j \equiv \bot$.

For example, `Nokia_Mobile_Phone` $\sqcap$ `Turing_Award_laureate` $\equiv \bot$ states that two categories are disjoint or incompatible, which is a particular type of definition, meaning in terms of sets of instances that `Nokia_Mobile_Phone` is in the complementary of `Turing_Award_laureate`.

---

[3] https://en.wikipedia.org/wiki/Category:Smartphones

Both types of definitions are useful for a practitioner aiming at contributing to *DBpedia*. Indeed, providing descriptions and then definitions to categories allows to be in agreement with knowledge representation principles, i.e. building sound and complete definitions of individual classes, as categories should be. In particular, this would help to find missing triples. For example, suppose that the definition Nokia_Mobile_Phone $\equiv$ Phone $\sqcap$ $\exists$manufacturer.Nokia is lying in *DBpedia*. Then, if an element x belongs to Nokia_Mobile_Phone, then this element should be a phone with manufacturer Nokia, i.e. x is an instance of Phone $\sqcap$ $\exists$manufacturer.Nokia ("necessary condition"). Conversely, if an element is an instance of Phone $\sqcap$ $\exists$manufacturer.Nokia, then x should be an instance of Nokia_Mobile_Phone ("sufficient condition"). This allows to complete incomplete triples if required.

In addition, specifying incompatible categories enables to track inconsistencies. Indeed, suppose there exits a triple in *DBpedia* asserting that Smartphones and Sports_cars are incompatible. Whenever a practitioner tries to associate the category Sports_cars to a resource related to the category Smartphones, she/he could be warned that both categories are incompatible. This will guide practitioners and help them having better practices.

2.3 A Practical Approach in FCA

Following the lines of [1] in the FCA framework, the discovery of category definitions relies on the construction of a context (G, M, I) from a set of triples denoted by ST. Given ST, G is the set of subjects, i.e. $G = \{s/\langle s, p, o \rangle \in ST\}$ and M is a set of pairs predicate-objects, i.e. $M = \{(p, o)/\langle s, p, o \rangle \in ST\}$. The incidence relation is defined as $sI(p, o) \Longleftrightarrow \langle s, p, o \rangle \in ST$.

Then the discovery process is based on a search for implications of the form $B_1 \Longrightarrow B_2$ where $B_1, B_2 \subseteq M$. Whenever an implication $B_1 \Longrightarrow B_2$ is discovered, the converse rule is checked. If $B_2 \Longrightarrow B_1$ is also an implication, then we have the definition $B_1 \equiv B_2$. If this is not the case, the set of triples involved in the context should be checked for potential incompleteness.

In the following, we present an alternative search for category definition based on "Redescription Mining", where the name of the category appears on the left hand side of the $\equiv$ symbol and a set of characteristics (composed of $\exists predicate.object$ expressions) appears on the right hand side.

3   Redescription Mining

3.1 Definitions

Redescription mining aims at searching for data subsets with multiple descriptions, as different views on the same set of objects [5,6]. Redescription mining takes as input a set of objects G and a set of attributes M partitioned into *views* V_i such as $M = V_1 \cup \cdots \cup V_n$ and $V_i \cap V_j = \emptyset$ if $i \neq j$. For example, the attributes can be partitioned w.r.t. the sources of the data or w.r.t. some criteria defined by a user. A value is associated to each pair $(object, attribute)$, which can be Boolean, numerical or nominal, and which depends on the domain of the attribute. An example of such a dataset is provided in Fig. 1.

Views	V_1			V_2
Attributes	a_1	a_2	a_3	a_4
f_1		2	3	Triangle
f_2		3	3	Triangle
f_3	×	0	3	Triangle
f_4	×	2	3	Triangle
f_5	×	2	4	Rectangle

a_1: Has a right angle (Boolean)
a_2: Max number of equal sides (numerical)
a_3: Total number of sides (numerical)
a_4: Type (nominal)

Fig. 1. An example of dataset for redescription mining, with objects $\{f_1, \ldots, f_5\}$ and attributes $\{a_1, a_2, a_3, a_4\}$.

Given a set of objects G, a partition of a set of attributes M, redescription mining aims at finding a pair of "queries" (q_1, q_2), where q_1 and q_2 correspond to logical statements involving attributes and their values. These statements are expressed in propositional logic with the conjunction, disjunction and negation connectors. Below, a redescription say RD based on the pair (q_1, q_2) is denoted by $RD = q_1 \longleftrightarrow q_2$ or $RD = (q_1, q_2)$.

Given a redescription $RD = q_1 \longleftrightarrow q_2$, the set of objects G can be partitioned w.r.t. the queries which are satisfied by a subset of objects. There are four possible partitions, denoted by E_{ij} with $i, j \in \{0, 1\}$, depending on the partition q_1 or q_2 which is satisfied. For example, $E_{10}(R)$ denotes the set of objects satisfying q_1 but not q_2.

Redescriptions are mined w.r.t. a support, the Jaccard coefficient, and a p-value. The support of a redescription $RD = (q_1, q_2)$ is the proportion of objects in the dataset satisfying both queries q_1 and q_2, i.e. $\text{support}(R) = \frac{|E_{11}(R)|}{|G|}$.

The similarity between two datasets corresponding to two queries q_1 and q_2 is measured thanks to the Jaccard coefficient:

$$\text{jacc}(q_1 \leftrightarrow q_2) = \frac{|E_{11}(R)|}{|E_{11}(R)| + |E_{10}(R)| + |E_{01}(R)|}$$

Let us consider for example the redescription $RD = (a_2 = 2) \longleftrightarrow (a_4 = Triangle)$ which is based on $q_1 = (a_2 = 2)$ and $q_2 = (a_4 = Triangle)$ w.r.t. the dataset in Fig. 1. We have that: $|E_{11}(R)| = |\{f_1, f_4\}| = 2$, $|E_{10}(R)| = |\{f_5\}| = 3$, $|E_{01}(R)| = |\{f_2, f_3\}| = 4$ and $|E_{00}(R)| = 0$. Then it comes that $\text{support}(RD) = \frac{2}{5}$ and $\text{jacc}(RD) = \frac{2}{2+3+4} = \frac{2}{9}$. This means that the redescription RD is not of very good quality.

By contrast, the redescription $(a_3 = 3) \longleftrightarrow \neg(a_4 = Rectangle)$ returns a Jaccard coefficient of 1 which is maximal, meaning this time that we have a very good redescription.

3.2 A Redescription Mining Algorithm

In this paper, we reuse the `ReReMi` algorithm to mine redescriptions [5]. `ReReMi` takes two files D_1 and D_2 as input, which correspond to two subsets of attributes or "views" V_1 and V_2 in the dataset, and returns a set of redescriptions.

Firstly, a "candidate redescription" based on a given set of pairs (q_1, q_2), where q_1 contains only one attribute $\{a_1\} \subseteq V_1$ and q_2 only one attribute $\{a_2\} \subseteq V_2$, is checked. The checking is not necessarily systematic for all possible pairs or combinations of pairs of attributes, as a set of initial pairs can be specified by an analyst. Doing so, the set of candidate redescriptions is progressively extended, i.e. one attribute is added at a time to one of the queries of the candidate redescription.

A query q can be extended with a new attribute a in four possible ways: $q_1 \wedge a$, $q_1 \vee a$, $q_1 \wedge \neg a$ or $q_1 \vee \neg a$. The redescription with the best Jaccard coefficient is added to the candidate redescriptions. However, this extension can be customized using for example only one of the possibilities, e.g. $q_1 \wedge a$. The algorithm continues until there is no more candidate available, i.e. until there is no way to increase the Jaccard coefficient of the current candidate redescription. Finally, the set of the candidate redescriptions is returned to the analyst.

3.3 Redescription Mining in Linked Open Data

For applying redescription mining to a set of linked data, i.e. a set of related RDF triples, we need first to transform this set of triples into a format that can be processed by the `ReReMi` algorithm. This operation is similar to the building of a context in the FCA framework. The attributes correspond to the predicates of the triples and they are separated into views.

Given a set of triples ST, we build an input "context" (G, M, I) where objects correspond to subjects of the RDF triples, i.e. $G = \{s/\langle s, p, o \rangle \in ST\}$) and attributes to the set of pairs "(predicate, object)", i.e. $M = \{(p, o)/\langle s, p, o \rangle \in ST\}$). The relation $I \subseteq G \times M$ is Boolean and we have $sI(p, o)$ is `true` whenever $\langle s, p, o \rangle \in ST$.

Next, the set of attributes is partitioned into two views as follows. $M = M_{subj} \cup M_{desc}$ and $M_{subj} \cap M_{desc} = \emptyset$. M_{subj} is the set of attributes (p, o) such that $p = $ `dct:subject` and the set M_{desc} is the complementary set in M (i.e. pairs (p, o) where $p \neq$ `dct:subject`). Based on that, searching for a category definition can be achieved in two complementary ways:

(i) by providing a description to the category: in this case, there is a search for redescriptions (q_1, q_2) where $q_1 = a$ with $a \in M_{subj}$ and q_2 is a query based on a set of one or more attributes from M_{desc}. Actually, this search should output a definition based on characteristics shared by all the resources of the category, actually a set of necessary and sufficient conditions for being a member of the category.

(ii) by determining which categories are incompatible: in this case, there is a search for categories which do not share any common resources, i.e. $C_i \sqcap$

$C_j \equiv \perp$. Then the redescriptions are only based on M_{subj} and the Jaccard coefficient of the categories in the output should be close to 0 instead of 1.

Table 1. Statistics on the datasets extracted.

D	Triples	Objects	$|M_{subj}|$	$|M_{desc}|$	Density
Turing_Award	2 642	65	503	857	3.9e−2
Smartphones	8 418	598	359	1 730	6.7e−3
Sports_cars	9 047	604	435	2 295	5.5e−3
French_films	121 496	6 039	6 028	19 459	7.9e−4

4   Experiments

4.1   Datasets

We extracted four different subsets of triples[4], corresponding to the domains Turing_Award_laureates, Smartphones, Sports_cars, and French_films in *DBpedia*, whose statistics are given in Table 1. The Turing_Award_laureates dataset is small with only 65 objects and less than 1500 attributes, meaning that there are less than 1500 unique pairs $(predicate, object)$ in the extracted triples. The dataset French_films is the largest, with more than 6000 objects and 25000 attributes. This dataset is rather sparse and the attributes have a weak support, and the density is very low as well. The datasets Smartphones and Sports_cars are similar in size, with roughly 600 objects and between 2000 and 2800 attributes.

For each dataset, the partition of the attributes is built as follows: M_{subj} is constructed from the subset of triples whose predicate is dct:subject whereas M_{desc} is the complementary set. Here, there are only Boolean attributes and only conjunction is used in RM. From M_{subj} and M_{desc}, two tabular files compliant with ReReMi input are created, namely D_{subj} which contains attributes of the view M_{subj}, D_{desc} which contains attributes of the view M_{desc}. The thresholds used are 0.5 for Jaccard similarity (jacc $\geqslant$ 0.5) and 3 for support (support $\geqslant$ 3).

The discovery of incompatible categories relies only on the use of M_{subj}, and D_{subj} is provided for both views. The thresholds used are 0.3 for Jaccard similarity with this time jacc $\leqslant$ 0.3 and 5 for support (support $\geqslant$ 5).

4.2   Extraction of Definitions

The ReReMi algorithm returns a set of redescriptions with their respective Jaccard coefficients. For measuring the precision of the algorithm, each redescription is manually evaluated by a domain expert. Hereafter, a redescription which is

---

[4] The datasets and the results of the experiments are available online, see https://gitlab.inria.fr/jreynaud/iccs19-redescriptions.

Table 2. Definitions extracted by ReReMi for each dataset, along with their corresponding Jaccard coefficient, written in a Description Logics-like formalism. If the evaluator answered true to the question, the symbol ≡ is used. Otherwise, the symbol ≢ is used.

N.	Redescription	jacc
Turing_Award_laureates		
R1	Harvard_University_alumni ≡ ∃almaMater.Harvard_University	.89
R2	Stanford_University_alumni ≡ ∃almaMater.Stanford_University	.56
R3	British_computer_scientists ≢ ∃award.Fellow_of_the_Royal_Society	.63
Sports_cars		
R4	McLaren_vehicles ≡ ∃manufacturer.McLaren_Automotive	.86
R5	McLaren_vehicles ≡ ∃assembly.Surrey	.75
R6	2010_automobiles ⊓ Audi_Vehicles ≢ ∃manufacturer.Audi	.55
Smartphones		
R7	Nokia_mobile_phones ≡ ∃manufacturer.Nokia	.82
R8	Samsung_Galaxy ≡ ∃manufacturer.Samsung_Electronics ⊓ ∃operatingSystem.Android_OS	.66
R9	MeeGo_Devices ≢ ∃operatingSystem.Sailfish_OS	.73
French_films		
R10	Films_directed_by_Georges_Méliès ≡ ∃director.Georges_Méliès	.98
R11	Film_scores_by_Georges_Delerue ≡ ∃musicComposer.Georges_Delerue	.82
R12	Films_directed_by_Georges_Méliès ≢ ∃director.Georges_Méliès ⊓ ∃language.Silent_Film	.50

considered as "valid" by the expert is called a definition. This allows us to compute the precision as the ratio of definitions to redescriptions (see in Sect. 4.4). Table 2 presents the redescriptions extracted along with their Jaccard coefficient.

In the Turing_Award_laureates dataset, most of the discovered definitions are about universities (redescriptions R1 and R2), whereas definitions discovered in the two datasets Sports_cars and Smartphones are mostly about manufacturers. In the dataset French_films, all the redescriptions except one are related to "Georges Méliès". This means that such attributes have a support high enough to supporting redescriptions.

Most of the "invalid" mined redescriptions are based on a description which is too "approximate", i.e. there are possibly too many exceptions to the rule. For example, a large proportion of British computer scientists are also fellows of the Royal Society, but not all are award winners (see rule R3). In some other cases, there are not enough counter-examples in the dataset. For example, in redescription R9, there are too few Meego smartphones which are not running Sailfish in the dataset.

4.3 Extraction of the Incompatible Categories

The results about the extraction of incompatible categories are a bit disappointing for the dataset Turing_Award_laureates. Indeed, most of the categories discovered by ReReMi are not incompatible. This is maybe due to the fact that this dataset is about persons. Then the categories are characterizations of these persons w.r.t. a part of their life (e.g. where they studied and when they were born). Thus, most of the categories in this dataset cannot be incompatible, and there are too few objects to provide counter-examples.

Table 3. Incompatibilities discovered by `ReReMi` for each dataset. In all reported cases jacc $= 0$. The axioms are written in a Description Logics-like formalism.

N.	Incompatible categories
Turing_Award_laureates	
R13	Harvard_University_alumni $\sqcap$ Scientist_from_California $\equiv \bot$
R14	Fellows_of_the_British_Computer_Society $\sqcap$ Jewish_American_scientists $\equiv \bot$
R15	Massachusetts_Institute_of_Technology_faculty $\sqcap$ IBM_Fellows $\equiv \bot$
Sports_cars	
R16	1970s_automobiles $\sqcap$ Cars_introduced_in_1998 $\equiv \bot$
R17	Kit_cars $\sqcap$ Coupes $\equiv \bot$
R18	1960s_automobiles $\sqcap$ Lotus_racing_cars $\equiv \bot$
Smartphones	
R19	Blackberry $\sqcap$ Nokia_mobile_phones $\equiv \bot$
R20	Mobile_phones_introduced_in_2013 $\sqcap$ Mobile_phones_introduced_in_2014 $\equiv \bot$
R21	Touchscreen_mobile_phone $\sqcap$ Nokia_platforms $\equiv \bot$
French_films	
R22	1980s_drama_films $\sqcap$ 1970s_comedy_films $\equiv \bot$

The other datasets provide better results. In the `Sports_cars` dataset, a lot of categories are incompatible because they denote cars from different time span, such as redescription `R16` in Table 3. In the `Smartphones` dataset, a lot of categories are incompatible because they denote phones from different brands, such as redescription `R19`. For these two datasets, the `ReReMi` algorithm discovers a lot of incompatible categories. Finally, only one redescription is returned for the `French_films` dataset.

4.4   Discussion

The number of extracted category definitions along with the number of incompatible categories are reported in Table 4. These results are specific and depends on the data domain, and thus cannot be generalized to the whole *DBpedia*. For discovering more general definitions, we probably need to process larger datasets, e.g. instead of `Turing_Award_laureates`, considering a dataset about `Person`. This would bring at the same time scalability issues that may be overcome with sampling or by using a pre-processing to select only a subset of predicates or by optimising the criteria used by the algorithm. Further experimentation in this direction could be considered in the future.

Discovered rules may look trivial, because DBpedia uses "explicit" labels for categories. However, in LOD, all categories are not labelled by an explicit name. In Wikidata, for example, the category corresponding to the French films is `Q393063`. Our approach do not use the semantics of the labels and can be generalised to other knowledge bases which do not use explicit labels.

Table 4. Results of the two experiments for each dataset. In the definition discovery settings, the number of extracted redescriptions ($|\mathcal{R}|$) and evaluated as true ($|\mathcal{D}|$) are reported, along with the precision ($\frac{|\mathcal{R}|}{|\mathcal{D}|}$). In the settings of incompatible categories, the number of disjunctions axioms extracted ($|\mathcal{N}|$) is reported.

	Nb triples	$|\mathcal{R}|$	$|\mathcal{D}|$	Prec.	$|\mathcal{N}|$
Turing_Award_laureates	2642	12	9	.75	30
Smartphones	8418	36	12	.67	121
Sports_cars	9047	98	57	.58	63
French_films	121496	52	30	.58	1

The experiments also demonstrate the difficulty of data selection. Here, we use datasets of various sizes and domains. Finding a set of categories allowing to extract a good set of triples w.r.t. the constraints of the experiments is not straightforward. This calls for complex SPARQL queries and this underlines the interest of having better information about categories.

Most of the time, there is only one attribute in the right side of a redescription, meaning that such an attribute is very discriminant and that redescriptions do not have any attribute in common. Then, it can be difficult to build a partial ordering between the defined categories. By contrast, in the Smartphones dataset, we have the redescription R8 and

$$\text{Samsung\_Mobile\_Phone} \equiv \exists \text{manufacturer.Samsung\_Electronics}$$

In this case, from these two redescriptions, we can infer that

$$\text{Samsung\_Galaxy} \sqsubseteq \text{Samsung\_Mobile\_Phone}$$

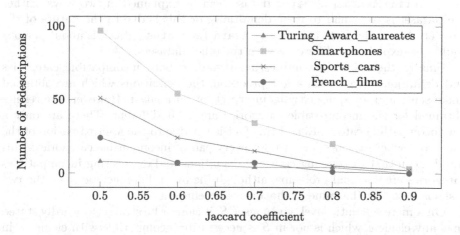

Fig. 2. Number of redescriptions extracted w.r.t. the Jaccard coefficient.

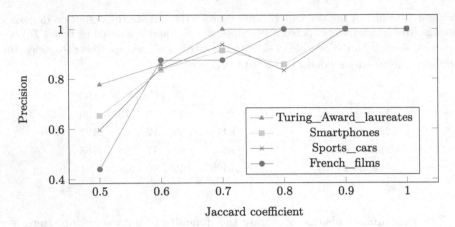

Fig. 3. Precision of the redescriptions w.r.t. the Jaccard coefficient.

Figure 2 shows the number of redescriptions found w.r.t. the Jaccard coefficient. Compared to association rules, the number of redescriptions is 2 to 10 times less [12]. The number of extracted redescriptions seems to be correlated with the density of the dataset, i.e. "the more dense the dataset is, the more redescriptions are extracted". This graduality becomes less important when the Jaccard coefficient increases.

Figure 3 shows the precision w.r.t. the Jaccard coefficient. The precision increases w.r.t. the threshold of the Jaccard coefficient, meaning that the Jaccard coefficient is a suitable measure for redescription mining in LOD. The precision depends on the datasets. It seems to be correlated to the size of the dataset and/or to the number of extracted redescriptions. However, further experiments should be performed to test this hypothesis. The low score of the Turing_Award_laureates dataset can be explained in two ways. Either the dataset is too small to mine definitions, or this is due to the nature of the dataset. Again, the fact that Turing_Award_laureates dataset is about persons could also explain the difference with the other datasets.

Finally, the results are interesting regarding both incompatible categories and definitions; Even with a low precision, the definitions which are obtained make sense and are quite easy to interpret for an analyst. However, the results obtained for the incompatible categories are a bit different. There are only a few incompatible categories and this fact is not due to the approximation of the Jaccard coefficient, since jacc = 0 for every pair of incompatible categories. This could mean that discovering category definitions and discovering incompatibles categories are not dual problems, although the main difference between the two tasks is based on the value of the Jaccard coefficient.

On a more semantic level, given a set S, it cannot be straightforwardly stated that any element which is not in S is necessarily incompatible with elements in S, especially if we work in terms of open world assumption. This last point is also matter to future work.

5 Related Work

In [14], authors rely on *evidential terminological decision trees* (EDTD) to classify instances w.r.t. assertions in which they are involved. An EDTD is a decision tree where nodes are labeled with a logical formula and a value in [0, 1] which can be interpreted as the probability of the logical formula to be true. This allows the authors to match a class with an assertion. The lower is the assertion in the tree, the more specific it is. To complete, the same authors in [13] search for a set of pairwise disjoint clusters in building a decision tree where each node corresponds to a concept description. Then, two concept descriptions at different leaf nodes are necessary disjoint.

By contrast, in [9], authors rely on rule mining and search for *obligatory class attributes*. Given a class, an obligatory attribute denotes a relation that every individual of the class should be involved in, e.g. every person has a birthdate, and then `hasBirthdate` is an obligatory attribute of class `Person`. While in [9], authors are not interested in the range of relations, authors in [1] take into account both relations and their range. They rely on FCA [8] and extracted association rules to define classes. Attributes are based on pairs $A_i = (\text{predicate}_i, \text{object}_i)$ and implications $A_i \Rightarrow A_j$ are searched. Only implications whose converse has a high support w.r.t. are kept as candidate definitions.

FCA and association rules are also used in [16], where authors build different formal contexts in order to discover specific relations, such as subsumption between two classes or transitivity of a relation for example.

In [11], authors aim to classify resources from RDF data, focusing on the relations existing between resources. For a resource s and a class C, they compute the probability of s to belong to C w.r.t. the relations in s. For example, resources with the relation `hasBirthdate` are instances of the class `Person`.

Contrasting other approaches, authors in [3, 4] consider the RDF graph and propose the algorithm AMIE+, which mainly focuses on relations, without considering domain and range. AMIE+ searches for implications between relations. For example, *people married to a person who lives in some place P also live in P* is the kind of rule that can be extracted by AMIE+.

We position ourselves in the continuity of these works. However, while most of the approaches search for implications, we search for definition and disjunctions using redescription mining. Regarding disjunction, authors in [15] propose a gold standard for class disjointness in DBpedia and compare a supervised approach based on machine learning and a statistical approach based on schema induction for learning disjointness. Their approach shows some similarities with our own approach as detailed in [12].

6 Conclusion and Future Work

In this paper, we present an original use of redescription mining for discovering definitions and disjunctions of categories in DBpedia. The approach involves RM in a very original task; The experimental results show that the approach is well-founded and comparable to related work approaches.

In future work, we would like to make more usage of the expressiveness of RM, i.e. using ¬ and ∨ Boolean connectors, for discovering more complex redescriptions. However, one problem could be the scalability when processing large sparse datasets. Moreover, another improvement would be to consider datatype properties such as dates or distances. Since ReReMi handles numerical data, we could discover redescriptions including literals such as "cars manufactured in 1997". Finally, another research direction is related to attributes which are partially ordered. This is possible in FCA thanks to pattern structures [7]. However, this is not yet integrated in RM. Such an extension would allow to discover SongWriter ≡ ∃isCreating.Song from the triples ⟨x, a, dbo : SongWriter⟩, ⟨x, isCreating, y⟩, and ⟨y, a, dbo : Song⟩.

References

1. Alam, M., Buzmakov, A., Codocedo, V., Napoli, A.: Mining definitions from RDF annotations using formal concept analysis. In: IJCAI, pp. 823–829 (2015)
2. Baader, F., Calvanese, D., McGuinness, D., Nardi, D., Patel-Schneider, P. (eds.): The Description Logic Handbook. Cambridge University Press, New York (2003)
3. Galárraga, L.A., Teflioudi, C., Hose, K., Suchanek, F.M.: AMIE: association rule mining under incomplete evidence in ontological knowledge bases. In: WWW 2013, pp. 413–422 (2013)
4. Galárraga, L.A., Teflioudi, C., Hose, K., Suchanek, F.M.: Fast rule mining in ontological knowledge bases with AMIE+. VLDB J. **24**(6), 707–730 (2015)
5. Galbrun, E., Miettinen, P.: From black and white to full color: extending redescription mining outside the Boolean world. Stat. Anal. Data Min. **5**(4), 284–303 (2012)
6. Galbrun, E., Miettinen, P.: Redescription Mining. Springer Briefs in Computer Science. Springer, New York (2017). https://doi.org/10.1007/978-3-319-72889-6
7. Ganter, B., Kuznetsov, S.O.: Pattern structures and their projections. In: Delugach, H.S., Stumme, G. (eds.) ICCS-ConceptStruct 2001. LNCS (LNAI), vol. 2120, pp. 129–142. Springer, Heidelberg (2001). https://doi.org/10.1007/3-540-44583-8_10
8. Ganter, B., Wille, R.: Formal Concept Analysis - Mathematical Foundations. Springer, Heidelberg (1999). https://doi.org/10.1007/978-3-642-59830-2
9. Lajus, J., Suchanek, F.M.: Are all people married? Determining obligatory attributes in knowledge bases. In: International Conference WWW (2018)
10. Lehmann, J., Isele, R., Jakob, M., et al.: Dbpedia-a large-scale, multilingual knowledge base extracted from wikipedia. Semantic Web **6**(2), 167–195 (2015)
11. Paulheim, H., Bizer, C.: Type inference on noisy RDF data. In: Alani, H., et al. (eds.) ISWC 2013. LNCS, vol. 8218, pp. 510–525. Springer, Heidelberg (2013). https://doi.org/10.1007/978-3-642-41335-3_32
12. Reynaud, J., Toussaint, Y., Napoli, A.: Three approaches for mining definitions from relational data in the web of data. In: Proceedings of the 6th International Workshop FCA4AI (IJCAI/ECAI), pp. 21–32 (2018)
13. Rizzo, G., d'Amato, C., Fanizzi, N., Esposito, F.: Terminological cluster trees for disjointness axiom discovery. In: Blomqvist, E., Maynard, D., Gangemi, A., Hoekstra, R., Hitzler, P., Hartig, O. (eds.) ESWC 2017. LNCS, vol. 10249, pp. 184–201. Springer, Cham (2017). https://doi.org/10.1007/978-3-319-58068-5_12

14. Rizzo, G., Fanizzi, N., d'Amato, C., Esposito, F.: Approximate classification with web ontologies through evidential terminological trees and forests. Int. J. Approx. Reason. **92**, 340–362 (2018)
15. Völker, J., Fleischhacker, D., Stuckenschmidt, H.: Automatic acquisition of class disjointness. J. Web Sem. **35**, 124–139 (2015)
16. Völker, J., Niepert, M.: Statistical schema induction. In: Antoniou, G., et al. (eds.) ESWC 2011. LNCS, vol. 6643, pp. 124–138. Springer, Heidelberg (2011). https://doi.org/10.1007/978-3-642-21034-1_9

Covering Concept Lattices
with Concept Chains

Ants Torim[(✉)], Marko Mets, and Kristo Raun

Software Science Department, Tallinn University of Technology,
Akadeemia tee 15a, 12618 Tallinn, Estonia
ants.torim@taltech.ee, metsmarko@outlook.com, kristo.raun@gmail.com

Abstract. The total number of concepts in a concept lattice tends to grow exponentially with the size of a context. There are numerous methods for selecting a subset of concepts based on some interestingness measure. We propose a method for finding interesting concept chains instead of interesting concepts. Concept chains also correspond to a certain visual rearrangement of a binary data table called a seriation. In a case study on the performance data of 852 students 80% of the corresponding formal context was covered by a single concept chain. We present three heuristic algorithms (MS-Chain, FL-Sort, KM-chain) for finding the concept chain cover in an efficient manner.

Keywords: Formal concept analysis · Interestingness measures · Concept chain · Case study · Data analysis · Data mining

1 Introduction

The fields of application for formal concept analysis (FCA) include linguistics [14], text retrieval and mining [1], data analysis [8,10,15], software engineering [5,16] and so on. It has solid mathematical [3] and philosophical foundations [19]. For example, when compared to clusters from cluster analysis, the formal concept does not only include a set of objects (extent), but also a set of attributes (intent, definition), and clear connections between the concepts.

Concept lattice diagrams (Hasse diagrams) provide a powerful ordered and structured visual representation of concepts and their relations. There are many tools for working with concept lattices: Concept Explorer [23] (and reimplementations), Galicia [18], FCART [12] etc.

One of the problems of FCA is that the number of concepts in the concept lattice increases exponentially with the size of the data set. Dias et al. [2] group the methods for dealing with such complexity into three categories:

1. **Redundant information removal** aims to produce a lattice that is isomorphic to original without redundant information.
2. **Simplification** abstracts the lattice into a high-level overview.

© Springer Nature Switzerland AG 2019
D. Endres et al. (Eds.): ICCS 2019, LNAI 11530, pp. 190–203, 2019.
https://doi.org/10.1007/978-3-030-23182-8_14

3. **Selection** means selecting a subset of concepts, objects and based on certain relevance or interestingness criterion.

Our approach is based on **selection**. There are several methods to select a subset of the most interesting concepts. Such interestingness measures, like stability and separation and their relations were recently reviewed by Kuznetsov et al. [7].

Real-world data sets may not have well-separated concepts with stable definitions, there may be many very similar concepts related by inclusion relations. These data sets are well described by concept chains where one chain can cover many related concepts without any duplication that may occur within the intents and extents of a set of *interesting* concepts. In our case study we look into one such data set that is well suited for concept chain description. Data about student course completion is inherently *triangle-like*: students have higher and lower capabilities, courses are harder and easier and there are also dependencies between the earlier and later courses. An advantage of concept chains over a selection of interesting concepts is that they preserve more of the structure of the concept lattice, having some relation to concept lattice simplification. The presence of numerous slight variations of the same concept is a problem when focusing on single concepts but these variations become a part of a concept chain in a structured manner. In general, concept chains seem to be an interesting alternative to other selection methods.

2   Basic Definitions and Examples

A basic knowledge of FCA [3,21] is assumed here. We denote objects and attributes by small letters g, m, a formal concept as a pair of its extent and intent $C = (A, B)$ and use the prime symbol $'$ for derivation operator like in g' or A'.

There are several measures for concepts interestingness, a thorough review and comparison is given by Kuznetsov et al. [7]. Here we use the measures of stability and separation.

A stability index is based on the idea of a dependency in a data set that can be reconstructed from different parts of the data set [9]. For a formal concept (A, B) the intentional stability index is the probability that B will remain closed when removing a subset of objects from extent A with equal probability [7]. The higher the stability index of a concept, the lower the influence that any single object has to its intent. The intentional stability is defined as:

$$Stab_i(A, B) = \frac{|\{C \subseteq A \mid C' = B\}|}{2^{|A|}} \qquad (1)$$

The 3×3 concept $(345, abc)$ from the Fig. 1(i) data set (lower left corner) has the intentional stability index of $\frac{4}{8} = 0.5$. The 3×3 concept $(345, cde)$ from the Fig. 1(ii) data set has the stability index of $\frac{7}{8}$.

The separation index $s(A, B)$ is meant to describe how well a concept sorts out the objects it covers from other objects and also how well it sorts out the attributes it covers from other attributes of the context [6]. The higher the separation index of a concept, the fewer the number of similar concepts in the context. It is defined as the ratio between the area covered by the concept and the total area covered by its objects and attributes.

$$s(A,B) = \frac{|A||B|}{\sum_{g \in A} |g'| + \sum_{m \in B} |m'| - |A||B|} \tag{2}$$

The 3×3 concept $(345, abc)$ from the Fig. 1(i) data set has the separation index of $\frac{3 \cdot 3}{12+12-9} = 0.6$. The 3×3 concept $(345, cde)$ from the Fig. 1(ii) data set has the separation index of $\frac{3 \cdot 3}{9+9-9} = 1.0$.

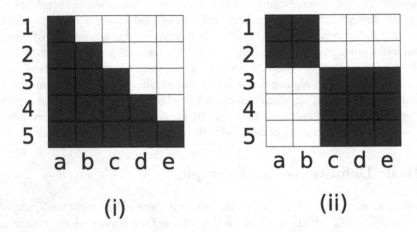

Fig. 1. Two binary data sets (formal contexts). Black = 1, white = 0.

As we can see the data set (i) has concepts with lower stability and separation than the data set (ii). Data set (ii) has two clearly separated concepts with non-zero areas while data set (i) has five greatly overlapping concepts. This example is small enough that we can deal with the full lattice, but if we want to reduce a large data set to a small number of interesting concepts, then it is unclear how such chains should be simplified. Should they be reduced to a single concept, or to several overlapping concepts? Another approach that is reviewed here is to partition the data set not into the concepts but into the chains.

A chain is defined as a subset of an ordered set in which any two elements are comparable [3]. A chain is complete when it is not possible to insert further elements into it [13]. A concept chain is a sequence of formal concepts ordered by containment (generality). A formal concept is defined by either its intent (set of attributes) or extent (set of objects), a concept chain is defined by a sequence (with no repetitions) of attributes or a sequence of objects. For example, the data set (i) is fully described by the chain $abcde$ while the data set (ii) requires two chains ab and cde. Concept chains are therefore easy to describe in text due

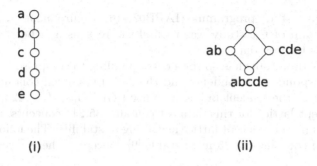

Fig. 2. Lattices corresponding to the data sets from Fig. 1

to their sequential nature which is helpful in data analysis and convenient as a unit of thought (Fig. 2).

Reordering binary contexts as those from Fig. 1 to reveal their internal structure visually is known as a **seriation** of matrices. Structure (i) is known as a Pareto seriation: data table can be reordered so that ones form a contiguous, usually triangle-like structure around one corner of the data table. Structure (ii) is known as a block diagonal seriation [22]: data table can be reordered so that ones form blocks (concepts or fuzzy concepts) around the diagonal. Pareto seriation is equivalent to a concept chain. Block diagonal seriation is an anti-chain (a set of concepts without any order relations between them), but not every anti-chain has a corresponding block diagonal seriation.

3   Context Covering Problem

For a sizable formal context the number of formal concepts in the lattice can be huge and such complexity is often managed by selecting the most interesting concepts according to a certain metric [7]. As different metrics give different results, the question of evaluating such a selection of concepts arises. Here, we are using the following definition for the context covering problem:

Definition 1. Given a formal context $K = (G, M, I)$ and a threshold δ, find the set of concepts C, so that for the set of errors $E = \{e \mid e \subseteq I, \forall (A, B) \in C :$ $e \notin (A \times B)\}$ the number of errors $|E|$ is less than or equal to δ, and the number of concepts, $|C|$, is minimal.

For example, for the set of concepts $\{(12345, a), (5, abcde)\}$ in Fig. 1(i) we have $|E| = 6$, for the set of concepts $\{(345, cde)\}$ in Fig. 1(ii) we have $|E| = 4$.

This problem is equivalent to δ-approx role mining problem described by Vaidya et al. [17] where it is also proven (through transformation to set basis problem) that this problem is NP-complete.

4   Case Study: Student Performance

We introduce a case study which is particularly suitable for concept chain coverage: a data set on student performance. The data was collected on students in a computer science study programme (IAPB02), in the enrolment years from 2009 to 2013. The aim of the study was to find the reasons and bottlenecks which cause students to drop out.

The binary data table has 33 rows corresponding to compulsory courses, 423 columns corresponding to students and the data table itself contains 6553 ones corresponding to the student failing a course ($|G| = 33, |M| = 423, |I| = 6553$). The full concept lattice for this data set contains 35,241 concepts.

We can prune this concept lattice according to stability. The following partial lattice (Fig. 3) contains the 25 most stable [9] concepts. These cover 84% of the data table.

Below we show the cumulative cover of the data table for those 25 concepts (Fig. 4).

General intuition why concept chains could be useful in this case is as follows: if it holds that we can rank students from strongest to weakest, and correspondingly courses from easiest to hardest, then data should logically form a single concept chain which runs from the hardest courses, having the most failures, to the easiest courses, having the least failures - and similarly, from the weakest students, failing the most courses, to the strongest students, failing the least courses. If there are several independent aspects (e.g. mental aptitude, physical aptitude), then we should have several corresponding concept chains. There are some confounding factors in our data, as all courses that have not been passed as required by the endpoint of data collection were denoted as failed, which could also be caused by failing a previous course which was a precondition, or the students just giving up on studying. Therefore, instead of pure difficulty, there is a mix of difficulty, as the student's semester in the study programme and dependencies to other courses seem to also influence the failure rate of a course.

It turns out that one of our heuristic algorithms (MS-Chain) finds a chain that covers 78% of this data table, and following chains add correspondingly 3%, 2%, 1% of extra cover. This chain is given below in Fig. 5.

As we can see, such a concept chain can give easy to read, compact, and semi-visual descriptions for certain formal contexts. Such a figure corresponds to a seriated Pareto-structure data table from where all the ones not contained in the chain have been removed.

While stability gave us quite a good and compact representation of an entire data set, the single chain has roughly the same coverage (78% vs 84%) and is even more compact, being essentially an ordered list of attributes (courses), which is also well suited for textual representation. We can interpret the fact that a single chain is so effective as a confirmation that students have a single dimension of *ability*, not several and the courses in this chain are ordered in the difficulty to pass, compounding actual difficulty with the position in the study programme (most of the courses at the top of the chain are given either in the last or the penultimate semester).

We can conclude from those results that there are some application areas where concept chain cover is an effective way of simplifying and understanding the context.

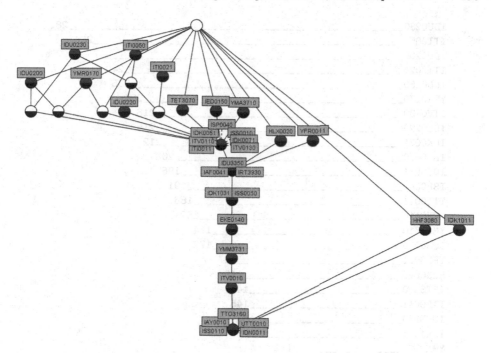

Fig. 3. A partial lattice with the 25 most stable concepts. Generated with Concept Explorer [23].

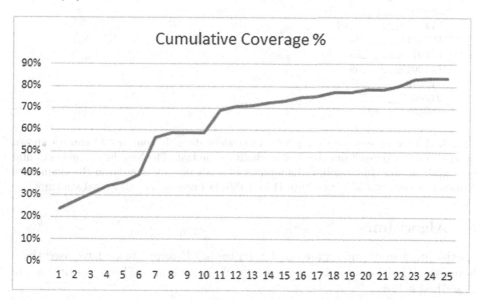

Fig. 4. Cumulative cover % for the 25 most stable concepts.

```
IDU0230_____282
ITI0050_____264
IDU0200_____247
ITI0021_____240
IED0150_____235
YMR0170_____224
ITV0130_____218
IDU0220_____216
IDK0051_____212
TET3070_____203
IDK0071_____196
ISP0040_____191
ITI0011_____186
ITV0110_____182
YMA3710_____174
ISS0010_____172
YFR0011_____157
HLX0020_____149
IRT3930_____145
IAF0041_____145
IDU3350_____143
IDK1031_____130
YMM3731_____112
ISS0050_____108
EKE0140_____100
HHF3080_____80
ITV0010_____70
IDK1011_____62
ISS0110_____59
IAY0010_____59
TTO3160_____56
UTT0010____52
IDN0011___47
```

Fig. 5. A concept chain covering 78% of student data. It contains 32 courses shown by their code ordered from the first in chain to the last. The lengths of the horizontal bars and the numbers describe the number of students at this point in the chain. The Number of concepts is 30 as IAF0041 and ISS0110 remove no additional students.

5   Algorithms

As the problem of finding maximal coverage is NP-complete we have used three heuristic algorithms for finding concept chain coverage. These algorithms are described below.

5.1   Monotone System Chain Algorithm

This algorithm, MS-Chain, is based on a monotone weight function from the theory of monotone systems [20] and gave best results in our case study.

A monotone weight function for an object is calculated based on the other objects in a monotone system and decreases (or increases) monotonically when any object is removed from the system.

Our monotone weight function $w()$ for an object g in the system (formal context) is following:

$$w(g) = \sum_{m \in g'} |m'| \tag{3}$$

That is, objects which contain many attributes contained in many objects have higher weights. As removal of any object can only decrease and never increase any $|m'|$, it is obvious that this weight function is monotonically decreasing. It is defined dually for attributes.

The **MS-Chain** algorithm takes context (G, M, I) as an input and returns sequence of objects $S = (g_1, g_2, ..., g_n)$ as an output. It is defined dually for attributes.

Algorithm 1. MS-Chain

$S \leftarrow \{\}$
while $S' \neq \{\}$ **do**
    Append g with minimal $w(g)$ from G to S and remove it from G.
    Recalculate the weights.
end while

From the sequence of objects $S = (g_1, g_2 ..., g_n)$ we generate the concept chain starting from the top (the object added last) as follows: $(g_1'', g_1'), (\{g_1, g_2\}'', \{g_1, g_2\}'), ... (\{g_1, g_2, ..., g_n\}'', \{g_1, g_2, ..., g_n\}')$ removing duplicate concepts.

It is easy to see that ordering of objects in the sequence S cannot violate the ordering of labels in the concept lattice, that is, there is no $g_i' \subset g_j'$ where $i < j$, because $g_i' \subset g_j'$ implies that $w(g_i) < w(g_j)$ for any set of objects.

Complexity of this algorithm depends on the number of recalculation operations necessary which is $|G|^2$.

5.2 Frequency-Lexicographic Sort Algorithm

FL-Sort algorithm orders the objects and attributes in a binary data table in two stages: first, by sorting them according to frequency, and second, by sorting them iteratively based on lexicographic order.

Frequency for an object g is $f|g'|$ and for attribute m is $f|m'|$. Lexicographic (for example alphabetic) order is defined for sorted data table so that row vector $(x_1, x_2, ..., x_n)$ is lexicographically greater than row vector $(y_1, y_2, ..., y_n)$ either if $x1 > y1$ or $x_1 = y_1$ and $(x_2, ..., x_n)$ is lexicographically greater than $(y_2, ..., y_n)$.

FL-Sort algorithm takes a binary data table D as an input and returns it rearranged. The algorithm is as follows:

Algorithm 2. FL-Sort

Sort all rows in D by frequencies.
Sort all columns in D by frequencies.
$SortByRows \leftarrow True$
while $D \neq D_{old}$ **do**
    $D_{old} \leftarrow D$
    if $SortByRows$ **then**
        Sort D lexicographically by rows
    else
        Sort D lexicographically by columns
    end if
    $SortByRows \leftarrow \neg SortByRows$
end while

Rearranged rows (dually columns) form a basis for object sequence S from which we can generate a concept chain. It is easy to see that ordering of objects in the sequence S cannot violate the ordering of labels in the concept lattice. Namely, there is no $g'_i \subset g'_j$ where $i < j$ because that would violate the lexicographic order.

Complexity of sorting is well known to be $n \log n$. Here, the number of lexicographic sort steps is not of crucial importance for algorithm's complexity. There cannot be infinite steps for non-infinite data table as lexicographic sorting by columns can only increase or keep the lexicographic weight of the first row (which is limited by maximum number of ones) and if the first row remains same, then it must increase or keep the lexicographic weight of the second row, etc. The same applies dually for columns.

Figure 6 shows the number of lexicographic sort steps for randomly generated binary data tables. These tend to remain constant between 5 and 10 even as the size of the data table increases. If this holds generally, then the FL-Sort algorithm would have a speed advantage over the MS-Chain algorithm and a general complexity of $n \log n$.

5.3   Meta-Algorithm for Finding Several Concept Chains

The MS-Chain and FL-Sort algorithms return one concept chain. Even though in our case study this had a pretty good coverage, it may not always be the case. What would be a solution to extend those algorithms to find several chains? One option, a simple greedy meta-algorithm, which we used also for our case study for students, is as follows:

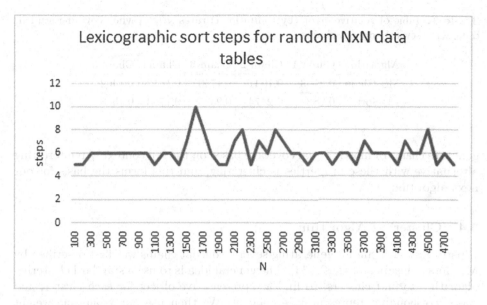

Fig. 6. Steps for lexicographic sort until data table is unchanged for random binary data tables.

Input: Context $K = (G, M, I)$, function $f(K)$ for finding the best concept chain C for context K, maximal number of errors δ (see concept coverage Definition 1). Output: Minimal (heuristic) sequence of concept chains $C_{seq} = (C_1, C_2, ..., C_n)$ so that the number of errors when covering a context K with those concepts is below δ.

Algorithm 3. Meta-algorithm

$C_{seq} \leftarrow ()$

while Number of errors $|E|$ for concepts in C_{seq} covering context K is smaller than δ (see def.1) **do**

    $C \leftarrow f(K)$ (get concept chain from the algorithm)

    Append C into C_{seq}

    Remove all concepts in C from K, that is for all $(A, B) \in C$ remove $A \times B$ from I.

end while

Results of applying this meta-algorithm, together with both the MS-Chain and FL-Sort, on student data are described in Table 1.

For this case study the MS-Chain algorithm had clear advantage when covering with 1–3 chains, but results evened out at 4–5 chains.

It was relatively easy to extend the existing algorithms to generate many concept chains, but the difference is that this greedy algorithm does not try to

Table 1. Table of relative error (by Definition 1) rates $|E|/|I|$ when covering student data with several concept chains.

Algorithm	Chain 1	Chain 2	Chain 3	Chain4	Chain 5
MS-Chain	0.2193	0.1941	0.1740	0.1613	0.1462
FL-Sort	0.2884	0.2474	0.2335	0.1763	0.1568

generate chains of mostly equal coverage based on the full context. An interesting alternative with these properties is clustering, and this forms the basis for our next algorithm.

5.4   Clustering Algorithm

Clustering algorithm for generating several concept chains was first described by M. Mets in his master thesis [11]. The general idea is to use a standard clustering algorithm to find clusters, to find a representative object for each cluster, and the corresponding representative concept. We then use our monotone weight function (Eq. 3) to order objects in the representative concepts extent, forming paths from this object to the infimum, and dually, order intent to give us chain to the supremum of the lattice. This relies on the property that every chain from the concept to the supremum can be described by the ordered intent, and dually, every chain from the concept to infimum can be described by the ordered extent. Also, as was described for the MS-Chain algorithm, the order of attributes and objects provided by our monotone weight function will not violate the order in the concept lattice.

The version of this algorithm that is based on k-modes clustering [4], called the **KM-Chain**, is as follows:

Input: Formal context (G, M, I), number of chains k
Output: Sequence of concept chains $C_{seq} = (C_1, C_2, ..., C_k)$

Algorithm 4. KM-Chain

$C_{seq} \leftarrow ()$
Use k-modes algorithm to generate k clusters (sets of objects) $(K_1, K_2, ..., K_k)$ from the context (G, M, I).
for all $K_i \in (K_1, K_2, ..., K_k)$ **do**
    Select representative object g_i so that $|g_i'| \leq |g'|$ for all $g \in K$
    Generate corresponding representative concept (g'', g')
    Sort all $g_j \in g''$ according to monotone weight $\sum_{m \in g_j'} |m'|$ to sequence B
    Sort all $m_j \in g'$ according to monotone weight $\sum_{g \in m_j'} |g'|$ to sequence T
    $C_i \leftarrow Chain(T), (g'', g'), Chain(B)$
    Append C_i to C_{seq}
end for

Time complexity of steps added to the clustering algorithm comes again from two sorting operations with the complexity $n \log n$. Unfortunately, this algorithm has not yet been applied to student data, but results with other data have been promising.

5.5 Comparing the Algorithms

We applied MS-Chain and FL-Sort with meta algorithm for generating several concept chains and KM chains algorithm to some well known data sets from UCI Machine Learning repository. Both MS Chain and FL Sort were configured to stop when less than 10% of the data table was uncovered, KM Chain was configured for 12 clusters (chains). In the Table 2 we provide running times and uncovered rates for 1, 6 and 12 concept chains.

Table 2. Table of spent time in seconds and uncovered rates for 1, 6, 12 concept chains.

Algorithm:	MS Chain				FL Sort				KM Chain 12			
Time (s), chains:	t	c1	c6	c12	t	c1	c6	c12	t	c1	c6	c12
house votes 84	76	0.92	0.57	0.4	5.2	0.83	0.51	0.1	2.3	0.89	0.56	0.38
student grades	131	0.93	0.78	0.66	5.0	0.6	0.32	0.11	4.1	0.86	0.86	0.67
instacart 600	516	0.98	0.93	0.87	43	0.84	0.67	0.55	5.4	0.98	0.92	0.78
grocery	12	0.88	0.61	0.41	2.0	0.83	0.55	0.38	0.37	0.85	0.58	0.48
e-commerce	305	0.89	0.63	0.45	47	0.89	0.65	0.47	3.8	0.96	0.88	0.57

We can see from the Table 2 that FL sort had distinctly superior uncovered rate than the other algorithms for house vote, student grade and instacart data. Running times were clearly the best for KM Chain while MS Chain was clearly the slowest. Time advantage for KM Chain is somewhat deceptive as the target uncovered rate 0.1 caused both MS Chain and FL Sort to generate many more chains than needed to match the uncovered rate of KM Chain: 0.38 to 0.57.

In general, FL sort seems to have the best coverage, but not strict superiority. MS Chain is clearly the slowest. No measured UCI data set was as readily covered by concept chains as the data from our case study.

6 Conclusions

Our case study of student results confirms that concept chains are a good option for reducing concept lattice complexity through selection. They are generally well suited to data tables which have a Pareto structure.

Though the exact problem of concept covering is NP-complete, we proposed three heuristic algorithms of which MS-Chain algorithm has $O(n^2)$ complexity and FL-Sort seems to have average case complexity of $O(n \log n)$. However, this is not proven for FL-Sort and requires further investigation. FL-sort seems to provide the best compromise of performance and quality of the three algorithms described. A more comprehensive study would also be needed on the relative merits of these algorithms, and alternatives in the form of case studies, their theoretical properties and alternative algorithms.

Acknowledgements. We would like to thank Marko Kääramees for helping to provide the student data and UCI Machine Learning Repository for providing the datasets used for algorithm comparison.

References

1. Carpineto, C., Romano, G.: Using concept lattices for text retrieval and mining. In: Ganter, B., Stumme, G., Wille, R. (eds.) Formal Concept Analysis. LNCS (LNAI), vol. 3626, pp. 161–179. Springer, Heidelberg (2005). https://doi.org/10.1007/11528784_9
2. Dias, S.M., Newton, J.V.: Concept lattices reduction: definition, analysis and classification. Expert. Syst. Appl. **42**(20), 7084–7097 (2015)
3. Ganter, B., Wille, R.: Formal Concept Analysis: Mathematical Foundations. Springer, Heidelberg (2012). https://doi.org/10.1007/978-3-642-59830-2
4. Hartigan, J.A., Wong, M.A.: Algorithm AS 136: K-means clustering algorithm. J. R. Stat. Soc. **28**, 100–108 (1979)
5. Hesse, W., Tilley, T.: Formal concept analysis used for software analysis and modelling. In: Ganter, B., Stumme, G., Wille, R. (eds.) Formal Concept Analysis. LNCS (LNAI), vol. 3626, pp. 288–303. Springer, Heidelberg (2005). https://doi.org/10.1007/11528784_15
6. Klimushkin, M., Obiedkov, S., Roth, C.: Approaches to the selection of relevant concepts in the case of noisy data. In: Kwuida, L., Sertkaya, B. (eds.) ICFCA 2010. LNCS (LNAI), vol. 5986, pp. 255–266. Springer, Heidelberg (2010). https://doi.org/10.1007/978-3-642-11928-6_18
7. Kuznetsov, S.O., Makhalova, T.: On interestingness measures of formal concepts. arXiv preprint arXiv:1611.02646 (2016)
8. Kuznetsov, S.O.: Galois connections in data analysis: contributions from the Soviet era and modern Russian research. In: Ganter, B., Stumme, G., Wille, R. (eds.) Formal Concept Analysis. LNCS (LNAI), vol. 3626, pp. 196–225. Springer, Heidelberg (2005). https://doi.org/10.1007/11528784_11
9. Kuznetsov, S.O.: On stability of a formal concept. Ann. Math. Artif. Intell. **49**(1–4), 101–115 (2007)
10. Lakhal, L., Stumme, G.: Efficient mining of association rules based on formal concept analysis. In: Ganter, B., Stumme, G., Wille, R. (eds.) Formal Concept Analysis. LNCS (LNAI), vol. 3626, pp. 180–195. Springer, Heidelberg (2005). https://doi.org/10.1007/11528784_10
11. Mets, M.: Simplifying concept lattices with concept chains. Master thesis in Estonian, Tallinn (2018)
12. Neznanov, A., Ilvovsky, D., Parinov, A.: Advancing FCA workflow in FCART system for knowledge discovery in quantitative data. Procedia Comput. Sci. **31**, 201–210 (2014)
13. Ore, O.: Chains in partially ordered sets. Bull. Am. Math. Soc. **49**(8), 558–566 (1943)

14. Priss, U.: Linguistic applications of formal concept analysis. In: Ganter, B., Stumme, G., Wille, R. (eds.) Formal Concept Analysis. LNCS (LNAI), vol. 3626, pp. 149–160. Springer, Heidelberg (2005). https://doi.org/10.1007/11528784_8
15. Torim, A., Lindroos, K.: Sorting concepts by priority using the theory of monotone systems. In: Eklund, P., Haemmerlé, O. (eds.) ICCS-ConceptStruct 2008. LNCS (LNAI), vol. 5113, pp. 175–188. Springer, Heidelberg (2008). https://doi.org/10.1007/978-3-540-70596-3_12
16. Torim, A.: Galois sub-hierarchies used for use case modeling. In: CLA, pp. 21–32 (2013)
17. Vaidya, J., Vijayalakshmi, A., Qi, G.: The role mining problem: finding a minimal descriptive set of roles. In: Proceedings of the 12th ACM Symposium on Access Control Models and Technologies. ACM (2007)
18. Valtchev, P., et al.: Galicia: an open platform for lattices. In: Using Conceptual Structures: Contributions to the 11th International Conference on Conceptual Structures (ICCS 2003) (2003)
19. Wille, R.: Formal concept analysis as mathematical theory of concepts and concept hierarchies. In: Ganter, B., Stumme, G., Wille, R. (eds.) Formal Concept Analysis. LNCS (LNAI), vol. 3626, pp. 1–33. Springer, Heidelberg (2005). https://doi.org/10.1007/11528784_1
20. Võhandu, L., et al.: Some algorithms for data table (re) ordering using Monotone Systems. In: Proceedings of the 5th WSEAS International Conference on Artificial Intelligence, Knowledge Engineering and Data Bases: 5th WSEAS International Conference on Artificial Intelligence, Knowledge Engineering and Data Bases (AIKED 2006) (2006)
21. Wille, R.: Restructuring lattice theory: an approach based on hierarchies of concepts. In: Rival, I. (ed.) Ordered Sets, pp. 445–470. Springer, Dordrecht (1982). https://doi.org/10.1007/978-94-009-7798-3_15
22. Liiv, I.: Pattern Discovery Using Seriation and Matrix Reordering: A Unified View, Extensions and an Application to Inventory Management. TUT Press, Tallinn (2008)
23. Yevtushenko, S. A.: System of data analysis "Concept Explorer". In: Proceedings of the 7th National Conference on Artificial Intelligence, KII 2000, Russia, pp. 127–134 (2000). (In Russian)

The Compositional Rule of Inference Under the Composition Max-Product

Nourelhouda Zerarka[1]([envelope])[ID], Saoussen Bel Hadj Kacem[1,2], and Moncef Tagina[1]

[1] National School of Computer Sciences, COSMOS Research Laboratory,
University of Manouba, 2010 Manouba, Tunisia
{nourelhouda.zerarka,Saoussen.BelHadjKacem,moncef.tagina}@ensi-uma.tn
[2] Faculty of Economic Sciences and Management of Nabeul,
University of Carthage, 8000 Nabeul, Tunisia

Abstract. Approximate reasoning is used in Fuzzy Inference Systems to handle imprecise knowledge. It aims to be close as possible to human reasoning. The main approach of approximate reasoning is the compositional rule of inference, which generates different methods by varying its parameters: a t-norm and an implication. In most cases, combinations of t-norms and implications do not fit human intuitions. Based on these methods, we suggest the use of the product t-norm in the compositional rule of inference. We combine this t-norm with different known implications. We then study these combinations and check if they give reasonable consequences.

Keywords: Fuzzy logic · Approximate reasoning ·
Compositional rule of inference · Max-product · Fuzzy implication

1 Introduction

Human reasoning is approximate rather than exact, since it handles imprecise information. For that, fuzzy logic was introduced by Zadeh in 1965 [9] where the main idea was to infer a result from fuzzy concepts. Systems using fuzzy logic have got a big success in this last decade in many fields like medical domain [6], damage detection [7]... etc.

Approximate Reasoning [11] imitates human reasoning in undefined situations, to solve complex problems that do not have a precise solution with traditional methods. It is used in control systems, expert systems or decision support systems to give actions from vague predicates. Compositional Rule of Inference (CRI) [2] is the first and the principal approximate reasoning approach. It allows inferring a result from a function which contains two operators: a t-norm and an implication. Triangular norm [1] (t-norm for short) is a binary function which is used as a conjunction function in fuzzy systems. Fuzzy implication [8] is a function that allows evaluating a rule from the values of its premise and conclusion. According to some authors [2–5], some combinations of t-norms and implications do not always fit the human intuitions. For that and to insure an appropriate

© Springer Nature Switzerland AG 2019
D. Endres et al. (Eds.): ICCS 2019, LNAI 11530, pp. 204–217, 2019.
https://doi.org/10.1007/978-3-030-23182-8_15

inference result, it is necessary to study all the possible combinations and their compatibility. This will establish a general guide for fuzzy inference systems developers when choosing its parameters.

We noticed after a literature review that some studies were made considering Zadeh t-norm [2,5], Lukasiewicz t-norm [4] and drastic product t-norm [3] with a set of known implications. Mizumoto et al. [3–5] have used six criteria in their works. These criteria were suggested by Fukami [2] to describe how the comportment of approximate reasoning should be in order to meet human reasoning. The authors have verified the satisfaction of the criteria by the treated combinations. They found that some combinations didn't verify all the criteria and it gave some incompatible ones.

According to our knowledge, no work in the compositional rule of inference was interested in the product t-norm. For that, our aim in this paper is to study the product t-norm in combination with some of the considered implications in [3–5]. We show the results obtained from different combinations, we also check if they verify the axiomatic of approximate reasoning. In addition to that, we summarize at the end the results of our study, with recommending compatible couples. Our study combined with the previous studies will be like a complete guide that could orientate a fuzzy inference system user in the choice of the t-norm and the implication.

The paper is organized as follows. In the second section, we present the compositional rule of inference, and we cite the existing work that studied combinations of t-norms and implications in the compositional rule of inference. The third section is dedicated to our work about the study of the product t-norm in combination with the principal implication operators. The last section concludes this work.

2 Literature Review

2.1 Compositional Rule of Inference

The compositional rule of inference (CRI) [11] was proposed by Zadeh, in order to give an approximate reasoning and to determine new deductions in a fuzzy inference system. The CRI is based on Generalized Modus Ponens (GMP) which gives us the possibility to infer by an observation different from the rule's premise. The GMP is of the following form:

Ant 1: If X is A then Y is B
Ant 2: X is A'

Cons: Y is B'

where X and Y are linguistic variables, A, A', B and B' are fuzzy sets. A and A' belong to the universe of discourse U. B and B' belong to the universe of discourse V. Using CRI, the membership function of the conclusion B' is calculated by the Eq. (1).

$$\forall v \in V, \mu_{B'}(v) = \sup_{u \in U} T(\mu_{A'}(u), I(\mu_A(u), \mu_B(v)))$$

(1)

where $\mu_A(u)$, $\mu_B(v)$, $\mu_{A'}(u)$ and $\mu_{B'}(v)$ are the membership functions of A, B, A' and B' respectively, T is a t-norm and I is an implication. Some of the most known t-norms and implications are illustrated in Tables 1 and 2.

Table 1. The most known t-norms.

Notation	Name	Function
∧	Zadeh	$min(u, v)$
⊙	Lukasiewicz	$max(u + v - 1, 0)$
.	Goguen	$u.v$
∧	Drastic	$\begin{cases} u \text{ if } v = 1 \\ v \text{ if } u = 1 \\ 0 \quad \text{else} \end{cases}$

To extend the fuzzy sets considered in the CRI, linguistic modifiers can be used. Linguistic modifier [10] is a tool to give a new characterization to a fuzzy set and to modify its meaning which is not far from the original. Mathematically, it is represented by α where $A' = A^\alpha$. From that, A' can have four values, $A' = A$, $A' = A^2$ when A' is very A, $A' = A^{0.5}$ if A' is more or less A, and $A' = 1 - A$ if A' is not A. The exponent of A is defined by:

$$A^\alpha = \int_U \mu_A^\alpha(u)/u \tag{2}$$

Table 2. The most used implications.

Notation	Name	Function
I_{ZM}	Zadeh	$max(1 - u, min(u, v))$
I_L	Lukasiewicz	$min(1 - u + v, 1)$
I_s	Rescher-Gaines	$\begin{cases} 1 \text{ if } u \leq v \\ 0 \text{ if } u > v \end{cases}$
I_g	Btouwer-Godel	$\begin{cases} 1 \text{ if } u \leq v \\ v \text{ if } u > v \end{cases}$

Example 1. To explain the concept of the CRI, we give a simple example.

Ant 1: If the temperature is *high* then the command is *cool*

Ant 2: The temperature is *very high*

Cons: The command is ? *cool*

To get the value of the command, we choose to use the min t-norm and Rescher-Gaines implication (I_s). The Eq. (1) becomes the following:

$$\forall v \in V, \mu_{B'}(v) = \sup_{u \in U} min(\mu_{very\ high}(u), I_s(\mu_{high}(u), \mu_{cool}(v))) \quad (3)$$

With u the temperature and v the power of the command. After executing the CRI, we find that "$B' = cool^2$" which allows concluding that the command is *very cool*. The representations of the fuzzy sets *high*, *very high*, *cool* and *very cool* are in Fig. 1.

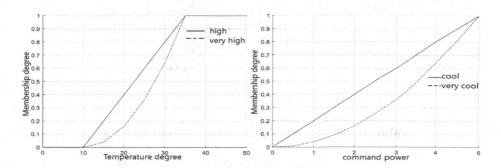

Fig. 1. Representation of the membership function of the fuzzy sets *high*, *very high* *cool* and *very cool*.

2.2   Fuzzy Reasoning Methods

The CRI was tested in [2–5] by Mizumoto et al. using the t-norms of Zadeh, Lukasiewicz and drastic product, with different implications. They tried to verify whether the combinations (T, I) satisfy a set of criteria defined by Fukami [2]. These criteria reflect simple human reasoning. Their general idea is that the behavior of the consequence B' depends on the behavior of B the same way as the behavior of A' depends on the behavior of A, except in two cases (C2-2 and C4-1). For the criterion C2-1 for example, if the observation A' is very A, we should find that the consequence B' is very B. The following are the criteria:

$$\textbf{C1: } A' = A \Rightarrow B' = B \text{ (modus ponens)} \quad (4)$$

$$\textbf{C2-1: } A' = \text{very } A \Rightarrow B' = \text{very } B \quad (5)$$

$$\textbf{C2-2: } A' = \text{very } A \Rightarrow B' = B \quad (6)$$

$$\textbf{C3: } A' = \text{more or less } A \Rightarrow B' = \text{more or less } B \quad (7)$$

$$\textbf{C4-1: } A' = \text{not } A \Rightarrow B' = \text{unknown} \quad (8)$$

$$\textbf{C4-2: } A' = \text{not } A \Rightarrow B' = \text{not } B \quad (9)$$

Mizumoto and Zimmermann [5] and Fukami et al. [2] have tested the CRI using the t-norm min of Zadeh with various implications. The authors have got the results where an extract is shown in Table 3. With the t-norm min, the implications I_{ZM} and I_L do not satisfy the criteria except C4-1, I_s satisfies C1, C2-1, C3 and C4-1, and finally I_g satisfies C1, C2-2, C3 and C4-1. This study allows affirming that t-norm min is not compatible with I_{ZM} and I_L, but compatible with I_s and I_g.

Table 3. Inference results under the composition max-min.

	A	Very A	More or less A	not A
I_{ZM}	$0.5 \vee \mu_B(v)$	$\frac{3-\sqrt{5}}{2} \vee \mu_B(v)$	$\frac{\sqrt{5}-1}{2} \vee \mu_B(v)$	1
I_L	$\frac{1+\mu_B(v)}{2}$	$\frac{3+2\mu_B(v)-\sqrt{5+4\mu_B(v)}}{2}$	$\frac{\sqrt{5+4\mu_B(v)}-1}{2}$	1
I_s	$\mu_B(v)$	$\mu_B^2(v)$	$\sqrt{\mu_B(v)}$	1
I_g	$\mu_B(v)$	$\mu_B(v)$	$\sqrt{\mu_B(v)}$	1

Table 4. Inference results under the composition max-$\odot$.

	A	Very A	More or less A	not A
I_{ZM}	$\mu_B(v)$	$\mu_B(v)$	$\frac{1}{4} \vee \mu_B(v)$	1
I_L	$\mu_B(v)$	$\mu_B(v)$	$\begin{cases} \mu_B(v) + \frac{1}{4} & \text{if } \mu_B(v) \leq \frac{1}{4} \\ \sqrt{\mu_B(v)} & \text{if } \mu_B(v) \geq \frac{1}{4} \end{cases}$	1
I_s	$\mu_B(v)$	$\mu_B^2(v)$	$\sqrt{\mu_B(v)}$	1
I_g	$\mu_B(v)$	$\mu_B(v)$	$\sqrt{\mu_B(v)}$	1

Table 5. Inference results under the composition max-$\wedge$.

	A	Very A	More or less A	not A
I_{ZM}	$\mu_B(v)$	$\mu_B(v)$	$\mu_B(v)$	1
I_L	$\mu_B(v)$	$\mu_B(v)$	$\sqrt{\mu_B(v)}$	1
I_s	$\mu_B(v)$	$\mu_B^2(v)$	$\sqrt{\mu_B(v)}$	1
I_g	$\mu_B(v)$	$\mu_B(v)$	$\sqrt{\mu_B(v)}$	1

In [4], Mizumoto has chosen the t-norm of Lukasiewicz ($\odot$) combined with the same set of implications. An extract of the results is shown in Table 4. The study shows that only I_s and I_g check the criteria of approximate reasoning, and therefore they are compatible with Lukasiewicz t-norm.

Mizumoto has proposed in [3] the use of the drastic t-norm ($\wedge$) with the same implications. Table 5 shows an extract of this study. We can see that in addition of I_s and I_g, I_L is also compatible with the drastic t-norm.

3   Proposal Methods with Product T-Norm

The choice of the t-norm and the implication in CRI is very important to get consequences that satisfy human intuitions. We have noticed that no work has studied the product t-norm (.) (see Table 1). For that, we propose to use the product as t-norm for the CRI to see the satisfaction of the criteria ((4)–(9)), in combination with the implications cited in Table 2. To get the membership function of the result B', we use the following equation:

$$\forall v \in V, \mu_{B'}(v) = sup_{u \in U} \; prod(\mu_{A'}(u), I(\mu_A(u), \mu_B(v))) \tag{10}$$

Where μ_A, $\mu_{A'}$, μ_B and $\mu_{B'}$ are membership functions of the fuzzy sets A, A', B and B' respectively.

Our aim is to evaluate the conclusion B' when using the couple (prod, I) to test the satisfaction of all the criteria ((4)–(9)). We want to find the best combination that satisfies these criteria. We should mention that our demonstrations in this paper follow the same principle and procedure used in [2–5]. We take the variable α with value 1 (if $A' = A$), 2 (if $A' = very$ A) or 0.5 (if $A' = more$ or $less$ A) where the membership function of the fuzzy set A' is $\mu_A^\alpha(u)$. Consequently, the conclusion B' is calculated by the following equation:

$$\vee v \in V, \mu_{B'}(v) = sup_{u \in U} \; prod(\mu_A^\alpha(u), I(\mu_A(u), \mu_B(v))) \tag{11}$$

3.1   The Case of the Implication of Zadeh

The first combination that we consider for the CRI is the product t-norm and Zadeh implication. We test the combination (prod, I_{ZM}) to verify the satisfaction of the criteria ((4)–(9)). The membership function of the result is calculated by the following function:

$$B'_{ZM} = \int_V \bigvee_{u \in U} (\mu_A^\alpha(u).((\mu_A(u) \wedge \mu_B(v)) \vee (1 - \mu_A(u))))/v \tag{12}$$

In order to evaluate the fuzzy set B', we first consider the function S_{ZM}:

$$S_{ZM}(\mu_A(u), \alpha) = \mu_A^\alpha(u).((\mu_A(u) \wedge \mu_B(v)) \vee (1 - \mu_A(u))) \tag{13}$$

Theorem 1. *The criterion C1 of modus ponens* (4) *is not satisfied by the combination* (prod, I_{ZM}).

Proof. C1 considers that $A' = A$, so $\alpha = 1$. Using the Eq. (13) with $\alpha = 1$ we get:

$$S_{ZM}(\mu_A(u), 1) = \mu_A^1(u).((\mu_A(u) \wedge \mu_B(v)) \vee (1 - \mu_A(u))) \tag{14}$$

Figure 2(a) shows the function $S_{ZM}(\mu_A(u), 1)$ in terms of $\mu_B(v)$ and $\mu_A(u)$. $\mu_A(u)$ and $\mu_B(v)$ take all the values in the interval [0,1] according to u and v varying over U and V respectively. For example, if $\mu_B(v) = 0.2$, the expression $S_{ZM}(\mu_A(u), 1)$ is indicated by "- - -" in Fig. 2(a). We can see that the maximum

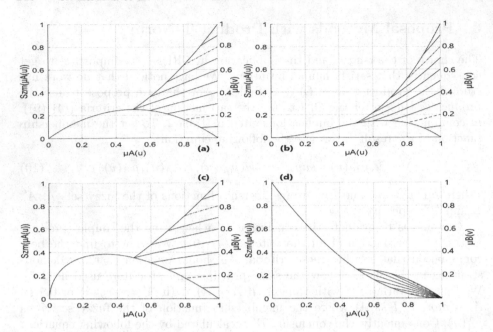

Fig. 2. Representation of the result $S_{ZM}(\mu_A(u), \alpha)$ when (a) $\mu_{A'} = \mu_A$, (b) $\mu_{A'} = \mu_A^2$, (c) $\mu_{A'} = \mu_A^{0.5}$, (d) $\mu_{A'} = 1 - \mu_A$.

value of $S_{ZM}(\mu_A(u), 1)$ for $\mu_B(v) = 0.2$ is $\frac{1}{4}$. On the other hand, when $\mu_B(v) = 0.8$, $S_{ZM}(\mu_A(u), 1)$ is shown by "-.-.-". The maximum value of this function for $\mu_B(v) = 0.8$ become 0.8. More generally, when $\mu_B(v)$ is bigger than $\frac{1}{4}$, the maximum value of $S_{ZM}(\mu_A(u), 1)$ is equal to $\mu_B(v)$. But if $\mu_B(v)$ is smaller or equal to $\frac{1}{4}$, the maximum value of $S_{ZM}(\mu_A(u), 1)$ becomes equal to $\frac{1}{4}$. We deduce that the value of $\bigvee_{u \in U} S_{ZM}(\mu_A(u), 1)$ is:

$$\bigvee_{u \in U} S_{ZM}(\mu_A(u), 1) = \begin{cases} \mu_B(v) & if \ \mu_B(v) > \frac{1}{4} \\ \frac{1}{4} & else \end{cases} \tag{15}$$

So from (15), we conclude that the membership function of the inferred result B' is different from B and is:

$$B'_{ZM} = \int_V \bigvee_{u \in U} S_{ZM}(\mu_A(u), 1)/v$$
$$B'_{ZM} = \int_V \mu_B(v) \vee \frac{1}{4}/v \tag{16}$$

Theorem 2. *The criteria C2-1 and C2-2 of (5) and (6) respectively, are not satisfied by the combination (prod, I_{ZM}).*

Proof. Criteria C2-1 and C2-2 concern the case when $A' = A^2$, then $\alpha = 2$. Using the Eq. (13) and with $\alpha = 2$, we get:

$$S_{ZM}(\mu_A(u), 2) = \mu_A^2(u).((\mu_A(u) \wedge \mu_B(v)) \vee (1 - \mu_A(u))) \tag{17}$$

From Fig. 2(b), we can see that:

$$\bigvee_{u \in U} S_{ZM}(\mu_A(u), 2) = \begin{cases} \mu_B(v) \ if \ \mu_B(v) > \frac{\sqrt{3}-1}{5} \\ \frac{\sqrt{3}-1}{5} \qquad else \end{cases} \tag{18}$$

We deduce that the value of B' is different from B^2 or B and is:

$$B'_{ZM} = \int_V \mu_B(v) \vee \frac{\sqrt{3}-1}{5} /v \tag{19}$$

Theorem 3. *The criterion C3 of (7) is not satisfied by the combination (prod, I_{ZM}).*

Proof. The criterion C3 considers that $A' = A^{0.5}$, so that $\alpha = 0.5$. Using the Eq. (13) and with $\alpha = 0.5$, we obtain:

$$S_{ZM}(\mu_A(u), 0.5) = \mu_A^{0.5}(u).((\mu_A(u) \wedge \mu_B(v)) \vee (1 - \mu_A(u))) \tag{20}$$

From Fig. 2(c), we get:

$$\bigvee_{u \in U} S_{ZM}(\mu_A(u), 0.5) = \begin{cases} \mu_B(v) \ if \ \mu_B(v) > \frac{3-\sqrt{5}}{2} \\ \frac{3-\sqrt{5}}{2} \qquad else \end{cases} \tag{21}$$

The value of the inferred result B' is then different from $\sqrt{B}$ and it is:

$$B'_{ZM} = \int_V \mu_B \vee \frac{3-\sqrt{5}}{2} /v \tag{22}$$

Theorem 4. *The criterion C4-1 of (8) is satisfied by the combination (prod, I_{ZM}).*

Proof. The criteria C4-1 and C4-2 suppose that $A' = 1 - A$, so we have:

$$S_{ZM}(\mu_A(u)) = (1 - \mu_A(u)).((\mu_A(u) \wedge \mu_B(v)) \vee (1 - \mu_A(u))) \tag{23}$$

From Fig. 2(d), we can see that, whatever the value of $\mu_B(v)$, S_{ZM} is always equal to 1. Which implies that the maximum value of S_{ZM} is 1 for all $\mu_B(v)$. We conclude that the inferred result B' is unknown:

$$B'_{ZM} = \int_V 1/v \tag{24}$$

3.2   The Case of the Implication of Lukasiewicz

The second combination that we treat for the CRI is the product t-norm and Lukasiewicz implication I_L (see Table 1). We show the consequence B' and we verify the satisfaction of the criteria ((4)–(9)).

$$B'_L = \int_V \bigvee_{u \in U} \mu_A^\alpha(u).((1 - \mu_A(u) + \mu_B(v)) \wedge 1)/v \tag{25}$$

and

$$S_L(\mu_A(u), \alpha) = \mu_A^\alpha(u).((1 - \mu_A(u) + \mu_B(v)) \wedge 1) \tag{26}$$

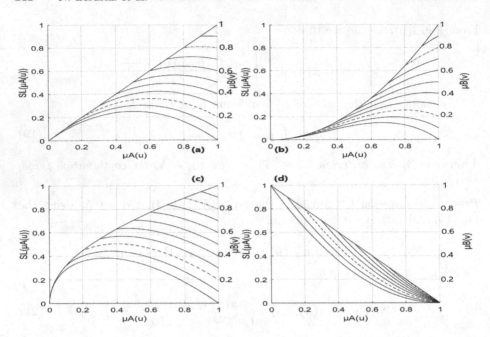

Fig. 3. Representation of the result $S_L(\mu_A(u), \alpha)$ when (a) $\mu_{A'} = \mu_A$, (b) $\mu_{A'} = \mu_A^2$, (c) $\mu_{A'} = \mu_A^{0.5}$, (d) $\mu_{A'} = 1 - \mu_A$

Theorem 5. *The criterion C1 of modus ponens (4) is not satisfied by the combination (Prod, I_L).*

Proof. By the Eq. (26) and when $\alpha = 1$, we can have:

$$S_L(\mu_A(u), 1) = \mu_A^1(u).((1 - \mu_A(u) + \mu_B(v)) \wedge 1) \tag{27}$$

From Fig. 3(a), we deduce that:

$$\bigvee_{u \in U} S_L(\mu_A(u), 1) = \frac{1 + \mu_B(v)(2 + \mu_B(v))}{4} \tag{28}$$

Therefore, the value of the inferred result B' is:

$$B'_L = \int_V \frac{1 + \mu_B(v)(2 + \mu_B(v))}{4} /v \tag{29}$$

Theorem 6. *The criteria C2-1 and C2-2 of (5) and (6) respectively, are not satisfied by the combination (Prod, I_L).*

Proof. Using the Eq. (26) with $\alpha = 2$, we get:

$$S_L(\mu_A(u), 2) = \mu_A^2(u).((1 - \mu_A(u) + \mu_B(v)) \wedge 1) \tag{30}$$

We can see from Fig. 3(b) that the inferred result B' is:

$$B'_L = \begin{cases} \int_V \mu_B(v)/v \ if \ \mu_B(v) \geq 0.5 \\ \int_V \frac{4^{\mu_B(v)}\sqrt{3}-1}{5}/v \qquad else \end{cases} \tag{31}$$

Theorem 7. *The criterion C3 of (7) is not satisfied by the combination (Prod, I_L).*

Proof. C3 concerns the case where $A^{\alpha} = A^{0.5}$. From the Eq. (26) with $\alpha = 0.5$, we get: $S_L(\mu_A(u), 0.5) = \mu_A^{0.5}(u).((1 - \mu_A(u) + \mu_B(v)) \wedge 1)$.

From Fig. 3(c), we see that the inferred result B' is:

$$B'_L = \begin{cases} \int_V \mu_B^{0.5}(v)/v \ if \ \mu_B(v) \geq 0.5 \\ \int_V \frac{3+\mu_B(v)-\sqrt{5-\mu_B(v)}}{2}/v \qquad else \end{cases} \tag{32}$$

Theorem 8. *The criterion C4-1 of (8) is satisfied by the combination (Prod, I_L).*

Proof. The criteria C4-1 and C4-2 concern the case when $A' = 1 - A$. So we have:

$$S_L(\mu_A(u)) = (1 - \mu_A(u)).((1 - \mu_A(u) + \mu_B(v)) \wedge 1) \tag{33}$$

From Fig. 3(d), we see that the maximum value of S_L is equal to 1 whatever the value of $\mu_B(v)$. Thus, the inferred result B'_L is undefined.

3.3 The Case of the Implication of Rescher-Gaines

The fourth combination discussed for the CRI is the product t-norm and Rescher-Gaines implication. The consequence B' is done by:

$$B'_s = \int_V \bigvee_{u \in U} \mu_A^{\alpha}(u).I_s(\mu_A(u), \mu_B(v))/v \tag{34}$$

Assuming that:

$$S_s(\mu_A(u), \alpha) = \mu_A^{\alpha}(u).I_s(\mu_A(u), \mu_B(v)) \tag{35}$$

Theorem 9. *The criteria C1, C2-2 and C3 of (4), (6) and (7) are satisfied by the combination (Prod, I_s).*

Proof. From the equation (35), we can get: $S_s(\mu_A(u), \alpha) = \mu_A^{\alpha}(u).I_s(\mu_A(u), \mu_B(v))$.

Having $\alpha = 1, 2$ and 0.5, we see from Fig. 4(a) (b) (c) that:

$$\bigvee_{u \in U} S_s(\mu_A(u), \alpha) = \mu_B^{\alpha}(v) \tag{36}$$

We conclude that the value of the inferred result B' is:

$$B'_s = \int_V \mu_B^{\alpha}(v)/v \tag{37}$$

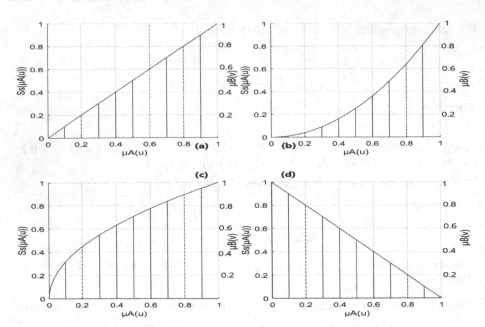

Fig. 4. Representation of the result $S_s(\mu_A(u), \alpha)$ when (a) $\mu_{A'} = \mu_A$, (b) $\mu_{A'} = \mu_A^2$, (c) $\mu_{A'} = \mu_A^{0.5}$, (d) $\mu_{A'} = 1 - \mu_A$.

Theorem 10. *The criteria C4-1 of* (8) *is satisfied by the combination* $(Prod, I_s)$.

Proof. The value of $S_s(\mu_A(u))$ is: $S_s(\mu_A(u)) = (1 - \mu_A(u)).I_s(\mu_A(u), \mu_B(v))$.

From Fig. 4(d), we get 1 as the maximum value of S_s for all $\mu_B(v)$, so B' is undefined.

3.4 The Case of the Implication of Btouwer-Godel

The fifth combination for the CRI that we consider is the product t-norm and Btouwer-Godel implication. The consequence B' is shown and the satisfaction of the criteria $((4)-(9))$ is verified.

$$B'_g = \int_V \bigvee_{u \in U} \mu_A^\alpha(u).I_g(\mu_A(u), \mu_B(v))/v \tag{38}$$

In this case, we have:

$$S_g(\mu_A(u), \alpha) = \mu_A^\alpha(u).I_g(\mu_A(u), \mu_B(v)) \tag{39}$$

Theorem 11. *The criteria C1* (4)*, C2-2* (6)*, C3* (7) *and C4-1* (8) *are satisfied by the combination* $(Prod, I_g)$.

Proof. The same way is used for the demonstration using Fig. 5.

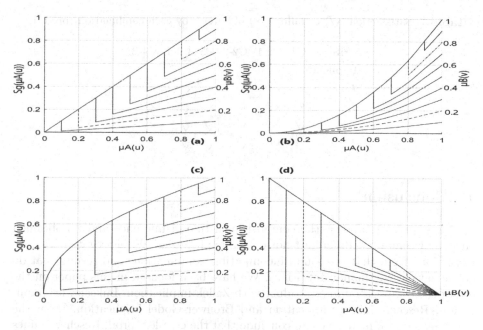

Fig. 5. Representation of the result $S_g(\mu_A(u), \alpha)$ when (a) $\mu_{A'} = \mu_A$, (b) $\mu_{A'} = \mu_A^2$, (c) $\mu_{A'} = \mu_A^{0.5}$, (d) $\mu_{A'} = 1 - \mu_A$

3.5   Comparison Table

The Table 6 shows the consequences obtained from all the combinations (product t-norm, implications) on the CRI treated in this paper.

Table 6. Inference results under the composition max-product.

	A	Very A	More or less A	not A
I_{ZM}	$\frac{1}{4} \vee \mu_B$	$\frac{\sqrt{3}-1}{5} \vee \mu_B$	$\frac{3-\sqrt{5}}{2} \vee \mu_B$	1
I_L	$\frac{1+\mu_B(2+\mu_B)}{4}$	$\begin{cases} \mu_B \ if \ \mu_B \geq \frac{1}{2} \\ \frac{4^{\mu_B}\sqrt{3}-1}{5} \ else \end{cases}$	$\begin{cases} \sqrt{\mu_B} \ if \ \mu_B \geq \frac{1}{2} \\ \frac{3+\mu_B-\sqrt{5-\mu_B}}{2} \ else \end{cases}$	1
I_s	μ_B	μ_B^2	$\sqrt{\mu_B}$	1
I_g	μ_B	μ_B	$\sqrt{\mu_B}$	1

Like shown in Table 7 and using the results from Table 6, some inference methods satisfy the criteria but others fail. Indeed, the best results were found using the implication I_s which satisfies the criteria C1, C2-1, C3 and C4-1, and the implication I_g which satisfies criteria C1, C2-2, C3 and C4-1. But the other implications do not verify all the criteria. The implications of Zadeh and Lukasiewicz satisfy only the criterion C4-1.

Table 7. Satisfaction ($\sqrt{}$) or failure ($\times$) of criteria by each combination (prod, I).

Criteria	C1	C2-1	C2-2	C3	C4-1	C4-2
Implication						
I_{ZM}	$\times$	$\times$	$\times$	$\times$	$\sqrt{}$	$\times$
I_L	$\times$	$\times$	$\times$	$\times$	$\sqrt{}$	$\times$
I_s	$\sqrt{}$	$\sqrt{}$	$\times$	$\sqrt{}$	$\sqrt{}$	$\times$
I_g	$\sqrt{}$	$\times$	$\sqrt{}$	$\sqrt{}$	$\sqrt{}$	$\times$

4   Conclusion

In this paper, we studied the compositional rule of inference and its obtained output by combining different t-norms and implications. We aggregated previous works, and from that, we found incompatible combinations and results that do not always fit the human intuitions. We have been focused in this paper on the use of the composition max-product with Zadeh implication, Lukasiewicz implication, Rescher-Gaines implication and Btouwer-Godel implication. From the different tests we made, we can conclude that the couples (prod, Rescher-Gaines implication) and (prod, Btouwer-Godel implication) could be among the best choices for approximate reasoning in fuzzy systems. Indeed, only these implications check all criteria of approximate reasoning, with difference comportment. Using them in fuzzy inference systems may thus yield a result close to that of the human expert. Therefore, for the future work we want to test new combinations using other implications.

References

1. Bandemer, H., Gottwald, S.: Fuzzy Sets, Fuzzy Logic, Fuzzy Methods. Wiley, Chichester (1995)
2. Fukami, S., Mizumoto, M., Tanaka, K.: Some considerations on fuzzy conditional inference. Fuzzy Sets Syst. **4**(3), 243–273 (1980)
3. Mizumoto, M.: Fuzzy inference using max-$\wedge$ composition in the compositional rule of inference. Approx. Reason. Decis. Anal., 67–76 (1982)
4. Mizumoto, M.: Fuzzy conditional inference under max-$\odot$ composition. Inf. Sci. **27**(3), 183–209 (1982)
5. Mizumoto, M., Zimmermann, H.J.: Comparison of fuzzy reasoning methods. Fuzzy Sets Syst. **8**(3), 253–283 (1982)
6. Nguyen, T., Khosravi, A., Creighton, D., Nahavandi, S.: Classification of healthcare data using genetic fuzzy logic system and wavelets. Expert. Syst. Appl. **42**(4), 2184–2197 (2014)
7. Sahu, S., Kumar, P.B., Parhi, D.R.: Intelegent hybrid fuzzy logic system for damage detection of beam-like structural elements. J. Theor. Appl. Mech. **55**(2), 509–521 (2017)
8. Tick, J., Fodor, J.: Fuzzy implications and inference processes. In: Computational Cybernetics, pp. 105–109 (2005)

9. Zadeh, L.A.: Fuzzy sets. Inf. Control. **8**(3), 338–353 (1965)
10. Zadeh, L.A.: A fuzzy-set-theoretic interpretation of linguistic hedges. J. Cybern. **2**(3), 4–34 (1972)
11. Zadeh, L.A.: The concept of a linguistic variable and its application to approximate reasoning-III. Inf. Sci. **9**(1), 43–80 (1975)

19. Zadeh, L.A.: Fuzzy sets. Inf. Control 8(3), 338–353 (1965)

Short Papers

Short Papers

Mining Social Networks from Linked Open Data

Raji Ghawi[✉][iD] and Jürgen Pfeffer[iD]

Bavarian School of Public Policy, Technical University of Munich, Munich, Germany
{raji.ghawi,juergen.pfeffer}@tum.de

Abstract. The richness and openness of Linked Open Data (LOD) make them invaluable resources of information, and create new opportunities for many areas of application. In this paper, we address the exploitation of LOD by utilizing SPARQL queries in order to extract social networks of entities. This enables the application of techniques from Social Network Analysis to study social interactions among entities, providing deep insights into their latent social structure.

Keywords: LOD · SNA · RDF · SPARQL algebra · Extraction patterns

1 Introduction

Linked Open Data (LOD) [1] refers to freely available data on the WWW that are typically represented using the Resource Description Framework (RDF) and standards built on it. The increasing adoption of LOD is turning the Web into a global data space that connects data from diverse domains and enables genuinely novel applications. LOD is an invaluable resource of information due to its richness and openness; hence it creates new opportunities for many areas of application. In this paper, we address how LOD can be exploited in order to extract social networks between entities. This will enable the application of de-facto techniques from *Social Network Analysis* (SNA) [7,12] to study social relations and interactions among entities, providing deep insights into their latent social structure. This paper is an attempt to bring together the two research areas of LOD and SNA. The main idea is to derive social networks from large datasets of LOD, such that extracted networks can be analyzed with SNA methods, and in return, additional knowledge is created that can be added to LOD.

Several works in literature have already attempted to combine SNA with semantic technologies. Flink [10] is an early system for semantic-based extraction and aggregation of online social networks. Martin et al. [11] proposed a model to represent social networks in RDF and showed how SPARQL can be used to query and transform networks. Other works have been proposed to use SPARQL and other semantic technologies not only to represent social networks, but also to perform social network analysis [2–4]. Groth and Gil [5] presented an approach

© Springer Nature Switzerland AG 2019
D. Endres et al. (Eds.): ICCS 2019, LNAI 11530, pp. 221–229, 2019.
https://doi.org/10.1007/978-3-030-23182-8_16

for extracting networks from Linked Data, where extracted networks can then be analyzed through network analysis algorithms, and the results of these analyses can be published back as Linked Data. Unlike these works, we focus on network extraction patterns from RDF, rather than on representing networks themselves. The contributions of this paper are as follows. We propose techniques to extract social networks from LOD and express those techniques in a formal way using SPARQL algebra (Sect. 2). Then we present a generic translation method that transform query results into networks (Sect. 3).

2   Extracting Networks

Social Networks. A social network consists of a set of actors and relations defined on them. Typically, networks are represented in terms of *graphs*. A graph G is a pair (V, E) that consists of a set V of vertices, and a set E of edges. While the elements of V represent the actors of the network, the ties between them are represented in E. Therefore, an edge is simply a pair of vertices $E = \{(v_i, v_j) \mid v_i, v_j \in V\}$. If the relation between a pair of vertices $i, j \in V$ is potentially asymmetric, we say the edges are directed (and so is the network). Otherwise, the edges are bidirectional and the network is said to be *undirected*. Relations among vertices could have a sort of strength, in this case, edges are given numeric *weights*, and we say the network is *weighted*. A weighted network is represented as a triple $G = (V, E, \omega)$ where: ω is a function that maps edges to their weight values $\omega : E \to \mathbb{R}$. In SNA literature, many metrics (indices) have been developed to characterize social networks [12].

SPARQL Algebra. We adopt the SPARQL algebra from Kaminski et al. [8, 9], which is based on the SPARQL 1.1 specification [6]. Let $\mathbf{I}, \mathbf{L}$, and $\mathbf{B}$ be pairwise disjoint sets of IRIs (Internationalized Resource Identifier), literals, and blank nodes, respectively. The set $\mathbf{T}$ of (RDF) terms is $\mathbf{I} \cup \mathbf{L} \cup \mathbf{B}$. An RDF triple is an element (s, p, o) of $(\mathbf{I} \cup \mathbf{B}) \times \mathbf{I} \times \mathbf{T}$, with s called the subject, p the predicate, and o the object. An RDF graph is a finite set of RDF triples. SPARQL algebra is based on three types of building blocks: expressions, patterns, and queries, that are built over terms $\mathbf{T}$ and an infinite set $\mathbf{X} = \{?x, ?y, \cdots\}$ of variables, disjoint from $\mathbf{T}$. A pattern in SPARQL can be a *basic graph pattern (BGP)* which is a set of triple patterns [9], i.e., elements of the set $(\mathbf{T} \cup \mathbf{X}) \times (\mathbf{I} \cup \mathbf{X}) \times (\mathbf{T} \cup \mathbf{X})$. Other types of patterns include: *union*, *join*, and *filter*. A group-aggregation construct is defined as: $GroupAgg(Z, ?x, f, E, P)$, where Z is a set of variables, called grouping variables, $?x$ is another variable, called aggregation variable, f is an aggregate function, E is an expression, and P is a pattern. Queries in SPARQL are expressions of the form $Project(X, P)$, for P a pattern and X a set of variables (called free variables). The semantics of SPARQL is defined in terms of (solution) mappings, that is, partial functions μ from variables $\mathbf{X}$ to terms $\mathbf{T}$. The solution of a SPARQL query Q over an RDF graph G is a multiset of mappings $\Omega = [\![P]\!]_G$, where $[\![.]\!]_G$ is an evaluation function that maps queries and RDF graphs to multisets of solution mappings.

In the following, we introduce techniques for extracting social networks from LOD using SPARQL. Those techniques are based on identification of common RDF triple patterns and how the network ties are inferred from such patterns. We classify those techniques based on the number of predicates and number of RDF triples in a pattern. We start with patterns having one predicate p, where we present possible patterns composed of one and two RDF triples, all having p as predicate. Then, we discuss patterns having two predicates p, q, where we present possible patterns for two, three, and four RDF triples.

2.1 Extraction Using One Predicate

We start with patterns having one predicate $p \in \mathbf{I}$. We present the possible patterns composed of one, and two RDF triples, having p as predicate.

Pattern with One Triple. Given certain predicate $p \in \mathbf{I}$, let $?u, ?v \in \mathbf{X}$ be two variables, then the BGP $(?u, p, ?v)$ represents a direct relation (tie) from a node represented by $?u$ to a node represented by $?v$ using the predicate p, as shown in Fig. 1-a. We call this case: *direct extraction*. To extract all such ties among nodes in the RDF graph using p, the following SPARQL query can be used: $Q_1 = Project(\{?u, ?v\}, \{(?u, p, ?v)\})$ which can be translated into SPARQL syntax as: **SELECT ?u ?v WHERE {?u p ?v.}**. The extracted relation in this case is always *directional*, hence, the extracted social network will be *directed*.

Example 1. The YAGO dataset[1] has a predicate **yago:influences** that relates persons to others who have influence on them (on their opinions or work). To extract a social network based on this *influence* relationship, we can use this query: $Q = Project(\{?u, ?v\}, \{(?u, \mathtt{yago:influences}, ?v)\})$

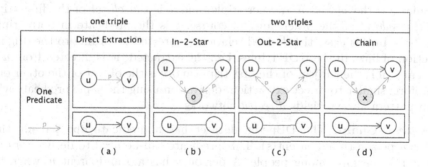

Fig. 1. Extraction patterns using one predicate p

---

[1] http://yago-knowledge.org.

Patterns with Two Triples. Social networks can be indirectly extracted from RDF data when the relation is *implicit* in the RDF graph. When we derive a tie between two nodes using two RDF triples, it does matter where the positions of those nodes in the RDF triples are: subject-subject, object-object, subject-object, or object-subject. Therefore, we distinguish three derivation patterns (variants), namely: in-2-star, out-2-star, and chain (Fig. 1).

In the first pattern *in-2-star*, a tie between two nodes u, v is derived when both nodes are linked to a third node o, that is, when u and v are in the *subject* position of two RDF triples having the same *object* o and the same predicate p (Fig. 1-b). With *out-2-star* pattern, a tie between two nodes u, v is derived when both nodes have incoming links from a third node s, that is, when u and v are in the *object* position of two RDF triples having the same *subject* s and the same predicate p (Fig. 1-c). In both in-2-star and out-2-star patterns, the derived relation is bidirectional, therefore, in contrast to direct extraction, derivation using the same predicate with these patterns always yields *undirected* networks.

Example 2. **In-2-Star.** The YAGO predicate `yago:actedIn` can be used to derive co-acting network among actors who acted in same movies. The query can be expressed as:

$Q = Project(\{?u, ?v\}, \{(?u, \texttt{yago:actedIn}, ?o), (?v, \texttt{yago:actedIn}, ?o)\})$

Example 3. **Out-2-Star.** The DBpedia dataset[2] has a predicate `dbo:starring` that relates a movie (or TV show) to people who have a starring role in it. This predicate can be used to derive a relationship among actors who have starring roles in same movies. The following query can be used for this purpose:

$Q = Project(\{?u, ?v\}, \{(?s, \texttt{dbo:starring}, ?u), (?s, \texttt{dbo:starring}, ?v)\})$

In *chain* pattern, a tie between two nodes u, v is derived when there is a chain of two links starting from one of these nodes, ending at the other, and traversing a third node x. This case for instance occurs when u is the *subject* of a triple, v is the *object* of another triple, and x is the *object* of the first triple and the *subject* of the other, and, of course, p is the predicate in both triples (Fig. 1-d). In this case, the derived relation is directed according to the original direction of links in the RDF triples. i.e., the extracted tie is directed from u to v, because u is the subject of the first triple and v is the object of the other one. Therefore, similar to direct extraction, derivation using the same predicate with chain pattern always yields *directed* networks.

Example 4. **Chain.** The DBpedia dataset has a predicate `dbo:parent` that relates a person to his parent(s). This predicate can be used to derive a *grandparent* relationship among people. A person u has a grandparent v, when the parent of u is x and the parent of x is v. The corresponding query is:

$Q = Project(\{?u, ?v\}, \{(?u, \texttt{dbo:parent}, ?x), (?x, \texttt{dbo:parent}, ?v)\})$

Table 1 shows the SPARQL queries that are used to extract ties among nodes in the RDF graph using the three patterns: in-2-star, out-2-star, and chain.

---

[2] https://wiki.dbpedia.org.

Table 1. Queries for extraction patterns with single predicate

Pattern		Query
Direct	$u \rightarrow v$	$Q_1 = Project(\{?\mathbf{u}, ?\mathbf{v}\}, \{(?\mathbf{u}, \mathbf{p}, ?\mathbf{v})\})$
In-2-Star	$u \rightarrow o \leftarrow v$	$Q_2 = Project(\{?\mathbf{u}, ?\mathbf{v}\}, \{(?\mathbf{u}, \mathbf{p}, ?o), (?\mathbf{v}, \mathbf{p}, ?o)\})$
Out-2-Star	$u \leftarrow s \rightarrow v$	$Q_3 = Project(\{?\mathbf{u}, ?\mathbf{v}\}, \{(?s, \mathbf{p}, ?\mathbf{u}), (?s, \mathbf{p}, ?\mathbf{v})\})$
Chain	$u \rightarrow x \rightarrow v$	$Q_4 = Project(\{?\mathbf{u}, ?\mathbf{v}\}, \{(?\mathbf{u}, \mathbf{p}, ?x), (?x, \mathbf{p}, ?\mathbf{v})\})$

Networks derived by the same predicate can be *weighted* when the number of co-occurrences of the in-2-star pattern is taken into consideration. For instance, in co-acting network, the weight of a tie between two actors is the number of movies they commonly acted in. In order to express this relation in a SPARQL query, we need a group-aggregation algebraic pattern. Kaminski's SPARQL algebra provides *GroupAgg* construct for this purpose. For example, to extract a weighted network using in-2-star pattern the needed query can be written as:

$Project(\{?\mathbf{u}, ?v, ?w\}, GroupAgg(\langle ?u, ?v \rangle, ?w, \mathbf{Count}, ?o, \{(?u, p, ?o), (?v, p, ?o)\}))$

In this query, the list of grouping variables is $Z = \langle ?u, ?v \rangle$ (as we want to count the number of their co-occurrences), the aggregation variable is $?w$, a fresh variable to store the weight of the tie, the aggregation function f is Count, the aggregation expression is simply the variable $?o$, and the pattern P is $\{(?u, p, ?o), (?v, p, ?o)\}$. Finally, we select the three variables u, v and w. The query can be syntactically expressed as:

`SELECT ?u ?v (COUNT(?o) AS ?w) WHERE {?u p ?o. ?v p ?o} GROUP BY ?u ?v`

2.2 Extraction Using Two Predicates

In this section, we discuss patterns having two predicates $p, q \in \mathbf{I}$. We present the possible patterns composed of two, three, and four RDF triples, having p and q predicates. All patterns presented here have *weighted* versions that we will not present for sake of brevity.

Patterns with Two Triples. In this type of derivation, a tie is extracted from two RDF triples having two different predicates $p, q \in \mathbf{I}$. Similarly to derivation using same predicate, we distinguish three patterns according to the positions of nodes in the triples, namely: in-2-star, out-2-star, and chain (Table 2). These patterns have respectively the same configurations as their corresponding patterns in the previous section, however, the difference here is that the two triples have different predicates p and q.

Patterns with Three Triples. Among different possible patterns of two predicates and three triples, we present two common patterns as shown in Fig. 2. With *parallel-in* pattern, a tie is extracted from a node u to another one v, when both

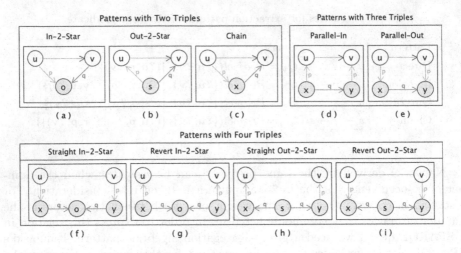

Fig. 2. Extraction patterns using two predicates p, q.

Table 2. Queries for extraction patterns with two predicates.

Pattern	Query
In-2-Star	$Project(\{?\mathbf{u}, ?\mathbf{v}\}, \{(?\mathbf{u}, \mathsf{p}, ?o), (?\mathbf{v}, \mathsf{q}, ?o)\})$
Out-2-Star	$Project(\{?\mathbf{u}, ?\mathbf{v}\}, \{(?s, \mathsf{p}, ?\mathbf{u}), (?s, \mathsf{q}, ?\mathbf{v})\})$
Chain	$Project(\{?\mathbf{u}, ?\mathbf{v}\}, \{(?\mathbf{u}, \mathsf{p}, ?x), (?x, \mathsf{q}, ?\mathbf{v})\})$
Parallel-In	$Project(\{?\mathbf{u}, ?\mathbf{v}\}, \{(?x, \mathsf{p}, ?\mathbf{u}), (?y, \mathsf{p}, ?\mathbf{v}), (?x, \mathsf{q}, ?y)\})$
Parallel-Out	$Project(\{?\mathbf{u}, ?\mathbf{v}\}, \{(?\mathbf{u}, \mathsf{p}, ?x), (?\mathbf{v}, \mathsf{p}, ?y), (?x, \mathsf{q}, ?y)\})$
Straight In-2-Star	$Project(\{?\mathbf{u}, ?\mathbf{v}\}, \{(?\mathbf{u}, \mathsf{p/q}, ?o), (?\mathbf{v}, \mathsf{p/q}, ?o)\})$
Revert In-2-Star	$Project(\{?\mathbf{u}, ?\mathbf{v}\}, \{(?x, \mathsf{p}, ?\mathbf{u}), (?y, \mathsf{p}, ?\mathbf{v}), (?x, \mathsf{q}, ?o), (?y, \mathsf{q}, ?o)\})$
Straight Out-2-Star	$Project(\{?\mathbf{u}, ?\mathbf{v}\}, \{(?s, \mathsf{q/p}, ?\mathbf{v}), (?s, \mathsf{q/p}, ?\mathbf{u})\}$
Revert Out-2-Star	$Project(\{?\mathbf{u}, ?\mathbf{v}\}, \{(?\mathbf{u}, \mathsf{p}, ?x), (?\mathbf{v}, \mathsf{p}, ?y), (?s, \mathsf{q}, ?x), (?s, \mathsf{q}, ?y)\})$

nodes have in-links (they are in object position in two triples with predicate p) from two other intermediary nodes x and y, that are linked to each other using the other predicate q. With *parallel-out* pattern, a tie is extracted from a node u to another one v, when both nodes have out-links (they are in subject position in two triples with predicate p) to two other intermediary nodes x and y, that are linked to each other using the other predicate q.

In both cases, the extracted relation is directional, such that the direction of the extracted tie (from u to v) is the same direction (parallel) of the relation between the corresponding intermediary nodes (from x to y).

Example 5. **Parallel-In** The Bibliographic Ontology[3] provides main concepts and properties for describing citations and bibliographic references on the

---

[3] http://bibliographic-ontology.org/.

Semantic Web. The predicate dc:contributor relates a document to its author, while bibo:cites relates a document to another document that cites the first document. Thus, using these predicates, we can extract a citation social network among authors, such that it relates an author to another one when the first writes a document that cites a document written by the second author. This network is extracted using the following query: $Q = Project(\{?u, ?v\}, \{(?x, \texttt{dc:contributor}, ?u), (?y, \texttt{dc:contributor}, ?v), (?x, \texttt{bibo:cites}, ?y)\})$

Patterns with Four Triples. Among different possible patterns of two predicates and four triples, we chose to present four common patterns as shown in Fig. 2. Networks extracted using these patterns are *undirected*. With *straight in-2-star* pattern, a tie between two nodes u and v is extracted when they are linked (using one predicate p) to two another nodes x and y that are in turn linked to a fifth node o using another predicate q (Fig. 2-f). In this pattern ($u \xrightarrow{p} x \xrightarrow{q} o \xleftarrow{q} y \xleftarrow{p} v$) the intermediary nodes make an in-2-star pattern using predicate q, and receive straight links from u, v using p (same direction as q). Using SPARQL property path, this pattern can be written as: $(?u, p/q, ?o), (?v, p/q, ?o)$. With *revert in-2-star* pattern, we extract a bidirectional tie between two nodes u and v if they have links (using one predicate p) from two other nodes x and y that are in turn linked to a fifth node o using another predicate q (Fig. 2-g). This pattern ($u \xleftarrow{p} x \xrightarrow{q} o \xleftarrow{q} y \xrightarrow{p} v$) is similar to the previous one, however, the links of predicate p are not in the same direction as q (hence the name *revert*). There are also another two patterns called: straight out-2-star and revert out-2-star, that are based on out-2-star configuration (Fig. 2-h, i.)

Example 6. **Straight In-2-Star.** In DailyMed dataset[4], the producesDrug predicate relates a pharmaceutical company to a drug it produces, and the predicate activeIngredient relates a drug to its active ingredient. Using these two predicates, we can extract a social network of competing pharmaceutical companies where competition is defined by selling drugs with the same active ingredient [5]. The required query can be written as: $Q = Project(\{?u, ?v\}, P)$ where $P = \{(?u, \text{producesDrug/activeIngredient}, ?o), (?v, \text{producesDrug/activeIngredient}, ?o)\}$ where $?u$ and $?v$ are companies producing $?x$ and $?y$ drugs, respectively, and the drugs both have the same active ingredient $?o$.

3   Translation into Networks

Binary Networks. In this case, the query should have two returned variables representing connected vertices. Thus, it has the form: $Q = Project(\{?u, ?v\}, P)$

---

[4] https://dailymed.nlm.nih.gov/dailymed/.

where P is some pattern (as described in previous section). Let $\Omega = [\![Q]\!]_D$ be a set of solution mappings $\{\mu\}$ of query Q. To translate Ω to a binary network: $H(V, E)$, we define a translation function tr: $tr(\Omega) = H(V, E)$, where $V = \{\mu(?u) \mid \mu \in \Omega\} \cup \{\mu(?v) \mid \mu \in \Omega\}$, and $E = \{(\mu(?u), \mu(?v)) \mid \mu \in \Omega\}$.

Weighted Networks. In this case, the query should have three returned variables: the first two represent connected nodes, and the third is the weight. Thus, the query has the form: $Q = Project(\{?u, ?v, ?w\}, P)$ where P is some pattern. Let $\Omega = [\![Q]\!]_D$ be a set of solution mappings $\{\mu\}$ of query Q. To translate Ω to a weighted network: $H(V, E, \omega)$, we define a translation function tr: $tr(\Omega) = H(V, E, \omega)$ where $V = \{\mu(?u) \mid \mu \in \Omega\} \cup \{\mu(?v) \mid \mu \in \Omega\}$, $E = \{e_\mu = (\mu(?u), \mu(?v)) \mid \mu \in \Omega\}$, and $\omega(e_\mu) = \mu(?w)$

4   Conclusion and Future Works

In this paper, we have presented a set of techniques to directly mine social networks from Linked Open Data. These techniques mainly correspond to common patterns found in RDF graphs, where new ties/relations are derived from existing ones that are explicitly represented by predicates. We consider the specification of such patterns as guidelines that help a user to figure out the appropriate formulation of the query to extract a desired network, and to understand the outcomes of different design choices: which predicates and how many triple patterns are needed, which is the appropriate direction of predicate of each triple pattern (subject-object), etc. Extraction patterns can also be used as building blocks to extract other types of social networks, such as: contextual networks and ego-centered networks. Our focus has been on complete networks, that cover an entire dataset w.r.t the relation to be extracted. However, in future work we will address mining of partial networks (that cover subset of the population defined by means of a specific context, e.g., time, location, or gender), and ego-centric networks (that address an identified individual/ego and her surrounding environment.

References

1. Bizer, C., Heath, T., Berners-Lee, T.: Linked data - the story so far. Int. J. Semantic Web Inf. Syst. **5**(3), 1–22 (2009)
2. Erétéo, G., Buffa, M., Gandon, F., Corby, O.: Analysis of a real online social network using semantic web frameworks. In: Bernstein, A., Karger, D.R., Heath, T., Feigenbaum, L., Maynard, D., Motta, E., Thirunarayan, K. (eds.) ISWC 2009. LNCS, vol. 5823, pp. 180–195. Springer, Heidelberg (2009). https://doi.org/10.1007/978-3-642-04930-9_12
3. Erétéo, G., Gandon, F., Corby, O., Buffa, M.: Semantic social network analysis. CoRR abs/0904.3701 (2009)
4. Ghawi, R., Schönfeld, M., Pfeffer, J.: Towards semantic-based social network analysis. In: 14th International IEEE Conference on Signal-Image Technologies and Internet-Based Systems (SITIS 2018). IEEE, November 2018

5. Groth, P.T., Gil, Y.: Linked data for network science. In: LISC. CEUR Workshop Proceedings, vol. 783. CEUR-WS.org (2011)
6. Harris, S., Seaborne, A.: SPARQL 1.1 Query Language. W3C Recommendation (2013)
7. Hennig, M., Brandes, U., Pfeffer, J., Mergel, I.: Studying Social Networks: A Guide to Empirical Research. Campus Verlag, Frankfurt (2012)
8. Kaminski, M., Kostylev, E.V., Cuenca Grau, B.: Semantics and expressive power of subqueries and aggregates in SPARQL 1.1. In: Proceedings of the 25th International Conference on World Wide Web, Geneva, Switzerland, pp. 227–238 (2016)
9. Kaminski, M., Kostylev, E.V., Grau, B.C.: Query nesting, assignment, and aggregation in SPARQL 1.1. ACM Trans. Database Syst. 42(3), 17:1–17:46 (2017)
10. Mika, P.: Flink: semantic web technology for the extraction and analysis of social networks. Web Semant. 3(2–3), 211–223 (2005)
11. San Martín, M., Gutierrez, C.: Representing, querying and transforming social networks with RDF/SPARQL. In: Aroyo, L., Traverso, P., Ciravegna, F., Cimiano, P., Heath, T., Hyvönen, E., Mizoguchi, R., Oren, E., Sabou, M., Simperl, E. (eds.) ESWC 2009. LNCS, vol. 5554, pp. 293–307. Springer, Heidelberg (2009). https://doi.org/10.1007/978-3-642-02121-3_24
12. Wasserman, S., Faust, K.: Social Network Analysis: Methods and Applications, 1st edn. Cambridge University Press, New York (1994)

Information Retrieval Chatbots
Based on Conceptual Models

Tatiana Makhalova[1,2(✉)], Dmitry Ilvovsky[1], and Boris Galitsky[3]

[1] National Research University Higher School of Economics, Moscow, Russia
{tpmakhalova,dilvovsky}@hse.ru
[2] Université de Lorraine, CNRS, Inria, LORIA, 54000 Nancy, France
[3] Oracle Corp., Redwood Shores, CA, USA
boris.galitsky@oracle.com

Abstract. Customer support systems based on chatbots gain an increasing popularity. Chatbots are becoming more and more important to a plethora of applications not only for social services. Modern information retrieval (IR) chatbots are based on simple queries to a database and do not ensure intelligent dialogues with users. In this paper we propose an IR-chatbot model that incorporates a concept-based knowledge model and an index-guided traversal through it to ensure the discovery of information relevant for users and coherent to their preferences. The proposed approach not only supports a search session, but also helps users to discover properties of items and sequentially refine an imprecise query.

Keywords: Formal Concept Analysis · Pattern Structures · Chatbots

1 Introduction

Dialogue systems and conversational agents – including chatbots, personal assistants and voice-control interfaces – are becoming ubiquitous in modern society. However, building intelligent conversational agents remains a major unsolved problem in artificial intelligence research.

There are two main directions in the chatbot development.

(1) *"Social chatbots"* are able to keep any kind of conversation, they usually do not follow a perfectly-defined trajectory and might be spontaneous. The development of the social chatbots implies accumulating a huge set of training dialogue data and feeding it to a deep learning network. The chatbot is expected to learn automatically "how to chat" [3].

(2) *"Task-oriented chatbots"* are expected to keep a natural-style conversation in a particular domain, e.g., restaurant information retrieval, booking a flight, providing automatic customer support [10,11]. They are developed with the help of a wide range of NLP and ML functionality. Domain-specific knowledge is incorporated in the model via explicitly-provided features and model-output

© Springer Nature Switzerland AG 2019
D. Endres et al. (Eds.): ICCS 2019, LNAI 11530, pp. 230–238, 2019.
https://doi.org/10.1007/978-3-030-23182-8_17

Table 1. A catalog fragment (a). Objects g_1–g_6 are smartwatches, g_7 is a dress and g_8 is a sweatshirt. The corresponding "is defined" formal context is given in (b), see details in Sect. 3.

(a)

	Brand	Avg. review	Price	Heart rate	GPS	Waterproof	Color	Material	Size
	a_1	a_2	a_3	a_4	a_5	a_6	a_7	a_8	a_9
g_1	TrainYS	3.6	105	yes	yes	yes	Black, Purple, White, Silver		
g_2	Youroach	4.8	180	yes	yes	no	Black, Pink, White, Silver		
g_3	BestWatch	2.1	50	no	yes	no	Black, White, Red		
g_4	Youroach	4.5	265	yes	yes	yes	Black, Red, White, Silver, Blue		
g_5	TrainYS	3.8	15	no	no	yes	Black		
g_6	CDream	4.8	250	yes	yes	yes	Black, White, Blue		
g_7	Brand X	3.9	140				White, Red, Violet	silk	XS
g_8	Brand Z	2.4	85				Green, Red	wool	S,M,L

(b)

	Brand	Avg. review	Price	Heart rate	GPS	Waterproof	Color	Material	Size
	a_1	a_2	a_3	a_4	a_5	a_6	a_7	a_8	a_9
g_1	×	×	×	×	×	×	×		
g_2	×	×	×	×	×	×	×		
g_3	×	×	×	×	×	×	×		
g_4	×	×	×	×	×	×	×		
g_5	×	×	×	×	×	×	×		
g_6	×	×	×	×	×	×	×		
g_7	×	×	×				×	×	×
g_8	×	×	×				×	×	×

restrictions [15], partially observable Markov decision processes [16] and other techniques [2,6].

Being unreliable and too brittle, these two approaches are unsuitable for enterprise chatbots.

In the epoch of web search engines, there is a need for a specific class of task-oriented chatbots – those who support web search in case of imprecise queries in specific domains, they are called information retrieval(IR)-chatbots. Their essential features are (i) ability to give a relevant and short list of items even when the user has only a general idea of the item he/she is searching for; (ii) flexibility, i.e., the user may change his/her mind about some preferences being provided with information from a chatbot, the chatbot should update a search strategy w.r.t. the user answers and (meta)data; (iii) efficiency, i.e., the user should get a satisfiable result within a short communication.

The existing IR-chatbots send queries to database to support web search and do not use any domain knowledge models. In this paper we propose a conceptual model of chatbots that is based on a knowledge model traversal rather than simply queries to database. We use Formal Concept Analysis (FCA) and Pattern Structures (PS) to build a knowledge model and stability index (its approximation) to ensure an efficient query refinement procedure (i.e., to satisfy user needs within a short communication). The paper is organized as follows. Below we provide a small example where IR-chatbots might be used. In Sect. 2 we present the basic notions of FCA and PS. Section 3 introduces a knowledge model that is the base of IR-chatbots. In Sect. 4 we discuss principles for the IR-chatbot functioning and present an algorithm for the interactive refinement of user queries. In Sect. 5 we conclude and give direction of future work.

Use Case. Let us consider a small use case where the IR-chatbots can be used. Given a catalog of objects (data) that are organized in categories (metadata) the user goal is to find a particular object(s) in the catalog. A fragment of a catalog and the corresponding hierarchy is given in Table 1(a) and Fig. 1, respectively.

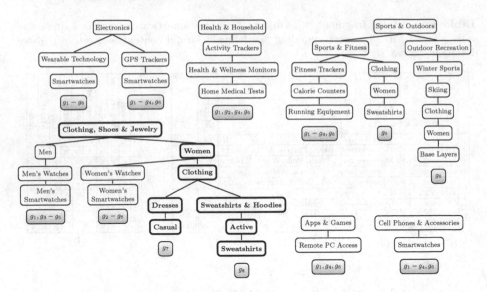

Fig. 1. A fragment of a hierarchy of categories for objects from Table 1. The category names for objects g_7 and g_8 are highlighted in bold.

Usually, objects are categorized ambiguously, i.e., are located in several leafs of a hierarchical tree. An object might belong to completely different or repetitive categories. That might lead users astray rather than improves search experience. For example, searching for "smartwatch" one can get a long list of categories (see paths with the leafs containing g_1–g_6 in Fig. 1). It is unclear beforehand if some items can be found in different categories. More than that, a web search engine usually proposes irrelevant attributes to refine and/or does not adjust user preferences w.r.t. available items.

Thus, the main problem is that in case of very general queries the search engine does not provide convenient tools to discover a variety of objects the user might be interested in.

In the next section we present a theoretical framework that allows us to remove ambiguity in metadata and improve the user experience by taking into account user-specified constraints and the variety of values of object satisfying given constraints.

2   Basic Notions

A *formal context* [8] is a triple (G, M, I), where $G = \{g_1, g_2, ..., g_n\}$ is a set objects, $M = \{m_1, m_2, ..., m_k\}$ is a set attributes and $I \subseteq G \times M$ is an incidence relation, i.e. $(g, m) \in I$ if the object g has the attribute m. The derivation operators $(\cdot)'$ are defined for $A \subseteq G$ and $B \subseteq M$ as follows:

$$A' = \{m \in M \mid \forall g \in A : gIm\}, \; B' = \{g \in G \mid \forall m \in B : gIm\}.$$

A' is the set of attributes common to all objects of A and B' is the set of objects sharing all attributes of B. A *(formal) concept* is a pair (A, B), where $A \subseteq G$, $B \subseteq M$ and $A' = B$, $B' = A$. A is the *extent* and B is the *intent* of the concept. A partial order $\leqslant$ is defined on the set of concepts as follows: $(A, B) \leqslant (C, D)$ iff $A \subseteq C (D \subseteq B)$, (A, B) is a subconcept of (C, D), (C, D) is a superconcept of (A, B).

Pattern Structure [9] is a generalization of the formal context, where objects are described by more complex structures. A *pattern structure* is a triple $(G, (D, \sqcap), \delta)$, where G is a set of objects, $(D, \sqcap)$ is a complete meet-semilattice of descriptions and $\delta : G \to D$ is a mapping of an object to a description. The Galois connection between a set of objects and their descriptions is defined as follows: $A^\square := \sqcap_{g \in A} \delta(g)$ for $A \subseteq G$, $d^\square := \{g \in G \mid d \sqsubseteq \delta(g)\}$ for $d \in D$. A pair (A, d) for which $A^\square = d$ and $d^\square = A$ is a *pattern concept*.

Intensional stability [12, 13] of concept (A, B) is the probability that B will remain closed when removing a subset of objects from extent A with equal probability: $stab((A, B)) = |\{C \subseteq A \mid C' = B\}|/2^{|A|}$. The concepts with high values of stability are more stable w.r.t. random removal of the objects.

The computing stability is $P\#$-complete [12]. In practice, one uses its approximations [1, 4]. One of the most popular approximations is Δ-measure [5]. That is defined as the minimal difference in supports between concept (A, B) and its nearest subconcepts, i.e., $\Delta((A, B)) = \min_{(A^*, B^*) \leqslant (A, B)} |A| - |A^*|$.

3 Building a Domain Knowledge Model

We propose to use a two-level knowledge model, where the upper level is used to navigate through groups of similar objects described in a very general way and the bottom level is used to search particular objects within a group of similar objects described in detail.

Upper Level: Coarse Categorization Model. Let G be a set of objects described by a set of attributes M, where every attribute $m \in M$ has a particular domain of values $dom(m)$. We define a binary relation I for $g \in G$ and $m \in M$ as follows: $gIm = 1 \Leftrightarrow g$ has m. We call I "is defined" relation, see example in Table 1.

We define *degree of homogeneity* of objects $A \subseteq G$ as the rate of their common attributes, i.e. $h(A) = |\{\{g\}' \mid g \in A\}|/|M|$, homogeneity is anti-monotonic. Partially ordered concepts (A, B) having $h(A) \in [h_1, h_2]$ make the upper level $\mathcal{M}_\mathcal{U}$. The lower bound h_1 prevents from creating too general groups of objects, while the upper bound h_2 ensures that very homogeneous (similar in sense of attributes M, not their values) objects will be treated in detail at the bottom level. For every concept (A, B) we add the names of categories of objects from A, these names are extracted from metadata, we denote it by $F(A)$. To build this set we need to collect all category names of each $g \in A$ from the roots to leafs in a given hierarchy (metadata). For example, the homogeneity rate of $(\{g_7, g_8\}'', \{g_7, g_8\}')$ is $6/9$. The category names to be collected for this concept are highlighted in bold in Fig. 1.

Bottom Level: Refined Categorization Model. For each set of objects A, where $(A, B) \in \mathcal{M_U}$, we build a pattern structure $\mathcal{M_B}(A)$ using the corresponding data fragment of the original dataset. The derivation operator $\square$ is defined specifically for different attribute types.

4   Interactive Query Refinement

4.1   Two-Stage Approach: Basic Idea

We propose an approach to query refinement where a user query is specified in an interactive manner. The procedure is adaptive w.r.t. both user constraints and the variability of attributes of objects satisfying the constraints.

The interactive query refinement consists of two main steps:

1. Navigating to a relevant concept $(A, B) \in \mathcal{M_U}$.
2. Query refinement within $\mathcal{M_B}(A)$.

The pseudocode of the procedure is given in Algorithm 1. For a given user query Q in natural language, we use standard NLP methods to extract a set of key words K and values V of some attributes from M (line 1). Then the concepts $(A, B) \in \mathcal{M_U}$ for which $F(A)$ matches with K (line 2) are chosen as most relevant concepts $\mathcal{F}$ and ranked w.r.t. Δ-measure. The iterative refinement starts from the top-ranked concept. At each iteration in lines 5–8 the algorithm tries to find the items relevant to the user among objects from A (line 7).

Input: Q, a user query in natural language; $\mathcal{M_U}$, the upper level of the knowledge model
Output: A^*, a subset of objects that meet user needs

1   $(K, V) \leftarrow ExtractWordsAndValues(Q)$
2   $\mathcal{F} \leftarrow$ NAVIGATETOCONCEPT$(\mathcal{M_U}, K)$ ▷ see Algorithm 2
3   $\mathcal{F}_{ord} \leftarrow sortByDelta(\mathcal{F})$
4   $A^* \leftarrow \emptyset$
5   **while** $A^* = \emptyset$ **do**
6 | $A \leftarrow next(\mathcal{F}_{ord})$
7 | $A^* \leftarrow$ REFINEQUERY$(\mathcal{M_B}(A), V)$ ▷ see Algorithm 3
8   **end**

Algorithm 1. TWO-STAGE QUERY REFINEMENT

4.2   The First Stage: Navigating to a Group of Relevant Homogeneous Objects

To find most relevant formal concepts we traverse $\mathcal{M_U}$ starting from most general concepts, see Algorithm 2. We compare the keywords K from the query with $F(A)$, $(A, B) \in \mathcal{M_U}$ (line 3). At each iteration we try to get more specific groups of objects from the set of lower neighbors of $(A, B) \in \mathcal{M_U}$, i.e., $LowerNeighbors(\mathcal{M_U}, A)$. We stop specifying concepts when no more specific concept (A_s, B_s) of (A, B) $(A_s \subset A)$ has the same number of matched keywords as (A, B), i.e. when $|K \cap F(A)| > |K \cap F(A_s)|$ (condition in line 3 is false for all $A \in \mathcal{F}$).

4.3   The Second Stage: Walk Through a Pattern Structure

Once $(A, B) \in \mathcal{M}_\mathcal{U}$ has been identified, the corresponding pattern structure $\mathcal{M}_\mathcal{B}(A)$ is chosen to support further query refinement, see Algorithm 3.

The idea of the refinement is a sequential questioning of the user, where a new user response is used to jump to the most promising pattern concept (A_r, d_r), d_r is analyzed by the *isVaried* function to identify the features that will be offered the user to refine.

On input the algorithm gets a pattern structure $\mathcal{M}_\mathcal{B}(A)$ and, optionally, values V of some attributes from M extracted from the query. We start from the most specific concept (A_s, d_s) whose description includes values from V (line 2). If V is empty, the most general (top) pattern concept is taken. Its lower neighbors $LowerNeighbors(A_s, d_s)$ ordered by Δ-measure and the number of lower neighbors. They are candidates for further refinement. The attributes M^* to be specified are chosen with help of the *isVaried* function (line 7). Boolean function *isVaried* checks if values for given objects are quite diverse to be specified by the user. Examples of *isVaried* function are given in Table 2, (a). M_{irrel} are attributes marked by the user as irrelevant.

Once attributes $M^* \subseteq M$ are identified (line 7) the chatbot asks the user to choose attributes $M^*_{spec} \subseteq M^*$ he/she wants to specify. Then the chatbot shows the user only particular values of M^*_{spec} depending on d_r instead of the whole rage of values $dom(\cdot)$. That facilitates the decision-making process. The specified values W_{spec} are used to find the next (A_s, d_s).

Example. Let us illustrate the principles of the query refinement using the running example given in Table 1. For query "smartwatch" the chatbot navigates to pattern structure $\mathcal{M}_\mathcal{B}(\{g_1, \ldots, g_6\})$. Since no attribute values V have been extracted we start from the top concept. The sequences of refinements is given in Fig. 2.

All lower neighbors of the top concept have Δ-measure equal to 1, thus we start from the pattern concept with extent $A_1 = \{g_1, g_2, g_3, g_4, g_6\}$ since it has the smallest number of lower neighbors. The attributes that meet *isVaried* requirements (see Table 2) are "Price" and "Waterproof". The user chooses "Waterproof" and the chatbot finds a concept with extent $A_2 = \{g_1, g_4, g_6\}$ that satisfies user preferences. Based on *isVaried* condition, the chatbot proposes to choose "Avg. review" or "Price" for refinement. The user choses highly

---

Input: K, a set of key words (category names); $\mathcal{A}$, a set of most general concepts
Output: $\mathcal{F}$, a set of concepts to be specified

```
1  F ← A
2  for A ∈ F do
3  |   if K ⊆ F(A) then
4  |   |   F* ← LowerNeighbors(M_U, A)
5  |   |   F ← F ∪ F*; F ← F \ {A}
6  |   end
7  end
```

Algorithm 2. NAVIGATETOCONCEPT

Input: $\mathcal{M}_\mathcal{B}(A)$, a pattern structure; V, attribute values extracted from the query
Output: *relevant*, a set of relevant objects

1 $run \leftarrow True$; $relevant \leftarrow \emptyset$; $M_{irrel} \leftarrow \emptyset$
2 $(A_s, d_s) \leftarrow findTheMostSpecificConcept(\mathcal{M}_\mathcal{B}(A), V)$
3 $GS_{ranked} \leftarrow sortByDelta(LowerNeighbors(A_s, d_s))$
4 **while** run **and** $GS_{ranked} \neq \emptyset$ **do**
5 $\quad (A_r, d_r) \leftarrow pop(GS_{ranked})$
6 $\quad relevant \leftarrow A_r$
7 $\quad M^* = \{M_i \mid M_i \in M \setminus M_{irrel}, M_i \in isVaried(A_r, M)\}$
8 $\quad$ **if** $M^* \neq \emptyset$ **then**
9 $\quad\quad M^*_{spec} = ask(M^*)$ $\triangleright$ ask the user for categories he/she wants to specify
10 $\quad\quad M_{irrel} \leftarrow M^* \setminus M^*_{spec}$
11 $\quad\quad S \leftarrow \{b \mid b \in values(M_i, d_r), M_i \in M^*_{spec}\}$ $\triangleright$ suggest particular values within chosen
        categories
12 $\quad\quad W_{spec} \leftarrow userChoice(S)$
13 $\quad\quad$ **if** $W_{spec} \neq \emptyset$ **then**
14 $\quad\quad\quad (A_s, d_s) \leftarrow findTheMostGeneralConcept(A_r, d_r, W_{spec})$
15 $\quad\quad\quad GS_{ranked} \leftarrow sortByDelta(LowerNeighbors(A_s, d_s))$
16 $\quad\quad$ **end**
17 $\quad$ **end**
18 **end**
19 **return** *relevant*

Algorithm 3. REFINEQUERY

rated items, i.e., the range $[4.0, 4.8]$ and get items g_4 and g_6 that are too expensive for him/her. The search refinement continues with next candidate $A_3 = \{g_1, g_2, g_3, g_5, g_6\}$. Then the objects are $A_4 = \{g_1, g_2, g_6\}$, the relevant item is g_1.

Table 2. The condition for *isVaried* boolean function (a) and the attributes that satisfy *isVaried* condition (highlighted in bold) and are offered the user to refine (b).

Condition on variability	Description
$\mathcal{E}_1 : v_1 < \frac{|m' \cap A|}{|A|} < v_2$	rate of objects having m
$\mathcal{E}_2 : v_1 < \frac{|A|}{|\{m(g) \mid g \in A\}|} < v_2$	relative number of different values for nominal attr.
$\mathcal{E}_3 : std([m(g) \mid g \in A]) > v$	standard dev., for real-valued attr.

(a)

Attribute	*isVaried*	A_1	A_2	A_3	A_4
Brand	$0.5 \leq \mathcal{E}_1 \leq 0.6$	0.8	1	0.8	1
Avg. review	$0.5 \leq \mathcal{E}_4 \leq 1.13$	1.15	**0.62**	**1.11**	**0.69**
Price	$50 \leq \mathcal{E}_3 \leq 100$	**92.4**	**88.36**	**95.7**	**72.5**
Heart rate	$0.5 \leq \mathcal{E}_1 \leq 0.6$	0.8	1	**0.6**	1
GPS	$0.5 \leq \mathcal{E}_1 \leq 0.6$	1	1	**0.6**	1
Waterproof	$0.5 \leq \mathcal{E}_1 \leq 0.6$	**0.6**	1	**0.6**	0.66
Color	$2 \leq \mathcal{E}_2 \leq 5$	7	6	7	6

(b)

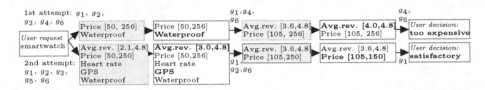

Fig. 2. A sequence of query refinements. Colored rectangles correspond to chatbot proposals, the attributes in bold in white rectangles are user choices. The sets of objects out of rectangles refer to the concepts chosen by the chatbot according to the user-specified preferences.

5 Conclusion

In this paper we introduce a new model of the IR-chatbot. To the best of our knowledge it is the first model that is based on traversal through a knowledge model rather than simple queries to database. We use Δ-measure to obtain satisfactory search results in a small number of steps. The proposed model has the following advantages w.r.t. traditional IR-chatbots: (i) it is adaptive to both user preferences and the range of items that satisfy user criterion; (ii) it helps users to discover relevant properties of the items he/she is searching for based on Δ-measure and *isVaried* function; (iii) it offers the user a small number of attributes to refine at each step, that simplifies the decision-making process.

The presented model can be incorporated in the developing project on discourse structure-driven dialog system and semantic-based web search tools [7,14].

Acknowledgements. Sections 3, 4.1 and 4.2 (algorithm to build a domain knowledge model, algorithm to navigate to a group of relevant objects) were written by Dmitry A. Ilvovsky and Tatiana Makhalova supported by the Russian Science Foundation under grant 17-11-01294 and performed at National Research University Higher School of Economics, Russia.

Sections 2 and 4.3 (chatbot investigations, model and algorithm of pattern structure walk) were prepared within the framework of the HSE University Basic Research Program and funded by the Russian Academic Excellence Project '5-100'. The rest of the paper was written and performed at Oracle Corp.

References

1. Babin, M.A., Kuznetsov, S.O.: Approximating concept stability. In: Domenach, F., Ignatov, D.I., Poelmans, J. (eds.) ICFCA 2012. LNCS (LNAI), vol. 7278, pp. 7–15. Springer, Heidelberg (2012). https://doi.org/10.1007/978-3-642-29892-9_7
2. Bordes, A., Boureau, Y.L., Weston, J.: Learning end-to-end goal-oriented dialog. arXiv preprint arXiv:1605.07683 (2016)
3. Bowden, K.K., Oraby, S., Misra, A., Wu, J., Lukin, S., Walker, M.: Data-driven dialogue systems for social agents. In: Eskenazi, M., Devillers, L., Mariani, J. (eds.) Advanced Social Interaction with Agents. LNEE, vol. 510, pp. 53–56. Springer, Cham (2019). https://doi.org/10.1007/978-3-319-92108-2_6
4. Buzmakov, A., Kuznetsov, S.O., Napoli, A.: Scalable estimates of concept stability. In: Glodeanu, C.V., Kaytoue, M., Sacarea, C. (eds.) ICFCA 2014. LNCS (LNAI), vol. 8478, pp. 157–172. Springer, Cham (2014). https://doi.org/10.1007/978-3-319-07248-7_12
5. Buzmakov, A., Kuznetsov, S.O., Napoli, A.: Sofia: how to make FCA polynomial? In: Proceedings of FCA4AI, vol. 1430, pp. 27–34 (2015)
6. Eric, M., Manning, C.D.: Key-value retrieval networks for task-oriented dialogue. arXiv preprint arXiv:1705.05414 (2017)
7. Galitsky, B.: Semantic tools. https://github.com/bgalitsky/relevance-based-on-parse-trees
8. Ganter, B., Wille, R.: Formal Concept Analysis: Mathematical Foundations. Springer, Heidelberg (1999). https://doi.org/10.1007/978-3-642-59830-2

9. Ganter, B., Kuznetsov, S.O.: Pattern structures and their projections. In: Delugach, H.S., Stumme, G. (eds.) ICCS-ConceptStruct 2001. LNCS (LNAI), vol. 2120, pp. 129–142. Springer, Heidelberg (2001). https://doi.org/10.1007/3-540-44583-8_10
10. Henderson, M., Thomson, B., Williams, J.D.: The second dialog state tracking challenge. In: Proceedings of SIGDIAL, pp. 263–272 (2014)
11. Hirschman, L.: Evaluating Spoken Language Interaction: Experiences from the Darpa Spoken Language Program 1990–1995. Spoken Language Discourse. MIT Press, Cambridge (2000)
12. Kuznetsov, S.O.: On stability of a formal concept. Ann. Math. Artif. Intell. **49**(1–4), 101–115 (2007)
13. Kuznetsov, S., Obiedkov, S., Roth, C.: Reducing the representation complexity of lattice-based taxonomies. In: Priss, U., Polovina, S., Hill, R. (eds.) ICCS-ConceptStruct 2007. LNCS (LNAI), vol. 4604, pp. 241–254. Springer, Heidelberg (2007). https://doi.org/10.1007/978-3-540-73681-3_18
14. Makhalova, T., Ilvovsky, D., Galitsky, B.: News clustering approach based on discourse text structure. In: Proceedings of the First Workshop on Computing News Storylines, pp. 16–20 (2015)
15. Williams, J.D., Asadi, K., Zweig, G.: Hybrid code networks: practical and efficient end-to-end dialog control with supervised and reinforcement learning. arXiv preprint arXiv:1702.03274 (2017)
16. Young, S., Gašić, M., Thomson, B., Williams, J.D.: POMDP-based statistical spoken dialog systems: a review. Proc. IEEE **101**(5), 1160–1179 (2013)

Semiotic-Conceptual Analysis
of a Lexical Field

Uta Priss[1](✉) [ID] and L. John Old[2] [ID]

[1] Zentrum für erfolgreiches Lehren und Lernen,
Ostfalia University, Wolfenbüttel, Germany
[2] Braunschweig, Germany
http://www.upriss.org.uk

Abstract. Semiotic-Conceptual Analysis (SCA) is a mathematical formalisation of semiotics which uses Formal Concept Analysis (FCA) as an
underlying formal model of conceptual structures. Previously SCA had
only been applied to formal languages. This paper discusses the applicability of SCA to natural languages using the example of the lexical field
of "cooking" in English and Maori.

1 Introduction

Semiotic-Conceptual Analysis (SCA) has been introduced by Priss (2017) as a
mathematical formalisation of semiotics which uses Formal Concept Analysis
(FCA) as a formalisation (Ganter and Wille 1999) of conceptual structures. It
has previously been shown how SCA can be applied to the analysis of programming languages and to investigations of why and how certain concepts are more
difficult to learn than others. This paper applies SCA to a natural language
example and argues that, contrary to purely linguistic analyses, a semiotic perspective that analyses conceptual structures in the form of concept lattices is
more promising.

According to SCA, a sign is a triple consisting of a representamen (for example a word or sentence), an interpretation (which can include information about
context, situation, speaker, listener and so on) and a denotation which represents
a meaning. A condition for signs is that a pair consisting of a representamen and
an interpretation uniquely identifies a denotation or, in other words, an interpretation is a partial function that maps representamens onto denotations. In this
paper, it is assumed that all denotations are concepts in some conceptual structure. Thus, the notions of "denotation" and "concept" can be used somewhat
interchangeably although, strictly, "denotation" is a role whereas "concept" is a
type or category. Concepts can be hypothetically constructed whereas, in SCA,
denotations must belong to signs that are actually used in communication. With
respect to natural languages this implies that the meanings of words are concepts and according to SCA they can be modelled as formal concepts using FCA.

L. J. Old—Independent Scholar.

© Springer Nature Switzerland AG 2019
D. Endres et al. (Eds.): ICCS 2019, LNAI 11530, pp. 239–247, 2019.
https://doi.org/10.1007/978-3-030-23182-8_18

Technically, denotations and concepts are signs as well because they must have representamens, interpretations and denotations themselves, leading to a semiotic chain where signs are parts of signs which are discussed using signs and so on. It is up to a researcher to decide which sets of representamens, denotations and interpretations to use and which to ignore in a particular application and how far to investigate semiotic chains. Using SCA it is feasible to construct denotational conceptual structures (hierarchies, concept lattices or other) and then to investigate how representamens are mapped into these conceptual structures.

The next section provides a brief explanation of the lexical field of cooking in English using a linguistic analysis. Section 3 compares this lexical field in English and Maori using a conceptual analysis. Section 4 then adds a semiotic analysis in the sense of SCA.

2   Linguistic Analysis

Figure 1 shows a reduced neighbourhood lattice of the English and Maori words for cooking. According to Priss and Old (2005) a bilingual neighbourhood lattice can be formed by starting with a word in one language (such as "to cook" in English) then looking up all translations of that word in another language (here Maori), then looking up all the translations of the translations and so. Because the sets grow with each iteration it is useful to constrain this mechanism by only selecting words which occur as translations more than once or by some other means of eliminating homographs. For example, Maori translations of "to boil" include words for how mud "boils" in geothermal hot pools. Such non-food related words have been manually eliminated from Fig. 1. The Norwegian researcher, Helge Dyvik, developed a similar "semantic mirrors method" which was formalised with FCA by Priss and Old (2005). Dyvik's idea was that semantic structures in two languages mirror each other and can be used to jointly construct a thesaurus for each of the languages.

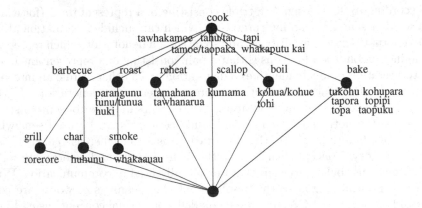

Fig. 1. A neighbourhood lattice for "cooking" words in English and Maori

Unfortunately, the resulting lattice in Fig. 1 is not very interesting. It is mostly just an antichain. The fact that some English words appear to correspond to many Maori words is an indication that the meanings of the Maori words might be distributed in a fairly different manner from the English words which is not obvious from the lattice. While Dyvik successfully detects mirrors comparing English and Norwegian words, this could be because both languages are linguistic and cultural close cousins. Thus a comparison of both demonstrates subtle differences which hint at underlying conceptual structures. Maori and English, however, are both culturally and linguistically far apart. We are arguing in this paper that a primarily linguistic method for deriving semantic information is insufficient if the underlying conceptual structures are far apart. Furthermore, even for languages which are closer related, Priss and Old (2007) observe that bilingual resources (such as corpora or dictionaries) may be inadequate for deriving semantic information if the bilingual resources do not already contain sufficient semantic details. Thus automatic extraction of semantic information from lexical databases that do not already encode semantic information is still a challenge. A hypothesis of SCA is that representamens point to conceptual structures but a significant amount of the information is implicit and not lexicalised. In order to extract semantic information, some sort of "decoding" practice needs to be employed which goes beyond a purely linguistic analysis.

In the 60s and 70s a method of "componential analysis" was developed and applied to lexical fields in order to decode underlying semantic information. An example of this method is Lehrer's (1969) lexical field of the English verbs of "cooking". He identifies a list of semantic features which are either present or absent for each word and which explain the semantic differences between the words. For example, "boiling" involves cooking in a non-fat liquid (e.g. water), contrary to frying which requires a fatty-liquid (e.g. oil). Both grilling and barbecuing employ direct heat, but in barbecuing a special sauce may be used. The result of componential analysis is essentially a formal context with words as formal objects and semantic features as attributes. Lehrer provides such a table in his paper which we have slightly simplified[1]. The corresponding concept lattice is presented in Fig. 2. The reason for colouring some of the nodes is explained further below. The main features for grouping English words of cooking appear to be whether heat is applied directly or indirectly, whether the food is meant to become brown on the surface and whether cooking is achieved with water or fat. Apart from the features that group words, at the lower nodes there is a long list of features that distinguish individual words. For example, cooking in a cream sauce and in a (scallop) shell is a unique characteristic of scalloping.

---

[1] We omitted a few of the attributes, for example, the length of cooking time, whether a vigorous action is required and whether it applies to liquids or solids. We omitted some compound cooking verbs and we renamed some of the attributes.

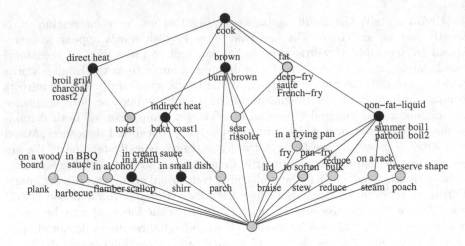

Fig. 2. The lexical field of "cooking" in English

3   Conceptual Analysis

In order to obtain a better understanding of the significance of the semantic features, we decided to compare this English lexical field to Maori again, but this time using semantic features. Polynesian people were isolated from other cultures from the early first millennium (Leach 1981). The Polynesian Maori arrived in New Zealand in the 13th/14th century and lived there in isolation until 1769[2]. Because their contact with foreigners was so recent and because the first Maori language newspapers were already printed in the 1840s, the impact of the contact with foreigners on the Maori language and culture are reasonably well documented. Therefore the Maori language is a good candidate for investigating conceptual differences and the linguistic and cultural changes that occurred after their first contact with "Pakeha" (which is the Maori word for people of European descent).

Although Polynesian people may have once had knowledge of pottery making, they abandoned this practice[3] long before they arrived in New Zealand (Leach 1981). Without pottery which provides heat-proof cooking vessels the most common types of English cooking (i.e., frying in a frying pan or cooking in a pot of water) are impossible. Beaton (2008) describes the six main types of Maori food preparation as: earth oven (hangi) cookery, Polynesian puddings, roasting, boiling, preserving and fermenting. Cooking in a hangi is the most important means of cooking for Maori and is described below. Polynesian puddings resemble bread, but require complicated steps to extract starch from plants, and are also ultimately baked in a hangi. Without heat-proof cooking vessels, boiling

---

[2] Abel Tasman's contact with them in 1642 was brief and hostile and did not likely have much, if any, impact on Maori culture.

[3] Leach speculates that the need for pottery making may be connected to growing grains neither of which Polynesian people did.

can only be achieved by placing hot stones into, for example, wooden vessels. It is not, however, possible to cook larger pieces of meat in such a manner and it is not clear whether Maori used boiling for food at all or only for dyeing fibre (Beaton 2008). But at least the concept of boiling in water exists in the Maori language. Preserving and fermenting are also in the list of food preparation styles because, for Maori, this lexical field is more about general food processing. Maori always had to conduct all the steps from obtaining the ingredients from nature to producing the final food product by themselves. This is contrary to an English concept of cooking which mainly refers to the part of the food processing act which happens in one's own kitchen. For Maori, roasting involves broiling, for example, shellfish on hot embers or smaller birds or fish on sticks over an open fire. This is a kind of Maori "fast food" and traditionally was not a favoured means of food preparation (Beaton 2008). Maori preferred to cook their food in a hangi which is an earth oven and is an extreme kind of "slow food". Preparing a hangi involves a large amount of time and labour: digging a hole, collecting (large amounts of) firewood, heating stones, placing food on the stones, pouring water over the stones to produce steam, covering the hole with wet woven mats or sacks, and finally placing earth dug from the hole over the top. The food can be placed in the hangi in vessels to gather the fat or wrapped in leaves for flavour. While the food itself stays in the hangi for 2–3 h the whole process takes a day. A hangi is a communal activity cooked for a larger group of people.

Figure 3 displays a concept lattice of a lexical field of cooking in traditional Maori language. The data collection method for Fig. 3 was simpler than for Fig. 2. We searched for cooking words in several dictionaries[4] and derived attributes from the dictionary definitions. Thus, the Maori data does not have the same detail as the English data. We then compared the English and the Maori lattices. The grey nodes are those for which we did not find a translation in the other language, and the black nodes are those which exist in both languages. Thus, words from either language can serve as representamens for the concepts that are coloured black. The grey nodes with a thicker border in Fig. 2 correspond to the three loanwords which can be found in the modern Maori language. They were derived from English (tiu: to stew, parai: to fry, whakatohi: to toast) after 1769. The comparison of the two languages shows that the general concepts (cooking, broiling, baking, boiling and burning) exist in both languages. For some reason the very specific term of cooking in a small shell exists in both languages as well (kumama and to scallop). It is probably a coincidence that this is practised in both cultures. Both cultures also appear to have a notion of baking something in a small vessel. The remaining two more general types of English cooking (toasting and frying) and a very stereotypical one (stewing) appeared in Maori culture only after contact with Europeans. Because basically all modern Maori are also native English speakers, it is quite likely that other specific English cooking terms (parching, braising, poaching and so on) are simply included as English words if they are mentioned in a Maori language conversation.

---

[4] Williams (1957) and https://maoridictionary.co.nz.

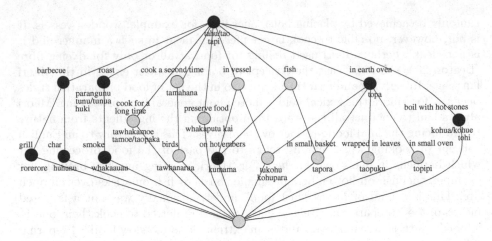

Fig. 3. The lexical field of "cooking" in Maori

Figure 3 shows that apart from the general words of cooking, boiling and baking (and the scalloping exception) only the Maori words in the subfield of barbecuing and roasting have English expressions. Maori distinctions, with respect to whether fish or birds are cooked or whether something is wrapped in leaves or baskets, have no English counterpart. Although "cooking for a long time" and "cooking a second time" might be expressed in English, in Maori the cooking process is much longer and cooking for a second time may not just be reheating but a required step of the food preparation process. Thus, it is not clear whether these Maori concepts really correspond to English concepts.

Hangis and other Maori food traditions are still practised within modern Maori communities. But while ethnic food (Chinese, Japanese, Italian and Indian) is popular in New Zealand, Maori restaurants are difficult to find apart from a few tourist locations where visitors can book the "whole Maori experience" including greeting ceremony and hangi. The reason for this is most likely, that the Maori "fast food" procedure of roasting something on an open fire does not have a sufficiently distinctive Maori quality. The slow food of a hangi, on the other hand, requires planning ahead for how many people will be eating, and does not allow people to select food from a menu which is then ready half an hour later. There are "oven hangis" (tasteless, according to some Maori) cooked in a modern oven but they still require 2–3 h of baking time. Thus, traditional Maori food is so different that it does not easily fit into a modern restaurant culture. Furthermore, because Maori did not practice large scale agriculture, none of their vegetables apart from their staple, kumara[5], would be available for a mass market. Thus, "hangi" and "kumara" are the main Maori words from the lexical field of cooking which have become loanwords in New Zealand English. In summary, the top concepts of the English lexical field of cooking can be expressed in Maori, but only a few concepts and the subfield of broiling of the Maori lexical

---

[5] A kind of sweet potato.

field of cooking can be expressed in English. It appears that English cooking influenced the life of modern Maori much more than vice versa.

4   Semiotic Analysis

The previous two sections describe the lexical field of cooking using linguistic and conceptual analyses. A linguistic analysis starts with words and their relationships to other words. Typical questions for a conceptual analysis focus on a conceptual modelling of the denotational structures. A semiotic analysis considers all three components of signs: representamens, denotations and interpretations. Typical semiotic questions focus on synonymy, polysemy, complexity, efficiency, the mapping of representamen relations, suitability, completeness and usability of signs. Because of the formal modelling with SCA and FCA, these questions become focused and to some degree measurable. The following list provides an overview of the approach:

- *Conceptual efficiency* increases if the total number of attributes in a lattice decreases. As mentioned before, we eliminated several attributes from Lehrer's (1969) original data because the lattice based on the original data had too many concepts which appeared to have no purpose with respect to most representamens.
- *Conceptual complexity* decreases if fewer attributes are needed to identify individual concepts. Lowering complexity tends to involve a decrease of efficiency. For example, in Fig. 2 the concept for "broil" is more complex than "toast" which can only be described by a combination of two attributes ("browning with direct heat").
- *Synonymy* refers to different representamens being attached to the same concept. A high degree of synonymy indicates that the conceptual modelling of the denotations may not be suitable or complete (see below).
- *Polysemy* refers to the same representamen belonging to different formal objects. In Fig. 2 this is indicated by adding a number after the word, such as "roast1" and "roast2". Polysemy is efficient, if it refers to the same representamen used in similar meanings in different concept lattices. Polysemy within a single concept lattice is somewhat acceptable if the words belong to closely related concepts (such as "boil1" and "boil2" in Fig. 2). The fact that the join and meet of "roast1" and "roast2" are the top and bottom concepts can indicate that there are missing attributes in the lattice.
- *Semiotic efficiency* increases if there is a high degree of polysemy (preferably not in one concept lattice but across different concept lattices). More polysemy requires using more interpretations.
- *Semiotic complexity* increases if a large number of interpretations is needed to disambiguate representamens. Figures 2 and 3 each represent an interpretation. But in Fig. 2 additional interpretations are needed to disambiguate "roast" and "boil".
- *Representamen relations* are more relevant for complex expressions such as phrases, sentences or larger texts. It would be possible to investigate word formation but that tends to be of interest mainly for historical analyses.

- *Suitability and completeness of a conceptual model* investigates how well a set of representamens can be described via their denotations within a conceptual model. For example, representamens that are mapped to the top or bottom concept are not very well described by the model. In the examples, in Figs. 2 and 3 only the very general cooking terms are mapped to the top concepts which is as expected. If the English representamens are mapped into the Maori lattice and vice versa, then many concepts are "lexical gaps" because they do not contain a representamen of the other language; furthermore many representamens would be synonyms because they are not sufficiently distinguished. For each representamen a definition can be generated from the lattice. For example, "to scallop" means to apply indirect heat to something cooked in a shell and adding a cream sauce. Such definitions can be compared to dictionary definitions with respect to how well they match.
- *Usability* is mainly relevant for sign systems that are purposefully and deliberately created. Language evolves over time and tends to self-adjust by incorporating new words and changing or forgetting existing words as needed.

The main categories related to cooking appear to be the physical process of cooking (e.g. using a frying pan), the intended result (e.g. brown) and the type of food that is cooked (e.g. type of animal). Some of the relationships between the attributes are causally related and not really of a linguistic nature. It would be of interest to compare the lattices in Figs. 2 and 3 to lattices derived from a more carefully designed formal ontology, but that is left for future research.

5   Conclusion

From an SCA view, representamens (e.g. words or phrases) are mapped onto denotations (which exist as conceptual structures) by interpretations. Interpretations can occur at different levels of granularity: corresponding to the utterances of one person in one specific context, or one person in general or to a group of people or a language. In this paper three main interpretations are considered: modern English, traditional Maori and modern Maori language. A purely linguistic analysis that compares translations from English into Maori and vice versa does not appear to provide detailed semantic insights. But if conceptual structures are constructed using some kind of method of decoding, then it is possible to show how representamens can be mapped into these conceptual structures. Using SCA questions about the quality of the representamens compared to the underlying denotational structures can be specified and investigated.

References

Beaton, S.: A contemporary Maori culinary tradition-does it exist?: an analysis of Maori cuisine. Dissertation, University of Otago (2008)

Ganter, B., Wille, R.: Formal Concept Analysis: Mathematical Foundations. Springer, Heidelberg (1999). https://doi.org/10.1007/978-3-642-59830-2

Leach, H.M.: Cooking without pots: aspects of prehistoric and traditional Polynesian cooking. In: National & Regional Styles of Cookery: Proceedings: Oxford Symposium 1981, vol. 1, p. 312 (1981)

Lehrer, A.: Semantic cuisine. J. Linguist. **5**(1), 39–55 (1969)

Priss, U.: Semiotic-conceptual analysis: a proposal. Int. J. Gen. Syst. **46**(5), 569–585 (2017)

Priss, U., Old, L.J.: Bilingual word association networks. In: Priss, U., Polovina, S., Hill, R. (eds.) ICCS-ConceptStruct 2007. LNCS (LNAI), vol. 4604, pp. 310–320. Springer, Heidelberg (2007). https://doi.org/10.1007/978-3-540-73681-3_23

Priss, U., Old, L.J.: Conceptual exploration of semantic mirrors. In: Ganter, B., Godin, R. (eds.) ICFCA 2005. LNCS (LNAI), vol. 3403, pp. 21–32. Springer, Heidelberg (2005). https://doi.org/10.1007/978-3-540-32262-7_2

Williams, H.: A Dictionary of the Maori Language, 6th edn. Government Printer, Wellington (1957)

Applying Semiotic-Conceptual Analysis to Mathematical Language

Uta Priss[✉] iD

Zentrum für erfolgreiches Lehren und Lernen,
Ostfalia University of Applied Sciences, Wolfenbüttel, Germany
http://www.upriss.org.uk

Abstract. This paper demonstrates how semiotic-conceptual analysis (SCA) can be applied to an investigation of mathematical language and notation. The background for this research is mathematics in higher education, in particular the question of why many students find mathematics difficult to learn. SCA supports an analysis on different levels: pertaining to the conceptual structures underlying mathematical knowledge separately from and in combination with the semiotic relationship between the representation and the content of mathematical knowledge. We believe that this provides novel insights into the structure of mathematical knowledge and presents a method of decoding which lecturers can employ.

1 Introduction

Semiotic-conceptual analysis (SCA) is a mathematical theory for investigating the use of sign systems which was developed by Priss (2017b). SCA provides a different angle compared to linguistic, semantic or usability analyses because it facilitates a separation of conceptual and semiotic aspects but also takes representations and interpretations into consideration. So far only a few applications of SCA have been described (Priss 2017b and 2016). This paper discusses how SCA can be applied to the language of mathematics itself. The purpose for this is to investigate further why many students perceive mathematics as a difficult subject to learn. The work of Priss (2018) which examines ambiguities in mathematical expressions and compares the structure of mathematical concepts with natural language concepts is extended in this paper.

The mathematical details of the formalisation of SCA are described by Priss (2017b) and shall not be repeated in this paper. The conceptual structures of SCA are modelled with formal concept analysis (FCA) whose mathematical details (cf. Ganter and Wille 1999) shall also not be repeated in this paper. In SCA a sign is a triple consisting of a representamen, a denotation and an interpretation so that the representamen and interpretation together uniquely identify the denotation. Or in other words, interpretations are partial functions that map representamens into denotations. Primarily these notions are role concepts which means that anything can be a representamen and so on if it is

© Springer Nature Switzerland AG 2019
D. Endres et al. (Eds.): ICCS 2019, LNAI 11530, pp. 248–256, 2019.
https://doi.org/10.1007/978-3-030-23182-8_19

used in that role. But it is not really useful to consider just any triple as a sign. Therefore, the mathematical definition can be extended by some less formal, fuzzy usage conditions: a sign should be something that is used in an act of communication; representamens should be physical representations (such as words, images, bits or neuron combinations), interpretations should contain some information about when, where, how, why and by whom a sign is used and denotations should describe meaning. Whoever designs an application decides what exactly the sets of representamens, denotations and interpretations are in that case. Signs can themselves be representamens, interpretations or denotations of other signs leading to a potential "semiotic chain".

Priss (2017b) defines formal contexts for denotations, representamens and interpretations but states that other conceptual structures can also be employed instead of or in addition to lattices. Interpretations can, for example, be modelled as temporal sequences or as possible paths through a computer program. Common structures on representamens are syntax and grammar. At least in the context of this paper where SCA is applied to mathematics, denotations should be modelled with FCA as formal concepts in concept lattices which can have additional features (axioms, functions or relations).

SCA has been elaborated in several publications (Priss 2016, 2017a, 2017b and 2018). The role of language in learning mathematics has been investigated by other researchers (cf. Schleppegrell's 2007 review) but not usually from a semiotic perspective. Other semiotic research in mathematics education (e.g. Presmeg et al. 2018) tends to be not as formal. In our view the mathematical model of semiotics that is most similar to SCA is provided by Goguen (1999). But unlike Goguen's formalisation, SCA separates conceptual and semiotic aspects. Thus, we believe that there is no existing research with the exact same focus as presented in this paper.

2 Differentiating Conceptual and Semiotic Analyses

Denotations can be modelled in some *domain* which consists of all relevant information: conceptual hierarchies, relations, axioms and so forth. For example, set theory is a mathematical domain. In this paper denotations are modelled as concepts which are formalised with FCA. In general, the difference between concepts and denotations is that "concept" is a structural notion whereas "denotation" is a role. In this paper the two notions can be used fairly interchangeably.

In the remainder of this paper the term *conceptual analysis* refers to an analysis of conceptual structures within a domain. The term *semiotic analysis* implies that different parts of a sign (representamens, denotations and interpretations) contribute to an analysis. Using this terminology, it is possible to investigate separate aspects of signs: their underlying conceptual structures and their semiotic aspects, such as, how well structures amongst representamens correspond to denotational structures. For example, proofs in analytic geometry being simpler than the corresponding proofs in Euclidean geometry is primarily a conceptual difference and not a semiotic one. In FCA, formal contexts and concept lattices are two different conceptual structures. But whether vectors in linear algebra are represented graphically or as n-tuples is not a conceptual but a semiotic difference. Typical questions for a conceptual analysis focus on denotational structures, what kinds of concepts can be constructed in a domain and the complexity and efficiency of such structures. Typical semiotic questions focus on synonymy and polysemy, complexity and efficiency of representamens compared to denotations, how representamen relations correspond to conceptual relations, how suitable and complete the conceptual domain is for the representamens and on the usability of signs.

Complexity and efficiency are relevant for both conceptual and semiotic analyses. From a conceptual view, compound concepts are more complex than atomic concepts which could be axioms or object and attribute concepts[1] in FCA. Reducing complexity is inverse to increasing efficiency because having more atomic concepts is less efficient but makes it easier to express compound concepts. For example, defining an equivalence relation as a "binary relation that is reflexive, symmetric and transitive" is not very complex because it relies on previously defined terms "binary", "relation", "reflexive", "symmetric" and "transitive". A definition via a set of formulas without relying on previously defined terms would be more efficient and more complex. Similarly, a programming language with a large set of predefined functions yields programs that are short and simple compared to programs, for example, written in assembly language. In FCA, a clarified, reduced lattice has maximum efficiency but if all concepts were atomic then they would have minimum complexity.

Complexity and efficiency can also be viewed semiotically. Synonyms are signs whose different representamens are mapped into the same denotation. Synonymy should be kept to a minimum because it is inefficient. Polysemy means that one representamen is mapped into different but related denotations under different interpretations. Polysemy occurs for example, when the value of a variable in a computer program is changed. Polysemy increases efficiency because it means that the set of representamens can be even smaller than the set of atomic concepts because interpretations disambiguate the representamens. An example of this is that natural languages can express a much larger number of concepts than they have words or word combinations because the contexts in which the words are used disambiguate them.

Correspondence between grammatical/syntactic relations and conceptual relations refers, for instance, to the ordering, sequence, topology and distances in a graphical representation compared to such structures in the denotational domain. Usability investigates how adequate representamens are for denotations (including structural and qualitative features). But the denotational domain should also be adequate for the representamens, for example, sufficiently complete. Different users can be modelled as different interpretations. In this paper, interpretations are not mentioned very often because Priss (2017a) argues that

---

[1] The object concept of an object is the smallest concept which has the object in its extension. Vice versa an attribute concept is the largest concept which has an attribute in its intension.

mathematical texts mainly employ only a single interpretation corresponding to the "correct" meaning of mathematical signs as considered by experts. Interpretations are relevant when it comes to explaining the view of students. Their interpretations are often different from expert interpretations and may be an indication of misconceptions. With respect to experts, interpretations may be useful if one wants to analyse personal preferences of using and interacting with mathematical signs.

3 Conceptual Analysis of Mathematical Signs

This section discusses mathematical signs from a conceptual viewpoint. Priss (2018) argues that many people find mathematics difficult to learn because mathematical concepts are formal and structurally very different from natural language concepts which are associative. Associative concepts depend heavily on the words used to express them and their situational contexts. For example, it is impossible to obtain a universal agreement about what "democracy" means. Priss (2017a) provides a definition of "formal concept" that is slightly wider than the usual FCA notion and essentially refers to concepts that have a necessary and sufficient definition. Apart from mathematical concepts other formal concepts are for example phylogenetic notions such as "Centaurea cyanus" because it provides necessary and sufficient conditions for whether something is a common cornflower or not. This paper addresses the question as to how such formal mathematical concepts can be modelled with FCA. The aim is not to apply FCA to mathematics which has been done numerous times before by Ganter and Wille (1999) and many others. Instead the aim is to obtain an understanding of what the concepts that underpin mathematical language themselves are like – by modelling them with FCA. For example, what is the extension and intension of a concept for "=" modelled with FCA?

We argue that denotations of mathematical signs are abstract concepts corresponding to mathematical equivalence classes because there can be many mathematically equivalent representamens for a mathematical sign. For example, after disambiguating a representamen "5" with respect to whether it is an integer, real number and so on, it can be assumed that there is a shared abstract notion of "5" which is independent of its representamen and situational context. Thus a single interpretation can be assumed for all representamens of the integer "5". This is contrary to "democracy" where such a shared abstract notion does not exist. It should be mentioned that mathematical concepts do develop over time. For example, the number "0" was historically invented (or discovered) much later than the natural numbers. Nevertheless we would argue that changes occur before a precise mathematical definition has been established. Once a mathematical concept has a formal definition, the meaning is exactly what is stated by the definition and only changes if the definition is changed.

Figure 1 shows two examples of formal concept lattices that represent mathematical concepts. The purpose of Fig. 1 is to create lattices where FCA concepts represent mathematical concepts and where attribute implications might correspond to mathematical implications. The formal objects of lattice A are all pairs of the numbers 1, 2, 3, and 4 and all triples of the numbers 1 and 2. The intensions use a placeholder notation: $1 refers to the first element of the vector, $2 to the second and so on. For example, the vector $(2, 2)$ fulfils the equation $1 = $2 because $2 = 2$. The lattice contains some attribute implications which are correct mathematical statements, for example $1 \prec $2 \Longrightarrow $1 \leq $2 (where "$\prec$" is the predecessor-successor relation). But there are also implications which are not generally true, such as $1 + $2 = $3 \Longrightarrow_? $1 = $2 and only appear in the lattice because of the very limited set of formal objects.

In theory, if it was possible to create lattice A for all pairs, triples and so on of natural numbers and all operations on them, then the attribute implications would be extensionally proven mathematical implications. But because such a lattice would be infinite and it is not clear what operations to include, this is not possible. Extensional proofs tend to only be possible if they pertain to finite sets or if there is some sort of construction mechanism that loops through an infinite set as is the case for mathematical induction. One interesting observation is that as soon as one enlarges the set of formal objects in lattice A many concepts emerge which are neither object nor attribute concepts. Many relationships in a larger version of lattice A appear to be coincidental. It is also questionable whether it is at all useful to combine pairs and triples in one set of formal objects because the resulting implications may not be interesting. In SCA the notion of *signature* is used to describe the length and datatypes of vectors that are used as formal objects. In lattice A the signature is length 2 or 3 with datatype natural numbers.

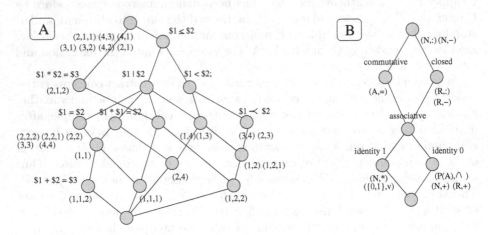

Fig. 1. Conceptual analysis of mathematical signs

Lattice B in Fig. 1 is constructed in a similar manner. In that case the signature of the formal objects describes a pair of a set with an operation. The letters "N" and "R" refer to the sets of natural and real numbers; "A" is a set and "P(A)" its powerset. The attributes are represented by words but the corresponding definitions should be clear. For example, "commutative" corresponds to $\forall_{x,y \in \$1} : x\$2y = y\$2x$. The formal object $(A, =)$ is unusual because it refers to a set A with the equals sign as a truth-valued operation. In that case the definition of relational symmetry $\forall_{x,y \in \$1} : x\$2y \iff y\$2x$ coincides with commutativity. This raises questions about adding some further restrictions about the formal attributes or objects in order to avoid combining notions such as commutativity and symmetry in one lattice.

A difference between the two lattices is that in lattice B, quantifiers are used in the intensions. Furthermore, the placeholder $\$2$ refers to operations and is thus somewhat more abstract. In lattice A an algorithm could be provided that iteratively generates the set of formal objects even if it is infinite. But in lattice A it is not clear whether the set of attributes is in any way complete. In lattice B it is impossible to discuss an infinite set of formal objects because that would involve a set of sets in the first component of the pairs. Furthermore, there could be other algebraic structures with operations which nobody has yet thought about. Nevertheless the set of attributes in lattice B is complete if it is meant to correspond to the axioms of commutative monoids. Priss (2017b) suggests the use of the notion "open set" (from linguistics) for a set for which it is basically known whether an item belongs to it or not but which cannot be listed in its entirety. The set of common cornflowers that currently exists on this Earth is such an open set. Thus, it appears that some mathematical concepts have an extension or intension that is "open" in some manner because an infinite version of the set of objects in lattice B and the set of attributes in lattice A cannot be provided.

In both lattices the relationship between formal objects and attributes requires proofs but in lattice B the proofs are somewhat more complex. It is conceivable that in lattice B there could even be relationships between formal objects and attributes which are unknown because nobody has yet been able to construct a proof. This may not be the case for elementary group theory, but it is the case in other mathematical domains. In cases where it is not possible to provide an algorithm for a set of formal objects, mathematicians tend to rather look for a structural description of the elements instead of generating a list. For example, it is known how many different structural types of monoids or groups exist for sets of a certain size. For expert mathematicians all of this is familiar. But first year university students experience a transition from school mathematics which relies somewhat on associations and intuitions to a purely formal mathematics. They need to learn about the nature of formal, mathematical concepts and what exactly is formal and precisely defined and what is not yet known, not provable or open.

4   Semiotic Analysis of Mathematical Signs

In addition to encountering the nature of formal mathematical concepts for the first time, first year university students also need to develop a tolerance for the ambiguity of mathematical notation. The textbooks used in schools tend to be more carefully designed and select a certain fairly consistent subset of mathematical notation. But at university level, students need to get accustomed to how mathematical language is used in a wider context of applications where different notations may be used. For example, the modulo operation can be written as: $a \bmod n$, $a\%n$, $a \pmod n$ and use $=$, $\equiv$ or $\equiv_n$. Notations such as using $1/n$ for inverse elements in modular arithmetics lead to examples such as $1/2 = 1$ (in $\mathbb{Z}_3$) which require students to unlearn some aspects of their school knowledge. Some notations always depend on context. For example an edge AB in a directed graph is different from an edge AB in an undirected graph (where it equals BA) even though both use the same notation.

But SCA considers more than just analysing notations. It involves first specifying the extensions and intensions of the denotational conceptual structures as presented in the previous section. Then, second, it involves considering all 3 components of the signs. This section provides an overview of using SCA for analysing mathematical signs as discussed in the literature and adds a further small example. Priss (2018) argues that mathematical signs are incomplete, polysemous, make frequent use of strong synonymy (contrary to natural language) and because of frequent use of visualisations raise questions of iconicity. Incompleteness is often strongest when it comes to defining the basics because these tend to require some meta-level formalisations or are at a higher level of difficulty[2]. Polysemy is discussed below. Strong synonymy means that two representamens have exactly the same denotations (Priss 2017b). In natural languages, synonyms such as "car" and "automobile" tend to be similar but not exactly the same whereas mathematically equivalent denotations belong to strong synonyms. The stylistic use of synonyms is different in mathematics as well because in natural languages exact repetitions are often considered bad style and students may be taught to rephrase by using synonyms. In mathematics, however, a sign can only be replaced by a strong synonym but not by non-strong synonyms. For example, the words "function" and "relation" cannot usually replace each other in mathematical sentences. Iconicity of visualisations refers to relationships such as left/right, inside/outside, near/far, above/below and distance which may be present in visualisations. For an iconic sign there is some similarity between such relationships in its visualisation and in its denotation. It can be challenging for students to determine which relationships in visualisations matter and which do not. For example, in a Hasse diagram of a concept lattice it matters which nodes are above other nodes and connected via an edge but the length of the edges does not matter (Priss 2017a). Formulas often lack the iconic quality of left/right corresponding to first/later because formulas may require the reader to jump across different elements of the formula instead of the usual left-to-right sequence (Priss 2018). Other semiotic aspects of mathematical language pertain to syntactic rules (e.g. precedence rules), and the special use of variables (Priss 2018).

A means for identifying polysemy of mathematical notations is by first disambiguating and then translating them into a formal language which specifies

---

[2] For example, definitions of "set", "$\Longleftrightarrow$" or the Peano axioms for natural numbers are challenging for first year students.

how the signs are to be calculated or operated with. Mathematical signs often contain a hidden task relating to what is meant to be done with the signs which is clear to expert mathematicians but not explicitly notated. There is some evidence that at least school children sometimes perform nonsense calculations if they are incorrectly associating a certain task with a certain type of problem (e.g. Puchalska and Semadeni 1987). The following table shows the steps of disambiguating and identifying tasks of the polysemous meanings of the equals sign (as discussed by Priss (2016)):

nr	Example	Disambiguation	Task
1	$1 + 2 = ?$		calculate $(1 + 2)$
2	$1 + 2 = 4$	"=" : Expr $\times$ Expr $\rightarrow$ {true, false}	eval_truth $(= (1 + 2, 4)))$
3	$1 + 1 + 1 = 1 + 2 = 3$	abbreviation for $1 + 1 + 1 = 1 + 2$,	eval_truth (...)
		$1 + 2 = 3$ and $1 + 1 + 1 = 3$	
4	$1 + 1 + 1 = 1 + 2 = 3$	$\{1 + 1 + 1, 1 + 2, 3\}$ is an equivalence class	observe equivalence

Example 1 presents an operational use of the equals sign. It conveys a request to perform a calculation similar to a function call in programming languages with the sum of 1 and 2 as input and the result 3 as output. Because example 2 is false its equals sign can only be interpreted as a truth-valued function that maps a pair of expressions $(1 + 2, 4)$ into the set of values "true" or "false". Example 3 is an abbreviation for two or three statements of example 2. But it could also be an indication of equivalence as represented by example 4. The equals signs in example 4 cannot be considered truth-valued functions because if $= (1 + 1 + 1, 2 + 1)$ yields "true" then it would result in "true $= 3$" which is meaningless. Example 4 is semiotically similar to $2 < 3 < 4$ and could also be interpreted as a graph where "=" or "<" are vertices and transitivity is implied similar to a Hasse diagram. The denotations of the four examples are similar. Thus, it is a case of polysemy. Specifying exactly what is meant by mathematical signs as in the table highlights subtle differences in meaning.

5   Conclusion

SCA provides insights into the nature of mathematical concepts and notations which mathematicians (apart from teachers) may not be aware of. SCA can be employed as one tool amongst others for decoding hidden difficulties in the mathematical subject matter. A conceptual analysis of mathematical signs shows that mathematical concepts are structurally different from natural language concepts and that there may be a divergence between extensional and intensional aspects of the mathematical domain. A semiotic analysis demonstrates that mathematical language can be ambiguous, context-dependent and full of synonymy and polysemy. Mathematical representamens hide a fair amount of detail about their underlying concepts and the tasks that are to be performed with them. Similar looking representamens can have totally different meanings.

One method of helping students to understand the intricacies of mathematical signs is to have students translate mathematical notations into a computer programming language. This is, for example, advocated by Priss and Riegler (2017). The reason for this is that in programming languages the structures and datatypes of all elements always need to be explicitly provided. Furthermore, a certain functional abstraction is required in order to implement tests for features such as commutativity where the operation itself is an input to a function. A disadvantage of teaching mathematics by programming is that the students need to learn a programming language in addition to the mathematical notation. But there are some programming languages (such as SETL or Python) which support expressions that are fairly close to mathematical language.

References

Ganter, B., Wille, R.: Formal Concept Analysis. Mathematical Foundations. Springer, Heidelberg (1999). https://doi.org/10.1007/978-3-642-59830-2

Goguen, J.: An introduction to algebraic semiotics, with application to user interface design. In: Nehaniv, C.L. (ed.) CMAA 1998. LNCS (LNAI), vol. 1562, pp. 242–291. Springer, Heidelberg (1999). https://doi.org/10.1007/3-540-48834-0_15

Presmeg, N., Radford, L., Roth, W.-M., Kadunz, G. (eds.): Signs of Signification. ICME-13 Monographs. Springer, Cham (2018). https://doi.org/10.1007/978-3-319-70287-2

Priss, U.: A semiotic-conceptual analysis of conceptual learning. In: Haemmerlé, O., Stapleton, G., Faron Zucker, C. (eds.) ICCS 2016. LNCS (LNAI), vol. 9717, pp. 122–136. Springer, Cham (2016). https://doi.org/10.1007/978-3-319-40985-6_10

Priss, U., Riegler, P.: Automatisierte Programmbewertung in der Mathematik-Ausbildung. In: Automatisierte Bewertung in der Programmierausbildung, Waxmann (2017)

Priss, U.: Learning thresholds in formal concept analysis. In: Bertet, K., Borchmann, D., Cellier, P., Ferré, S. (eds.) ICFCA 2017. LNCS (LNAI), vol. 10308, pp. 198–210. Springer, Cham (2017a). https://doi.org/10.1007/978-3-319-59271-8_13

Priss, U.: Semiotic-conceptual analysis: a proposal. Int. J. Gen. Syst. **46**(5), 569–585 (2017b)

Priss, U.: A semiotic-conceptual analysis of conceptual development in learning mathematics. In: Presmeg, N., Radford, L., Roth, W.-M., Kadunz, G. (eds.) Signs of Signification. IM, pp. 173–188. Springer, Cham (2018). https://doi.org/10.1007/978-3-319-70287-2_10

Puchalska, E., Semadeni, Z.: Children's reactions to verbal arithmetical problems with missing, surplus or contradictory data. For Learn. Math. **7**(3), 9–16 (1987)

Schleppegrell, M.J.: The linguistic challenges of mathematics teaching and learning: a research review. Read. Writ. Q. **23**(2), 139–159 (2007)

Mathematical Similarity Models: Do We Need Incomparability to Be Precise?

Anna Serr, Moritz Schubert, and Dominik Endres[✉]

Philipps University Marburg, Gutenbergstr. 18, 35032 Marburg, Germany
{serr,moritz.schubert}@students.uni-marburg.de,
dominik.endres@uni-marburg.de

Abstract. The expanded version of Tversky's feature model by Geist, Lengnink and Wille (GLW) provides a compelling representation of similarity by adding an incomparability option. However, previous research has found the GLW model lacking when compared with participants' responses. We present several new models based on the GLW model and validate them on data from previous similarity experiments. The results indicate that human similarity perception is not well described by a partial order.

Keywords: Similarity · Knowledge structure · Order theory

1 Introduction and Theory

Perceived similarity between objects can be used as an indicator for how humans structure their knowledge about the world. It relies on sensory attributes as well as semantic concepts and the history of each individual.

The *contrast model* by Tversky [4] attempts to formalize similarity in a mathematical model using attribute sets to represent each considered object. It was further developed by Geist, Lengnink and Wille [2] into the *GLW model* (see Table 1, left). A first evaluation [3] showed a high precision of the model, but it failed to make useful predictions in most cases because of its restrictive conditions for comparability.

This study introduces several new models, which were developed based on [2]. For evaluation of these new models preexisting data from two similarity experiments was used.

In Sect. 2 we detail the methods used in the experiments, which generated our data and present the new models. In Sect. 3 we present different empirical measures to assess the quality of the models. We discuss these measures and possible implications for future research in Sect. 4.

2 Methods

2.1 Experiments

The first data set, the *rating experiment*, was collected by students during a research practical, the second, the *comparison experiment*, is described in [3].

© Springer Nature Switzerland AG 2019
D. Endres et al. (Eds.): ICCS 2019, LNAI 11530, pp. 257–261, 2019.
https://doi.org/10.1007/978-3-030-23182-8_20

Rating Experiment. The stimulus set comprised of 11 grayscale photos of various objects (e.g. a monkey, a pumpkin, a hammer) taken from the stimulus set that had previously been used in the fMRI experiment in [1]. They were adjusted for size along the main diagonal, luminance and contrast. The experiment consisted of a feature selection and a rating task. During the feature selection task each of the stimuli was presented to the participants (N = 49) next to a list of 35 words, constituting potential features of the objects. Participants were tasked with selecting any number of features that they thought best described the presented stimulus. In the rating task, participants were presented with pairs of stimuli and rated their similarity on a scale from 1 to 7.

Comparison Experiment. A new stimulus set was created for this experiment. It consisted of 10 colored photos of different fruit types that were only adjusted for size. We chose the new stimulus set to increase overall similarity and thus comparability between stimuli. We also expected the stimuli to appear more natural than the grayscale photos. The study consisted of two experiments. The goal of the first experiment (N = 22) was to generate a feature list for all stimuli. This experiment resulted in 48 features. The second experiment (N = 60) consisted of a feature selection task and a comparison task. Participants could assign any number of features from the feature list, generated from the first experiment, to each presented stimulus. During the comparison task they were presented a pair of pairs (or *quadruplet*) of stimuli. They were then asked to indicate by keypress which pair was more similar, or if the pairs were equally similiar, or incomparable. For further details see [3].

2.2   Similarity Models

Condition Recombination. All tested similarity models were based on the GLW model [2] and Table 1. In a first step the four ordering conditions of the GLW model were recombined to distinguish their respective contribution to precision and comparability. Conditions two and three were not separated, because they measure the same aspect of similarity. This way seven combinations of the four conditions were tested. The only combination previously evaluated in [3] is model (1). Object pairs are comparable if and only if all conditions listed next to a model in Table 1, right, hold. Thus, models tend to predict less comparability if they are a conjunction of many conditions.

Cardinality Models. Cardinality Models do not compare the elements of the subsets but only their cardinality, i.e. the number of elements in each subset. The first condition of GLW, $A \cap B \supseteq C \cap D$, would be $|A \cap B| \geq |C \cap D|$ in a cardinality model. The same seven combinations of conditions were used. Cardinality models with only one condition produce a total order. Models with more than one condition predict incomparability only whenever conditions are fulfilled in opposing directions.

Table 1. Left: GLW model. Small letters denote objects, capital letters corresponding attribute sets. $s(a, b)$ is the similarity between object a and object b. **Right:** GLW condition recombinations tested in this study. For details, see text.

Definition of the GLW model:

$s(a, b) \geq s(c, d)$ whenever:

$$A \cap B \supseteq C \cap D \tag{1}$$

$$\bar{A} \cap B \subseteq \bar{C} \cap D \tag{2}$$

$$A \cap \bar{B} \subseteq C \cap \bar{D} \tag{3}$$

$$\bar{A} \cap \bar{B} \supseteq \bar{C} \cap \bar{D} \tag{4}$$

Recombined Models

Model	Conditions used		
1)	(1)	(2),(3)	(4)
2)	(1)	(2),(3)	-
3)	(1)	-	(4)
4)	-	(2),(3)	(4)
5)	(1)	-	-
6)	-	(2),(3)	-
7)	-	-	(4)

Index Model. We also experimented with an index model in an attempt to reconcile the GLW conditions with a total order. It is derived from the *Jaccard index* J: the cardinality of the intersection of two sets divided by the cardinality of their union, see Eq. 5. The Jaccard index depends on both shared (numerator) and separating (denominator) attributes. Thus, it can serve as a similarity measure derived from GLW conditions one, two and three. Equation 6 expresses the mean similarity of A to all other objects, i.e. the context (GLW condition four). This context has a normalizing effect on the similarity between A and B in Eq. 7, which defines our index model.

$$J(A, B) = \frac{|A \cap B|}{|A \cup B|} \tag{5}$$

$$mA = \frac{1}{n}(J(A, A) + J(A, B) + \dots + J(A, N)) \tag{6}$$

$$s(a, b) \geq s(c, d) \text{ whenever:} \quad \frac{\left(\frac{|A \cap B|}{|A \cup B|}\right)}{\left(\frac{mA + mB}{2}\right)} > \frac{\left(\frac{|C \cap D|}{|C \cup D|}\right)}{\left(\frac{mC + mD}{2}\right)} \tag{7}$$

3 Results

For every model two results were computed. First, the fraction of incomparable cases i. The fraction of incomparability ratings from participants in [3] is $\bar{x} = .11(\pm.13)$. Second, the precision p under exclusion of trivial cases. A case is trivial if the model prediction is implied by the stimulus combination alone (e.g. [aa, aa] or [ab, ab]). The fraction of trivial cases t is different for the two data sets. For the data set of the rating experiment it is $t = .05$, for the comparison experiment it is $t = .11$. This is important because trivial cases are always comparable and were not excluded from i. The values of i and p for the different models are reported in Table 2.

Table 2. Values of i and p for each model, applied to the data set of the rating and the comparison experiment, respectively. Numbers indicate condition combination, C for cardinality model, I for index model. Human reported incomparability is ≈ 0.11.

	(1)	(C1)	(2)	(C2)	(3)	(C3)	(4)	(C4)	(5)	(C5)	(6)	(C6)	(7)	(C7)	(I)
i(rating)	.95	.29	.87	.26	.93	.15	.95	.24	.25	.00	.81	.22	.93	.00	.00
i(comparison)	.88	.58	.86	.53	.87	.48	.88	.53	.75	.00	.73	.47	.86	.00	.00
p(rating)	.94	.87	.99	.87	.93	.85	.95	.85	.85	.84	.99	.85	.91	.77	.85
p(comparison)	.65	.71	.92	.70	.64	.64	.83	.67	.59	.50	.95	.67	.61	.45	.62

4   Discussion

The recombination of ordering conditions shows that the conditions contributing most to precision (condition 2 and 3) are not the same as those causing the highest incomparability (condition 4). Regardless, all partially ordered models yield much more incomparability than participants do.

On the other hand, the models producing a total order all have lower precisions than the partially ordered models. This might be due to cardinality of attribute sets being too unspecific a measure for similarity. Comparing the cardinality of sets instead of single elements treats different types of attributes, e.g. category, color or function, as equally important.

Furthermore, an analysis of participants' incomparability ratings revealed a lack of systematicity in those ratings. 18% of the participants did not use the rating at all, those who used it assigned it to cases very different from one another and even to trivial cases. At least for quadruplets of stimuli there seems to be no general consensus about incomparability between participants.

These findings lead us to the conclusion that the current formalization of incomparability is not suitable for the description of human (in)comparability perception. Future research should aim at models that predict substantially more comparability than current models, while trying to maintain high levels of precision. This might e.g. be feasible with typed attributes.

Acknowledgement. This work was supported by the DFG SFB/TRR 135 "Cardinal Mechanisms of Perception", project C6.

References

1. Endres, D., Adam, R., Giese, M.A., Noppeney, U.: Understanding the semantic structure of human fMRI brain recordings with formal concept analysis. In: Domenach, F., Ignatov, D.I., Poelmans, J. (eds.) ICFCA 2012. LNCS (LNAI), vol. 7278, pp. 96–111. Springer, Heidelberg (2012). https://doi.org/10.1007/978-3-642-29892-9_13
2. Geist, S., Lengnink, K., Wille, R.: An order-theoretic foundation for similarity measures. In: Lengnink, K. (ed.) Formalisierungen von Ähnlichkeit aus Sicht der Formalen Begriffsanalyse, pp. 75–87. Shaker Verlag (1996)

3. Schubert, M., Endres, D.: Empirically evaluating the similarity model of Geist, Lengnink and Wille. In: Chapman, P., Endres, D., Pernelle, N. (eds.) ICCS 2018. LNCS (LNAI), vol. 10872, pp. 88–95. Springer, Cham (2018). https://doi.org/10.1007/978-3-319-91379-7_7
4. Tversky, A.: Features of similarity. Psychol. Rev. **84**(4), 327–352 (1977). https://doi.org/10.1037/0033-295X.84.4.327

Conceptual Graphs Based Modeling of MongoDB Data Structure and Query

Viorica Varga$^{(\boxtimes)}$, Camelia-Florina Andor, and Christian Săcărea

Babes-Bolyai University, str. Kogalniceanu 1, 400081 Cluj Napoca, Romania
{ivarga,andorcamelia}@cs.ubbcluj.ro,
csacarea@math.ubbcluj.ro

Abstract. NoSQL data stores do not enforce any structural constraints on the data, they are usually referenced as schema-less data. On the other hand, for managing and retrieving data, its inherent structure proves to be significant. Especially for modeling purposes, conceptual design of semi-structured data proves to be an important task. MongoDB document store is the most popular of NoSQL systems, ranked December 2018 on the first place among similar systems by DB-Engines (www.db-engines.com). In this paper, we present a modeling method for MongoDB data structure based on Conceptual Graphs (CGs). A common interface is proposed for data structure modeling and queries in MongoDB.

1 Introduction and Related Work

NoSQL data stores vary not only in their data but also in their query model. The most common categorization of these systems is by their data model, distinguishing key-value stores, document stores, column-family stores, and graph databases [1]. Document based NoSQL systems are based on the semi-structured data model, but most NoSQL data stores do not enforce any structural constraints on the data; they are usually referenced as schema-less data. On the other hand, for managing and retrieving data, its inherent structure proves to be significant. Without a general structure of the data, tasks like application development or data analysis are quite difficult. Especially for modeling purposes, conceptual design of semi-structured data proves to be an important task [2].

Motivated by [4], our research is focused on modeling various databases using FCA and CGs [3,5], and we propose a Conceptual Graph based modeling of JSON data structure in MongoDB. Starting with version 3.6, MongoDB supports JSON Schema validation. We propose a CG based data modeling tool which gives the possibility to design MongoDB data structure in form of CG and to transform it into JSON Schema, which can be used to validate in MongoDB with **validator** expression the structure of the data. Since Conceptual Graphs are also suitable to be used for Visual Query Systems, we propose a graphical interface for query design in MongoDB using CGs.

© Springer Nature Switzerland AG 2019
D. Endres et al. (Eds.): ICCS 2019, LNAI 11530, pp. 262–270, 2019.
https://doi.org/10.1007/978-3-030-23182-8_21

2 Graphic Representation of MongoDB Data Structure by Conceptual Graphs

Data in MongoDB is stored in documents and similarly structured documents are typically organized into collections. Choosing the right database schema for an application impacts performance. In this section, we present MongoDB data schema using Conceptual Graphs (referenced as JSON Schema CG in the following). Every object is modeled as a CG **concept** and then graphically represented. The relationships between objects are represented as **relations**, we recall from [5] the relations: hasOne, hasMore, hasKey, refers, IsOptional.

Step 1. Identify all complex properties. Every property (complex or simple), the type of a node or an enumeration will be modeled as a **concept**. More precisely, the **concept type** represents: a *property* (P), a *root* (R), the *type of the data* (T) or an *enumeration constraint* (N). The **concept referent** can be: the *name of* the corresponding *node* (property), the *data type of a property*, the *set of acceptable values* of the corresponding *property*, in the case of enumeration. Remark that, in this particular case, the concept name will be composed by the predefined values of the enumeration, separated by (|). For details, see the isEnum relation and the detailed example.

Step 2. As earlier defined, the relationship between two or more **concepts** will be represented by means of a CG **relation**. The arcs are directed such that they highlight the ascendant-descendant relationship: **from the root to the leaf** levels. The relations presented in [5] are adaptable to the JSON schema. Hence, we enumerate only the additional relations. This list can be extended with other types of relations:

- refers: represents a linkage between two or more complex properties. In the case of JSON Schema, this relation can not be expressed explicitly, but we consider that it is important to have it when working with CGs.
- IsOptional: designs the case when the minimum number of occurrences of a property is zero. If this relation is omitted, the default value of the number of occurrences (of the corresponding property) is one.
- hasType: defines the BSON data type of a property. If the *hasKey* relation is set, this relation can be omitted.
- oneOf and isPossibility: specify the child elements of a oneOf compositor. oneOf compositor allows only one of the schema contained in the declaration to be present within the containing property.
- anyOf and isPossibility: specify the child elements of an anyOf compositor. The anyOf compositor allows at least one of the elements contained in the declaration to be present within the containing property.
- isEnum: represents the enumeration constraint, which limits the content of a property to a set of acceptable values.

The hierarchical structure of JSON data gives a natural representation of the one-to-many relationships. The many-to-many relationship is not supported directly by JSON. There are a couple of possible solutions to model it, for details, see [5].

Step 3. Identify all child elements of the complex properties, defined at *Step 1*, give the BSON data type for each one and specify also the potential restrictions of the properties.

3   An Example to Illustrate the Representation of MongoDB Schema with Conceptual Graphs

In this section, we exemplify previously developed methods on a graphical representation of JSON Schema using Conceptual Graphs through a detailed example. For this, we use data from Computer Science bibliography[1], which is stored in XML documents. Then, we import the data in MongoDB. Because of the complexity of the initial data from `dblp`, only a part of it is represented. In the following, we analyze the representation method step-by-step.

Step 1. We start the design with the specification of fundamental properties. We define a concept, called `DBLP`, which will represent the root of the JSON Schema. The root `DBLP` contains some different child properties, e.g. `proceedings`, `article`, `inproceedings`, `book`, etc., which are all complex properties. Hence, we construct their descendants and we define the relationships between them.

Step 2. In the initial XML data, the one-to-many relationship between the objects `proceedings` and `inproceedings` is modeled by the `crossref` property of `inproceedings`, which contains the `key` of a `proceedings`. The flat representation of this relationship is modeled by the `refers` relation[2]. The embedded structure is recommended in MongoDB documentation, if it is possible. Therefore, we propose an embedding of `inproceedings` in `proceedings`, such that the parent-child relationship is represented by the `hasMore` relation, see Fig. 1. Notice that a `hasMore` relation can connect a complex property with a simple one, e. g. the relation between `proceedings` and `editors` properties.

Step 3. A detailed design for the complex properties is illustrated in Fig. 1. We add a rating[3] property for conference proceedings to illustrate the enumeration constraint. We model the ISBN property as optional, because not every proceeding has an ISBN number. Objects `proceedings` and `inproceedings` are very complex, so we omit some properties on the flat representation and others on the embedded one.

We consider in MongoDB a database named DBLP and the collections: *article*, *proceedings*, *book*, etc. In MongoDB we have the possibility to perform schema validation in a *collection* during data inserts and updates. Due to obvious space reasons, we have not included the corresponding MongoDB `createCollection` function. It can be consulted at[4].

---

[1] https://dblp.uni-trier.de.

[2] http://www.cs.ubbcluj.ro/~ivarga/ConceptualGraph/FlatRefersStructure.png.

[3] http://valutazione.unibas.it/gii-grin-scie-rating/.

[4] http://www.cs.ubbcluj.ro/~ivarga/ConceptualGraph/cgMongoSchema.txt.

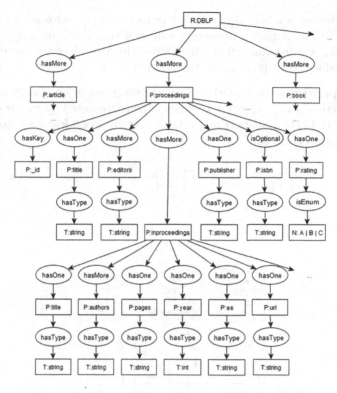

Fig. 1. The embedded **DBLP** JSON Schema CG

4 MongoDB Query Conceptual Graph

In the following, we recall the definition of an XQuery Conceptual Graph from [3] and we adapt it for MongoDB queries. A **concept type** can be: a (simple or complex) *property* (P), a condition (C), an aggregate operator (F), the result of the Query (out). The **concept referent** can denote: the *name of the* corresponding *property* or the *denomination of the aggregate operator*. Furthermore, a **relation** can be:

- ○ **has**: permits the navigation from parent to child concept (in MongoDB with dot notation). Notice that, in this case we are not interested in the type of the relationship (**hasOne** or **hasMore**).
- ○ **return**: links the concepts which we want to return as the result of the query with the **out** concept: in the case of $n-1$ returning nodes, it will be represented by an n-adic relation, where the first $n-1$ arcs point toward the relation (and are numbered from 1 to $n-1$), while the last arc points away.
- ○ **filter**: connects the property concept with the condition concept;
- ○ **get**: binds the property concept to the aggregation concept;
- ○ **equal**: expresses the join operation between two concept nodes with common values;

○ `groupby`: between a complex concept property node and one of its children property. The aggregation operators will refer to a child property.
○ `filter$all`: verifies that all specified values for this filter are included in the array of values corresponding to the concept node.

Selection operation. MongoDB permits the filter condition specification using the `find` function. In the Query CG this will be represented by means of `filter` relations. The `filter` relation is a relation between one leaf level node of CG and the condition concept.

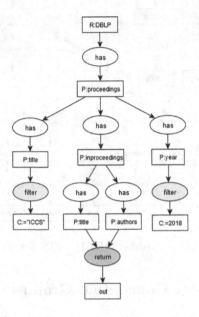

Fig. 2. Query CG for a given proceeding on embedded structure

Example 1. Consider a first query (Q1): 'Find the title and authors of *inproceedings* papers from *proceedings* of ICCS from year 2018!' In Fig. 2 we can see the corresponding CG for the embedded structure of Fig. 1. As we detailed earlier, the root, the simple and complex properties become concepts. The hierarchical structure is also accentuated here with the help of the `has` relation. The filter condition is a relation and the result is given by the `return` relation. The corresponding MongoDB function is:

```
db.proceedings.find({"title":"ICCS", "year":2018},
  {"inproceedings.title":1, "inproceedings.authors":1, "_id":0})
```

Example 2. Let query (Q2) be: 'Find the title of *proceedings* with rating **B** where authors: "Simon Andrews", "Simon Polovina", have published *inproceedings* papers together, give also in the result the title, year and pages of the paper!' The corresponding Query CG is constructed for the embedded structure, see Fig. 3. MongoDB offers the `$all` operator, which selects the documents

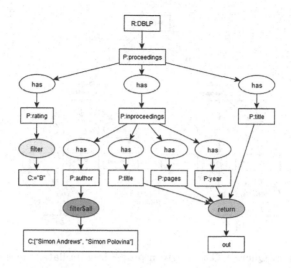

Fig. 3. Query CG for query Q2

where the value of a field is an array that contains all the specified elements. We use the `filter$all` relation to the `authors` concept for the condition of the two given authors. The result is given by the `return` relation. The query in MongoDB is:

```
db.proceedings.aggregate([{$unwind:"$inproceedings"},
 {$match:{"rating":"B",
  "inproceedings.authors":
          {$all:["Simon Andrews","Simon Polovina"]}}},
 {$project:{"_id":0, "title":1, "inproceedings.title":1,
    "inproceedings.pages":1, "inproceedings.year":1}}])
```

Join operation. The join operation implies at least two concept nodes with common values. Usually, these concepts with common values are related in the JSON schema CG by the **refers** relation. The user has to navigate from root to one of the concepts, then to the second concept and select the **equal** relation between them. Each of the concepts can be selected either as first or as second argument of the relation **equal**.

Example 3. Consider the query (Q1) for the flat structure. In Fig. 4 we can see the corresponding Query CG. The corresponding query in MongoDB will be more complex:

```
var proceedings_ids = db.proceedings.find({"title":"ICCS",
  "year":2018},{"_id":1}).map(function(item){return item._id})
 db.inproceedings.find({"crossref":{$in:proceedings_ids}},
  {"title":1,"authors":1,"_id":0})
```

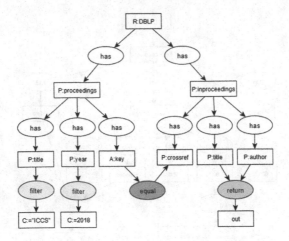

Fig. 4. Query CG for a given proceeding on flat structure

Aggregation operation. The grouping operator from SQL is available in MongoDB too. Some common aggregate operators are: `min()`, `max()`, `avg()`, `count()` and `sum()`. The GROUP BY operator is also implemented in Query CG as a relation. The `groupby` relation will be between a complex concept property node **P** and one of its children **C**. The result will be the grouping of the property **P** by the picked **C** property. These aggregation operators are represented in the Query CG by the help of the `get` relation: the arc pointing toward the relation marks the property **A** a child of property **P** subject to the aggregation, while the arc pointing away from the relation marks the operator itself. The property **A** - the subject of aggregation - has to be a simple property for the `min()`, `max()`, `avg()` and `sum()` operators. For the `count()` operator we can choose property **A** a simple property or one which is in many to one relation with property **P**. (**P** *hasMore* **A**). We also can count the documents in **P**, which is a complex property. The implementation of the `count()` operator is different from the other aggregation operators in MongoDB, it is solved with operator `$sum`, see query (Q3).

Example 4. (Q3) "Let us calculate the number of papers for every publisher in publication of type proceeding after year 2010". The corresponding Query CG is displayed in Fig. 5a for the embedded structure of Fig. 1. The MongoDB query is:

```
db.proceedings.aggregate([{$match:{"year":{$gt:2010}}},
      {$unwind:"$inproceedings"},
   {$group:{"_id":"$publisher","count":{$sum:1}}},
   {$project:{"_id":0, "publisher":"$_id","count":1}}])
```

The aggregation operators can be used without group by operator.

Example 5. (Q4) "Calculate the number of papers of author Uta Priss published in Springer publications of type proceeding after 2010!" The corresponding Query CG is displayed in Fig. 5b for the embedded structure of Fig. 1. The corresponding MongoDB query is:

```
db.proceedings.aggregate([{$unwind:"$inproceedings"},
  {$match:{"publisher" : "Springer","year":{$gt:2010},
     "inproceedings.authors":"Uta Priss"}},
  {$group:{"_id": null, "count":{$sum:1}}},
  {$project:{"_id":0,"count":1}} ])
```

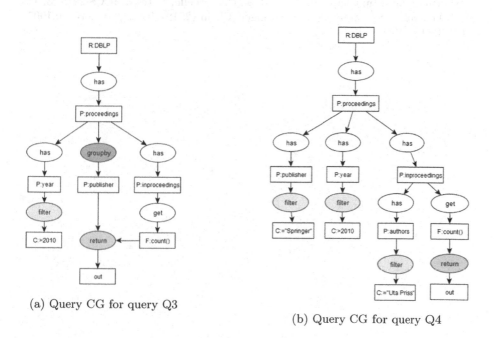

(a) Query CG for query Q3

(b) Query CG for query Q4

Fig. 5. Illustrating aggregation

5   Conclusions and Future Work

Interaction with computers becomes more and more important in our daily life. The goal of Conceptual Graphs is to provide a graphical representation for logic which is able to support human reasoning. This article proposes an application which provides a graphical interface for MongoDB Data Design in form of Conceptual Graphs. We implemented a software for MongoDB Data Design and we have provided a proof of concept how queries can be represented as Conceptual Graphs.

References

1. Cattell, R.: Scalable SQL and NoSQL data stores. SIGMOD Rec. **39**(4), 12–27 (2010)
2. Klettke, M., Strl, U., Scherzinger, S.: Schema extraction and structural outlier detection for JSON-based NoSQL data stores. In: (BTW), pp. 425–444. GI (2015)
3. Molnar, A., Varga, V., Sacarea, C.: Conceptual graphs based modeling and querying of XML data. In: SoftCOM, pp. 23–28. IEEE (2017)
4. Sowa, J.F.: Conceptual graphs for a data base interface. IBM J. Res. Dev. **20**(4), 336–357 (1976)
5. Varga, V., Săcărea, C., Molnar, A.E.: Conceptual graphs based modeling of semi-structured data. In: Chapman, P., Endres, D., Pernelle, N. (eds.) ICCS 2018. LNCS (LNAI), vol. 10872, pp. 167–175. Springer, Cham (2018). https://doi.org/10.1007/978-3-319-91379-7_13

Author Index

Author Index

Printed in the United States
by Booklanders

Printed in the United States
By Bookmasters